Censored

Censored

A Literary History of Subversion and Control

Matthew Fellion and Katherine Inglis

MCGILL-QUEEN'S UNIVERSITY PRESS

MONTREAL & KINGSTON / CHICAGO

Copyright © 2017 Matthew Fellion and Katherine Inglis

ISBN 978-0-7735-5127-5 (cloth)
ISBN 978-0-7735-5188-6 (ePDF)
ISBN 978-0-7735-5189-3 (ePUB)

Legal deposit fourth quarter 2017
Bibliothèque nationale du Québec

Published simultaneously outside North America by The British Library

Printed and bound in Malta by Gutenberg Press

McGill-Queen's University Press acknowledges the support of the Canada Council for the Arts
for our publishing program. We also acknowledge the financial support of the Government of
Canada through the Canada Book Fund for our publishing activities.

Library and Archives Canada Cataloguing in Publication
Fellion, Matthew, 1985–, author
Censored : a literary history of subversion and control / Matthew Fellion and Katherine Inglis.

Includes bibliographical references and index.
Issued in print and electronic formats.
ISBN 978-0-7735-5127-5 (hardcover) ISBN 978-0-7735-5188-6 (ePDF) ISBN 978-0-7735-
5189-3 (ePUB)

1. English literature–Censorship–History.
2. American literature–Censorship–History.
3. Censorship–Great Britain–History.
4. Censorship–United States–History.
5. Literature and society–Great Britain–History.
6. Literature and society–United States–History.
    I. Inglis, Katherine, 1980–, author II. Title.

Z658.G7F45 2017   025.2'130941   C2017-902566-X
C2017-902567-8

Illustrations copyright © 2017 British Library Board except for those on the page numbers
listed below.

158 Fox Photos/Getty Images; 176 Gisele Freund/The LIFE Images Collection/Getty Images;
192 Keystone/Getty Images; 204 Reproduced courtesy of the National Library of Ireland; 216
Photo Gordon Parks, FSA/OWI Collection, Library of Congress, Washington, D.C. (LC-USW3-
030297-D); 230 © William M Gaines Agent Inc.; 248 William Jacobellis/New York Post Archives/©
NYP Holdings, Inc. via Getty Images; 276 Photo courtesy Twice Sold Tales Used Books, Seattle,
WA (www.twicesoldtales.com); 288 Photo Hulton Archive/Getty Images; 306 Photos © Andreas
Hansen; 318 Courtesy Samuel S. Lin; 338 Ronald Grant Archive/Mary Evans Picture Library; 352
Photo Uwe Anspach/dpa picture alliance archive/Alamy Stock Photo; 364 © Marjane Satrapi,
courtesy Penguin Random House; 382 Photo © Chris Summitt

Typeset by IDSUK (DataConnection) Ltd
Jacket designed by Jason Anscomb, Rawshock Design

For those who, free to speak,
are powerless to be heard

Contents

Acknowledgements

Writing a history of censorship makes one conscious of all the people who work to bring books into the world, many of whom have been on the front lines in the struggle between subversion and control. We would like to thank Rob Davies of British Library Publishing for thinking of this book, giving us the opportunity to write it, and allowing it room to grow. He has been receptive and supportive at every step. We are grateful to our editor Jon Crabb and copy-editor Jacqueline Harvey for making the text pristine (and sorry for the headaches that our endnotes will have given them), to image editors Pauline Hubner and Sally Nicholls for the illustrations, to Jason Anscomb for the visual style, as well as the typesetter, proofreader, and indexer. Thanks to Emma O'Bryen, Maria Vassilopoulos and Abbie Day for publicity, marketing and sales; and thanks to Natalie Blachere, Filomena Falocco, Amy Hemond, Jennifer Roberts, Jack Hannan and others at McGill-Queen's University Press for marketing and distributing the North American edition. We would also like to thank the printers and everyone else involved in delivering this book into readers' hands, especially the independent booksellers who continue to serve their communities despite the economies of scale.

The welcoming staff at the National Library of Scotland have made working there a pleasure, and have patiently fielded what must have seemed like endless requests for a motley selection of resources. Special thanks to Suzy Pope and Mike Saunders, Reference Services, for help in finding tabloids. Thanks, too, to the cafe staff for the coffees and teas that kept us going. The University of Edinburgh Interlibrary Loan staff, particularly Louise Dutnell, have gone beyond the call of duty in tracking down and summoning elusive books, some of which we consulted with the help of staff at the Centre for Research Collections. We are grateful to Liz Stevenson, Academic Support Librarian at the University of Edinburgh Law Library for teaching us how to navigate case law, and Shenxiao Tong, Academic Support Librarian at the Main Library, for advice. Janet Black, Gavin Douglas, and Fiona Carmichael of the University of Edinburgh created an environment for Dr Inglis to conduct secure research. Anne Marie Menta and June Can at Yale's Beinecke Rare Book and Manuscript Library processed our request for and supplied us with images of papers from the James Kirkup archive. Nathalie Mathieu at Library and Archives Canada guided us to the Radclyffe Hall material in the Lovat Dickson bequest. Marie Moser, Cat Anderson, and the other lovely people at the Edinburgh Bookshop have sourced various hard-to-find books for us, including *Black Voices from Prison*. Robert Inglis overcame technological barriers on our behalf.

We are deeply grateful to those who read chapters of the book or otherwise made contributions: James Eli Adams, Owen Boynton, Denise Chung Guerrero, David Fellion, Holly Furneaux, Keith Hughes, Carole Jones, Michelle Keown, Michele Moody-Adams, Tom Mole, Steve Pinkerton, Cory Rushton, Shari Sabeti, Paul Sawyer, Suzanne Trill, and Jonathan Wild. Anne Marie Hagen organized a workshop that allowed us to give material on *Jenny Lives with Eric and Martin* an early airing. The University of Edinburgh students who have taken Dr Inglis's course on censorship have also contributed through their enthusiasm for the subject and their challenging questions. They chose to study *Beloved* and *Persepolis*, both of which appear in this book. We would like to extend special thanks to Mayra Feliciano for allowing us to use her image in chapter 25, and to the photographer Chris Summitt for providing a window into community protest in Tucson. All views expressed in this book are our own, as are any errors that we have made.

Thanks, finally, to our families and friends for their support, and to everyone who has expressed interest in this project along the way. We hope you enjoy the book.

Introduction

When we refer to the freedom of speech, we do not mean the freedom to go out into the wilderness and whisper to the night sky or scribble in the sand. If nobody will hear or read our words, we may express anything, but can communicate nothing. The freedom of communication is what counts, and communication requires one or more recipients. It is something that people do with other people, and such actions are constrained by the rights, freedoms, and often the wishes of everyone involved, as well as by the social norms that shape what we can say, and even what it occurs to us to say.[1] Those involved in a particular communication include the speaker or speakers, the audience, and others who may be affected even if they do not participate directly, such as the one who is being spoken about. Though censorship is something of a dirty word, and nobody wants to be called a censor, censorship is inevitable because people impose limits on each other's actions.

Isn't speech fundamentally different from action, though? What harm can words do? This reasoning can lead to the conclusion that speech should never be restricted because it cannot actually hurt anyone, and that those who believe they have been harmed by speech simply need to grow a thicker skin. We find this position unconvincing. Speech involves action, and has tangible effects, though these are rarely easy to predict or control. The same power that exposes a corrupt government can incite mob violence against a vulnerable person. A state can declare

AREOPAGITICA;

A

SPEECH

OF

Mr. JOHN MILTON

For the Liberty of VNLICENC'D
PRINTING,

To the PARLAMENT of ENGLAND.

Τἐλεύθερον δ' ἐκεῖνο, εἴ τις θέλει πόλει
Χρησόν τι βέλευμ' εἰς μέσον φέρειν, ἔχων,
Καὶ ταῦθ' ὁ χρήζων, λαμπρός ἐσθ', ὁ μὴ θέλων,
Σιγᾷ, τί τέτων ἐστὶν ἰσαίτερον πόλει;

Euripid, Hicetid.

This is true Liberty when free born men
Having to advise the public may speak free,
Which he who can, and will, deserv's high praise,
Who neither can nor will, may hold his peace;
What can be juster in a State then this?

Euripid. Hicetid.

LONDON,
Printed in the Yeare, 1644.

The title page of John Milton's *Areopagitica*, in which he argues against print licensing but endorses the destruction of mischievous books.

war, a judge can pass a sentence, and anybody can give names to things. As the philosopher Judith Butler argues, the names that others use for us, whether categories like 'man', 'woman', 'Black', and 'White', or any number of terms of abuse, add up over time to become the stuff that our sense of self is made of. There is some room to push back against these names, change them, make them our own, and reject them. There is no way to escape them.[2] Because speech is powerful, our freedom to speak must be defended from unjust restrictions. Because speech is powerful, however, that freedom cannot be absolute. Like action, speech will always raise ethical and legal questions.

Whether through laws, regulations, policies, or social conventions, people restrict speech because of the actions that they believe it to be performing. To give a few examples, laws have historically prohibited speech that incites crime or violence, betrays the state, foments political dissent, reveals classified information, disturbs the peace, corrupts morals, promotes hatred against groups, denies genocides, damages reputations or business interests, steals intellectual property, extorts money, insults rulers, questions religious doctrine, attacks religious figures or gods, invades privacy, and harasses, abuses, threatens, blackmails, or defrauds individuals. Are these restrictions good or bad? Unless you happen to accept the possible consequences of every imaginable speech act, then you will find some restrictions reasonable and others arbitrary, ill conceived, oppressive, or unethical. We suggest that most people are actually okay with many different kinds of censorship. *Censored* deals with more contentious cases, in which those whose speech was restricted have struggled against the constraints.

Our aim is to tell stories that reveal how the censorship of literature has developed over time. We strive to be fair and accurate, but not neutral. There are many instances of injustice and the abuse of power in this book, as well as cases that are more difficult to call. *Hit Man*, for instance, presents itself as a handbook for would-be assassins. When its instructions were used to commit a murder, an appeals court found that the First Amendment of the US Constitution, which guarantees the freedom of speech, did not protect *Hit Man*'s publisher from a civil lawsuit. Given that the publisher admitted that he intended the book to be used to commit crimes, was this a reasonable limitation of his liberties or a slippery slope leading to the censorship of crime novels and films? We invite you to consider the perspectives we present, and to think about where you would draw your own lines.

The Scope of This Book

This book examines censorship in two countries that claim an ancient tradition of free expression and political liberty. Anti-censorship writers in the United Kingdom and the United States tend to identify John Milton, the author of *Paradise Lost*, as the almost mythic forefather of this tradition. In 1641, when the English Parliament abolished the Star Chamber that King Charles I had used to punish dissidents and control the country, it overturned the Decree of 1637, under which no books could be printed without state approval. But Parliament decided that it wanted its own censorship powers, and in 1643 reintroduced a licensing system to control the press. Milton wrote *Areopagitica* in 1644 in an attempt to persuade Parliament to reject censorship. He wrote:

> As good almost kill a Man as kill a good Book; who kills a Man kills a reasonable creature, Gods image; but hee who destroyes a good Booke, kills reason it selfe, kills the Image of God, as it were in the eye.[3]

Nick Cohen, a British journalist and anti-censorship writer, identifies the 1640s as the time when 'the English unleashed the contemporary idea of freedom of speech', and sees *Areopagitica* as the first expression of a modern critique of censorship. Milton's words, he finds, 'still have the power to bring a tear to English eyes'.[4] On the other side of the Atlantic, in the *Banned Books* reference guide published by the American Library Association and sponsored by other US anti-censorship organizations, Milton keeps company with Supreme Court judges and Benjamin Franklin in a gallery of 'First Amendment Quotations'.[5] The attorney who defended D. H. Lawrence's *Lady Chatterley's Lover* and John Cleland's *Memoirs of a Woman of Pleasure* in court, Charles Rembar, explains that '*Areopagitica* is a fundamental document in the history of liberty'. Rembar recognized, however, that Milton did not extend the freedom of speech to everyone.[6] Milton was most concerned with giving Puritans access to the press, and did not argue that people of other creeds should have the same freedom.[7] In fact, he did not actually argue against censorship, only censorship prior to publication. Few anti-censorship writers quote Milton's acknowledgement that books can be dangerous, and can sow discord and violence. He accepts that the church and government have a duty to monitor books, and if necessary to 'confine, imprison, and do sharpest justice on them as malefactors'. He thought that the best way to regulate the press was to prohibit anonymous publication, advising that if anonymous books 'be found mischievous and libellous, the fire and the executioner will be the timeliest and most effectual remedy'.[8] Just as Milton's attack on censorship is much more limited than is usually recognized, the freedom of speech, vital as it is, has been limited in many ways. In telling the history of the censorship of printed literature in the Anglo-American tradition, this book exposes the gap between the freedom of speech that has been celebrated in soaring Miltonian rhetoric, and the social, economic, and legal reality on the ground, where those whose writing challenges the status quo, especially religious, political, and sexual norms, have risked having 'sharpest justice' done to them and their books. Booksellers, printers, and publishers have often been first in the line of fire.

In addition to the United States and the United Kingdom, China, Australia, Canada, Iran, India, Pakistan, Turkey, and France make appearances in this book, while Ireland, with its distinctive Censorship of Publications Board, has its own chapter. The literature we examine is (mostly) written in English or translated into English, and we interpret 'literature' broadly enough to include autobiography, some non-fiction writing, the Bible, magazines, and comic books, as well as poetry, fiction, and a little bit of drama.

We do not cover, except in passing, live performances and new media, such as radio, television, film, and computer software, which give rise to different censorship processes. Many of these processes involve licensing offices, broadcasting authorities, ratings agencies, or other bodies that screen content before it is released to the public. The internet is a special case, which we shall discuss in the afterword. From 1737 to 1968, the law required that spoken drama performed in theatres in the United Kingdom be approved and licensed by the Office of the Lord Chamberlain, which was a means of continual state control over the moral and political content of plays.[9] In contrast, ever since press licensing ended in 1695, printed literature has tended to be one of the least restricted media in the United Kingdom and, subsequently, the United States. The written word is the proving ground of the freedom of speech. What cannot be acted out on stage or broadcast into the living rooms of the nation may still be written in a book, and what cannot be written in a book tells us much about the limits of speech at a particular place and time.

Each chapter focuses on a work of literature, though we mention other books along the way and sometimes discuss issues that are much bigger than the suppression of a single book. The chapters can stand alone or be read in any order. Taken together, they describe a range of censorship practices while tracing the censorship of literature down to the present from the Middle Ages in the United Kingdom and from the nineteenth century in the United States.

Our sources are thoroughly referenced in the endnotes, which contain only references. Readers who skip the notes will not miss any other information. In order to avoid the inaccuracies that creep in when information is compressed too many times, we have avoided citing encyclopaedic works about censorship, and have gathered our information from primary sources and more specialized secondary sources. Several encyclopaedic works have, however, been invaluable for identifying censorship cases and providing leads for further research.[10]

What Is Censorship?

'Censorship' once referred only to the state suppression of speech. This idea still lingers in the American Library Association's definition of censorship as 'Official prohibition or restriction of any type of expression believed to threaten the political, social, or moral order'.[11] In ordinary usage, however, people no longer reserve the term 'censorship' for 'official' actions, and have not done so for a long time. A newspaper can censor your comment on an article. A friend can censor your words when repeating them to someone else. You can censor yourself. We believe that this broader concept is more useful in practice, but it is also much more difficult to pin down in theory. We are tempted to define censorship in the same way that US Supreme Court Justice Potter Stewart defined hard-core pornography: 'I know it when I see it.'[12]

One way to understand censorship is to imagine a chain of communication stretching from a speaker to their audience. A simplified version of the chain, for a book published in the traditional way, might look like this: author—publisher—printer—retailer—reader.[13] In reality the chain is more complicated. The 'publisher' includes distinct people, such as editors, lawyers, and sometimes translators. The 'retailer' includes distributors, wholesalers, and merchants. An institution, such as a library, school, or prison, might intervene between the retailer and the reader, and various agents of law and order, such as customs officials, postal inspectors, police officers, and self-appointed moral crusaders, can intercept the communication, inserting themselves into the chain. The reader might continue the chain, returning the book to circulation by selling it or giving it away. And the author may choose a different method of circulation altogether, such as self-publishing or sharing work with a coterie of friends. Nevertheless, at every link in the chain, the substance of the communication can be altered or destroyed.

The chain of communication may be disrupted in various ways, and this disruption does not automatically constitute censorship. Editors have authors cut and revise manuscripts in order to improve them. Retailers decline to stock books that they don't think they can sell. Librarians pulp superfluous or outdated material. We do not usually consider these practices to be censorship, even if they prevent an author's original words from reaching their target. Censorship occurs when the chain is disrupted for certain reasons: because a communication 'threaten[s] the political, social, or moral order' (in the American Library Association's words); because it could harm or offend readers or third parties; because it reveals forbidden information; or because somebody believes that the author does not deserve to be heard. In many cases there is no single 'censor' making these judgements about speech. For instance, printers might refuse to print a book if they believe a judge would find it obscene in court. Perhaps they do not object to the manuscript themselves, but the law holds the printers responsible for their part in publishing it, so they censor it pre-emptively, and the judge never has to make the call. Moreover, censorship is not always possible to isolate from other interruptions to a chain of communication. A publisher may reject a book because it is bad, unmarketable, and immoral. Any one of these reasons would be enough to reject the book, but only the third is reason to censor it. What if the publisher thinks the book is bad and unmarketable *because* it is immoral? The boundaries of censorship are blurry.

The most famous cases of censored literature tend to involve books defended in court, such as James Joyce's *Ulysses* and Radclyffe Hall's *The Well of Loneliness*, and books removed from school libraries or curricula, such as Mark Twain's *Adventures of Huckleberry Finn* and Marjane Satrapi's *Persepolis*. Catalogues of such 'banned books' often look suspiciously like reading lists for introductory undergraduate literature courses. Stocked as they are with 'great books', these lists can be misleading, because they make censorship look rather ineffective. The full text of *Lady Chatterley's Lover*, completed in 1928, could not safely be published in the United Kingdom until Penguin Books won a court case in 1960, but the novel is now freely available and has become entrenched in the canon of English literature. Censorship can even backfire, calling further attention to the object being censored. This phenomenon is known as the 'Streisand effect', after Barbra Streisand, who popularized photographs of her California home by attempting to suppress them. Sometimes communication is less like a chain and more like a river: block the flow here, and it bursts its banks over there.

The effects of censorship, however, are not always easy to see. In 1988, following a moral panic about Susanne Bösche's children's book *Jenny Lives with Eric and Martin*, the UK government passed Section 28 of the Local Government Act. Section 28 declared that local authorities, such as town and city councils, could not 'promote homosexuality' or 'promote the teaching in any maintained school of the acceptability of homosexuality as a pretended family relationship'. This patently homophobic law was vague and remained unenforced, but it successfully hampered discussions of same-sex relationships in schools, because teachers avoided the topic out of fear of violating a law that was difficult to understand. Similarly, laws forbidding obscenity, blasphemy, sedition, and defamation affect not only those who end up in court but also those who are careful not to. As the human rights barrister Geoffrey Robertson has said on the topic of UK libel law, 'We do not have free speech in Britain, we have expensive speech.'[14] Risks are fine for those who can afford to take them. Everybody else usually plays it safe. This form of widespread, defensive self-censorship is known as 'chilling effect'. Chilling effect is usually invisible, a black hole that can be detected only by the absence of the light that it devours. For every successful defence of a book in court, there may be many more books that were never written in the first place, or never published, printed, or sold, because of the potential repercussions.

The threat of legal penalties is not the only reason writers censor themselves. Self-censorship is a normal part of communication, but it is not always voluntary, and can result from the writer's lack of social or political power. Inequalities along axes of race, gender, sexuality, class, religion, and ability are forces that create censorship, and these forces are all the more potent because no single censoring authority is orchestrating them. The author and playwright Frances Burney had a successful literary career, but repeatedly stifled her plays out of deference to the two father figures in her life, who ensured that her writing remained within the limits of acceptable feminine conduct. Social inequality continues to affect writers' work long after they have died. Some works of literature endure through the centuries and become fixtures in schools, universities, and lists of classic books, through a process known as 'canon formation'. While it is comforting to think that the survival of a work is solely a measure of its merit, this is simply not true. The taste-makers who built the canon of English literature, including critics in the nineteenth and early twentieth centuries, stacked the deck in favour of White male authors, selectively forgetting others, and it is only in the last fifty years that literary scholars have made significant progress in recovering the work of people like Burney.

Institutions, including schools, have their own regulations and hierarchies, which affect the forms that censorship takes. The American Library Association's catalogue of censorship incidents, *Banned Books*, consists mostly of challenges and bans in US schools, where parents, school boards, educators, politicians, and students themselves have fought to determine what material students ought to read. Other institutions can exercise much more severe censorship. Prison policies, for example, restrict the kind of material that can be sent to incarcerated people, how this material can be delivered, and what can be held in prison libraries. The poet Etheridge Knight's collection *Black Voices from Prison* discusses prison censorship and was later subject to it. One of the most comprehensive systems of censorship is slavery, which robs enslaved people of their rights and their autonomy. Mary Prince, a survivor of British slavery in the West Indies, was able to preserve her history only by putting it into the hands of abolitionists, who shaped it into a tool to serve their own purposes.

We have attempted to strike a balance between different kinds of stories in this book, but we do not wish to pretend that all censorship is equal. What makes censorship matter is power, and the people who suffer most from the censorship of literature are those with the least power to speak and the least freedom to read.

Notes

1. See Pierre Bourdieu, 'Censorship and the Imposition of Form', in *Language and Symbolic Power*, ed. John B. Thompson, trans. Gino Raymond and Matthew Adamson (Cambridge: Polity, 1992; repr. 2002), pp. 137–59 (p. 138).

2. See Judith Butler, *Excitable Speech: A Politics of the Performative* (New York: Routledge, 1997), pp. 14–15, 29–30, 33, 36–38, 49, 153–54, 155, 157–59, 162–63.

3. John Milton, *Areopagitica: A Speech of Mr. John Milton for the Liberty of Unlicenc'd Printing, to the Parlament [sic] of England* (London, 1644), in *Censorship and the Press, 1580–1720*, ed. Geoff Kemp and Jason McElligott, 4 vols (London: Pickering & Chatto, 2009), II: *1640–1660*, ed. McElligott, pp. 93–125 (p. 96).

4. Nick Cohen, *You Can't Read This Book: Censorship in an Age of Freedom*, 2nd edn (London: Fourth Estate, 2013), pp. 131–33.

5. Robert P. Doyle, *Banned Books: Challenging our Freedom to Read* (Chicago: American Library Association, 2014), p. 71.

6. Charles Rembar, *The End of Obscenity: The Trials of Lady Chatterley, Tropic of Cancer, and Fanny Hill* (London: Deutsch, 1969), p. 8.

7. Jason McElligott, 'Introduction', in *Censorship and the Press*, II, xi–xxvi (p. xxi).

8. Milton, pp. 96, 124.

9. Dominic Shellard and others, *The Lord Chamberlain Regrets . . . : A History of British Theatre Censorship* (London: British Library, 2004), pp. 9–10, 173.

10. See Margaret Bald, *Banned Books: Literature Suppressed on Religious Grounds*, rev. edn (New York: Facts on File, 2006); *Censorship: A World Encyclopedia*, ed. Derek Jones, 4 vols (London: Fitzroy Dearborn, 2001); Jonathon Green and Nicholas J. Karolides, *Encyclopedia of Censorship*,

new edn (New York: Facts on File, 2005); Nicholas J. Karolides and others, *120 Banned Books: Censorship Histories of World Literature* (New York: Checkmark Books, 2005); Nicholas J. Karolides, *Banned Books: Literature Suppressed on Political Grounds*, rev. edn (New York: Facts on File, 2006); Dawn B. Sova, *Banned Books: Literature Suppressed on Sexual Grounds*, rev. edn (New York: Facts on File, 2006); Dawn B. Sova, *Banned Books: Literature Suppressed on Social Grounds*, rev. edn (New York: Facts on File, 2006).

11. Doyle, p. 60.
12. Jacobellis v. Ohio, 378 U.S. 184, 197 (1964) (Stewart, J., concurring).
13. See Robert Darnton, 'What Is the History of Books?', *Daedalus*, 111.3 (1982), 65–83 (p. 68).
14. Geoffrey Robertson, 'QC's View: "Media Must Fight Harder for its Freedom"', *Guardian*, 10 November 2009, https://www.theguardian.com/uk/2009/nov/10/qc-views-of-media-freedom, accessed 31 December 2016.

1

The English Bibles
John Wyclif, William Tyndale, and Others

The first complete English Bible was born out of heresy in the late fourteenth century. The sect that produced it, the Wycliffites, posed such a threat to Catholic orthodoxy that Thomas Arundel, Archbishop of Canterbury, prohibited the translation of scripture and the state burned heretics alive. Over a hundred years later, when the reformer William Tyndale printed his English New Testament, biblical translation was still proscribed. After Tyndale was burned as a heretic by the Holy Roman Emperor, Henry VIII authorized the Great Bible, spreading vernacular scripture throughout the new Church of England. He then imposed restrictions on reading it. Though the barriers to translation were now breached, particular translations would continue to be suppressed under subsequent rulers.

John Wyclif was a parish priest and Oxford theologian with a rebellious streak, and the censorship of the Wycliffite Bible was only one part of the censorship of his ideas. He believed that the Bible conveyed the ultimate authority of the Christian God. Where the Catholic Church departed from the truth of scripture—for instance, by amassing worldly goods in monasteries or recognizing the leadership of a Pope who was in a state of sin—the church was wrong.[1] The whiff of heresy in Wyclif's ideas attracted the attention of Pope

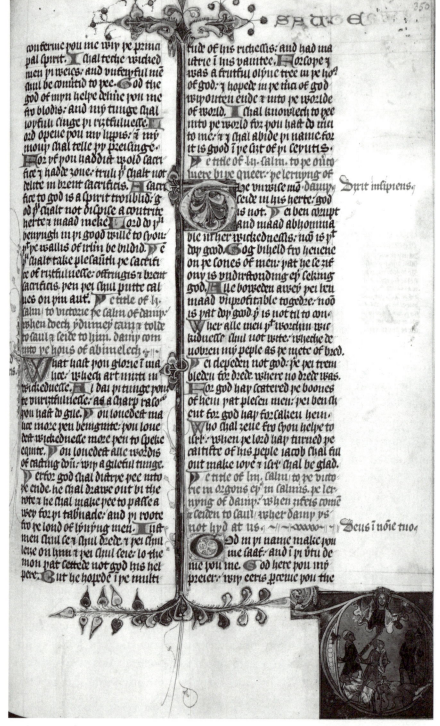

A page of the Psalter in a complete Wycliffite Bible from the early fifteenth century (Arundel MS 104).

Gregory XI and the English bishops, though they failed to condemn the priest, partly because he had the protection of John of Gaunt, the Duke of Lancaster.[2] Wyclif's teaching became still more dangerous when he concluded that the doctrine of transubstantiation was false: priests did not turn bread and wine into Christ's flesh and blood during the sacrament of the Eucharist, and the power to transform one substance into another was one of the powers they had wrongly claimed.[3] In 1381 a committee led by Oxford chancellor William Barton prohibited two of Wyclif's claims or 'theses' from being disseminated at the university. Though he did not stop writing, Wyclif left Oxford, returning to his parish at Lutterworth in Leicestershire, where he escaped official condemnation until his death in 1384.[4]

In Wyclif's absence, a movement based on his thought was gathering momentum at Oxford, and recent events made it an especially urgent threat. In 1378 the Great Schism had yielded two competing Popes, strengthening Wyclif's criticism of the church. In 1381 English commoners had risen up in the Peasants' Revolt.[5] One of the leaders of the revolt, John Ball, was described as a follower of Wyclif, and some linked the civil unrest to Wyclif's ideas,[6] which wandering 'poor preachers' were said to be spreading outside the university.[7] In 1382 William Courtenay, Archbishop of Canterbury, called a council of clerics and academics in London, known as the Blackfriars Council, which condemned several of these ideas as errors or heresies. A crackdown ensued at Oxford. Wycliffites were suspended, imprisoned, and excommunicated. Richard II ordered the chancellor of the university to yield up Wycliffite writings to Courtenay.[8] Yet the movement, which became known by the pejorative term 'Lollardy', was not eradicated. It gained traction among lay people outside the university, and sympathizers remained at Oxford.[9]

Here the Bible makes its appearance. Throughout the rise of the Wycliffite heresy, the English Bible was in progress. The translation from the Latin Vulgate was a team effort, probably involving Wyclif himself and some of his Oxford associates.[10] At first, the translators rendered the Latin into English as literally as possible, with stilted results. Known as the Early Version, these texts began to appear in the early 1380s.[11] The Later Version, which began to be copied around 1390,[12] is a more natural translation.[13] Though some copies contained prefaces in which the Wycliffites advanced their arguments, the translations themselves were orthodox and true to the Vulgate text.[14] The Book of Genesis in the Later Version opens with the following words, alien yet familiar:

> In the bigynnyng God made of nouȝt heuene and erthe. Forsothe the erthe was idel and voide, and derknessis weren on the face of depthe; and the Spiryt of the Lord was borun on the watris. And God seide, Liȝt be maad, and liȝt was maad.[15]

The Wycliffites translated the Bible in order to make it available to the common people. Though French had been the language of literature and politics since the Norman Conquest in 1066, by the end of the fourteenth century Middle English, used by writers such as Geoffrey Chaucer, John Gower, and William Langland, was gaining ground. Yet the standard text of the Bible was still in Latin, an elite language. Scripture had been translated into Anglo-Saxon before the Conquest, but this version of English was no longer in use. There were some partial French and Middle English translations, and possibly a complete French translation.[16] Most English people did not, however, have access to the Bible in a language they knew, and needed to rely on the clergy for religious instruction. The Wycliffites, who considered the clergy fallible and corrupt, wanted to bring scripture directly to the laity. When Courtenay examined the Wycliffite John Aston for heresy, he commanded Aston to speak in Latin. An audience of lay sympathizers had intruded on the interrogation, and Courtenay did not want them to understand what was being said. Aston did, so he spoke in English.[17]

Biblical translation was not yet forbidden, but some considered it undesirable. Around 1401, academics at Oxford debated the question. Some objected to putting scripture in the hands of ordinary people, especially women and peasants, who might be tempted to preach—and would inevitably, these scholars thought, preach error. They considered English an inferior language to Latin, and saw translation as a threat both to the meaning of the text and to the church hierarchy. The Oxonian Richard Ullerston, though he was no heretic, defended English and the laity's capacity to understand scripture, arguing that it was right for women to instruct each other and for peasants to educate their families.[18] Elitism ran deep, however, and not just among Ullerston's opponents. The chronicler Henry Knighton complained (in Latin) about the effects of translating 'the gospel that Christ gave to the clergy and doctors of the church' into English:

> the gospel has become more common and more open to laymen and even to women who know how to read than it customarily is to moderately well-educated clergy of good intelligence. Thus the pearl of the gospel is scattered abroad and trodden underfoot by swine.[19]

The poet Thomas Hoccleve recommended that women who wanted to debate scripture sit down, spin yarn, and cackle about something else, 'for your wit | Is al to feeble to dispute of it!'[20]

Most of the English-speaking commoners were illiterate, and the Wycliffite Bible, which was copied out by hand, was neither cheap nor easy to acquire. It often circulated in sections rather than as a complete text.[21] Still, networks of Wycliffites (or 'Lollards') formed, in households and villages, around those who could read portions of the Bible aloud or who had learned passages by rote. Wycliffites met for preaching and, in the scholar Margaret Aston's words, 'underground reading parties'—outdoors, in churches where priests were sympathetic, in taverns, and in private houses. There were wandering preachers, books and editions, and schools.[22] Scripture and heresy circulated together. And they did, as detractors had feared, reach women, some of whom became preachers. Hostile sources claimed that women were even celebrating Mass, which was theoretically possible. One of the 'Twelve Conclusions of the Lollards', nailed to the door of Westminster Hall in 1395, denies transubstantiation and claims that 'every true man and woman in God's law [may] make the sacrament of the bread without any such miracle'.[23]

As the movement spread, church and state legislation targeted both the heretics and their books. In the 1380s and 1390s, there were further attempts to suppress works by Wyclif.[24] A 1395 mandate from Pope Boniface IX called for action against the sect.[25] In 1401 Henry IV's parliament passed a statute known as *De heretico comburendo*, which prescribed execution by burning for heretics who refused to abjure their heresy or who relapsed after abjuring. The statute also required that heterodox books be relinquished to the church on pain of punishment for heresy.[26] In 1409 Courtenay's successor Thomas Arundel issued his Constitutions, which the scholar Nicholas Watson describes as 'one of the most draconian pieces of censorship in English history'. Arundel prohibited unlicensed preaching; restricted the topics that parish priests, preachers, and teachers could discuss; and confined religious debate to the universities. He required that every student at Oxford be examined for orthodoxy once a month. He had new books screened and approved at the universities in a process that he himself would oversee. And he prohibited all translations of scripture from Wyclif's time or later, except those that were allowed by special permission. Even reading an unlicensed translation was forbidden.[27] Arundel had an Oxford committee examine Wyclif's works and report on the heresies they contained. By 1411, the committee had found 267 heresies and errors, and Wyclif's works were destroyed in a bonfire at Carfax.[28] Arundel sent the list of heresies to antipope John XXIII, who in 1412 prohibited reading or possessing texts by Wyclif and called for them to be burned[29]—which they were (again) at St Paul's in 1413.[30] The condemnation of John Wyclif reached its climax two years later in the Council of Constance, where he and the Bohemian reformer Jan Hus were formally declared heretics. Hus was burned alive and Wyclif's bones were burned, as were, once more, his books.[31]

Nothing further could be done to Wyclif, but the persecution of the Wycliffites and the suppression of the English Bible were only beginning. Under Arundel's Constitutions, merely possessing religious writings in English or knowing prayers and scripture in English could be evidence of heresy, and under the *De heretico comburendo* heresy meant death by fire for those who relapsed or refused to recant. Though Wycliffites learned to equivocate in trials, and most renounced their heresy if convicted, some died for their beliefs. A London skinner named John Claydon, who could not read, had Wycliffite literature copied out and read to him. In his 1415 trial, one of these books, *The Lanterne of Liʒt*, was held as evidence against him, and he admitted that he agreed with its contents. Because he had already recanted once before, he was sentenced to death.[32] In 1494 a woman of over eighty, Joan Boughton, refused to recant, and 'said she was soo belovid wiþ God and his holy angelys that all the fyre in London shuld not hurt hyr'. She did not survive the fire, and the night after she was executed her followers gathered up her ashes.[33] When heretics were convicted, their books were destroyed.[34] One burned his own books pre-emptively lest 'his bookes should burne him'.[35] Enforcement appears to have been selective: orthodox people of higher status, especially royalty and the clergy, owned English Bibles without consequences, yet the London bookseller Thomas Marlborough was indicted for possession of a Bible that had belonged to Henry IV.[36] Records suggest that persecution fell most heavily on those below the ranks of the elite and above the peasantry, such as artisans and their families, who became a major part of the movement.[37] Laywomen who made a public display of their religious devotion risked being taken for Wycliffites even if they were not, as in the case of Margery Kempe. An orthodox mystic who travelled on pilgrimages, preached in English, and defended women preachers, Kempe was repeatedly accused of being a Lollard and threatened with burning.[38] Occasional acts of resistance by the Wycliffites renewed the fears of church and state. The Lollard Disendowment Bill, proposed in Parliament around 1410 and again in 1414, called for the state to confiscate ecclesiastical wealth and put it to other uses, such as funding fifteen new universities, 100 almshouses, and new aristocrats.[39] In 1414 the Lollard knight Sir John Oldcastle led an armed uprising against the crown, which provoked increased persecution of the heretics,[40] and the weaver William Perkins led another unsuccessful revolt in 1431.[41] After the Oldcastle rising, sixty-nine people were sentenced to execution as traitors, though a number of these were pardoned. Records are incomplete, but the historian John A. F. Thomson lists nearly five hundred and fifty major prosecutions for heresy, resulting in over thirty executions, between the rising and 1522.[42]

Owning books could attract suspicion, and records of one trial mention possession of Chaucer's *Canterbury Tales*, though the scholar Andrew Cole calls this 'the exception that proves no rule'.[43] On a large scale, it is likely that Arundel's Constitutions had a chilling effect on English literature dealing with religion, which often quoted scripture in translation. Watson argues that the Constitutions led to 'an atmosphere in which self-censorship was assumed to be both for the common good and (for one's own safety) prudent'.[44] The Wycliffites and their Bible endured, despite the persecution. Over two hundred and fifty manuscripts of Wycliffite scripture survive today. About twenty of them are complete Bibles.[45] By the 1520s, however, both the English language and the landscape of Christianity had changed. The Protestant Reformation was under way, and England needed a new vernacular

Bible. By 1526, one was available, and the Wycliffites John Tybal and Thomas Hilles of Steeple Bumpstead could travel to London to trade up their scriptures for William Tyndale's New Testament. The man who sold them their New Testaments, the friar Robert Barnes, told them to keep the books hidden. Barnes had recently recanted his Lutheranism and was confined to the Augustinian house in London. Tybal and Hilles were tried in 1528.[46] Barnes burned in 1540, having fled into exile, risen into Henry VIII's favour, and then fallen out of it again.[47]

New heresy, imported from Continental Europe, rubbed shoulders with old. The new reformers shared some theological and political concerns with the Wycliffites, and adopted several of their books for the cause.[48] They, too, believed that scripture should be available in the language of the people, a principle that the Dutch humanist Erasmus expressed, though he remained orthodox himself:

> Christ wishes his mysteries published as openly as possible. I would that even the lowliest women read the Gospels and the Pauline Epistles. And I would that they were translated into all languages so that they could be read and understood not only by Scots and Irish but also by Turks and Saracens.[49]

Erasmus was a leader of the new biblical scholarship, which returned to the Hebrew and Greek sources on which the Latin versions had been based. His edition of the Greek New Testament became the foundation for Protestant translations such as Martin Luther's New Testament in German, printed in 1522.[50] The printing press, which was invented in 1440, but which had not been available to the Wycliffites, enabled Protestant texts to spread rapidly.

The reformer William Tyndale, who was also committed to vernacular scripture, based his English New Testament on Erasmus's edition of the Greek. Tyndale had hoped to undertake his translation project in the house of Cuthbert Tunstall, Bishop of London, but Tunstall turned him down. Tyndale relocated to the Continent and began to print the New Testament in Cologne, but he had to flee to Worms when an enemy informed on him, leaving the first edition incomplete. At Worms, Tyndale printed a complete second edition in a run of several thousand, which merchants smuggled into England and Scotland, often in shipments of cloth. A printer in Antwerp ran off a few thousand more pirated copies, some of which also ended up in England. Tyndale also began to translate the Old Testament from Hebrew, publishing the Pentateuch in 1530, though he would not have the chance to finish his work.[51] His Genesis opens, with modernized spelling:

> In the beginning God created heaven and earth. The earth was void and empty, and darkness was upon the deep, and the spirit of God moved upon the water.
>   Then God said: let there be light and there was light.[52]

Tyndale's style had a significant impact on later translations of the Bible and, through them, on the English language. Scholars have calculated that 83 per cent of the New Testament in the King James Version is Tyndale's.[53]

More conservative clergy still thought that vernacular Bible translators were casting pearls before swine.[54] Like the Wycliffite Bible, however, Tyndale's translations were censored, above all, because of their links to heresy. In his New Testament, Tyndale, faithful to the Greek text, used terms that differed significantly from those of the Vulgate, such as 'congregation' for 'church', 'seniour' (later 'elder') for 'priest', 'love' for 'charity', 'favour' for 'grace', and 'repentance' for 'penance'.[55] Sir Thomas More complained in his 1529 *Dialogue concerning Heresies*, in the voice of the character called the 'Master Chancellor', that these choices helped further Tyndale's and Luther's heresies. Tyndale made readers believe that orthodox preachers had 'englyshed the scrypture wronge to lede the people purposely out of the ryght way'. Licensed by Tunstall to read heretical texts and write about them, More roundly condemned both the Wycliffite Bible and the Tyndale New Testament, and defended Arundel's Constitutions.[56]

More's writings were one strategy in the most recent campaign against heresy. In response to news of the English New Testament, the Lord Chancellor, Cardinal Thomas Wolsey, ordered searches for Lutheran books. In 1526 More led a raid at the Steelyard in London on European cloth merchants, four of whom were arrested for heresy (plus one for coin cutting). There was also a raid on Cambridge University, but reformers there had advance warning, and the search turned up nothing except Robert Barnes, the man who would soon give Tybal and Hilles of Steeple Bumpstead their New Testaments. He was arrested for heretical preaching. Wolsey staged a spectacle at St Paul's, where books were burned in a bonfire. Barnes and the merchants, having abjured, carried faggots as penance.[57] Bishop Tunstall followed Wolsey's lead. He reiterated an earlier order to London booksellers not to publish, import, or sell books without approval from the Lord Chancellor, the Archbishop of Canterbury, or Tunstall himself. He bought up copies of the Tyndale New Testament in order to destroy them, and held another bonfire at St Paul's Cross, in which New Testaments were destroyed. Wolsey arranged to have copies burned overseas, and William Warham, the Archbishop of Canterbury, sought the help of the bishops in buying up copies to burn.[58] Because the printing press now made it easier to convert money into more books, purchasing the New Testament for destruction may well have helped fund future editions.[59]

Authorities issued several lists of forbidden books on which Tyndale's translations appeared.[60] People who were buying, selling, and reading the Tyndale scriptures, among other reformist literature, faced heresy proceedings during which the *De heretico comburendo* continued to hang like a sword over their heads. Nobody burned while Wolsey was Chancellor, however, perhaps because Lutheranism was percolating mainly among the university-educated, and church authorities preferred to deal with it quietly.[61] This policy would change around 1529–30, when More became Lord Chancellor and John Stokesley became Bishop of London.[62] More argued in his *Dialogue* (through the 'Master Chancellor') that the church had stretched the limits of clemency, and concluded that it must turn heretics over to the state for punishment, which was the law of the *De heretico comburendo*.[63] As Lord Chancellor, More issued a proclamation against heresy and heretical books. Warham and Bishop Fisher of Rochester condemned Thomas Hitton to die in 1530, and several more people were burned during More's chancellorship.[64]

In 1531 the King's chief minister Thomas Cromwell sent a messenger to bring Tyndale back to England, promising safe conduct and mercy. Tyndale replied that, if Henry VIII would only authorize an English Bible, he would stop writing and return to submit himself to the King's will.[65] While Tyndale was bombarding the kingdom with treatises and English scripture, Henry was attempting to divorce Catherine of Aragon and marry Anne Boleyn, against the wishes of Pope Clement VII and the Holy Roman Emperor, Charles V. This

conflict culminated in Henry's excommunication and the creation of
the Church of England, with the King at its head. It was a dangerous time not only for heretics like Tyndale, but also for people like
More—an orthodox Catholic close to Henry who disapproved of
his remarriage and still considered the Pope to be the leader of the
church. More was beheaded for treason in 1535. Tyndale had criticized Henry's divorce in his tract *The Practice of Prelates*, but he never
had the chance to test Henry's mercy. In Antwerp, an Englishman
named Henry Phillips betrayed Tyndale to the court of Charles V at
Brussels, which proceeded against him as a Lutheran heretic. Tyndale
was strangled to death before he was burned at the stake in 1536.[66]
The Protestant martyrologist John Foxe records his last words as 'Lord
open the king of Englands eyes.'[67]

If Tyndale had lived a year longer, he would have seen English Bibles
circulating freely. Miles Coverdale's Bible was dedicated to Henry
VIII, and one version of it was printed with his licence. John Rogers's
'Matthew's Bible' was also dedicated to the King and printed with his
licence. Rogers had used Tyndale's translation to make Matthew's Bible,
filling in the incomplete portions with Coverdale's. There was no mention of the real translator on its title page. Rather, the translation was
attributed to the non-existent 'Thomas Matthew'. Cromwell pushed
bishops to place Matthew's Bible in the churches of their dioceses, but
it contained tell-tale signs of Tyndale's influence: his divergence from
the Vulgate on certain key words, and the initials 'WT' on the last page
of the Old Testament. Cromwell had Coverdale revise Matthew's Bible
instead. The result, an authorized 'Great Bible', would be a large book,
with no annotations, printed to high standards in France. France proved
a hostile environment, however. After interference from the Inquisition,
the publishers saved what they could, completed the project in England,
and began to sell the Great Bible in 1539. According to Cromwell's
Second Injunctions, every parish in England was required to display a
copy.[68] Yet the winds of politics, always changeable under Henry VIII,
soon turned against Cromwell, and he was executed for heresy and
treason in a 1540 purge that also sent Barnes to the fire.[69]

The story of the Great Bible has one final twist. Beginning in
1539, Henry's parliament took steps to enforce the new religious
orthodoxy. In 1543 the Act for the Advancement of True Religion

created fines for possessing books that were heretical or that questioned official doctrine, re-established the ban on Tyndale's translation, and prohibited Bibles with any annotations or prefaces.[70] The Act forbade everybody except the clergy from reading the Bible aloud in public, and restricted reading by rank and sex: men of the nobility or gentry could read the Bible aloud in their households, while merchants and women of the nobility or gentry could read it in private. The 'people of the lower sort' were forbidden to read the Bible altogether.[71] This Act meant that people were more likely to turn to the new doctrinal guide, the *King's Book*.[72] It may also have reflected official concerns about unruly Bible readers, who would get into fights over the interpretation of scripture.[73] In a speech to Parliament, Henry said, 'I am very sorry to know and hear, how unreverently that most precious word of God is disputed, rhymed sung and jangled in every alehouse and tavern.'[74] The Bible-reading prohibition was not widely enforced, though there is evidence that commoners were aware of it. A shoemaker was arrested in 1546 for reading the Bible aloud to two companions in Norwich Cathedral.[75] The first examination of the Protestant writer Anne Askew, in which she was exonerated, included charges of reading the Bible aloud.[76] (After a second examination, she was tortured on the rack and executed for heresy.[77]) In 1546 Henry proclaimed a fresh prohibition on Tyndale's and Coverdale's translations. Edmund Bonner, Bishop of London, had copies burned at St Paul's Cross, for good measure.[78]

Under Henry VIII's successor, Edward VI, the English Bible flourished, and forty editions of the complete scriptures or the New Testament were printed. No Bibles were printed during the reign of Mary I, who launched the Counter-Reformation to restore Catholicism in England, and the first of the almost three hundred people she executed was Rogers, the man behind Matthew's Bible. At least two large Bible-reading assemblies, however, were able to gather without consequences during her reign.[79] The accession of Elizabeth I marked the end of the long association between heresy and biblical translation in English, though certain translations were dangerous for political reasons. Under the censorship regimes of Elizabeth and James I, 'Popish' writing could be treasonous or seditious, and Catholic books were driven underground, including the Rheims New Testament and the Douai–Rheims Bible, uniquely Catholic translations designed to counteract the Protestant ones.[80] Around 1624 a printer named Peter Smith, who was reprinting the Rheims New Testament domestically, was arrested, and the government-sanctioned Stationers' Company destroyed his printing press and type.[81] James also took against the enormously popular Geneva Bible because of certain 'seditious' notes that challenged the divine right of kings. This opposition to the Geneva Bible provided some of the impetus for the King James Version, which was not annotated.[82] Bishop William Laud of London, soon to be Archbishop of Canterbury, forbade the printing of the Geneva Bible, and a man was imprisoned for importing copies in 1632.[83] In a comparatively minor incident, Laud also fined the printers of the 'Wicked Bible' three hundred pounds in 1631. A King James Version with a difference, the Wicked Bible merrily instructs Christians, 'Thou shalt commit adultery.'[84]

Notes

1. Maurice Keen, 'Wyclif, the Bible, and Transubstantiation', in *Wyclif in his Times*, ed. Anthony Kenny (Oxford: Clarendon Press, 1986), pp. 1–16 (pp. 3–4).

2. G. R. Evans, *John Wyclif* (Oxford: Lion, 2005), pp. 161–80. See also Joseph H. Dahmus, *The Prosecution of John Wyclyf* (New Haven: Yale University Press, 1952), pp. 7–73.

3. Keen, pp. 4–16. See also Dahmus, p. 129.

4. Evans, pp. 188–89, 191–92, 200, 210–12. See also Dahmus, pp. 129–54.

5. Dahmus, pp. 78–85.

6. Evans, pp. 192–93.

7. Anne Hudson, *The Premature Reformation: Wycliffite Texts and Lollard History* (Oxford: Clarendon Press, 1988), pp. 62–73. See also Andrew Cole, *Literature and Heresy in the Age of Chaucer* (Cambridge: Cambridge University Press, 2008), pp. 7–18; Dahmus, p. 85.

8. Dahmus, pp. 89–128.

9. Hudson, pp. 62, 82–110.

10. Mary Dove, *The First English Bible: The Text and Context of the Wycliffite Versions* (Cambridge: Cambridge University Press, 2007), pp. 2, 79–80.

11. David Daniell, *The Bible in English: Its History and Influence* (New Haven: Yale University Press, 2003), pp. 76–83.

12. Dove, p. 150.

13. Daniell, *The Bible in English*, pp. 78–81, 83–84.

14. Hudson, p. 23.

15. *The Holy Bible, Containing the Old and New Testaments, with the Apocryphal Books, in the Earliest English Versions Made from the Latin Vulgate by John Wycliffe and his Followers*, ed. Josiah Forshall and Frederic Madden, 4 vols (Oxford: Oxford University Press, 1850), I, 79 (Genesis 1. 1–3) [HathiTrust e-book].

16. Daniell, *The Bible in English*, pp. 56–65.

17. Dahmus, pp. 116–17.

18. Nicholas Watson, 'Censorship and Cultural Change in Late-Medieval England: Vernacular Theology, the Oxford Translation Debate, and Arundel's Constitutions of 1409', *Speculum*, 70.4 (1995), 822–64 (pp. 840–46). See also Kantik Ghosh, *The Wycliffite Heresy: Authority and the Interpretation of Texts* (Cambridge: Cambridge University Press, 2002), pp. 86–111.

19. *Knighton's Chronicle, 1337–1396*, ed. Geoffrey H. Martin (Oxford: Clarendon Press, 1995), pp. 242–44, quoted in Dove, p. 6.

20. Thomas Hoccleve, 'To Sir John Oldcastle', in *Hoccleve's Works: The Minor Poems*, ed. Frederick J. Furnivall and I. Gollancz, rev. Jerome Mitchell and A. I. Doyle, EETS ES 61 and 73 (London, 1892 and 1897, rev. 1970), ll. 148–49, quoted in Watson, p. 848.

21. Margaret Aston, 'Lollardy and Literacy', *History*, 62.206 (1977), 347–71 (pp. 347, 354).

22. Aston, 'Lollardy and Literacy', p. 353. See also Aston, 'Lollardy and Literacy', pp. 350–53, 355–60, 363–66, 369; Hudson, pp. 134–44, 153–57, 180–208, 421–30.

23. *Rogeri Dymmok Liber*, ed. H. S. Cronin (London: Wyclif Society, 1922), pp. 89–90, quoted in Margaret Aston, 'Lollard Women Priests?', *Journal of Ecclesiastical History*, 31.4 (1980), 441–61 (p. 454). See also Aston, 'Lollard Women Priests?', pp. 441–61; Dove, p. 110.

24. Hudson, pp. 177–78.

25. A. K. McHardy, '*De Heretico Comburendo*, 1401', in *Lollardy and the Gentry in the Later Middle Ages*, ed. Margaret Aston and Colin Richmond (Stroud: Sutton Publishing, 1997), pp. 112–26 (p. 113).

26. James Simpson, 'The Constraints of Satire in "Piers Plowman" and "Mum and the Sothsegger"', in *Langland, the Mystics and the Medieval English Religious Tradition: Essays in Honour of S. S. Hussey*, ed. Helen Phillips (Cambridge: Brewer, 1990), pp. 11–30 (p. 18).

27. Watson, pp. 826–29 and notes.

28. Hudson, pp. 83–84.

29. Dahmus, p. 153.

30. Hudson, p. 84 note 148.

31. Dahmus, pp. 153–54.

32. Hudson, pp. 158–61, 166, 211–13.

33. *The Great Chronicle of London*, ed. A. H. Thomas and I. D. Thornley (London, 1938), p. 252, quoted in Hudson, p. 161. See also Hudson, pp. 134, 160–61, 172.

34. Hudson, p. 168.

35. John Foxe, *The Acts and Monuments Online* (1570 edn) (Sheffield: HRI Online Publications, 2011), p. 998, http://www.johnfoxe.org, accessed 29 November 2016.

36. Dove, pp. 1, 44, 53–55. See also Margaret Aston and Colin Richmond, 'Introduction', in *Lollardy and the Gentry*, ed. Aston and Richmond, pp. 1–27 (p. 21).

37. Hudson, pp. 129–33. See also Margaret Aston, *Lollards and Reformers: Images and Literacy in Late Medieval Religion* (London: Hambledon Press, 1984), pp. 19–20.

38. Cole, pp. 155–82. See also Hudson, pp. 435–36.

39. Aston, *Lollards and Reformers*, pp. 20–21; Hudson, pp. 114–15, 174.

40. John A. F. Thomson, *The Later Lollards, 1414–1520* (Oxford: Oxford University Press, 1965), pp. 4–5. See also Hudson, pp. 116–19.

41. Claire Cross, *Church and People, England 1450–1660*, 2nd edn (Oxford: Blackwell, 1999), pp. 16–17.

42. Thomson, pp. 6–7, 237–38.

43. Cole, p. 83. See also Thomson, pp. 243–44.

44. Watson, p. 831.

45. Daniell, *The Bible in English*, p. 66.

46. Craig W. D'Alton, 'Cuthbert Tunstal and Heresy in Essex and London, 1528', *Albion*, 35.2 (2003), 210–28 (pp. 224, 227). See also Aston, *Lollards and Reformers*, pp. 231–32; Hudson, p. 480; Korey D. Maas, *The Reformation and Robert Barnes: History, Theology and Polemic in Early Modern England* (Woodbridge: Boydell Press, 2010), pp. 19–20.

47. Maas, pp. 21–41.

48. Hudson, pp. 488–94.

49. Desiderius Erasmus, 'Paraclesis', in *Christian Humanism and the Reformation: Selected Writings; with The Life of Erasmus, by Beatus Rhenanus*, ed. and trans. John C. Olin (New York: Harper Torchbooks, 1965), pp. 92–106 (p. 97).

50. Daniell, *The Bible in English*, pp. 113–19.

51. Daniell, *William Tyndale*, pp. 83–87, 108–11, 134, 175–76, 186–87, 283, 316–17.

52. *Tyndale's Old Testament: Being the Pentateuch of 1530, Joshua to 2 Chronicles of 1537, and Jonah*, trans. William Tyndale, ed. David Daniell (New Haven: Yale University Press, 1992), p. 15 (Genesis 1. 1–2).

53. Daniell, *The Bible in English*, pp. 134–39, 136 note 13.

54. Gillian Brennan, 'Patriotism, Language and Power: English Translations of the Bible, 1520–1580', *History Workshop*, 27 (1989), 18–36 (p. 18).

55. William A. Clebsch, *England's Earliest Protestants, 1520–1535* (New Haven: Yale University Press, 1964), pp. 143–44.

56. Thomas More, *The Complete Works of St. Thomas More*, 15 vols (New Haven: Yale University Press, 1963–97), VI. I: *A Dialogue concerning Heresies*, ed. Thomas M. C. Lawler and others (1981), 290. See further pp. 284–90, 314–16, 340–41.

57. Craig W. D'Alton, 'The Suppression of Lutheran Heretics in England, 1526–1529', *Journal of Ecclesiastical History*, 2 (2003), 228–53 (pp. 229–34, 236). See also Allan G. Chester, 'Robert Barnes and the Burning of the Books', *Huntington Library Quarterly*, 14.3 (1951), 211–21 (pp. 212–13, 220–21).

58. Daniell, *William Tyndale*, p. 175. See also D'Alton, 'The Suppression of Lutheran Heretics in England', pp. 240–41.

59. D'Alton, 'The Suppression of Lutheran Heretics in England', p. 241.

60. Clebsch, pp. 260, 262–70.

61. D'Alton, 'The Suppression of Lutheran Heretics in England', pp. 229, 241, 247–53. See also D'Alton, 'Cuthbert Tunstal and Heresy in Essex and London, 1528', pp. 212, 221, 224, 227.

62. Daniell, *William Tyndale*, pp. 182–84.

63. Craig W. D'Alton, 'Charity or Fire? The Argument of Thomas More's 1959 *Dyaloge*', *Sixteenth Century Journal*, 33.1 (2002), 51–70 (p. 52 and note 6, pp. 67–68).

64. Peter Ackroyd, *The Life of Thomas More* (London: Vintage, 1999), pp. 291, 295–99. See also Daniell, *William Tyndale*, pp. 182–85.

65. Daniell, *William Tyndale*, pp. 208–17.

66. Daniell, *William Tyndale*, pp. 201–5, 361–84.

67. John Foxe, *The Acts and Monuments Online* (1576 edn) (Sheffield: HRI Online Publications, 2011), p. 1076, http://www.johnfoxe.org, accessed 29 November 2016.

68. Daniell, *The Bible in English*, pp. 176, 180, 193–95, 198–204.

69. Alec Ryrie, *The Gospel and Henry VIII: Evangelicals in the Early English Reformation* (Cambridge: Cambridge University Press, 2003), p. 21.

70. Ryrie, pp. 15, 27–28, 46–47.

71. J. F. Mozley, *Coverdale and his Bibles* (London: Lutterworth Press, 1953), pp. 283–4, quoted in Brennan, p. 29. See also Brennan, pp. 29–30; Ryrie, p. 47.

72. Ryrie, p. 47.

73. Brennan, pp. 26–27.

74. Edward Hall, *The Union of the Two Noble and Illustrie Families of York and Lancaster*, facsimile reproduction (Scolar Press, 1970), p. cclxii, quoted in Brennan, p. 29.

75. Ryrie, p. 49.

76. Elizabeth Malson-Huddle, 'Anne Askew and the Controversy over the Real Presence', *Studies in English Literature, 1500–1900*, 50.1 (2010), 1–16 (p. 11).

77. Ryrie, p. 5.

78. Daniell, *The Bible in English*, p. 229.

79. Daniell, *The Bible in English*, pp. 132, 192, 229, 245, 263–64.

80. Leona Rostenberg, *The Minority Press and the English Crown: A Study in Repression, 1558–1625* (Nieuwkoop: De Graaf, 1971), pp. 31–39, 43–50, 78–90, 106, 118, 206. See also Alexandra Walsham, '"Domme Preachers"? Post-Reformation English Catholicism and the Culture of Print', *Past & Present*, 168 (2000), 72–123 (pp. 87–88).

81. Rostenberg, pp. 98–99.

82. Christopher Hill, *The English Bible and the Seventeenth-Century Revolution* (London: Penguin, 1994), p. 64. See further pp. 58–65.

83. Hill, p. 58. See also Dean George Lampros, 'A New Set of Spectacles: The *Assembly's Annotations*, 1645-1657', *Renaissance and Reformation / Renaissance et Réforme*, 19.4 (1995), 33–46 (p. 35).

84. F. F. Bruce, *History of the Bible in English: From the Earliest Versions*, 3rd edn (Guildford: Lutterworth Press, 1979), p. 108.

2

Memoirs of a Woman of Pleasure (Fanny Hill)
John Cleland

It is easy to see how state prohibitions against heresy, blasphemy, and sedition come about. These categories of speech directly challenge religious or secular authority. Obscenity, on the other hand, is more nebulous. Is it possible to threaten the state simply by writing about sex? English authorities answered 'yes' to this question in the late seventeenth century, when printers and publishers began to be prosecuted for publishing obscene works, including Continental erotica and posthumous editions of the Earl of Rochester's racy poetry. Elizabeth Latham was imprisoned for publishing a Rochester edition in 1693, and five years later a man named Hill fled the country to escape prosecution at the King's Bench for 'printing ſome obſcene poems of my lord *Rocheſter*'s tending to the corruption of youth'.[1] Though judges had ruled in 1708 that obscenity was a matter for the ecclesiastical courts, not the secular ones, the rationale for an obscenity offence was settled decisively in 1727 when the bookseller Edmund Curll was convicted for publishing an erotic dialogue between two nuns entitled *Venus in the Cloister; or, The Nun in her Smock* and *A Treatise on the Use of Flogging in Venereal Affairs*. This case established that publishing obscenity was indeed a criminal offence in English common law, specifically a type of libel, like blasphemous, defamatory, or seditious libel.[2] As the Attorney General argued,

Fanny Hill and Charles as depicted in an edition of *Memoirs of a Woman of Pleasure* 'with a set of elegant engravings' (London, 1766).

obscene libel 'tends to corrupt the morals of the King's subjects, and is against the peace of the King'.[3] When John Cleland's erotic novel *Memoirs of a Woman of Pleasure* appeared in 1748, it immediately fell foul of obscenity law, and it would continue to do so in England and the United States for over two hundred years.

The book is often known by the name of its heroine, Fanny Hill, who tells her story in the form of letters to another woman. A naïve country girl of fifteen who has lost her parents to the smallpox, Fanny unwittingly becomes the protégée of the madam of a brothel in London, where she undergoes a series of sexual initiations: she is molested by one of the prostitutes, watches people have sex, learns to masturbate, and fends off a hideous old man who has paid to take her virginity. She flees the brothel with a young man named Charles, who becomes her first lover. Charles is soon summoned abroad, Fanny miscarries of their child, and their unscrupulous land-lady forces her back into the sex trade, where she works alternately as a kept mistress and in a brothel until she achieves financial inde-pendence and moves in with an older man. After an absence of over two years, Charles returns, they are married, and Fanny decides that sex with love is better than sex without it.

Although Fanny does have complexity of character, Cleland's focus is clearly on the erotic episodes. At one point, Fanny's fellow prostitutes take turns recounting how they lost their virginity, for no other reason than to pass the time. So many incidents end in sex that Fanny worries her correspondent will be 'cloy'd and tired with the uniformity of adventures and expressions, inseparable from a subject of this sort'.[4] Having acknowledged the danger of boredom, Cleland varies his descriptions of acts and body parts, sometimes using the language of picturesque landscape painting, sometimes using elaborate metaphors and euphemisms. For instance, when Fanny has sex with a sailor who has accosted her on the street, the theme is distinctly maritime:

> stirr'd up so fiercely as I was, I got the start of him, and went away into the melting swoon, and squeezing him, whilst in the convulsive grasp of it, drew from him such a plenteous bedewal of balmy sweets, as join'd to my own effusion, perfectly floated those parts, and drown'd in a deluge all my raging conflagration of desire.[5]

Despite the abundant detail, Cleland completely avoids the Anglo-Saxon or four-letter vocabulary of sex. He does not even use clinical terms. The penis, by far the most prominent body part in the book, is variously a 'machine', an 'engine', a 'splitter', a 'maypole', a 'master member of the revels', a 'nipple of Love'.

Cleland perhaps thought that this delicate diction would protect his novel from the law. At any rate, delicacy is the reason for the novel's existence—delicacy, and debt. Cleland first conceived *Memoirs of a Woman of Pleasure* with a Scot named Charles Carmichael when they were working in colonial Bombay. Cleland was about twenty. The two men had been reading an erotic French work entitled *L'École des filles*, and wondered if it were possible to write erotica without resorting to vulgar words. Cleland later claimed, in his own defence, that Carmichael had outlined the first part of the work around 1730. It would not be published, however, until 1748, when Carmichael was dead and Cleland was in England, imprisoned in the Fleet for debt. To one of his creditors, Thomas Cannon, Cleland owed eight hundred pounds. Attempting to convert what resources he had into cash, he finished his novel, and Fenton Griffiths published it anonymously in two volumes, disguising his own identity under the ingenious pseudonym 'G. Fenton'. The author and the second volume of his book were both released in 1749. Later that year, Cleland and Fenton's brother Ralph Griffiths were arrested for publishing an obscene libel. Cleland initially denied authorship, then accepted responsibility. Nobody appears to have been punished.[6] In fact, the person who came out worst was Cleland's creditor, Cannon. In a letter to the Secretary of State's law clerk, Lovel Stanhope, Cleland argued that, if the authorities wanted to suppress his work, they should not have drawn attention to it. To prove his point, he cited the 'mad and wicked' Cannon's *Ancient and Modern Pederasty*, a book compiling various texts on the topic of sex between men. Thanks to Cleland, the authorities moved against Cannon, who fled the country for three years to avoid prosecution.[7]

In 1750, now in debt to Ralph, Cleland once more attempted to skirt the law by revising *Memoirs of a Woman of Pleasure* into a one-volume, expurgated edition called *Memoirs of Fanny Hill*.[8] The new Fanny is more reticent, and avoids explicit sexual narration with formulas such as 'I shall here draw the curtain' or 'I leave it to your imagination'.[9] Thighs are banished from the text. Sometimes Cleland blanks out phrases with asterisks. Although designed to avoid obscenity, *Memoirs of Fanny Hill* still got into trouble. The Bishop of London, Thomas Sherlock, urged the government to prosecute Cleland.[10] He also published an open letter in which he blamed two recent earthquakes on the people's moral corruption, citing the publication of stories about prostitutes among many other evils.[11] Proceedings were initiated but apparently not completed, since Griffiths continued to advertise the expurgated book openly.[12]

Less openly, versions of the original *Memoirs of a Woman of Pleasure* also circulated. Cleland had disavowed the work in his letter to Stanhope, saying he wished to be free of 'a Book I disdain to defend, and wish, from my Soul, buried and forgot'—but it was an underground hit, and he never lived it down.[13] Whether or not Griffiths printed further editions, as some contemporaries alleged, literary pirates certainly did. Some of these new editions contained illustrations.[14] They did not, however, contain one particularly dangerous passage from the original.[15] Late in the narrative, Fanny spies on two young men having anal sex, an act outlawed as 'sodomy'. She finds the sight both fascinating and abhorrent. After watching until the top partner finishes, she hurries to inform on the men, but trips and knocks herself out, allowing them to escape. In the original text, despite making a show of denouncing the act, Fanny describes it with her usual relish:

> and now passing one hand round his minion's hips, he got hold of his red-topt ivory toy, that stood perfectly stiff, and shewed, that if he was like his mother behind, he was like his father before; this he diverted himself with, whilst with the other, he wanton'd with his hair, and leaning forward over his back, drew his face, from which the boy shook the loose curls that fell over it, in the posture he stood him in, and brought him towards his, so as to receive a long-breath'd kiss, after which, renewing his driving, and thus continuing to harrass his rear, the height of the fit came on with its usual symptoms, and dismiss'd the action.[16]

In later editions, instead of recounting the details, Fanny simply says, 'they now proceeded to such lengths as soon satisfied me what they were'.[17] The complete episode became apocryphal, and some believed that a bookseller named Samuel Drybutter had inserted it, and been put in the pillory for doing so.[18]

Memoirs of a Woman of Pleasure is often considered to be the first work of literature to be prosecuted for obscenity in the United States.[19] In 1821 the Supreme Judicial Court of Massachusetts affirmed the conviction of Peter Holmes for publishing and distributing copies of the book, apparently with illustrations.[20] The novel would again be subject to state censorship in the United States in the 1960s, by which time the US Supreme Court had developed a test for obscenity that broke with the English model.

The case of Edmund Wilson's *Memoirs of Hecate County* reached the Supreme Court in 1948, but one justice recused himself and the others were evenly split, which meant that the publisher's conviction was automatically upheld, and the court provided no guidance on the issue of obscenity.[21] The Supreme Court would finally weigh in on the censorship of literature in *Roth* v. *United States* in 1957, where it considered whether obscenity prohibitions violated the First Amendment of the Constitution, which guarantees the freedom of speech. The publisher Samuel Roth was often on the wrong side of the law. He had published an unauthorized *Ulysses* in the United States,[22] and appeared before the Senate Subcommittee Hearings on Juvenile Delinquency during the comic book scare in 1954—where he declined to testify because he was under arrest at the time (see Chapters 11 and 15).[23] In the case the Supreme Court was reviewing, he had been sentenced to five years in prison and fined five thousand dollars for mailing an issue of the erotic magazine *American Aphrodite* and several advertisements.[24] The joint dissenting opinion of Justice Douglas and Justice Black in *Roth* was a strong attack on moral censorship: 'The legality of a publication in this country should never be allowed to turn either on the purity of thought which it instills in the mind of the reader or on the degree to which it offends the community conscience.'[25] Nevertheless, the court affirmed Roth's conviction and that of another mail-order bookseller, David Alberts. Writing for the majority, Justice Brennan established that the First Amendment did not protect obscenity, because 'implicit in the history of the First Amendment is the rejection of obscenity as utterly without redeeming social importance'.[26] A new test, however, would be required to determine what was obscene. The court rejected the prevailing Hicklin standard, based on the English case *R* v. *Hicklin* (1868), which determined that obscene material had the tendency to deprave and corrupt those open to immoral influences and into whose hands it might fall. This standard was unconstitutional, because it required all publications to be tailored to the most impressionable people, such as children. The Roth test would ask instead 'whether to the average person, applying contemporary community standards, the dominant theme of the material taken as a whole appeals to prurient interest'.[27]

The Roth test was not easy to apply. Were the community standards supposed to be local or national? Was there necessarily a connection between appealing to prurient interest and utterly lacking redeeming social importance? Legal interpretations of the test were still in flux, and several literary works would soon be subjected to it. Allen Ginsberg's poem *Howl* and Grove Press's edition of *Lady Chatterley's Lover* were judged not to be obscene in 1957 and 1960 (see Chapter 12 for *Lady Chatterley*). Henry Miller's *Tropic of Cancer*, also published by Grove Press, sparked over sixty legal cases around the United States before the Supreme Court ruled that it was not obscene in 1964, without elaborating in an opinion. The attorney Charles Rembar, who had defended *Lady Chatterley* in court and been involved with the defences of *Tropic of Cancer*, advanced a particular interpretation of the Roth test under which *only* books that were utterly without social value could be deemed obscene. Fortunately for Cleland's novel, this interpretation had gained some traction by the time G. P. Putnam's Sons asked Rembar to defend their edition of *Memoirs of a Woman of Pleasure*.[28]

The social value test was the most likely mechanism by which to save the book. Unlike *Lady Chatterley* and *Tropic of Cancer*, *Memoirs of a Woman of Pleasure* seemed obviously designed to arouse. But could it nevertheless have social value? Could a book be literature *and* pornography? The Putnam editors used the expurgated version of the gay sex scene, believing the full scene to be apocryphal, but their edition still contained multiple instances of rape and detailed descriptions of a variety of sexual practices that were considered taboo, including prostitution, adultery, lesbian mutual masturbation, voyeurism, and flagellation. Expecting that juries would be likely simply to decide whether the novel was a 'dirty book', Rembar avoided jury trials. He hoped that judges would be better able to focus on the First Amendment question.[29] *Memoirs of a Woman of Pleasure* was a dirty book, and only the Constitution could protect it.

Putnam's *Memoirs of a Woman of Pleasure* was tried in three states: New York, New Jersey, and Massachusetts. All three states had provisions for proceeding against books themselves instead of prosecuting the author, publisher, or printer. *Memoirs of a Woman of Pleasure* would be on trial, and Putnam's president, Walter J. Minton, would risk only legal expenses and the cost of publishing a book he might be required to destroy.

Rembar was permitted to call literary experts to give testimony about the book. In New York, Louis Untermeyer drew an analogy to literature about war: just as a war novel was about exploring human responses to conflict rather than just recounting the details of battles, Cleland's novel was about exploring human responses to sex rather than just describing sex. In Boston, asked by the prosecution if he would use Cleland's language 'over the breakfast table with your wife', Norman Holland replied: 'I would, were I so skilled to speak it.' In Hackensack, New Jersey, Fred Holley Stocking defended the educational value of the book and said, if an undergraduate 'were to read this book in a course of mine and his chief response were the arousal of sexual passion and that dominated every other response, he would flunk my course'. The New Jersey trial was notable for a unique tactic: the state called medical experts to testify to a link between reading literature about 'abnormal sex'—which included sex outside of marriage—and engaging in it. One of these experts, William P. Reilly, who happened also to be the president of the anti-obscenity group Citizens for Decent Literature, cited the authority of psychiatrist Fredric Wertham.[30] Wertham believed that exposure to sex and violence in the media helped drive children into delinquency, and he was one of the leaders of the anti-comic book movement in the 1940s and 1950s. The New York court ruled that *Memoirs of a Woman of Pleasure* was not obscene. The Massachusetts and New Jersey courts ruled that it was.

After the Supreme Judicial Court of Massachusetts affirmed the decision in that state, Putnam requested review from the US Supreme Court, which heard the case on the same day as two other obscenity cases involving publishers of erotica, *Ginzburg* v. *United States* and *Mishkin* v. *New York*. The Supreme Court justices decided six to three in favour of *Memoirs of a Woman of Pleasure*. As Justice Brennan made clear, writing for a plurality of three, even a 'modicum of social value' was enough to protect a book under the First Amendment, and the Supreme Judicial Court of Massachusetts had admitted that the book had 'some minimal literary value'.[31] Justices Black and Douglas, who continued to reject government censorship of obscenity altogether, concurred in the holding that the book was protected. So did Justice Stewart, who believed that the government could only censor hard-core pornography, which *Fanny Hill* wasn't. (As he claimed in the landmark film censorship case, *Jacobellis* v. *Ohio*, he knew it when he saw it.[32]) One of the three dissenting justices, Clark, questioned the expert testimony on the value of the book, and cited several authorities, including Wertham, on the link between pornography and 'criminal sexual behaviour or other antisocial conduct'. '*Memoirs*', Justice Clark wrote, 'is no work of art.'[33] His condemnation did not matter. *Fanny Hill* was free, and Rembar hailed the decision as 'the end of obscenity'. He meant that, in practice, 'serious' literary writers no longer needed to worry about being convicted of obscenity: unless their work was *utterly* without social value, it would survive the Roth test. William S. Burroughs's *Naked Lunch*, banned in 1962, was cleared in 1966 under the precedent set by *Memoirs*.[34]

The line between art and pornography had merely been redrawn, however, and Putnam's victory was a defeat for those who remained on the other side of the line. Ralph Ginzburg and Edward Mishkin were the casualties of the day: their publications became examples of what *could* be censored, and, unlike Minton, Ginzburg and Mishkin were facing criminal penalties. Mishkin had been sentenced to three years and fined twelve thousand dollars under New York law for publishing fifty books, with titles such as *Screaming Flesh*, *Bound in Rubber*, and *The Cult of the Spankers*. He specialized in pulp erotic fiction with gay, lesbian, and BDSM (bondage, discipline, sadism, and masochism) content.[35] Ginzburg's material was highbrow, and he had previously written a history of erotica. He had been sentenced to five years, later reduced to three, and fined forty-two thousand dollars under the Comstock Act, a federal obscenity statute, for mailing the fourth issue of a hardcover magazine called *Eros*, a newsletter called *Liaison*, and

Lillian Maxine Serett's sexual autobiography *The Housewife's Handbook on Selective Promiscuity*.[36] The issue of *Eros* included a series of photographs by Ralph M. Hattersley Jr., depicting a Black man and a White woman posing together in the nude. A caption explained that the 'photographic tone poem on the subject of interracial love', entitled 'Black and White in Color', was 'presented with the conviction that love between a man and a woman, no matter what their races, is beautiful'.[37]

Mishkin's case was not fought over social value, but Ginzburg's was. Expert witnesses had testified to the artistic and educational merit of his publications, and Serett had testified that she wanted *The Housewife's Handbook* to teach women 'that various forms of sexual expression are normal and healthy things to do, and also that women do have sexual rights'.[38] The trial judge, Ralph C. Body, took particular offence at a scene in *The Housewife's Handbook* in which Serett receives oral sex, an act he described as 'sodomy'[39]—which, in many states, it technically was.[40] Having convicted Ginzburg, and declining to arrest the judgment or to permit a new trial, Judge Body complained that 'Black and White in Color' 'constitutes a detailed portrayal of the act of sexual intercourse between a completely nude male and female, leaving nothing to the imagination'.[41] (This is a gross mischaracterization. In the photographs the models are kissing, embracing, and lying alongside each other. Their genitals are not visible.) In order to uphold Ginzburg's conviction, which an appeals court had affirmed, the US Supreme Court found an additional complication inside the Roth test. In 'close cases', the court decided, they could consider the manner in which the publications were marketed. If there was evidence of 'pandering'—openly appealing to 'erotic interest'—the publications could be deemed obscene. In short, if it looked like obscenity and was marketed as obscenity, it was obscenity, even if it had some small amount of value. Ginzburg had attempted to mail material with the postmarks of the towns Blue Ball and Intercourse, Pennsylvania, and had successfully mailed material with the postmark of Middlesex, New Jersey. This fact, along with Ginzburg's advertising, which 'stressed the sexual candor of the respective publications', was seen as evidence of pandering.[42] Against the strong dissenting opinions of the more libertarian justices, the Supreme Court upheld both Ginzburg and Mishkin's convictions.

Reflecting on his trial, Ginzburg wondered 'whether future generations of Americans, looking back at the obscenity trials of the nineteenth and twentieth centuries, would regard as depraved those who had stood before the bar of justice—or those who stood behind it'.[43] He was sent to prison in 1972, and a group called the Committee for a Free Press took out a full-page ad in the *New York Times* in which literary, artistic, and legal luminaries protested his sentence. Ginzburg made parole after eight months of what he described as the 'complete psychic castration' of prison life.[44] For Ginzburg, the liberation of *Memoirs of a Woman of Pleasure* in the United States was a far cry from the 'end of obscenity'.

Frank depictions of sex did not fare better in the United Kingdom, where speech was free in principle but protections were less robust than the First Amendment of the US Constitution. Since the nineteenth century, the obscenity law of England and Wales had run in two distinct channels: the common law, under which obscene libel was a criminal offence; and the Obscene Publications Act 1857, which permitted magistrates to order the seizure and destruction of books regardless of whether anyone was charged with a crime. In 1959 a new Obscene Publications Act combined both of these functions into a single statute while creating a public good defence for publications that were in the 'interests of science, literature, art or learning, or of other objects of general concern'.[45] According to Peter Rawlinson, Solicitor General, there were fifteen proceedings against *Memoirs of a Woman of Pleasure* from 1950 to 1964, eight of which were prosecutions of individuals and seven of which were destruction orders. Some of these proceedings were jury trials, and every one of them was decided against Cleland's novel or the people distributing it.[46]

The best known of these cases occurred in 1964, when the publisher Mayflower released the book in an inexpensive (three shillings and six pence) paperback edition. A police officer was offered a copy, reportedly without asking for it, in the Magic Shop, Tottenham Court Road, London,[47] where a sign advertised the book as 'Banned in America'.[48] The officer obtained a warrant to seize the 171 copies in stock,[49] and Ralph Gold was summoned to give cause why they should not be destroyed. Though eighty-two thousand copies were already in circulation, Mayflower stopped distributing the novel and intervened to defend it.[50]

The publishers asked to be prosecuted, which would have led to a more climactic jury trial, like Penguin's in the *Lady Chatterley's Lover* case.[51] The result of such a trial might have been more conclusive. A seizure order, however, only concerned the stock of a particular bookseller, and even if that stock survived another magistrate could order another seizure somewhere else. Or, if Gold's stock was destroyed, other retailers, perhaps with more cautious advertising, might continue to sell the book. The publishers were committed to supporting retailers who got into trouble over *Memoirs of a Woman of Pleasure*, but, as managing director Lionel Fennelly said, 'No publisher can afford to fight a case in a series of magistrates' courts.'[52] The Director of Public Prosecutions (DPP) denied their request: since Mayflower had behaved so responsibly in stopping distribution of the book, it would be 'oppressive' to prosecute them.[53] Labour, Liberal, and Conservative members of parliament united to condemn this decision, which denied the publishers the jury trial they desired, and left the survival of the book in the hands of a magistrate.[54] In fact, the DPP might have had trouble prosecuting even if he had wanted to. Before 1963, obscenity prosecutions in the United Kingdom often began with the sale of a book to a police officer. In 1963, however, a court had ruled that the police were, by virtue of their work, morally incorruptible, and that the sale of a book to an officer could not, therefore, be grounds for an obscenity prosecution. Much to the Solicitor General's frustration, the 'incorruptible police constable' made the criminal offence in the Obscene Publications Act much harder to enforce.[55] This loophole would not be closed until the Obscene Publications Act 1964 criminalized possession of an obscene publication with a view to publishing it.

A seize-and-destroy order it was, then, and the battle for *Fanny Hill* would play out in Bow Street Magistrates' Court. Experts, including Marghanita Laski, Peter Quennell, and H. Montgomery Hyde, testified to the novel's literary and historical merit, and defended its portrayal of sex—which meant stressing Fanny's enjoyment of 'normal and ordinary' vaginal intercourse.[56] Mervyn Griffith-Jones, who had prosecuted Penguin in the *Lady Chatterley's Lover* trial, presented the case against *Fanny Hill*. (When asked if it horrified him that girls in the book enjoy sex, Quennell said, 'It horrifies me less than it does Mr Griffith-Jones'.[57]) The magistrate ordered that the 171 copies be destroyed.[58]

Mayflower issued a statement saying that they had decided not to appeal, rather than go through another hearing, 'again without a jury', that would be 'open to precisely the same objections as before'.[59] A victory would not necessarily have prevented further action against the book, such as proceedings in Manchester, where thousands of copies were also seized and destroyed,[60] and in Swadlincote, Derbyshire, where market bookseller Barry Bramley had sold sixty-nine copies and forfeited three.[61] Instead, the publishers followed Cleland's example and released an expurgated edition, which was distinguished by its green cover from the orange-covered original. Even Mayflower's green edition, however, turned out to be vulnerable to censorship. In Edinburgh, where Scots law and local statutes governed obscenity, a baillie fined bookseller George Halliday Bertram for selling the green edition.[62] (This prosecution was part of a crackdown on Leith Walk that year in which four booksellers were convicted. The contentious books also included the *Kama Sutra* and *The Perfumed Garden*.[63]) While Mayflower's editions were being seized, a different publisher, Luxor Press, released a slightly expurgated 'de luxe edition' of *Memoirs of a Woman of Pleasure* 'intended for people who like good books', priced to ride above the controversy at forty-five shillings.[64] The authorities were not especially worried about what the wealthy were reading.

Mayflower's struggle to publish *Memoirs of a Woman of Pleasure* ended in 1970. By then the book had been cleared by the highest court in the United States. The United Kingdom had no comparable process for declaring a book immune to further prosecution. Mayflower simply tried again to release their unexpurgated edition, and this time the authorities took no action against it. *Memoirs of a Woman of Pleasure* outlived its scandal, however, and Penguin and Oxford published academic editions in 1985. Informed by more recent scholarship, these editions finally undid the most enduring censorship of Cleland's original text: they printed the gay sex in full.

Notes

1. Sir John Strange, *Reports of Adjudged Cases in the Courts of Chancery, King's Bench, Common Pleas, and Exchequer* (London, 1755), II, 790, quoted in Jim McGhee, 'Obscene Libel and the Language of "The Imperfect Enjoyment"', in *Reading Rochester*, ed. Edward Burns (Liverpool: Liverpool University Press, 1995), pp. 42–65 (p. 50). See also McGhee, pp. 48–56.

2. Colin Manchester, 'A History of the Crime of Obscene Libel', *Journal of Legal History*, 12.1 (1991), 36–57 (pp. 36–40).

3. *R v Curl* (1727) 2 Str 788, 789, quoted in Manchester, p. 39.

4. John Cleland, *Memoirs of a Woman of Pleasure*, ed. Peter Sabor (Oxford: Oxford University Press, 1985; repr. 1999), p. 91.

5. Cleland, *Memoirs of a Woman of Pleasure*, p. 141.

6. Hal Gladfelder, *Fanny Hill in Bombay: The Making and Unmaking of John Cleland* (Baltimore: Johns Hopkins University Press, 2012), pp. 15–20, 46, 49–50.

7. John Cleland to Lovel Stanhope (13 November 1749), London, The National Archives, SP 36/III, ff 157–59, quoted in Gladfelder, pp. 52–53; see also Gladfelder, pp. 8–9, 11, 51–53, 59.

8. Gladfelder, p. 50.

9. John Cleland, *Memoirs of Fanny Hill* (London, 1750), quoted in Peter Sabor, 'The Censor Censured: Expurgating *Memoirs of a Woman of Pleasure*', in *'Tis Nature's Fault: Unauthorized Sexuality during the Enlightenment*, ed. Robert Purks Maccubbin (Cambridge: Cambridge University Press, 1987), pp. 192–201 (p. 195).

10. Sabor, 'The Censor Censured', pp. 192–99.

11. Thomas Sherlock, *A Letter from the Lord Bishop of London to the Clergy and People of London and Westminster; on Occasion of the Late Earthquakes* (London, 1750), pp. 4, 11 [Internet Archive e-book].

12. Sabor, 'The Censor Censured', pp. 192–94.

13. Cleland to Stanhope (13 November 1749), quoted in Peter Sabor, 'Introduction', in Cleland, *Memoirs of a Woman of Pleasure*, pp. vii–xxvi (p. xiii).

14. Sabor, 'Introduction', pp. vii–viii, ix.

15. Gladfelder, p. 81.

16. Cleland, *Memoirs of a Woman of Pleasure*, pp. 158–59.

17. John Cleland, *Fanny Hill: Memoirs of a Woman of Pleasure. The Complete Unexpurgated Edition* (London: Mayflower, 1970), p. 189.

18. Gladfelder, pp. 81–82.

19. A Book Named "John Cleland's Memoirs of a Woman of Pleasure" v. Attorney Gen., 383 U.S. 413, 425 n. 1 (1966) (Douglas, J., concurring).

20. Harriet L. Turney, 'The Road to Respectability: A Woman of Pleasure and Competing Conceptions of the First Amendment', *University of Dayton Law Review*, 5.2 (1980), 271–99 (pp. 271–72 and note 7).

21. Edward de Grazia, *Girls Lean Back Everywhere: The Law of Obscenity and the Assault on Genius* (New York: Vintage, 1993), pp. 227–28.

22. Kevin Birmingham, *The Most Dangerous Book: The Battle for James Joyce's 'Ulysses'* (London: Head of Zeus, 2015), pp. 278–83.

23 *Hearings Before the Subcomm. to Investigate Juvenile Delinquency of the S. Comm. on the Judiciary*, 83rd Cong. 195–96 (1954) (testimony of Samuel Roth, Publisher, New York, N.Y.) [Internet Archive e-book].

24. De Grazia, pp. 281, 295.

25. Roth v. United States, 354 U.S. 476, 513 (1957) (Douglas, J., and Black, J., dissenting).

26. *Roth*, 354 U.S. at 484.

27. *Roth*, 354 U.S. at 489.

28. Charles Rembar, *The End of Obscenity: The Trials of 'Lady Chatterley', 'Tropic of Cancer', and 'Fanny Hill'* (London: Deutsch, 1969), pp. 55–58, 169, 180, 191, 205–8.

29. Rembar, pp. 337–39.

30. Rembar, pp. 256–57, 267, 330, 342–44, 348, 365–69, 388.

31. *Memoirs*, 383 U.S. at 420, 426 (plurality opinion).

32. Jacobellis v. Ohio, 378 U.S. 184, 197 (1964) (Stewart, J., concurring).

33. *Memoirs*, 383 U.S. at 447, 452 (Clark, J., dissenting).

34. Attorney Gen. v. A Book Named "Naked Lunch", 218 N.E.2d 571 (Mass. 1966).

35. Mishkin v. N.Y., 383 U.S. 502, 504–6, 514–15 (1966).

36. 'Ginzburg Sentence of 3 Years Upheld by Appeals Court', *New York Times*, 4 February 1971, http://www.nytimes.com/1971/02/04/archives/ginzburg-sentence-of-3-years-upheld-by-appeals-court.html, accessed 12 March 2017; United States v. Ginzburg, 224 F. Supp. 129, 134 (E.D. Pa. 1963).

37. Ralph M. Hattersley Jr., 'Black & White in Color', *Eros* 1.4 (1962).

38. 'The Trial of Eros Magazine', *Realist*, October 1963, p. 19, The Realist Archive Project, http://www.ep.tc/realist/44/19.html, accessed 14 March 2017.

39. Ralph Ginzburg, *Eros on Trial* (New York: Fact Magazine, 1966), pp. 21–23.

40. William N. Eskridge Jr., *Dishonorable Passions: Sodomy Laws in America 1861–2003* (New York:Viking, 2008), p. 91.

41. *Ginzburg*, 224 F. Supp. at 135.

42. Ginzburg v. United States, 383 U.S. 463, 467, 468 (1966).

43. Ginzburg, *Eros on Trial*, p. 61.

44. Ralph Ginzburg, *Castrated: My Eight Months in Prison* (New York: Avant-Garde Books, 1973), p. 20.

45. Obscene Publications Act 1959, s 4(1).

46. HC Deb 3 June 1964, vol 695, cols 1214–15.

47. 'Fanny Hill "Atmosphere"', *Guardian*, 21 January 1964, p. 1.

48. 'Court Says "Fanny Hill" is Obscene', *Guardian*, 11 February 1964, p. 10. See also 'Author Says Novel "Fanny Hill" Not Pornography', *The Times*, 21 January 1964, p. 7.

49. 'Fanny Hill "Atmosphere"', p. 1.

50. 'Court Says "Fanny Hill" is Obscene', p. 10.

51. 'Author Says Novel "Fanny Hill" Not Pornography', p. 7.

52. 'Court Says "Fanny Hill" is Obscene', p. 10.

53. 'Author Says Novel "Fanny Hill" Not Pornography', p. 7.

54. 'MPs Attack "Fanny Hill" Decision', *Guardian*, 13 February 1964, p. 1.

55. HC Deb 3 June 1964, vol 695, col 1183.

56. '"Fanny Hill" a Gay Little Book, Says Miss Laski', *Observer*, 2 February 1964, p. 3. See also 'Q.C. and a Witness Taken to Task', *Guardian*, 28 January 1964, p. 7.

57. 'Q.C. and a Witness Taken to Task', p. 7.

58. 'Court Says "Fanny Hill" is Obscene', p. 10.

59. '"Fanny Hill"—No Appeal by Publishers', *Guardian*, 15 February 1964, p. 1.

60. '"Fanny Hill" Dismembered', *Guardian*, 26 June 1964, p. 22.

61. 'Man Sold 69 Copies of "Fanny Hill"', *Guardian*, 26 August 1964, p. 2.

62. 'Court Rules "Fanny Hill" Indecent', *Guardian*, 23 October 1964, p. 6.

63. Roger Davidson and Gayle Davis, *The Sexual State: Sexuality and Scottish Governance, 1950–80* (Edinburgh: Edinburgh University Press, 2012), p. 237.

64. 'Dearer Edition of "Fanny Hill"', *The Times*, 30 November 1963, p. 6.

3

The Witlings

Frances Burney

In 1779 Frances (Fanny) Burney was one of the most critically acclaimed and popular novelists in Britain. Her first novel, *Evelina*, had gone through multiple editions in one year.[1] As *Evelina* had shown, Burney had a talent for comedy and dialogue, and she was intimately acquainted with the leading actors and playwrights of her day, who were eager to offer practical support and advice. Her admirers encouraged her to try writing for the theatre. But she faced an insuperable obstacle to a successful career as a playwright: the disapproval and fears of her father, Dr Charles Burney, and her mentor Samuel Crisp, whom she called her second 'daddy'. Charles Burney and Crisp feared that her satire of contemporary manners would anger powerful people. They argued that Burney was risking not only her professional reputation as a writer, but also her personal reputation, her position in society, and by extension her father's social standing. Their strong opposition drove Burney to suppress her first comic play, *The Witlings*. Later critics regurgitated Charles Burney and Crisp's condemnation of her dramatic work, and it has been only relatively recently that Burney's plays, including *The Witlings*, have been rediscovered and performed. Few women writers of Burney's time saw their plays performed, and of those who did fewer were remembered by literary history. The prejudices that affected Burney in her lifetime and after exemplify the

Frances Burney in 1782. Engraving by Charles Turner from a painting by Edward Francis Burney, Frances Burney's cousin.

way in which much of women's writing has been lost to history. It is
Burney's exceptional status in literary history, as a novelist of recognized importance, that drove later scholars to investigate and revive her
suppressed plays. Many other women writers await rediscovery.

Burney wrote in conditions governed by censorship and censorious attitudes. New plays could be performed only with the approval
of the examiner of plays, who, on behalf of the Lord Chamberlain,
authorized plays for performance in licensed theatres.[2] The only
one of Burney's plays performed in her lifetime, *Edwy and Elgiva*,
was approved by the examiner.[3] During the Napoleonic Wars,
when she was living in France, Burney relied upon smuggled correspondence for news of family and friends in England because
of the French government's censorship of communications,[4] and
she had great difficulty bringing the manuscript of *The Wanderer*,
her last novel, out of France.[5] In terms of its impact on her literary career and critical reputation, however, Burney's self-censorship
was of greater significance than any censorship by the state. She
was under personal and social pressure, especially from her father
and Crisp, to obey the rules of feminine conduct, and this pressure
shaped her career. As her biographer Margaret Anne Doody writes,
'it was to be easier to smuggle anti-Revolutionary manuscripts past
Napoleon's soldiers than to smuggle a comic play out to the public
past Dr. Burney's barriers'.[6]

Burney began suppressing her writing early in her life. Aged fourteen, she completed her first novel, *The History of Caroline Evelyn*, but
was ashamed of what she called her 'scribbling'. She had developed
literacy late, not learning to write until the age of ten, and then only in
illegible handwriting, which she kept secret for fear of ridicule. Even
as her skill developed, she retained that early sense of embarrassment
about her writing. She recalled that 'her pen, though her greatest, was
only her clandestine delight'. The only person allowed to read her
work was her sister Susanna. The 'stolen moments of their secret readings' were 'the happiest of their adolescent lives'.[7] But it was not proper
for young women to enjoy clandestine pleasures. Burney felt that her
urge to write was degrading, describing it as an 'inclination at which I
blushed', as if it were a masturbatory habit. Writing was a 'propensity'
that 'impelled' her, which she had 'struggled against' from childhood

into adolescence.[8] Setting the pattern for later acts of self-suppression, the young Burney decided it was her 'duty to combat this writing passion'.[9] On her fifteenth birthday, she made a bonfire of her manuscripts and burned *Caroline Evelyn*. Her sister watched and wept.[10]

Evelina was born from the ashes of *Caroline Evelyn*, and escaped its predecessor's end, but Burney took elaborate precautions to conceal her identity and prevent anyone apart from Susanna and her other sisters from learning that she was *Evelina*'s author. She found the idea of being known to be an author intolerable. As a private individual, Burney was deferential, shy, and quietly observant. In contrast, she complained, 'An *Authoress* must always be supposed to be flippant, assuming & loquacious!—And, indeed, the dread of these kind of censures have been my principal motives for wishing *snugship*', a state of cosy anonymity.[11] There was a theoretical risk that her handwriting could have been identified by a printer, because she had worked as an amanuensis and secretary for her father, so she copied out the manuscript in a false hand. Burney and her sisters formed a committee to manage their dealings with publishers, and had their brothers communicate with booksellers. The sisters routed their correspondence through a coffee house, once with the help of one of the brothers disguised in an old greatcoat and hat. Not until her plans were firmly in motion did Burney seek her father's permission to publish, but even then she did not tell him what she had written, allow him to see the manuscript, or tell him the title. Laughing, he gave his permission. He had no idea that she had already written a novel, and would not discover that she was the author of *Evelina* until its success was confirmed.[12] The novel was published anonymously, and its preface nudged readers and reviewers to believe that a man had written it: because of the work of others who had come before, 'no man need blush' to be a novelist, Burney wrote.[13] The novel's reviewers took the bait. *Evelina*'s author was compared favourably to eminent male authors, and the book was judged on its merits.[14] For a brief time, Burney experienced the (sometimes pleasurable) discomfort of hearing her work discussed by family members and acquaintances who did not know of her authorship. When her identity was eventually revealed, by her father and through literary gossip, she felt the loss of privacy deeply. Had she been able to, she would have prolonged her 'snugship' indefinitely.

Being a known 'Authoress' had its advantages. Burney was welcomed into literary coteries—select groups bound together by the
exchange of original literary work, criticism, and mutual support.[15]
Coteries provided access to writers, critics, and powerful patrons
like Elizabeth Montagu, the leader of the network known as 'the
bluestockings'. The term 'bluestocking' originally referred to any of
Montagu's visitors, but by the 1770s it had come to mean an intellectual woman. Montagu was particularly interested in supporting
women writers.[16] Though she helped authors who sought to publish
in print, and had published criticism herself, her coterie was known
for the private circulation of manuscripts within its social circle.[17]
In contrast, the Streatham set, which met at the Streatham home of
Hester Lynch Thrale, and was identified with its leading light, Samuel
Johnson, cultivated a more masculine and distinctly professional
identity. It favoured the public circulation of printed texts.[18] Burney
preferred the Streatham set's professionalism,[19] and found the identity of 'bluestockinger' an awkward fit, a label to laugh at rather than
embrace.[20] At Streatham, Burney was encouraged to attempt writing
for the stage, and specifically to write a comedy. The painter Joshua
Reynolds assured her she would succeed at dialogue, and praised
her 'knack at Characters'. The playwright Richard Brinsley Sheridan
made a grand offer to produce anything Burney gave him, '*Unsight
unseen*', as Reynolds put it.[21] The author of *The Rivals* and *The School
for Scandal*, Sheridan was one of the most popular playwrights of
his day, and also the manager of the Drury Lane theatre in London.
His offer was an unusual mark of confidence in a woman writer,
but not one that Samuel Crisp was able to appreciate. If Sheridan
had produced a comedy by Burney, she would have joined a small
group of professional women playwrights. Although the late eighteenth century saw a marked increase in the writing and production
of plays by women, particularly of comedies, there were twelve to
fourteen plays by men for every play by a woman. The comedies of
Hannah Cowley and Elizabeth Inchbald were popular and successful, and earlier writers such as Susannah Centlivre and Aphra Behn
had shown that it was possible for a woman to live by her pen.[22] But
Crisp thought that Burney's move from the novel to the stage risked
her personal and professional reputation. He sent a letter warning

her of the difficulty women writers faced in bringing comedies to the stage. Successful comedies had qualities that were out of bounds to 'Ladies of the strictest Character' like Burney. Comedy required 'lively Freedoms', 'waggeries', and 'Salt & Spirit'. Without this masculine saltiness, Burney would only be able to produce a poor play 'Void Of blood & Spirits'.[23] Too much blood and spirit, and Burney risked losing her character; too little, and she risked writing a flop. Burney assured Crisp that she 'would a thousand Times rather forfeit my character as a *Writer*, than risk ridicule or censure as a *Female*'.[24] Crisp and Charles Burney would soon force her to choose between the Writer and the Female.

By August 1779, Burney had a script. The actor Arthur Murphy had read part of it with approval.[25] It was too long, Burney recognized, but it was a work in progress and would be cut in rehearsal. Unfortunately, Burney shared the script with her father and Crisp before showing it to Sheridan, and asked them to offer their opinions of it as if it were not 'a play in manuscript, & *capable* of alterations'.[26] This was unwise: by inviting Charles Burney and Crisp to treat the script as a finished play rather than as an evolving work, Burney allowed them to judge her work more harshly than was appropriate for an early draft. The first read-through of *The Witlings* would be its last performance. The venue was Crisp's house, the reader was Charles Burney, and the audience consisted of Burney's sisters, Crisp, and members of Crisp's household.[27] The author was absent, and waited to receive their judgement by letter.

What Charles Burney read out was a comedy of manners that portrayed a literary coterie and its satellites through the distorting lens of satire. *The Witlings* laughs at the intellectual pretensions of the upper classes and their fawning dependents, such as untalented artists and gossipy businesswomen. The play depicts a coterie of pseudo-critics called the Esprit Party, who puff inadequate modern writers while unfairly criticizing major authors. No one listens to anyone else, no one ever manages to finish what they are saying, and no one really minds. The plot (which is secondary to the satire) hangs on the separation and reconciliation of two young lovers. They are forbidden from marrying by the young man's aunt, Lady Smatter, the wealthy and foolish leader of the Esprit Party, who struggles to understand the poems she criticizes. Her nemesis, Censor, genuinely respects English literature, and despises Lady Smatter. Censor brings about the resolution of the play by threatening her with public humiliation. If she disinherits her nephew or prevents him from marrying his fiancée, Censor will publicly lampoon her:

> This lady with Study has muddled her head;
> Sans meaning she talk'd, and sans knowledge she read,
> And gulp'd such a Dose of incongruous matter
> That Bedlam must soon hold the Carcase of Smatter.[28]

Censor makes Smatter an offer she cannot refuse: if Smatter supports the lovers, Censor promises, 'I will burn all I have written.'[29] Censor is true to his word and his name. Through his self-censorship, the lovers are reunited and Smatter's undeserved reputation as a literary critic is preserved. Burney transforms her own anxieties about privacy and reputation, and her tendency to self-censor, into comedy. According to its title page, *The Witlings* is written 'by a sister of the order': Burney calls herself a witling.

The first reading of the play at Crisp's house seemed to go well. Susanna wrote to Frances straight away to advise her that the fourth act needed work, but that the play had something for everyone: serious audience members were 'struck with Censor's Character', their sister 'Charlotte laugh'd till she was almost black in the face', and everyone—including Crisp—had found the play funny. But Crisp had taken the manuscript to his room, and Burney was to expect a separate communication from him and her father.[30] After this positive report, Burney was surprised by the letter she received from the two men, which she described as a 'Hissing, groaning, catcalling Epistle'.[31] Rather than give her the kind of constructive notes her sister had provided, they advised the complete suppression of the play.

The Witlings was, Crisp claimed, a poor imitation of Molière's *Les femmes savantes*.[32] For Burney's father, the most serious problem was what he called the 'Stocking-Club-Party'.[33] Charles Burney detected a satire on Elizabeth Montagu and the bluestockings in Lady Smatter and her coterie. In fact, Smatter is not a simple caricature of Montagu, who was known for her *Essay on the Writings and Genius of Shakespear*, which defended Shakespeare against 'the presumptuous invasions of our rash critics, and the squibs of our witlings'.[34] In contrast, Smatter, who is certainly a rash critic, attacks Shakespeare.[35] But there are points of resemblance between *The Witlings*'s Esprit Party and Montagu and her coterie, such as their private circulation of manuscripts and Smatter's control over her nephew, who was, like Montagu's nephew, her heir.[36] Charles Burney feared offending Montagu and her circle, even by association. It was not enough for Burney to revise her play or give it up. She must prevent anyone finding out she had written a satire on literary coteries at all. 'As it is,' he urged his daughter, 'not only the Whole Piece, but the *plot* had best be kept secret, from every body.'[37] Crisp went further: 'it would be the best *policy*, but for pecuniary advantages', for Burney 'to write no more'.[38]

Burney's response to the hissing epistle was carefully worded. She had 'expected many Objections to be raised, a thousand errors to be pointed out, & a million of alterations to be proposed;—but—the *suppression of the piece* were words I did *not* expect'.[39] Her letter deflected Crisp's attempt to prevent her from writing, saying that it was good advice and she quite agreed, but *now* was not the time to stop: she wanted to show that she understood her father's good intentions, and could only do that by writing, not by sulking in silence. She accepted her father's decision to suppress the play, but, notably, made no comment on the literary merits or demerits of the script. She agreed to withdraw *The Witlings* on the grounds that her father's reputation was inextricable from her '*Authorshipness*':

> What ever appears with your *knowledge*, will be naturally supposed to have met with your *approbation*, & perhaps with your *assistance*;—& therefore, though all *particular* censure would fall where it *ought*, upon *me*,—yet any *general* censure of the *whole*, & the *Plan* would cruelly, but certainly, involve *you* in it's [sic] severity.[40]

The suppression of *The Witlings* was, for Burney, the act of a loving and dutiful daughter. 'The fatal knell then, is knolled!' she wrote, '& down among the Dead Men sink the poor Witlings,—for-ever & for-ever & for-ever!'[41]

The Witlings still had its champions. Hester Thrale encouraged Burney to revise rather than suppress the script.[42] Arthur Murphy was astonished at Burney's decision and, Burney recalled, '*flew*' at her: 'What! cried he, condemn in *this* manner!—give up such writing!—such Dialogue! such Character!—No; it *must not* be,—shew it *me*, you *shall* shew it me.' She would not show it him. Sheridan also tried to catch a glimpse of the text, but could only communicate with Burney via her father. Even so, he was able to impress upon her—and her father—that dramatists should not attempt to judge their scripts at such an early stage of their development. He would 'much rather see pieces before their Authors were contented with them than afterwards, on account of sundry small changes always necessary to be made by the managers, for Theatrical purposes'. Burney wrote to Crisp, in some distress, that Sheridan 'would not *accept* my refusal—he beg'd my Father to tell me that he could take no denial to *seeing* what I had done.'[43]

Sheridan's demand prompted a flurry of activity: Burney rewrote the fourth act, which had been the least effective in the family read-through, and sent Crisp a list of proposed revisions which, she hoped, would defuse the danger of offending Elizabeth Montagu.[44] Crisp was not satisfied, but if Burney chose to give the play to Sheridan even so, Crisp insisted she 'require him to observe the strictest Secresy, that it shou'd not be known among strangers that he has seen it, & indeed not one of your Family told'. Burney had so much to lose, he warned, and her 'delicate & tender Frame of mind' would be unable to sustain the shock of failure.[45] Unfortunately, Burney never gave the revised script to Sheridan. Had she allowed him to rehearse the play, redundant material would have been cut, dramatic effects added, and the overall coherence of the piece strengthened. Plays are finished in their performance, through the interaction of the actors, the director, and designers with the script in a performance space. Sheridan understood that the script of *The Witlings* was not the final version of the play, and that it should not be judged as a finished work. But Burney could not, or would not, overrule her father and Crisp.

By this point, the thought of the theatre gave her 'more Fear than hope, & Anxiety than pleasure'.[46] Yet she continued writing. She published three more novels, and wrote seven more plays—three comedies and four tragedies, one incomplete. She wrote the tragedies during a

miserable period when she worked at court as deputy keeper of Queen
Charlotte's robes, a position she had taken unwillingly to gratify her
father.[47] One of the plays written at court, *Edwy and Elgiva*, was eventually performed at the Drury Lane theatre, but closed after the first night.
Most of the actors were underprepared (one remembered only two of
his lines), and the prompter was audible throughout the performance.
Burney, who had been recovering from the birth of her son, had been
unable to collaborate with the performers in the rehearsal process or
to cut extraneous material. She recognized, like the reviewers and the
underwhelmed audience, that the play showed her inexperience as a
dramatist, and her response was neither shame nor embarrassment but
a professional's desire to improve a flawed work. She assumed that she
would have the chance to revise the script and see a better version performed. Encouraged by Elizabeth Montagu, she planned to publish a
revised script, and made some progress towards this, but the script was
never passed to a publisher, and the play was not revived.[48]

One of Burney's comedies, *Love and Fashion*, came tantalizingly close
to performance, but was, like *The Witlings*, suppressed at her father's command. Susanna Burney had just died, and Charles Burney declared that
it would be unseemly to present a comedy so soon after a death in the
family. Burney had again written in secrecy, taking elaborate precautions to preserve her anonymity. Her brother, Charles Jr., acted as her
agent, and she discussed the play with him and her sisters using code:
the play was described as a 'table' and the theatre manager as a 'Broker'
and 'Upholsterer'.[49] Via her brother, Burney approached the upholsterer
of the Covent Garden theatre, Thomas Harris, who was perplexed. He
saw through the charade at once, and did not understand why Burney,
a famous author, insisted upon secrecy. Burney and her siblings continued to write in code, but Harris did not play along.[50] He advertised in
the newspapers that 'Madame d'Arbley [*sic*], *Ci-devant* Miss Burney' had
'a Comedy forthcoming' at his theatre.[51] This alarmed Burney's father.
He announced his disapproval, citing Susanna's death as grounds to suppress the play.[52] Challenging him more forcefully than she had ever dared
before, Burney described his displeasure as 'unaccountable but most
afflicting'. She was guilty of no 'crime' in 'doing what I have all my life
been urged to, & all my life intended, writing a Comedy'. This time,
Burney conveyed to her father what the theatre meant to her: 'I thought

the field more than open—inviting to me. The chance held out golden dreams.' And she strove to impress upon him that the play posed no risk to her character. 'Nothing in the principles, the moral, or the language' could disgrace her. If the play failed, it could only cause '*disappointment*'. She hoped he would '*disencourage*' her no more.[53] Yet Charles Burney was immovable, and she persuaded Harris to postpone production to another year.[54] Unsurprisingly, she never told her father about her other comedies, which she was thinking of offering to the Drury Lane and Covent Garden theatres. These last two comedies, *A Busy Day* and *The Woman-Hater*, revive some of the characters from *The Witlings*, and are rather acidic in their depiction of inadequate parents. Even had she been prepared to overrule Charles Burney over these plays, war prevented her from ever bringing them, or *Love and Fashion*, to the stage. In 1802 she was living in France with her husband and son, and when war broke out with England she was unable to send correspondence across the Channel. Burney did not return to England until 1812, after which her father continued to shape her career from beyond the grave. She revised and improved her plays, but her principal writing project, in her last years, was a posthumous biography of her father. While writing the biography, she carried out one final act of censorship, cutting and scribbling out passages from Charles Burney's letters, sometimes even altering the text in an imitation of his handwriting.[55] She burned the portion of her father's papers that she thought was irrelevant or mischievous in its criticism of the Burney family.[56] When she died in 1840, at the age of eighty-seven, Frances Burney's critical reputation still rested on her novels, which were, by then, emblems of a past age.

The judgement of posterity is not impartial. It is shaped by the prejudices, biases, and assumptions of the arbiters of taste. In Burney's case, early critics, who had not even read her scripts, praised Crisp and Charles Burney for their interference, then focused on her novels, diaries, and memoirs.[57] The suppression and neglect of her dramatic work is not unusual. It is typical of the process Clifford Siskin has called 'The Great Forgetting'—the failure of nineteenth-century literary critics to recognize women's writing, compounded by the failure of early twentieth-century critics to question a 'Great Tradition' that largely excluded women. Academic scholarship has, until relatively recently, tended to define the 'literature' of Burney's time as that which was printed and published, excluding the privately circulated manuscripts of the bluestockings, and closing off serious examination of Burney's plays, which existed only as manuscripts.[58] The suppression of Burney's plays in her own time, and the subsequent critical neglect, are a particularly clear example of how women's writing can disappear from the 'literary canon'—'those authors', in M. H. Abrams's words, 'who, by a cumulative consensus of critics, scholars, and teachers, have come to be widely recognized as "major"', and so are likely to be discussed, read, and taught.[59] But Burney's example is available largely because of her status as a canonized woman writer. Had Burney not already made her name as the author of *Evelina*, the story of the suppression of her dramatic works might have been lost to history. Even so, for two centuries, the dramatic works of an important eighteenth-century writer were suppressed, ignored, or forgotten.

We owe our present knowledge of Burney's plays to the Berg Collection of the New York Public Library, which acquired her papers in 1941, making her plays available to scholars. Critical editions began to appear in the 1950s, and the study of Burney's work gathered momentum in the late 1980s, when feminist scholars began to re-examine it. Doody's reappraisal of *The Witlings* in her biography of Burney proved particularly influential, revealing the supposedly unperformable play to be rich in comic potential.[60] Peter Sabor's collected edition of Burney's complete plays appeared in 1995. *The Witlings* had its premiere at the College of Staten Island, City University of New York, on 9 November 1994,[61] and there have been further productions at Main Street Theatre in Houston, Texas, and Theatre Erindale in Mississauga, Ontario, Canada. Reviews expressed surprise at the strength of the suppressed play, commenting on the witty dialogue, eccentric cast of characters, skewering of hypocrisy, and effectiveness of the central combat between Smatter and Censor.[62] Other plays have also been performed, most notably *A Busy Day*, which ran for four weeks at the Hen and Chicken Theatre, Bristol, in 1993, and five weeks at the King's Head Theatre in London in 1994. Reviews praised Burney's satiric eye and acerbic humour.[63] These successful performances vindicate Burney's determination to continue working on her plays, despite the 'disencouragement' of her daddies, her deference to their judgement and to codes of feminine conduct, and the neglect of early critics.

Notes

1. Stewart Cooke, 'Preface', in Frances Burney, *Evelina; or, The History of a Young Lady's Entrance into the World*, ed. Stewart J. Cooke (New York: Norton, 1998), pp. ix–x (p. x).

2. Barbara Darby, *Frances Burney, Dramatist: Gender, Performance, and the Late-Eighteenth-Century Stage* (Lexington: University Press of Kentucky, 1997), pp. 18–19.

3. Peter Sabor, 'Textual Introduction', in Frances Burney, *The Complete Plays of Frances Burney*, ed. Sabor, 2 vols (London: Pickering & Chatto, 1995), i: *Comedies*, xlii–xlv (p. xliii).

4. Joyce Hemlow, *The History of Fanny Burney* (Oxford: Clarendon Press, 1958), pp. 317–18, 320.

5. Margaret Anne Doody, *Frances Burney: The Life in the Works* (Cambridge: Cambridge University Press, 1988), pp. 315–16; Hemlow, p. 325.

6. Doody, p. 312.

7. Madame d'Arblay [Frances Burney], *Memoirs of Doctor Burney, Arranged from his Own Manuscripts, from Family Papers, and from Personal Recollections*, 3 vols (London: Moxon, 1832), ii, 123–25 [Google e-book].

8. Frances Burney, *The Wanderer; or, Female Difficulties*, 5 vols (London: Longman, Hurst, Rees, Orme, and Brown, 1814), i, xx–xxi, quoted in Doody, pp. 35–36.

9. D'Arblay, p. 125.

10. Burney, *The Wanderer*, quoted in Doody, pp. 35–36.

11. Frances Burney to Susanna Burney (3 September 1778), in *The Early Journals and Letters of Fanny Burney*, ed. Lars E. Troide and Stewart J. Cooke, 5 vols (Oxford: Clarendon Press, 1988–2012), iii, ed. Troide and Cooke (1994), 123–36 (p. 135). See also Jane Spencer, *Literary Relations: Kinship and the Canon 1660–1830* (Oxford: Oxford University Press, 2005), p. 52.

12. D'Arblay, pp. 126–37.

13. Burney, *Evelina*, p. 6.

14. Vivien Jones, 'Burney and Gender', in *The Cambridge Companion to Frances Burney*, ed. Peter Sabor (Cambridge: Cambridge University Press, 2007), pp. 111–29 (p. 117).

15. Betty A. Schellenberg, *Literary Coteries and the Making of Modern Print Culture, 1740–1790* (Cambridge: Cambridge University Press, 2016), p. 2.

16. Elizabeth Eger, *Bluestockings: Women of Reason from Enlightenment to Romanticism* (Basingstoke: Palgrave Macmillan, 2010), pp. 11–13, 80–87.

17. Schellenberg, *Literary Coteries*, pp. 63–64, 74–81.
18. Cassandra Ulph, 'Frances Burney's Private Professionalism', *Journal for Eighteenth-Century Studies*, 38.3 (2015), 377–93 (pp. 377–78).
19. Betty A. Schellenberg, *The Professionalization of Women Writers in Eighteenth-Century Britain* (Cambridge: Cambridge University Press, 2005), pp. 144, 146–47.
20. Jones, p. 120.
21. Frances Burney to Susanna Burney (11 January [1779]), in *The Early Journals and Letters of Fanny Burney*, III, 215–37 (p. 235).
22. Judith Phillips Stanton, '"This New-Found Path Attempting": Women Dramatists in England, 1660–1800', in *Curtain Calls: British and American Women and the Theater, 1660–1820*, ed. Mary Anne Schofield and Cecilia Macheski (Athens: Ohio University Press, 1991), pp. 325–54 (pp. 326, 331–37).
23. Samuel Crisp to Frances Burney (8 December 1778), in *The Early Journals and Letters of Fanny Burney*, III, 186–90 (pp. 187–88).
24. Frances Burney to Samuel Crisp (*c.*7 January 1779), in *The Early Journals and Letters of Fanny Burney*, III, 210–14 (p. 212).
25. Peter Sabor, 'General Introduction', in Burney, *The Complete Plays of Frances Burney*, I: *Comedies*, xi–xli (p. xviii).
26. Frances Burney to Samuel Crisp ([29]–30 July [1779]), *The Early Journals and Letters of Fanny Burney*, III, 339–43 (p. 343).
27. Susanna Burney to Frances Burney (3 August 1779), in *The Journals and Letters of Susan Burney: Music and Society in Late Eighteenth-Century England*, ed. Philip Olleson (Farnham: Ashgate, 2012), pp. 68–69.
28. Frances Burney, *The Witlings*, in Burney, *The Complete Plays of Frances Burney*, I, 1–101 (v. 778–81).
29. Burney, *The Witlings*, v. 844.
30. Susanna Burney to Frances Burney (3 August 1779), pp. 68–69.
31. Frances Burney to Samuel Crisp (*c.*13 August 1779), in *The Early Journals and Letters of Fanny Burney*, III, 348–50 (p. 350).
32. Frances Burney to Charles Burney (*c.*13 August 1779), in *The Early Journals and Letters of Fanny Burney*, III, 345–48 (p. 345).
33. Charles Burney to Frances Burney ([29 August] 1779), in *The Letters of Dr Charles Burney*, ed. Alvaro Ribeiro (Oxford: Clarendon Press, 1991–), I (1991), 279–81 (p. 280).
34. Elizabeth Montagu, *An Essay on the Writings and Genius of Shakespear, Compared with the Greek and French Dramatic Poets. With Some Remarks*

upon the Misrepresentations of Mons. de Voltaire, 5th edn (London: Dilly, 1785), pp. 14–15, quoted in Eger, p. 123.

35. Burney, *The Witlings*, II. 45–46.

36. Frances Burney to Samuel Crisp (22 January [1780]), in *The Early Journals and Letters of Fanny Burney*, IV. 2, ed. Betty Rizzo (2003), 6–15 (p. 9 note 28); Schellenberg, *Literary Coteries*, p. 161.

37. Charles Burney to Frances Burney ([29 August] 1779), p. 280.

38. Frances Burney to Charles Burney (*c.*13 August 1779), p. 347.

39. Frances Burney to Charles Burney (*c.*13 August 1779), p. 347.

40. Frances Burney to Charles Burney (*c.*13 August 1779), p. 346.

41. Frances Burney to Charles Burney (*c.*13 August 1779), p. 345.

42. Samuel Crisp to Frances Burney (29 August 1779), in *The Early Journals and Letters of Fanny Burney*, III, 351–53 (p. 352).

43. Frances Burney to Samuel Crisp (22 January [1780]), pp. 8, 13.

44. Frances Burney to Samuel Crisp (22 January [1780]), pp. 8–9.

45. Samuel Crisp to Frances Burney (23 February 1780), in *The Early Journals and Letters of Fanny Burney*, IV. 2, 16–19.

46. Frances Burney to Samuel Crisp (22 January [1780]), p. 9.

47. Doody, pp. 169–70.

48. Sabor, 'General Introduction', pp. xiii–xvii.

49. Darby, pp. 111–12.

50. Frances Burney to Esther Burney (19 November 1799), in *The Journals and Letters of Fanny Burney (Madame D'Arblay)*, 12 vols (Oxford: Clarendon Press, 1972–84), IV, ed. Joyce Hemlow (1973), 360–63.

51. *Morning Chronicle*, 29 January 1800.

52. Peter Sabor, 'The Rediscovery of Frances Burney's Plays', *Lumen: Selected Proceedings from the Canadian Society for Eighteenth-Century Studies*, 13 (1994), 145–56 (pp. 146–47).

53. Frances Burney to Charles Burney ([10] February 1800), in *The Journals and Letters of Fanny Burney*, IV, 394–95.

54. Frances Burney to Esther Burney (*c.*11 February 1800), in *The Journals and Letters of Fanny Burney*, IV, 396–97.

55. Alvaro Ribeiro, 'Textual Introduction', in *The Letters of Dr Charles Burney*, xxx–xxxiv (p. xxx).

56. Doody, pp. 376–78.

57. Sabor, 'Rediscovery', p. 149.

58. Clifford Siskin, *The Work of Writing: Literature and Social Change in Britain, 1700–1830* (Baltimore: Johns Hopkins University Press, 1998), p. 195.

59. M. H. Abrams, *A Glossary of Literary Terms*, 6th edn (Fort Worth, TX: Harcourt, Brace, 1993), pp. 19–20.

60. Sabor, 'Rediscovery', pp. 150–53.

61. Peter Sabor, 'The Witlings', in Burney, *The Complete Plays of Frances Burney*, I, 3–5 (p. 5).

62. Christopher Hole, review of *The Witlings*, *Stage Door*, 3 March 2014, http://www.stage-door.com/Theatre/2014/Entries/2014/3/3_The_Witlings.html, accessed 1 January 2017; Odai Johnson, review of *The Witlings*, *Theatre Journal*, 50.4 (1998), 543–44.

63. Sabor, 'General Introduction', pp. xi–xii.

4

Queen Mab
Percy Bysshe Shelley

In 1813 Percy Shelley was a twenty-year-old radical. He had been expelled from Oxford two years earlier in a conflict over his co-authored essay on 'The Necessity of Atheism'. He had since distributed subversive publications on the streets of Dublin, in glass bottles set adrift at sea, and in hot air balloons. He once dropped a pamphlet into a passing woman's hood. His fifteen-year-old servant, Dan Healy, also known as Dan Hill, had been arrested in 1812 and imprisoned for six months for putting up posters.[1] Shelley's latest work, a long poem called *Queen Mab*, looked at first glance like a flight of fancy: Mab, the fairy queen, appears to a human woman in a vision, and reveals truths about the universe. These truths, however, contain some of the author's unorthodox opinions, which Shelley elaborated at length in endnotes. Advocating atheism, free love, and vegetarianism, while challenging the sovereignty of monarchs, *Queen Mab* prophesied a future in which

> Woman and man, in confidence and love,
> Equal and free and pure together trod
> The mountain-paths of virtue, which no more
> Were stained with blood from many a pilgrim's feet.[2]

Shelley was not calling for a revolution like the ones that had occurred in the United States and France. A 'class traitor' (as scholar Timothy Morton calls him) born into the gentry, he advocated social equality in theory.[3] Yet,

QUEEN MAB.

―――――

I.

How wonderful is Death,
    Death and his brother Sleep !
One, pale as yonder wan~~ing~~ moon   *& horned moon*
    With lips of lurid blue ;
The other, ~~rosy as the~~   *glowing like the vital morn*
    When throned on ocean's wave
It ~~blushes o'er~~ the world :   *breathes over*
    Yet both so passing wonderful !   *strange*
                        ^

    Hath then the ~~gloomy Power~~ *iron-sceptred Skeleton*
Whose reign is in the tainted sepulchres
    ~~Seized on her sinless soul?~~ *To the helldogs that crouch beneath his*
    ~~Must thou that peerless form~~ *cast that fair prey. must that divinest form*

B

The first page of the 1813 *Queen Mab*, with Percy Shelley's revisions for a much shorter and less dangerous version of the poem entitled *The Daemon of the World* (published 1816).

he believed that 'the change should commence among the higher orders, or anarchy will only be the last flash before despotism'.[4] He instructed the publisher of *Queen Mab*, 'I expect no success.—Let only 250 Copies be printed. A small neat Quarto, on fine paper & so as to catch the aristocrats: They will not read it, but their sons & daughters may.'[5] He had his own name and his father-in-law's address appear on the title page instead of the printer's, and often clipped out this information when sending copies to his select list of recipients.[6] Distributing a publication with a false imprint or none at all was illegal, and this had been the charge against Shelley's servant Healy, but the practice shielded the printer from prosecution.[7] In 1817, after Harriet Shelley, whom Percy had left for Mary Wollstonecraft Godwin, killed herself, her parents used the poem as evidence in a successful suit for custody of Harriet and Percy's two children.[8] Aside from this personal fall-out and some published excerpts, the poem might simply have bided its time in private libraries, awaiting the curiosity of future generations of aristocratic firebrands.[9] Instead, *Queen Mab* found an audience that its author had never intended. In the early nineteenth century a more purposeful form of rebellion than Shelley's was taking shape in the United Kingdom. Radical pirate publishers were selling subversive books at affordable prices and in mass quantities to a dramatically expanding reading public that included the working class.[10]

From the late eighteenth century into the nineteenth, in an effort to prevent a hungry and discontented public from turning to civil unrest or revolution, British authorities cracked down on dissent.[11] In 1787 George III issued a proclamation against 'all Manner of Vice, Profaneness, and Immorality', ordering his subjects 'to suppress all loose and licentious Prints, Books, and Publications, dispersing Poison to the Minds of the Young and Unwary, and to punish the Publishers and Venders thereof'.[12] To help enforce this proclamation, the politician and abolitionist William Wilberforce founded an organization for moral reform called the Proclamation Society, later the Society for the Suppression of Vice. This voluntary group, which was the pattern for organizations such as Anthony Comstock's New York Society for the Suppression of Vice (see Chapter 6), policed a variety of practices, including obscene publications, working on the Sabbath, and prostitution.[13] The society was run by the elite, and the writer Sydney Smith complained that, while the group was punishing the transgressions of the poor, 'The peer ruins himself and his family with impunity'.[14]

In this climate of suppression, radical publishing was an especially
risky industry. While Britain, having discarded formal print licensing
in 1695, now prided itself on its freedom of the press, the Seditious
Societies Act 1799 made it easier for the government to monitor publishers by requiring them to register their presses, put their
imprint on everything they printed, keep copies of their printed
material, and maintain lists of clients.[15] English common law prohibited four different kinds of criminal libel (defamatory, obscene,
blasphemous, and seditious), and the period from the mid-1790s into
the early nineteenth century saw a spike in criminal libel trials as
authorities shifted their attention from prosecuting high treason to
controlling associations and the press. There were over a hundred
and twenty libel prosecutions between 1819 and 1821, compared
to about seventy from 1760 to 1790.[16] Penalties for illegal printing
included fines and prison sentences, and cheap publications tended
to be targeted.[17] (Mary Wollstonecraft Shelley's father, William Godwin, wrote his own seditious book, entitled *Political Justice*, in 1793.
Godwin claimed that Prime Minister William Pitt had advised against
prosecuting it because it was too expensive for the working class.[18])
In the 1790s, spurred on by propaganda, loyalist citizens monitored
and intimidated their neighbours, sometimes burning radical publications, including *Rights of Man* by the revolutionary writer Thomas
Paine. 'Church and King' mobs physically attacked newspaper offices
and bookshops.[19] Into the nineteenth century, 'taxes on knowledge',
including paper taxes on books and rising stamp duties on newspapers, helped to keep reading material out of the hands of workers,
while the window tax encouraged landlords to block up windows,
limiting their tenants' light.[20] Those who responded to economic
exploitation with direct action, such as the Luddites, who destroyed
textile-manufacturing equipment in the 1810s, could face death by
hanging.[21]

By this time, several prominent poets, including William Wordsworth, Samuel Taylor Coleridge, and Robert Southey, had retreated
from their youthful radicalism. (Shelley wrote of Wordsworth, 'thou
leavest me to grieve, | Thus having been, that thou shouldst cease to
be'.[22]) Southey had written a verse drama in the 1790s called *Wat Tyler*,
which dealt with the abuses of royal power that had led to the Peasants'

Revolt of 1381. In the play, the rogue priest John Ball addresses the commoners, spurring them to rebellion:

Have you not often in your conscience ask'd
Why is the difference, wherefore should that man,
No worthier than myself, thus lord it over me,
And bid me labour, and enjoy the fruits?[23]

Southey never published the play, and by the time a pirated version appeared in 1817 under the imprint of Sherwood, Neely, and Jones, he was Poet Laureate, arguing against universal suffrage in the Tory *Quarterly Review*. Southey did not regret his past, but the play was being used to attack him in Parliament, and he applied to the Lord Chancellor for an injunction to suppress it. Lord Eldon ruled that, because the work might well be libellous, the law could not protect Southey's share in the profits. Southey could not assert his copyright unless the publisher were to defend the book successfully in a libel trial.[24] This counter-intuitive decision created a legal loophole for radical literary piracy: the more subversive a publication, the less the publisher needed to worry about copyright. Other unauthorized editions of *Wat Tyler* soon followed. Within a year the price had dropped from two shillings to two pence, at a time when the usual cost of a comparable book was over ten shillings. This low price enabled the book to reach a mass market.[25]

In 1819, when the publisher Richard Carlile asked Shelley if he could reprint *Queen Mab*, Shelley declined.[26] Shelley did not undergo a political reversal like Southey's, but he had not meant the whole poem to be circulated widely, and was wary of the potential consequences.[27] Carlile, on the other hand, was one of the pirate publishers who had profited from *Wat Tyler*.[28] He had been a tin-worker for fifteen years but struggled to find steady work, and moved into writing and publishing in 1817.[29] The following year he reprinted *Age of Reason* by Thomas Paine, who had himself been prosecuted for seditious libel for his treatise *Rights of Man*. Charged with blasphemous libel for publishing *Age of Reason* and Elihu Palmer's *Principles of Nature*, Carlile read the entire *Age of Reason* aloud in court so that the jury could decide if it was in fact libellous. This performance was also an attempt to have the text further published in court reports. Imprisoned for six years, Carlile continued to operate his business through friends and family, some of whom joined him in prison, including his sister, Mary-Anne Carlile, and his wife, Jane Carlile.[30] Between them, Richard Carlile and his associates were incarcerated for a total of two hundred years.[31] Carlile even published material about birth control, though this topic proved too controversial for his readership.[32]

Nevertheless, Carlile initially refrained from publishing *Queen Mab*, as Shelley had requested.[33] The first, relatively expensive, pirated edition appeared in 1821, published by William Clark, a bookseller and former employee of Carlile. Clark also published a cheaper edition and an expurgated one. The Society for the Suppression of Vice brought a private prosecution for blasphemous libel against Clark, who yielded up copies of the book to be destroyed and was ordered to maintain good behaviour. Arrested again for further sales, he was sentenced to four months in prison.[34] While *Queen Mab* was potentially seditious as well as blasphemous, the explicit argument for atheism in the notes was its most obvious challenge to the status quo. Invoking the scientist Sir Isaac Newton, Shelley argues that God is not a valid hypothesis for explaining the world: 'The being called God by no means answers with the conditions prescribed by Newton; it bears every mark of a veil woven by philosophical conceit, to hide the ignorance of philosophers even from themselves.'[35] Seditious and blasphemous libel were different shades of the same crime, which was, in essence, publishing matter that would tend to cause a breach of the peace. Sedition was an offence against the state, while blasphemy was an offence against Christianity, the religion on which the laws of the realm were understood to rest.[36] Though some scholars believe that Shelley was actually glad to see the poem circulated,[37] he publicly disowned *Queen Mab* in the *Examiner*:

> I doubt not but that it is perfectly worthless in point of literary composition; and that in all that concerns moral and political speculation, as well as in the subtler discriminations of metaphysical and religious doctrine, it is still more crude and immature. I am a devoted enemy to religious, political, and domestic oppression; and I regret this publication not so much from literary vanity, as because I fear it is better fitted to injure than to serve the sacred cause of freedom.

Shelley explained that he had sought an injunction against the pirated edition, but did not hope to obtain one because of the *Wat Tyler* precedent.[38]

Neither the Society for the Suppression of Vice nor Shelley was able to prevent further circulation of the poem. Carlile, who saw radical publishing as a form of intellectual 'warfare' and condemned Clark for not fighting the libel charges in a jury trial, stepped in, publishing another unexpurgated *Queen Mab* using Clark's sheets. Carlile did not entirely agree with Shelley's ideas, but did not want 'to give the least encouragement to the hypocrites and villains who would stifle all discussion, and suppress every valuable publication, because it tends to unmask them, and to put a stop to their robberies upon the industrious multitude'.[39] Other publishers followed suit, including Jane Carlile.[40]

Not yet thirty, Shelley died in 1822, and the pirated *Queen Mab* became his initial legacy. (The Tory magazine *John Bull* announced, 'Mr. Bysshe Shelley, the author of that abominable and blasphemous book called *Queen Mab*, was lately drowned in a storm somewhere in the Mediterranean.'[41]) From 1821 to 1840, there were at least fourteen pirated editions of the poem.[42] The price dropped, reaching a shilling and six pence in 1832. While people of all classes read *Queen Mab*, its price made it available to those who could not afford more expensive books, and with whom its politics resonated.[43] The playwright George Bernard Shaw records that *Queen Mab* was known as the 'Chartists' Bible' because of its popularity with members of the working-class Chartist movement, who agitated for political reforms that included extending the vote to all men and removing property requirements for parliamentary membership.[44] The Owenite socialists also made use of *Queen Mab* and Shelley's other poems in their publications.[45] In the 1830s an apprentice wood-engraver named Henry Vizetelly found himself in a London workroom where the 'most democratic opinions were current' and the workers read 'forbidden books, furtively obtained', including *Wat Tyler*, *Rights of Man*, and *Age of Reason*. Vizetelly found *Queen Mab* to hold 'the greatest fascination': 'At that time we did not read Shelley as he is now read, for his poetic imagery and mellifluous diction, but because this ostracised poem of his teemed with agnostic and republican ideas boldly expressed in impassioned language.'[46] Fifty years later, Vizetelly would be a publisher himself, convicted of obscene libel for publishing inexpensive English translations of works by the French novelist Émile Zola (see Chapter 8).

The success of *Queen Mab* led to over twenty-six pirated editions of Shelley's poetry between 1822 and 1841,[47] and some of his other works also became part of a tradition of political protest, especially *The Mask of Anarchy*.[48] This poem was written on the occasion of the Peterloo Massacre at St Peter's Field, Manchester, in 1819, when British cavalry charged into a peaceful assembly of tens of thousands of people who were calling for parliamentary reform, killing over ten and wounding hundreds. (Richard Carlile was present at the massacre, and his account of it spurred the government's prosecution of him.[49]) Shelley's response concludes with a galvanizing call to action:

> Rise like lions after slumber
> In unvanquishable number—
> Shake your chains to earth like dew
> Which in sleep had fallen on you—
> Ye are many—they are few.[50]

Shelley submitted *The Mask of Anarchy* to Leigh Hunt for publication in the *Examiner*, but Hunt declined to print it until 1832.[51] The political associations of Shelley's poetry persisted through the twentieth century and spread internationally.[52] The last line of his 'Ode to the West Wind', 'If Winter comes, can Spring be far behind?', became a communist slogan in the 1958 novel *The Song of Youth* (*Qingchun zhi ge*) by Chinese author Yang Mo.[53] During the pro-democracy student protests in China in 1989, a week before the Tiananmen Square massacre on 4 June, the line was posted on Liaoning University's Democracy Forum wall.[54]

The pirated editions of Shelley did not all emphasize the poet's radicalism. In 1830 Stephen Hunt published an unauthorized, expurgated edition of *Queen Mab* that omitted the notes and eight hundred lines, declaring on the title page that this was a 'Revised Edition Free from All The Objectionable Passages'. He included this version in an anthology entitled *The Beauties of Percy Bysshe Shelley*, which also promised that it was free of the objectionable passages of *Queen Mab*.[55] These versions were aimed at conservative working-class readers.[56] A struggle over the author's reputation was taking place in the editions of his texts, and while the pirates were marketing their versions of Percy Shelley, Mary Wollstonecraft Shelley, author of *Frankenstein*, was shaping a different legacy, at a higher price point, for her late husband.

Mary's first edition of Percy's works was the 1824 *Posthumous Poems*, which she hoped would 'be a specimen of how he could write without shocking any one'.[57] The pirated *Queen Mab* had attracted the wrath of conservative critics, which Mary attempted to mitigate by releasing some of the poet's less overtly political works.[58] Here, at fifteen shillings, was a safer Percy for the middle and upper classes.[59] Mary intended to publish complete editions of Percy's prose and poetry, but her disapproving father-in-law, Sir Timothy Shelley, required her to withdraw the remaining copies of *Posthumous Poems*, and forbade her from further circulating Percy's work, threatening to cut off her financial maintenance.[60]

Mary Shelley finally published *The Poetical Works of Percy Bysshe Shelley* in 1839, by which time enough pirated versions of the complete works had appeared that she was able to secure permission from Sir Timothy.[61] The first edition, in four volumes, was expurgated. At the insistence of her respectable publisher, Edward Moxon, Mary omitted dangerous passages about religion from *Queen Mab*, including all of Canto VII, in which Mab claims:

> The exterminable spirit it contains
> Is nature's only God; but human pride
> Is skilful to invent most serious names
> To hide its ignorance.[62]

Later that year, preparing a one-volume edition, Mary convinced Moxon to restore the censored passages. She writes:

> The notes also are reprinted entire; not because they are models of reasoning or lessons of truth; but because Shelley wrote them. And that all that a man, at once so distinguished and so excellent, ever did, deserves to be preserved. The alterations his opinions underwent ought to be recorded, for they form his history.[63]

Mary attempts to strike a careful balance in this edition. She does not disguise Percy's radical politics, but she is almost apologetic about the more revolutionary implications of his work: 'He had been from youth the victim of the state of feeling inspired by the reaction of the French Revolution.' Mary's Percy is like Plato, 'taking more delight in the abstract and the ideal, than in the special and tangible'.[64] Though in *Queen Mab* he had made 'the whole universe the object and subject of his song', physical illness had subsequently made him 'turn his eyes inward'.[65] While *The Mask of Anarchy* showed that 'still his warmest sympathies were for the people' and that he 'was a republican, and loved a democracy', his 'first eager desire to excite his countrymen to resist openly the oppressions existent during "the good old times" had faded with early youth'.[66] The radical Percy is still here but tempered by a more mature, lyrical, and idealized version of him.[67]

Mary Shelley contextualized works like *Queen Mab* and 'Oedipus Tyrannus'—a satire on the royal family that the Society for the Suppression of Vice had quashed with threats of prosecution in 1820—as moments in the short but evolving career of a poetic genius. At twelve shillings, her collection was expensive, and therefore less accessible to the working-class readers who were consuming *Queen Mab* in its pirated form and whose resistance the government feared.[68] Moxon might have got away with the unexpurgated *Poetical Works* were it not for a rival publisher who was trying to make a point.

In 1841 a radical newspaper publisher and bookseller named Henry Hetherington was charged with blasphemous libel for selling *Haslam's Letters to the Clergy of All Denominations*, which attacked the Old Testament of the Bible. In response, Hetherington brought private prosecutions against Moxon and booksellers who sold Shelley's complete works.[69] Moxon's defence counsel, Thomas Noon Talfourd, tried to counter the charges of blasphemous libel by arguing that *Queen Mab* was different from 'a cheap and popular work of alleged blasphemy' like *Haslam's Letters*, which was 'prepared, calculated, and intended by the author to shake the religious principles of the uneducated and the young'. *Queen Mab* had appeared in Moxon's edition not to stir up unrest, but to illustrate the development of a poet who, though he 'fancies himself irreligious', 'everywhere falters or trembles into piety'.[70] Depicting Shelley's oeuvre as a winding stream of genius, Talfourd asked:

> shall we [...] be forbidden to ascend with painful steps its narrowing
> course to its furthest spring, because black rocks may encircle the spot
> whence it rushes into day, and demon shapes—frightful but powerless
> for harm—may gleam and frown on us beside it?[71]

The jury did not buy Talfourd's distinction between cheap blasphemy and a voyage into the perilous springs of genius. They convicted Moxon, and, though he was not punished, he returned to printing expurgated editions of Shelley. Hetherington was convicted, too.[72]

By the end of the nineteenth century, the split in Shelley's reputation remained. Anglo-American critics were largely dismissive of Shelley's radicalism, and effaced the politics, admired him despite them, or belittled him because of them. Matthew Arnold wrote, quoting himself:

> The man Shelley, in very truth, is not entirely sane, and Shelley's poetry
> is not entirely sane either. The Shelley of actual life is a vision of beauty
> and radiance, indeed, but availing nothing, effecting nothing. And in
> poetry, no less than in life, he is 'a beautiful *and ineffectual* angel, beating
> in the void his beautiful wings in vain'.[73]

T. S. Eliot, who found Shelley thoroughly adolescent, wrote: 'I can only regret that Shelley did not live to put his poetic gifts, which were certainly of the first order, at the service of more tenable beliefs— which need not have been, for my purposes, beliefs more acceptable to me.'[74] Others were more receptive to the radical Shelley, including the poet Algernon Charles Swinburne, German Marxists, and socialists like George Bernard Shaw, who wished 'that in future the bogus Shelley', the sanitized version of him, 'be buried and done with'.[75] Friedrich Engels wrote in 1845:

> Shelley, the genius, the prophet, Shelley, and Byron, with his glowing
> sensuality and his bitter satire upon our existing society, find most of
> their readers in the proletariat; the bourgeoisie owns only castrated
> editions, family editions, cut down in accordance with the hypocritical
> morality of today.[76]

One of Shelley's most famous lyric poems, 'Ode to the West Wind', calls on the wind to spread the poet's words around the world:

> Drive my dead thoughts over the universe
> Like withered leaves to quicken a new birth!
> And, by the incantation of this verse,
>
> Scatter, as from an unextinguished hearth
> Ashes and sparks, my words among mankind![77]

While these lines can be interpreted as a plea to a nature spirit for poetic inspiration, it is worth remembering that the difference Shelley wished to make in the world was not so abstract. He wrote 'Ode to the West Wind' in 1819, a month after *The Mask of Anarchy*. The words that he wanted the wind to scatter like sparks included his call to the British people to rise up in response to state violence at St Peter's Fields: 'Ye are many—they are few.'

Notes

1. Richard Holmes, *Shelley: The Pursuit* (London: HarperCollins, 1994), pp. 54–55, 119–20, 132, 148–50, 158–59. See also Andrew Franta, *Romanticism and the Rise of the Mass Public* (Cambridge: Cambridge University Press, 2007), pp. 114–15; Michael Henry Scrivener, *Radical Shelley: The Philosophical Anarchism and Utopian Thought of Percy Bysshe Shelley* (Princeton: Princeton University Press, 1982), p. 57.

2. Percy Bysshe Shelley, *Queen Mab: A Philosophical Poem, with Notes*, in *The Complete Poetry of Percy Bysshe Shelley*, ed. Donald H. Reiman and Neil Fraistat, 3 vols (Baltimore: Johns Hopkins University Press, 2003–12), II (2004), 163–312 (IX. 89–92).

3. Timothy Morton, 'Introduction', in *The Cambridge Companion to Shelley*, ed. Morton (Cambridge: Cambridge University Press, 2006), pp. 1–13 (p. 3).

4. Percy Bysshe Shelley to Thomas Love Peacock ([24] August [1819]), in Percy Bysshe Shelley, *The Letters of Percy Bysshe Shelley*, ed. Frederick L. Jones, 2 vols (Oxford: Clarendon Press, 1964), II: *Shelley in Italy*, 115.

5. Percy Bysshe Shelley to [Thomas Hookham] ([March 1813]), in Percy Bysshe Shelley, *The Letters of Percy Bysshe Shelley*, I: *Shelley in England*, 361.

6. Donald H. Reiman and Neil Fraistat, commentary for *Queen Mab: A Philosophical Poem*, in *The Complete Poetry of Percy Bysshe Shelley*, II, 491–594 (pp. 495–96).

7. Holmes, p. 158.

8. Kim Wheatley, *Shelley and his Readers: Beyond Paranoid Politics* (Columbia: University of Missouri Press, 1999), pp. 83–84.

9. Reiman and Fraistat, p. 508.

10. William St Clair, *The Reading Nation in the Romantic Period* (Cambridge: Cambridge University Press, 2004), pp. 10–13, 311–17.

11. St Clair, *The Reading Nation*, pp. 308–9.

12. *An Address to the Public, from the Society for the Suppression of Vice, Instituted in London, 1802*, in *Blasphemy in Britain and America, 1800–1930*, ed. David Nash, 4 vols (London: Pickering & Chatto, 2010), I: *The Blasphemous Enlightenment to 1810*, 83–112 (pp. 83, 84).

13. Edward J. Bristow, *Vice and Vigilance: Purity Movements in Britain since 1700* (Dublin: Gill & Macmillan, 1977), pp. 37–42. See also St Clair, *The Reading Nation*, p. 311.

14. [Sydney Smith], review of *Statement of the Proceedings of the Society for the Suppression of Vice* and *An Address to the Public from the Society for the Suppression of Vice*, *Edinburgh Review*, 13.26, 2nd edn (January 1809), 333–43 (p. 341) [Google e-book].

15. St Clair, *The Reading Nation*, p. 311. See also Alan Booth, '"The Memory of the Liberty of the Press": The Suppression of Radical Writing in the 1790s', in *Writing and Censorship in Britain*, ed. Paul Hyland and Neil Sammells (London: Routledge, 1992), pp. 107–22 (pp. 114–15).

16. Franta, pp. 144–45, 148–49, 151–52.

17. Booth, pp. 111–13; St Clair, *The Reading Nation*, pp. 310–11.

18. William St Clair, *The Godwins and the Shelleys: The Biography of a Family* (London: Faber & Faber, 1989), p. 85.

19. Booth, pp. 115–19.

20. St Clair, *The Reading Nation*, pp. 309–10. See also Booth, p. 114.

21. Scrivener, pp. 54, 56, 58–59.

22. Percy Bysshe Shelley, 'To Wordsworth', in *The Major Works*, ed. Zachary Leader and Michael O'Neill (Oxford: Oxford University Press, 2003), pp. 90–91 (ll. 13–14).

23. Robert Southey, *Wat Tyler* (Oxford: Woodstock Books, 1989), p. 29 (Act II).

24. Mark Storey, *Robert Southey: A Life* (Oxford: Oxford University Press, 1997), pp. 67, 253–57. See also St Clair, *The Reading Nation*, pp. 316–17.

25. St Clair, *The Reading Nation*, pp. 317–18.

26. Reiman and Fraistat, pp. 508–9.

27. See Scrivener, pp. 55–59.

28. St Clair, *The Reading Nation*, p. 317.

29. Philip W. Martin, 'Carlile, Richard (1790–1843)', *Oxford Dictionary of National Biography* (Oxford: Oxford University Press, 2004; online edn 2005), http://www.oxforddnb.com/view/article/4685, accessed 2 January 2017.

30. David Nash, *Blasphemy in Modern Britain, 1789 to the Present* (Aldershot: Ashgate, 1999), pp. 83–87. See also Martin; David Nash, 'General Introduction', in *Blasphemy in Britain and America, 1800–1930*, I, vii–xxxvi (p. xviii); St Clair, *The Reading Nation*, p. 313.

31. Scrivener, p. 55.

32. Martin.

33. Reiman and Fraistat, pp. 508–9.

34. R[ichard] Carlile, 'Prosecutions for Blasphemy', *Republican*, 18 March 1825, p. 350 [Google e-book]; Editor [Richard Carlile], 'Queen Mab', *Republican*, 1 February 1822, pp. 146–47 [Google e-book]. See also Reiman and Fraistat, pp. 509–11; Wheatley, p. 85.

35. Percy Bysshe Shelley, *Queen Mab*, p. 268 (author's note to VII. 13).

36. Nash, 'General Introduction', pp. xv, xviii.

37. Wheatley, p. 85 and note 70.

38. Percy B. Shelley to the editor of the *Examiner* (22 June 1821), in *The Poetical Works of Percy Bysshe Shelley*, ed. Mrs [Mary] Shelley (London: Moxon, 1840), p. 40 [HathiTrust e-book].

39. Editor [Richard Carlile], 'Queen Mab', pp. 147, 148. See also Reiman and Fraistat, p. 510.

40. Reiman and Fraistat, pp. 511–16. See also St Clair, *The Reading Nation*, pp. 680–81.

41. *John Bull*, 12 August 1822, quoted in Susan J. Wolfson, 'Editorial Privilege: Mary Shelley and Percy Shelley's Audiences', in *The Other Mary Shelley: Beyond 'Frankenstein'*, ed. Audrey A. Fisch and others (New York: Oxford University Press, 1993), pp. 39–72 (p. 46).

42. Reiman and Fraistat, p. 509.

43. St Clair, *The Reading Nation*, pp. 319–22, 680–81.

44. [George] Bernard Shaw, 'Shaming the Devil about Shelley', in *Pen Portraits and Reviews* (London: Constable, 1932; repr. 1949), pp. 236–46 (p. 244).

45. Jen Morgan, 'Uses of Shelley in Working-Class Culture: Approximations and Substitutions', *Key Words*, 13 (2015), 117–37 (pp. 117–20).

46. Henry Vizetelly, *Glances Back through Seventy Years: Autobiographical and Other Reminiscences*, 2 vols (London: Kegan Paul, Trench, Trübner, 1893), I, 121.

47. Neil Fraistat, 'Illegitimate Shelley: Radical Piracy and the Textual Edition as Cultural Performance', *PMLA*, 109.3 (1994), 409–23 (p. 412).

48. Timothy Morton, 'Receptions', in *The Cambridge Companion to Shelley*, pp. 35–42 (pp. 40–41).

49. Leonard W. Levy, *Blasphemy: Verbal Offense against the Sacred from Moses to Salman Rushdie* (New York: Knopf, 1993), p. 356.

50. Percy Bysshe Shelley, *The Mask of Anarchy*, in *The Major Works*, pp. 400–11 (ll. 368–72).

51. Mary Shelley, 'Note on the Poems of 1819. By the Editor', in *The Poetical Works of Percy Bysshe Shelley*, pp. 251–53 (p. 251).

52. Morton, 'Receptions', pp. 40–41.

53. Xiaomei Chen, *Occidentalism: A Theory of Counter-Discourse in Post-Mao China*, 2nd edn, rev. and expanded (Lanham, MD: Rowman & Littlefield, 2002), p. 74.

54. Anne Gunn, '"Tell the World about Us": The Student Movement in Shenyang, 1989', in *The Pro-Democracy Protests in China: Reports from the Provinces*, ed. Jonathan Unger (Armonk, NY: East Gate, 1991), pp. 64–78 (p. 74).

55. St Clair, *The Reading Nation*, p. 681.

56. Wheatley, p. 108.

57. Mary Wollstonecraft Shelley to Leigh Hunt (20 October [1823]), in Mary Wollstonecraft Shelley, *The Letters of Mary Wollstonecraft Shelley*, ed. Betty T. Bennett, 3 vols (Baltimore: Johns Hopkins University Press, 1980–88), I: *'A Part of the Elect'* (1980), 397.

58. Wheatley, pp. 59, 86–100, 104–7.

59. Fraistat, p. 412.

60. Emily W. Sunstein, *Mary Shelley: Romance and Reality* (Baltimore: Johns Hopkins University Press, 1989), pp. 232–33, 260–61.

61. Sunstein, pp. 340–42.

62. Percy Bysshe Shelley, *Queen Mab*, p. 214 (VII. 23–26). See Reiman and Fraistat, pp. 517–18; Sunstein, p. 343; Wolfson, p. 50.

63. Mary Shelley, 'Note on Queen Mab. By the Editor', in *The Poetical Works of Percy Bysshe Shelley*, pp. 37–40 (p. 37).

64. Mary Shelley, 'Preface. By the Editor', in *The Poetical Works of Percy Bysshe Shelley*, pp. vii–xi (pp. viii, ix).

65. Mary Shelley, 'Note on Alastor. By the Editor', in *The Poetical Works of Percy Bysshe Shelley*, p. 47.

66. Mary Shelley, 'Note on the Poems of 1819. By the Editor', p. 251.

67. See Sunstein, pp. 345–46; Wolfson, pp. 39–45, 48–56.

68. St Clair, *The Reading Nation*, p. 682.

69. 'The Laws against Blasphemy. Mr. Serjeant Talfourd's Defence of Moxon', *Law Magazine; or, Quarterly Review of Jurisprudence*, 26 (1841), 139–52 (pp. 144–45). See also Hans Ostrom, 'Moxon, Edward (*bap.* 1801, *d.* 1858)', *Oxford Dictionary of National Biography* (Oxford: Oxford University Press, 2004; online edn 2014), http://www.oxforddnb.com/view/article/19463, accessed 2 January 2017.

70. 'The Laws against Blasphemy', pp. 149, 150.

71. 'The Laws against Blasphemy', pp. 148–49.

72. Ostrom.

73. Matthew Arnold, *Essays in Criticism: Second Series* (London: Macmillan, 1893), pp. 251–52 (emphasis original) [HathiTrust e-book].

74. T. S. Eliot, *The Use of Poetry and the Use of Criticism: Studies in the Relation of Criticism to Poetry in England*, 2nd edn (London: Faber & Faber, 1964), p. 97.

75. Shaw, p. 245. See also Morton, 'Receptions', pp. 38, 39–40.

76. Friedrich Engels, *The Condition of the Working Class in England*, ed. David McLellan (Oxford: Oxford University Press, 1993; repr. 2009), p. 247.

77. Percy Bysshe Shelley, 'Ode to the West Wind', in *The Major Works*, pp. 412–14 (ll. 63–67).

5

The History of Mary Prince
Mary Prince

In defiance of the mass censorship that slavery entailed, Mary Prince recorded the story of her enslavement in Bermuda, the Turks Islands, and Antigua. *The History of Mary Prince* is the only known slave narrative, as the genre is called, told in English by a woman enslaved in the West Indies.[1] Prince's voice is one trace of the millions that slave-holding nations stifled by abducting African people, denying their humanity and autonomy, subjecting them to violence, preventing them from testifying in court against their self-styled masters, restricting their access to education and literacy, and subordinating their oral cultures to ones in which authority and history depended on the written word in European languages. Prince's escape from slavery was an escape from historical silence but not from censorship. Though she told her story, her White benefactors in Britain would shape its form and content, fashioning it into a tool to be used in the cause of abolition. Prince dictated her narrative in 1831 to the poet Susanna Strickland, who was a guest in the London home of Thomas Pringle—poet, secretary of the Anti-Slavery Society, and former South African colonist. Pringle edited Strickland's transcription, appended various supplementary documents to it, and published it as *The History of Mary Prince*. This publication process had a significant impact on the resulting book.

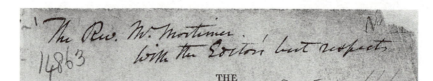

THE

HISTORY OF MARY PRINCE,

A WEST INDIAN SLAVE.

RELATED BY HERSELF.

___

WITH A SUPPLEMENT BY THE EDITOR.

___

To which is added,

THE NARRATIVE OF ASA-ASA,

A CAPTURED AFRICAN.

___

" By our sufferings, since ye brought us
To the man-degrading mart,—
All sustain'd by patience, taught us
Only by a broken heart,—
Deem our nation brutes no longer,
Till some reason ye shall find
Worthier of regard, and stronger
Than the colour of our kind." COWPER.

___

LONDON:
PUBLISHED BY F. WESTLEY AND A. H. DAVIS,
STATIONERS' HALL COURT;
AND BY WAUGH & INNES, EDINBURGH.

___

1831.

The title page of the first edition of *The History of Mary Prince*, containing a supplement by Thomas Pringle and a second slave narrative.

In the first place, Prince is likely to have censored herself. Her audience consisted of Strickland, Pringle, and a White British public for whom Prince would be both a witness of atrocity and the representative of a race.[2] Even those readers committed to the anti-slavery movement had their share of racism and moralistic prejudice, which would have created a double bind. Caught between authenticity and acceptability, Prince had to recount the horrors of her experience while remaining worthy, in the eyes of her readers, of their sympathy. She needed to present herself as a model victim, someone who had passed through the degradations of enslavement while still living up to the mores of the nineteenth-century British middle class.[3] As the novelist Toni Morrison explains, in order to make the events of their lives 'palatable' to abolitionists, authors of slave narratives 'were silent about many things, and they "forgot" many other things'.[4] Relating how she intervened when one of her former masters, Mr D——, was beating his daughter, Prince says, 'I can't repeat his answer, the words were too wicked—too bad to say.'[5] She could not appear to share D——'s wickedness by quoting him.

There is no mention in *The History of Mary Prince* of revolts among the enslaved population of the West Indies, which Prince may have known about, but which it would have been impolitic to discuss.[6] Prince had to moderate her tone carefully to engage her readers rather than record her subjective experience fully. As Morrison writes, authors of slave narratives needed 'to appear as objective as possible—not to offend the reader by being too angry, or by showing too much outrage, or by calling the reader names'.[7] At the age of twelve, Prince was separated from her family and sold, and she gently incriminates White bystanders in her account of the auction:

> They were not all bad, I dare say, but slavery hardens white people's hearts towards the blacks; and many of them were not slow to make their remarks upon us aloud, without regard to our grief—though their light words fell like cayenne on the fresh wounds of our hearts. Oh those white people have small hearts who can only feel for themselves.[8]

One might expect Prince's own words to be more searing than this, but she is careful not to offend.

As the person transcribing Prince's speech, Strickland also had the opportunity to alter it, and may have omitted references to Prince's sexual relationships, which were later revealed in court. In editing Strickland's manuscript, Pringle certainly changed it. He omitted the full names of several of Prince's masters, leaving only their initials on the grounds that they were deceased and naming them could only harm their families. In his preface, he assures readers that Strickland recorded Prince's narrative 'with all the narrator's repetitions and prolixities', but says he then 'pruned' the text 'into its present shape; retaining, as far as was practicable, Mary's exact expressions and peculiar phraseology'. Claiming not to have subtracted any 'fact of importance' or added 'a single circumstance or sentiment', Pringle writes that Prince's history is 'essentially her own, without any material alteration farther than what was requisite to exclude redundancies and gross grammatical errors, so as to render it clearly intelligible'.[9]

Scholars are suspicious of this condescending disclaimer. 'Pruned' makes Pringle sound like a gardener operating on an unruly hedge. He adjusted Prince's language to make it more like the Standard English he was familiar with, but Prince may actually have spoken a West Indian patois, in which the repetitions that Pringle considered redundant served expressive purposes.[10] In a footnote to the final paragraph of the narrative, Pringle writes, 'The whole of this paragraph especially, is given as nearly as was possible in Mary's precise words.'[11] Here, Prince concludes her story by condemning slavery:

> We don't mind hard work, if we had proper treatment, and proper wages like English servants, and proper time given in the week to keep us from breaking the Sabbath. But they won't give it: they will have work—work—work, night and day, sick or well, till we are quite done up; and we must not speak up nor look amiss, however much we be abused. And then when we are quite done up, who cares for us, more than for a lame horse? This is slavery. I tell it, to let English people know the truth; and I hope they will never leave off to pray God, and call loud to the great King of England, till all the poor blacks be given free, and slavery done up for evermore.[12]

How near to Prince's words is as near as possible, and how much farther from them did the rest of the narrative stray?

Aside from these alterations, Pringle encased Prince's story in an editorial apparatus that, by the third edition, included a preface, footnotes, a supplement, an appendix, a second slave narrative, and a postscript. Much of this matter, which in total takes up slightly more space than the history itself, is meant to authenticate Prince's words and refute attacks by pro-slavery opponents. After Pringle published the first edition of the *History*, the Birmingham Ladies' Society for the Relief of Negro Slaves wrote to ask for a description of the scars on Prince's body. Margaret Pringle, Thomas's wife, inspected Prince's scars, then did it a second time with Strickland, Margaret's sister, and another woman present as witnesses.[13] The resulting description, which was printed as an appendix to future editions of the *History*, demonstrates how Pringle and other anti-slavery activists were using Prince's words and her body as exhibits in a battle for public opinion.

Other Black authors also endured processes of authentication. In 1773 the poet Phillis Wheatley, enslaved in the United States, could not publish her *Poems on Various Subjects* without first appearing before a panel of eminent Bostonians, who verified that she had written it. Even then, she had to travel to England to publish the book. In 1770 Ukawsaw Gronniosaw had gone through a similar examination, every Thursday for seven weeks, before Calvinist ministers in Holland.[14] Frederick Douglass's 1845 *Narrative of the Life of Frederick Douglass, an American Slave*, Harriet Ann Jacobs's 1861 *Incidents in the Life of a Slave Girl*, and other slave narratives were, like Prince's, packaged in supplementary texts by White abolitionists, though less densely.[15] (Douglass, who was famous as a public speaker and abolitionist, obtained greater control over his *Narrative* in the second version of the 1846 edition. Published in Dublin, out of the ambit of White American abolitionists, this version includes a preface by Douglass and an appendix in which he argues with a pro-slavery opponent.[16]) These practices of certification indicate the White reading public's fundamental distrust of Black writers' veracity and intelligence.

The History of Mary Prince, with all its pruning and framing, tells us much of what we know of Prince's life. She was born enslaved at Brackish Pond in Bermuda, where she recalls having been a happy child. She was with her mother and siblings, her 'harsh, self-ish' master was often away, and her mistress, Mrs Williams, was 'a kind-hearted good woman'. She adds: 'I was too young to under-stand rightly my condition as a slave, and too thoughtless and full of spirits to look forward to the days of toil and sorrow.' Mr Williams sold Prince when she was twelve, and Prince describes the auction, where she was 'surrounded by strange men, who examined and handled me in the same manner that a butcher would a calf or a lamb he was about to purchase, and who talked about my shape and size in like words'. For nearly thirty years, Prince suffered the violence of a series of brutal slaveholders, and her narrative exposes the atrocities they perpetrated. She survived frequent beatings, saw others killed or maimed, and performed forced labour that damaged her body, including ten years of shovelling in the salt ponds of the Turks Islands, where the brine raised boils 'which eat down in some cases to the very bone'.[17] In what scholars suspect to be another instance of either self-censorship or editorial censorship, Prince understates the sexual abuse she is likely to have experienced.[18] She says she was often flogged naked, and appeals to her readers' sense of shame: 'There is no modesty or decency shown by the owner to his slaves; men, women, and children are exposed alike.'[19] Tellingly, she describes D— as an 'indecent man', and says:

> He had an ugly fashion of stripping himself quite naked, and ordering
> me then to wash him in a tub of water. This was worse to me than all
> the licks. Sometimes when he called me to wash him I could not come,
> my eyes were so full of shame. He would then come to beat me.[20]

This behaviour drove Prince to defy D— and take refuge overnight in a 'neighbouring house', but she 'went home again, not knowing what else to do'.[21] She eventually prevailed on John Wood to purchase her and take her to Antigua, where she would spend the remaining years of her enslavement. There, she became ill with rheumatism and an affliction known as St Anthony's fire. Amid ongoing physical and verbal abuse, Prince began to save up money by buying and selling goods. Having previously been baptized in the Anglican Church, she secretly began to attend meetings and classes in the Moravian Church, where she learned to read. She also married a free Black man named Daniel James, which infuriated Wood and his wife. Prince accompanied the Woods to England, hoping the climate would relieve her rheumatism and expecting to return to her husband.

Once Prince entered the jurisdiction of English law, she could not be taken back to the colonies against her will. In 1772 Lord Chief Justice Mansfield had ruled that James Somerset, a man who escaped enslavement while in England, could not be detained and forcibly taken to Jamaica to be sold. Some interpreted this decision to mean that slavery was illegal in England. At the very least, it meant that Prince was effectively free.[22] In London, the Woods continued to force Prince to do washing, though the task became increasingly painful for her, and when she complained they told her to leave. She could walk out the door and never look back, but she would be alone in a vast city with no way to make a living. She wanted instead to purchase her freedom with the money that she had saved, and sail back to Antigua. The Woods denied her this, saying she was already free. After spending two or three months in this limbo, Prince left. She was now a solitary, working-class Black British woman in 1828, which posed its own difficulties. Working people were struggling in a newly industrialized society that did not ensure humane conditions for labourers or adequate support for the poor, and the ten thousand to fifteen thousand free Black people in London lived mostly, in the scholar Jenny Sharpe's words, as 'servants, street entertainers, and beggars'.[23] To make matters worse, John Wood had written Prince a negative letter of reference claiming that she 'does not evince a disposition to make herself useful'.[24] She obtained assistance from the Moravians, the Anti-Slavery Society, and a group of Quaker women. A shoeblack and his wife took her in. She worked as a charwoman but was unable to find another position when her employer moved away, and finally became a domestic servant to the Pringles. Pringle published three editions of The History of Mary Prince in 1831, and added a postscript to the second edition that mentions Prince's

progressively deteriorating eyesight. He urges readers to promote
the book, the proceeds of which would 'provide a little fund for her
future benefit'.[25]

Strict British libel laws and a litigious publishing culture were yet
another obstacle for marginalized people like Prince who wished to
tell their stories. Once in circulation, *The History of Mary Prince* func-
tioned as anti-slavery propaganda.[26] It entered a cut-throat world of
pre-existing political and literary feuds. One of the abolitionists' most
vocal opponents, James McQueen, responded to the book by attacking Pringle and Prince in the *Glasgow Courier*, which he edited, and
in *Blackwood's Edinburgh Magazine*.[27] He denied facts of the narrative,
particularly the allegations against the Woods, accused Prince of being
a 'prostitute' and a 'dissolute female', and questioned Pringle's selective quotation from a letter that supported the Woods. McQueen
quoted sources, including two free Black servants, four medical doctors, and Prince's husband, who testified to the Woods' good conduct
and Prince's bad character, and he claimed that Prince's husband had
remarried.[28]

The most extensive of these attacks was an open letter in *Blackwood's* to the Prime Minister, Charles, the second Earl Grey. Claiming
it to be impossible 'that people, who put so much in the power of
their slaves, and treated them so confidentially, would treat them either
with severity or cruelty', McQueen suggests that John Wood take legal
action against Pringle on his own behalf and, on Mrs Wood's behalf,
flog Pringle through the city with an ox whip. McQueen also insinu-
ates that Pringle's 'secret closetings and labours with Mary' involved
sexual impropriety, since 'in London maid-servants are not removed
from the washing-tub to the parlour without an object'. The rest of
the letter is a defence of colonial slavery on economic and military
grounds. McQueen attempts to portray the real victim of slavery as
the slaver, who undertakes 'to enlighten and to civilize the African
barbarians', a 'heavy burden' that was 'imposed upon the West India
colonist without any remuneration for his labour'.[29] This example of
racist, pro-slavery rhetoric in a leading Edinburgh periodical illustrates
how important it was for Pringle to depict Prince as a stainless victim
of slavery. His enemies would be keen to depict her as an ungrateful
beneficiary of it.

McQueen was a regular contributor to *Blackwood's*, and the appearance of his attack there would have been all the more galling, since Pringle had been a co-founding editor of the magazine. The Tory bookseller William Blackwood established the periodical in 1817 to rival the Whig *Edinburgh Review*. Pringle being a Whig, it was a bad fit. He and his co-editor, James Cleghorn, quarrelled with Blackwood, who fired them after six issues, and hired the Oxford-educated wags John Wilson (alias Christopher North) and John Gibson Lockhart.[30] The next issue featured a biblical parody called 'Translation from an Ancient Chaldee Manuscript' that pilloried the Edinburgh intellectual scene, casting Tories and Whigs as warring forces of beasts, animals, and mythical figures, while mocking the physical disabilities of Pringle and Cleghorn, who both walked with crutches. The 'Chaldee MS' sparked libel suits (one of them from Pringle), an assault, and a duel, and the issue was reprinted without it. Pringle found himself unable to support his family on the money he earned editing magazines and copying records at Register House, and the author Sir Walter Scott helped him secure a land grant in South Africa, where he would lead a settlement of twenty-four Scots, oversee violence against the indigenous San people, defend the freedom of the press from the authoritarian governor in Cape Town, and find the anti-slavery vocation that he later pursued in London.[31]

Perhaps some of this acrimonious history lay underneath the surface when, in response to McQueen's letter, Pringle sued the London publisher of *Blackwood's*, Thomas Cadell, for libel. In turn, James Wood sued Pringle for libel over *The History of Mary Prince*. The first case was heard on 21 February 1833, and Prince appeared as a witness. The defence having withdrawn its pleas of justification at the last minute, she was not cross-examined. The judge awarded Pringle nominal damages of five pounds and costs.[32]

The second case, heard six days later, was more involved. In Wood's suit, he challenged the allegation that he and his wife were cruel to Prince, as well as several claims and omissions Pringle had made in the editor's supplement to the *History*.[33] In that supplement, Pringle quotes a letter from Wood that mentions Mary's 'depravity'.[34] Censoring the details of the accusation out of consideration for his lady readers, Pringle merely calls it 'in all probability, a vile calumny'.

He also expresses doubt that Prince's husband had remarried.[35] To justify the claims in the *History*, Prince would have to discuss her private life on the witness stand. She testified that, before marrying James, she had cohabited with two other men in Antigua, a free Black man named Oyskman and a White colonist named Captain Abbot. The example of 'depravity' that Pringle blanked out of Wood's letter involved a fight between Prince and another woman, whom she found in bed with Abbot. Prince also testified that she had mentioned these sexual relationships to Strickland—which suggests that either Strickland or Pringle omitted them from the finished narrative.[36] Pringle had to pay Wood twenty-five pounds, but not legal costs. *The Times* recorded that Pringle lost on all points, though the *Christian Advocate* mentioned that he had some success in justifying the allegations of the Woods' cruelty to Prince.[37]

Pringle died in December of 1834, having lived to see the purpose of his final years fulfilled when the Abolition Act came into effect that August.[38] (Slavery in the United States was formally abolished after the Civil War, with the ratification of the Thirteenth Amendment of the Constitution in 1865.) Strickland married John Moodie in 1831, with Prince in attendance, and emigrated to Canada.[39] As Susanna Moodie, she became a foundational figure in the history of Canadian literature in English, writing the memoirs *Roughing It in the Bush* and *Life in the Clearings versus the Bush*. She inspired the Canadian author Margaret Atwood's poetry collection *The Journals of Susanna Moodie*, and her account of the murderer Grace Marks was the basis for Atwood's novel *Alias Grace*.

We wish we could give similar closure to Mary Prince's story. The Abolition Act would have made it possible for her to return to Antigua, where the enslaved populations were emancipated immediately.[40] In contrast, most colonies implemented a transitional 'apprenticeship' period, during which formerly enslaved people were kept in servitude for a further six years.[41] An edition of *The History of Mary Prince* by Moira Ferguson brought scholarly attention to Prince in 1987, and there have been further editions by Sara Salih and Henry Louis Gates Jr. In 1992 the poet Gale Jackson published a poem entitled 'mary prince bermuda. turks island. antigua. 1787', in which she imagines Prince hearing rumours of uprisings in the colonies.[42]

Prince was made a National Hero of Bermuda in 2012.[43] Scholars do not know, however, what happened to her after she appeared at the libel trials in 1833. Having narrated as much of her life as she was permitted or legally obligated to, she vanished into the silence of unrecorded history.

Notes

1. Janice Schroeder, "'Narrat[ing] Some Poor Little Fable": Evidence of Bodily Pain in *The History of Mary Prince* and "Wife-Torture in England"', *Tulsa Studies in Women's Literature*, 23.2 (2004), 261–81 (p. 266).

2. Toni Morrison, 'The Site of Memory', in *Inventing the Truth: The Art and Craft of Memoir*, ed. William Zinsser (Boston: Houghton Mifflin, 1987), pp. 101–24 (pp. 104–5).

3. Jenny Sharpe, *Ghosts of Slavery: A Literary Archaeology of Black Women's Lives* (Minneapolis: University of Minnesota Press, 2003), pp. 120–23, 133–34.

4. Morrison, p. 110.

5. Mary Prince, *The History of Mary Prince, A West Indian Slave*, ed. Sara Salih (London: Penguin, 2004), p. 24.

6. Moira Ferguson, 'Introduction', in Mary Prince, *The History of Mary Prince*, ed. Ferguson (London: Pandora, 1987), pp. 1–41 (p. 3).

7. Morrison, p. 106.

8. Prince, *The History of Mary Prince*, ed. Salih, p. 11.

9. Thomas Pringle, 'Preface', in Prince, *The History of Mary Prince*, ed. Salih, pp. 3–5 (p. 3).

10. Jessica L. Allen, 'Pringle's Pruning of Prince: *The History of Mary Prince* and the Question of Repetition', *Callaloo*, 35.2 (2012), 509–19 (pp. 510, 513–16).

11. Prince, *The History of Mary Prince*, ed. Salih, p. 37 Pringle's note.

12. Prince, *The History of Mary Prince*, ed. Salih, p. 38.

13. 'Appendix', in *The History of Mary Prince*, ed. Salih, pp. 64–65.

14. Sara Salih, 'Introduction', in Prince, *The History of Mary Prince*, ed. Salih, pp. vii–xxxiv (pp. xiii–xiv).

15. Barbara Baumgartner, 'The Body as Evidence: Resistance, Collaboration, and Appropriation in *The History of Mary Prince*', *Callaloo*, 24.1 (2001), 253–75 (p. 261 and note 19).

16. Patricia J. Ferreira, 'Frederick Douglass in Ireland: The Dublin Edition of his "Narrative"', *New Hibernia Review / Iris Éireannach Nua*, 5.1 (2001), 53–67.

17. Prince, *The History of Mary Prince*, ed. Salih, pp. 7, 11, 19.

18. Salih, 'Introduction', p. ix.

19. Prince, *The History of Mary Prince*, ed. Salih, p. 37.

20. Prince, *The History of Mary Prince*, ed. Salih, p. 24.

21. Prince, *The History of Mary Prince*, ed. Salih, p. 24.

22. David Brion Davis, *The Problem of Slavery in the Age of Revolution, 1770–1823* (New York: Oxford University Press, 1999), pp. 23, 480–81, 500 and note 56, 501.

23. Sharpe, p. 127. See also Ferguson, p. 1.

24. Thomas Pringle, 'Supplement to the History of Mary Prince by the Editor', in Prince, *The History of Mary Prince*, ed. Salih, pp. 39–63 (pp. 39–40). See also Prince, *The History of Mary Prince*, ed. Salih, p. 34.

25. Thomas Pringle, 'Postscript—Second Edition', in Prince, *The History of Mary Prince*, ed. Salih, pp. 4–5 (p. 4).

26. Salih, 'Introduction', p. xxx.

27. Sue Thomas, 'Pringle v. Cadell and Wood v. Pringle: The Libel Cases over *The History of Mary Prince*', *Journal of Commonwealth Literature*, 40.1 (2005), 113–35 (pp. 114–18).

28. James McQueen, 'The Anti-Slavery Society and the West-India Colonists', *Glasgow Courier*, 26 July 1831, p. 1; James Macqueen [*sic*], 'The Colonial Empire of Great Britain, Letter to Earl Grey, First Lord of the Treasury, &c. &c.', *Blackwood's Edinburgh Magazine*, 30.187 (November, 1831), 744–64 (p. 750). See also Macqueen, 'The Colonial Empire of Great Britain', pp. 744–52.

29. Macqueen, 'The Colonial Empire of Great Britain', pp. 747, 750, 757.

30. Randolph Vigne, *Thomas Pringle: South African Pioneer, Poet and Abolitionist* (Woodbridge: James Currey, 2012), pp. 29–33.

31. Vigne, pp. 35–60, 76, 84, 123–31, 151–53.

32. Thomas, pp. 114, 126.

33. Thomas, p. 127.

34. John A. Wood to Charles Taylor (20 October 1830), quoted in Pringle, 'Supplement', p. 44.

35. Pringle, 'Supplement', p. 44 Pringle's note. See also p. 47.

36. *The Times*, 1 March 1833, quoted in Sara Salih, 'Appendix Three', in Prince, *The History of Mary Prince*, ed. Salih, pp. 100–3.

37. Thomas, pp. 114, 128.

38. Vigne, pp. 207, 247.

39. Charlotte Gray, *Sisters in the Wilderness: The Lives of Susanna Moodie and Catharine Parr Traill* (London: Duckworth, 2001), pp. 38, 41–48.

40. Thomas, p. 130.

41. Robin Blackburn, *The Overthrow of Colonial Slavery, 1776–1848* (London: Verso, 1988), pp. 456–60.

42. Sharpe, pp. 135–36.

43. Owain Johnston-Barnes, 'Mary Prince Is Made a National Hero', *Royal Gazette*, 16 June 2012, http://www.royalgazette.com/article/20120616/ NEWS/120619988, accessed 30 November 2016.

6

Leaves of Grass

Walt Whitman

In the 1881 edition of *Leaves of Grass*, Walt Whitman writes:

> SHUT not your doors to me proud libraries,
> For that which was lacking on all your well-fill'd shelves, yet needed
>   most, I bring,
> Forth from the war emerging, a book I have made,
> The words of my book nothing, the drift of it every thing,
> A book separate, not link'd with the rest nor felt by the intellect,
> But you ye untold latencies will thrill to every page.[1]

Whitman had good reason to make such a plea. While he exaggerated in saying his book was 'not link'd with the rest', the unruly poetry collection pushed boundaries from its first appearance, self-published, in 1855. Just as its sprawling lines of free verse broke with poetic convention, its frank approach to sex challenged middle- and upper-class decorum. A reviewer in the *Christian Examiner* wrote that, 'in point of style, the book is an impertinence towards the English language; and in point of sentiment, an affront upon the recognized morality of respectable people'.[2] One passage depicts a woman watching from her window as twenty-eight naked men bathe in the sea. She imagines joining them as the twenty-ninth bather:

Walt Whitman as he appears in the frontispiece of the first edition of *Leaves of Grass* and several subsequent editions. Engraving by Samuel Hollyer from a daguerreotype by Gabriel Harrison.

The young men float on their backs, their white bellies bulge to the
    sun, they do not ask who seizes fast to them,
They do not know who puffs and declines with pendant and bend-
    ing arch,
They do not think whom they souse with spray.[3]

Ignoring the warnings of his mentor, Ralph Waldo Emerson, Whitman
added further erotic content to subsequent editions.[4] He considered
there to be two available perspectives on sex in the nineteenth-century
United States, both of them harmful. The first was the 'conventional'
view of 'good folks and good print', which avoided any explicit reference to sex, resulting in 'states of ignorance, repression, and covered-
over disease and depletion'. The second view was that of 'common
life', found 'in the wit, or what passes for wit, of masculine circles, and
in erotic stories and talk', which aimed at 'merely sensual voluptuous-
ness'. Whitman offered a third way, showing that 'motherhood, father-
hood, sexuality, and all that belongs to them' could be affirmed 'openly,
joyously, proudly, "without shame or the need of shame"'.[5]

An 1881 review described Whitman as 'the poet and priest of democracy—the American type of democracy; the democracy based upon
individuality, though not, perhaps, the ultimate democracy; the democracy based upon I, the individual; not the democracy based upon
we, the sum of all individuals'.[6] The expansive 'I' of his poems observes
and moves among Americans of various walks of life. Sometimes he
celebrates physical pleasure as an end in itself, the 'curious sympathy
one feels, when feeling with the hand the naked meat of his own body,
or another person's body'. Sometimes he depicts sex as the means of
generating the nation's future: 'The drops I distil upon you shall grow
fierce and athletic girls, new artists, musicians, and singers.'[7] Some of
Whitman's poetry, especially the sequence of Leaves of Grass entitled
'Calamus', is now recognized as homoerotic, and the sexologist Havelock Ellis noted this interpretation in his book Sexual Inversion, itself
a target of censorship and an influence on Radclyffe Hall's The Well of
Loneliness (see Chapter 10).[8] Whitman denied the homoeroticism, and
his contemporaries did not widely acknowledge it, but in a review of
the 1855 edition of Leaves of Grass, the critic Rufus W. Griswold suggested, using a Latin phrase, that the cause of his disgust with the book

and its author was 'That horrible sin not to be mentioned among Christians'.[9] The sexual content of *Leaves of Grass* may have been what cost Whitman his job as a clerk in the Bureau of Indian Affairs in 1865. He claimed that a copy of the 1860 edition in his desk scandalized the new Secretary of the Interior, James Harlan, who was in the process of culling his staff. Whitman's resourceful friend William Douglas O'Connor helped secure him a position in the Attorney General's Office and published a defence of his poetry, dubbing Whitman the 'Good Gray Poet'.[10]

Leaves of Grass did not meet its greatest resistance until 1882, though it was not the 'proud libraries' that Whitman, now living in Camden, New Jersey, had to fear: it was Anthony Comstock, champion of the moral reform movement. 'Saint Anthony', as Whitman called him, descended from the New England Puritans, and upheld stringent moral standards that the world around him failed to meet.[11] During the Civil War he served in the Union army in Florida, where he eschewed the swearing, drinking, and smoking of his comrades and officers. He was appointed an agent for the Christian Commission, and organized church services for his regiment. His principles did not make him popular with his fellows.[12] After the war, working as a dry goods clerk in New York City, he found himself similarly surrounded by a culture he abhorred. A vice industry marketed at young men sowing their wild oats was thriving in the Northeastern United States, and moral reformers opposed this culture through organizations such as the Young Men's Christian Association (YMCA), of which Comstock became an active member. Moral reform was driven by upper-class and upper-middle-class men, and directed towards a threat that they believed to originate primarily in working-class immigrant communities.[13] Comstock soon found his niche as the reformers' enforcer, upholding laws against pornography, gambling, and abortion by entrapping and arresting perpetrators. By writing freely about sex, Whitman had become an unwilling combatant in a culture war between the reformers and their opponents.

Comstock's campaigns against obscene literature brought him into conflict with a group of radicals known as 'free lovers' (or 'free lusters', as he called them). Free lovers wanted to abolish the institution of marriage, through which the state regulated the sexual activity of individuals, especially women, who were expected to submit to their husbands. The free-love movement stood for women's suffrage, gender equality, access to birth control, and the necessity of freely given consent in sex.[14] At a time when the 'freedom of the press' was generally understood to apply only to political speech, free-love advocates and other libertarian radicals argued for a broad interpretation of the First Amendment, under which all ideas, no matter how unpopular, would be protected from state and federal government suppression.[15] When James Harlan fired Whitman, he said that Whitman 'was a free lover'.[16]

As far as Comstock was concerned, the free lovers were as bad as the pornographers. He believed that free-love publications were among the traps the devil had laid to corrupt young boys and girls. He wrote that the free lovers

> publish their false doctrines and theories, hold public meetings where foul-mouthed women address audiences of males—principally youth and old men—and the result of this seed-sowing is an enervated, lazy, shiftless, corrupt breed of human beings, devoid of common decency, not fit companions, in many cases, to run with swine.[17]

One of these so-called 'foul-mouthed women', Victoria Woodhull, became an early target of Comstock's. A proponent of free love and women's suffrage (and the first woman to run for US President), Woodhull had publicized the preacher Henry Ward Beecher's extra-marital affair in her newspaper, *Woodhull & Claflin's Weekly*. Comstock requested a copy of the offending issue under an assumed name, and then had Woodhull arrested for sending an obscene publication by post. When the case against Woodhull fell through because the existing law did not apply to newspapers, the YMCA gave Comstock greater authority, creating a Committee for the Suppression of Vice, which paid him a salary.[18] This committee later seceded from the YMCA, becoming the New York Society for the Suppression of Vice (NYSSV), whose logo depicted the jailing of an offender and the burning of a pile of books.

Backed by the YMCA's new committee, and armed with an exhibition of obscene literature and contraceptive devices, Comstock lobbied Congress for stronger postal legislation. The result was the 1873 Act for the Suppression of Trade in, and Circulation of, Obscene Literature and Articles of Immoral Use—the 'Comstock Act' for short. The Act significantly expanded the scope of Section 148 of the 1872 Post Office Act, extending the obscenity prohibition not only to newspapers but also to contraceptive and other 'immoral' devices, abortifacients, and advertisements for any of the prohibited items. Comstock was made a special agent of the US Post Office and tasked with enforcing the law, which he undertook with a vengeance. By 1874, Comstock was reported by the YMCA to have confiscated and destroyed 194,000 images, 60,300 'rubber articles', and over sixty thousand kilograms of books.[19] Free lovers and other progressive intellectuals banded together as the National Defense Association, and petitioned against the Comstock Act, but were unsuccessful in achieving its repeal.[20] Comstock's targets also included abortionists, of whom he claimed to have arrested over sixty. When one of them, known as Madame Restell, killed herself before her trial, Comstock noted, 'A bloody ending to a bloody life'.[21]

Whitman's work, being serious poetry, might have seemed outside the moral reformers' purview. Comstock and his associates were on firm footing when pursuing free-love pamphlets and cheap pulp fiction, such as dime novels, because public opinion and powerful social conservatives were on their side, but they risked losing support by attacking Whitman.[22] Nevertheless, Comstock considered art fair game, writing that the terms '"art" and "classic" are made to gild some of the most obscene representations and foulest matters in literature, regardless of their results to immature minds'.[23] His campaigns against art nudes, which he considered obscene when displayed or reproduced anywhere but in the protected space of galleries, attracted outrage and ridicule in the press.[24] Comstock characterized *Leaves of Grass* as 'an attempt by an author of our own time to clothe the most sensual thoughts, with the flowers and fancies of poetry, making the lascivious conception only more insidious and demoralizing'.[25] In 1882, after reading a letter from Comstock, the New England Society for the Suppression of Vice (NESSV) began to move against Whitman. (This Bostonian scion of Comstock's New York society would later be known as the Watch and Ward Society.) On this occasion, the NESSV appealed to Boston District Attorney Oliver Stevens, who wrote to Whitman's publisher, James R. Osgood and Company, warning that *Leaves of Grass* would be subject to prosecution for obscenity unless it was expurgated. Osgood suggested altering lines and omitting several poems, including 'To a Common Prostitute' and 'A Woman Waits for Me'.[26] Whitman had insisted from the outset that the sixth edition must include 'the old pieces, the *sexuality* ones, about which the original row was started & kept up so long', and, while he was willing to make minor changes, censoring whole poems was out of the question.[27] Osgood returned the plates and the remaining stock to Whitman, who had the book published in Philadelphia instead.[28]

In the ensuing months, several supporters of Whitman defied the censors. The freethinker and ex-minister George Chainey attempted to reprint the poem 'To a Common Prostitute' along with the text of a lecture defending Whitman. Allegedly at Stevens's urging, Boston postmaster Edward Tobey refused to mail the poem, deeming it obscene. Tobey sought confirmation from the Postmaster General, who declared the poem fit to be mailed.[29] In the *New York Tribune*, Comstock accused Chainey of being a free lover, and, claiming that the Postmaster General's decision applied only to Chainey's pamphlet, warned that he would 'certainly take steps to suppress' *Leaves of Grass* if he found it for sale in New York.[30] The friend who had helped Whitman when he was fired in 1865, William O'Connor, attacked Comstock in the *Tribune* and challenged him to follow through with his threat:

> But let him dare to throw into his night-cart that pearl of great price, the book of any honest author, let him venture to carry out his wicked menace in regard to the work of the good gray poet, and he will quickly find himself the centre of a tornado which will only pass to leave the United States Post Office without its scavenger.[31]

Two of the book's other defenders were indeed free lovers. Anarchist Benjamin Tucker published an advertisement for 'The Suppressed Book!' in newspapers, including his own periodical *Liberty*. Addressed to Stevens, Comstock, Tobey, Massachusetts Attorney General George

Marston, and all 'other enemies of Liberty whom it may concern', the
advertisement declared: 'You are hereby distinctly notified—all of you
in general, and you, Oliver Stevens, in particular—that I have in my
possession, and do now offer for sale, copies of the work advertised
above.'[32] Tucker got away with it, several newspapers in Boston sided
with *Leaves of Grass*, and the book was reportedly sold in New York
City and Boston without restriction.[33]

Ezra Heywood, who edited the radical magazine the *Word*, flew closer
to the sun. He reprinted and distributed the poems 'A Woman Waits for
Me' and 'To a Common Prostitute', along with an advertisement for a
douching device he called a 'Comstock syringe' and a free-love treatise
entitled *Cupid's Yokes*. He had already been imprisoned under the Comstock Law in 1878 for distributing *Cupid's Yokes*, and served six months
of his two-year sentence before free-love activist Laura Kendrick, on
behalf of the National Defense Association, helped obtain a pardon from
President Hayes. Arrested once again by Comstock, Heywood now
faced a more liberal judge, who dismissed the obscenity charges against
Whitman's poems and the treatise outright. Heywood was permitted to
call witnesses, defend his ideas in court, and make a plea for the freedom
of speech. The jury acquitted him of the syringe charges.[34] O'Connor
wrote to Whitman that 'When you bear in mind that Heywood had
really in the syringe matter, flatly broken a statute, his acquittal by the
jury in the very face of the evidence against him, shows the prejudice
against Comstock, and makes the victory remarkable'.[35] (The loophole
through which the jury permitted Heywood to escape was either that
they did not find Comstock credible or that they did not think the prosecution had proven that the vaginal syringe was specifically being marketed as a form of contraception.) Despite his defeat, Comstock would
continue to pursue Heywood for various publications, eventually securing another conviction in 1890. Heywood was prosecuted for distributing a letter from a physician that discussed oral sex and condemned
spousal rape, a letter from a mother describing the sexual education of
her daughter, and an article by Angela Heywood, Ezra's wife and fellow
traveller, defending women's right to birth control. In poor health, Ezra
did two years of hard labour, and died one year after his release.[36]

Though Heywood wrote to Whitman during the 1882 incident,
the poet washed his hands of the matter. The spirit of Whitman's

poetry was compatible with free love in some respects, but he found the politics extreme and did not want to associate himself with the movement.[37] As editor of the *Brooklyn Daily Times*, he had claimed in an editorial that the 'sacredness, the divine institution of the marriage tie lies at the root of the welfare, the safety, the very existence of every Christian nation'. He had even railed, in Comstockian fashion, against 'the influence of a loose popular literature in debauching the popular mind'.[38] O'Connor thought Heywood had needlessly baited Comstock, and wrote that Whitman '*did perfectly right* in keeping aloof and not contributing to the defence. Your connection could not help him and might hurt you'.[39] Whitman himself was fine: in an instance of the Streisand effect, scandal seems to have helped sales, and, though the Wanamaker's department store refused to stock it, the Philadelphia edition of *Leaves of Grass* was a financial success.[40]

In 1888, his health failing, Whitman revisited the controversy with his friend Horace Traubel. Traubel read O'Connor's description of Heywood as a 'stupendous jackass' to Whitman, who exclaimed in belated sympathy with the free lover, 'O William! how often I have been called by that pleasant name!'[41] Whitman recalled Emerson's warning that *Leaves of Grass* would get him 'tangled up with' the free-love 'heresy', but he believed that Emerson secretly approved of his obstinacy: Emerson 'must have known as well as I knew that it would have been decenter to throw the book away than to mutilate it'.[42] When Traubel pressed Whitman on his opinion of free love, the poet asked, 'What do you call free love? There's no other kind of love, is there?'[43]

Notes

1. Walt Whitman, *Leaves of Grass* (Boston: Osgood, 1881), p. 17, in The Walt Whitman Archive, http://www.whitmanarchive.org/published/LG/1881/whole.html, accessed 14 December 2016.

2. *Christian Examiner*, June 1856, pp. 6–7, in *Walt Whitman: The Critical Heritage*, ed. Milton Hindus (London: Routledge, 1997), pp. 62–64 (p. 62).

3. Walt Whitman, *Leaves of Grass* (Brooklyn: Fowler & Wells, 1856), p. 20, in The Walt Whitman Archive, http://www.whitmanarchive.org/published/LG/1856/whole.html, accessed 14 December 2016.

4. Jerome Loving, *Walt Whitman: The Song of Himself* (Berkeley: University of California Press, 1999), p. 241.

5. Walt Whitman, 'Memorandum at a Venture', *North American Review*, 134.307 (1882), 546–50 (pp. 546, 547, 548). See also Whitman, *Leaves of Grass* (1856), p. 323.

6. 'Leaves of Grass', *Boston Globe*, 13 November 1881, p. 8, in The Walt Whitman Archive, http://www.whitmanarchive.org/criticism/reviews/lg1881/anc.00209.html, accessed 14 December 2016.

7. Walt Whitman, *Leaves of Grass* (Boston: Thayer & Eldridge, 1860–61), pp. 301, 304, in The Walt Whitman Archive, http://whitmanarchive.org/published/LG/1860/whole.html, accessed 14 December 2016. See also Rosemary Graham, 'The Prostitute in the Garden: Walt Whitman, *Fanny Hill*, and the Fantasy of Female Pleasure', *ELH*, 64.2 (1997), 569–97 (p. 573).

8. Havelock Ellis, *Studies in the Psychology of Sex* (Philadelphia: Davis), II: *Sexual Inversion*, 2nd edn (1901), 24–26 [HathiTrust e-book].

9. [Rufus W. Griswold], *New York Criterion*, 10 November 1855, in *Walt Whitman: The Critical Heritage*, ed. Hindus, pp. 31–33 (p. 33 note). See also Ellis, pp. 24–25; Loving, pp. 238, 241.

10. David S. Reynolds, *Walt Whitman's America: A Cultural Biography* (New York: Knopf, 1995), pp. 455–57. See also Loving, pp. 290–91.

11. Horace Traubel, *With Walt Whitman in Camden*, 9 vols (1906–96), IV, ed. Sculley Bradley (Philadelphia: University of Pennsylvania Press, 1953), 92, in The Walt Whitman Archive, http://whitmanarchive.org/criticism/disciples/traubel/WWWiC/4/whole.html, accessed 7 March 2017.

12. Heywood Broun and Margaret Leech, *Anthony Comstock: Roundsman of the Lord* (London: Wishart, 1928), pp. 38, 48–62.

13. Nicola Beisel, *Imperiled Innocents: Anthony Comstock and Family Reproduction in Victorian America* (Princeton: Princeton University Press, 1997), pp. 37–38, 104–6.

14. Martin Henry Blatt, *Free Love and Anarchism: The Biography of Ezra Heywood* (Urbana: University of Illinois Press, 1989), pp. 109–10.

15. Mary M. Cronin, 'The Liberty to Argue Freely: Nineteenth-Century Obscenity Prosecutions and the Emergence of Modern Libertarian Free Speech Discourse', *Journalism and Communication Monographs*, 8.3 (2006), 163–219 (pp. 166, 171, 174, 179, 201–2).

16. Reynolds, p. 456.

17. Anthony Comstock, *Traps for the Young*, ed. Robert Bremner (Cambridge, MA: Belknap Press, 1967), p. 163.

18. Helen Lefkowitz Horowitz, 'Victoria Woodhull, Anthony Comstock, and Conflict over Sex in the United States in the 1870s', *Journal of American History*, 87.2 (2000), 403–34 (pp. 403, 431).

19. Broun and Leech, p. 165.

20. Cronin, pp. 187–89.

21. Records of the New York Society for the Suppression of Vice, Library of Congress, I, 111–12, quoted in Beisel, p. 46; see also Beisel, pp. 46–48.

22. Beisel, p. 164.

23. Comstock, p. 168.

24. Beisel, pp. 168, 169–72.

25. New York Society for the Suppression of Vice, *Eighth Annual Report*, 1882, p. 6, quoted in Beisel, p. 164.

26. Beisel, p. 165.

27. Walt Whitman to James R. Osgood (8 May 1881, emphasis original), in The Walt Whitman Archive, http://www.whitmanarchive.org/biography/correspondence/tei/hun.00047.html, accessed 15 December 2016.

28. Beisel, p. 165.

29. William Douglas O'Connor, 'Another Recovered Chapter in the History of *Leaves of Grass*', *Conservator*, 12 (1896), 99, in *Conserving Walt Whitman's Fame: Selections from Horace Traubel's 'Conservator', 1890–1919*, ed. Gary Schmidgall (Iowa City: University of Iowa Press, 2006), pp. 58–64.

30. 'Whitman's "Leaves of Grass"', *New York Tribune*, 6 August 1882, p. 8.

31. William O'Connor, 'Mr. Comstock as Cato the Censor', *New York Tribune*, 27 August 1882, p. 5.

32. Benjamin Tucker, *Liberty*, 22 July 1882, p. 4.

33. Blatt, pp. 142–43; 'Whitman's "Leaves of Grass"', p. 8.

34. Blatt, pp. 117–18, 129–32, 142–47. See also Cronin, pp. 190–94.

35. William D. O'Connor to Walt Whitman (17 April 1883), in Traubel, IV, 91.

36. Blatt, pp. 147, 162–71.

37. Blatt, pp. 143–44.

38. Walt Whitman, 'The Marriage Tie', in *I Sit and Look Out: Editorials from the 'Brooklyn Daily Times' by Walt Whitman*, ed. Emory Holloway and Vernolian Schwarz (New York: Columbia University Press, 1932), pp. 113–14 (p. 113). See also Kenneth M. Price, 'Walt Whitman, Free Love,

and the "Social Revolutionist"', *American Periodicals*, 1.1 (1991), 70–82 (pp. 75–79).

39. William D. O'Connor to Walt Whitman (1 April 1883, emphasis original), in The Walt Whitman Archive, http://www.whitmanarchive.org/biography/correspondence/tei/loc.05693.html, accessed 20 February 2017.

40. Loving, pp. 416–17.

41. Traubel, III, ed. Sculley Bradley (New York: Kennerley, 1914), 566, in The Walt Whitman Archive, http://www.whitmanarchive.org/criticism/disciples/traubel/WWWiC/3/whole.html, accessed 15 December 2016.

42. Traubel, III, 440.

43. Traubel, III, 439.

7

Adventures of Huckleberry Finn
Mark Twain

Huck Finn has always been a contentious text, though for different reasons at different times, and several people have tried their
hand at improving it. Offensive to some nineteenth-century readers
because of its impropriety, the book was later expurgated and removed
from school curricula because of its handling of race. The novel depicts
a White boy from Hannibal, Missouri, abused by his alcoholic father
and indoctrinated by a racist society, who encounters vice and folly
while travelling down the Mississippi on a raft in the company of Jim,
a Black man fleeing enslavement. The author, Samuel Clemens—better
known by his pseudonym Mark Twain—was 'his own worst censor',
and revised the manuscript extensively to tone down language that
was likely to offend his readers. Out came a reference to prostitution
and some undue kissing of girls by the con man known as 'the king'.
Oaths were softened, religious irreverence more scrupulously avoided.[1]
Twain's wife, Olivia Langdon Clemens, provided the second line of
defence. She would 'expergate' the proofs, as daughter Susy Clemens
wrote: 'and I remember so well, with what pangs of regret we used
to see her turn down the leaves of the pages which meant, that some
delightfully terrible part must be scratched out.'[2]

Twain also vetted Edward W. Kemble's illustrations, rejecting one
featuring the king (a 'lecherous old rascal') kissing a girl at an evan-
gelical camp meeting. Twain decided the whole scene, in which the

He bounced up and stared at me wild. Then he drops down on his knees, and puts his hands together and says :

"Doan' hurt me—don't ! I hain't ever done no harm to a ghos'. I awluz

JIM AND THE GHOST.

liked dead people, en done all I could for 'em. You go en git in de river agin, whah you b'longs, en doan' do nuffn to Ole Jim, 'at 'uz awluz yo' fren'."

Well, I warn't long making him understand I warn't dead. I was ever so glad to see Jim. I warn't lonesome, now. I told him I warn't afraid of *him* telling the people where I was. I talked along, but he only set there and looked at me ; never said nothing. Then I says :

"It's good daylight. Le's get breakfast. Make up your camp fire good."

"What's de use er makin' up de camp fire to cook strawbries en sich truck ? But you got a gun, hain't you ? Den we kin git sumfn better den strawbries."

"Strawberries and such truck," I says. "Is that what you live on ?"

"I couldn' git nuffn else," he says.

"Why, how long you been on the island, Jim ?"

"I come heah de night arter you's killed."

In one of Edward Kemble's illustrations to *Adventures of Huckleberry Finn*, Jim mistakes Huck, who has escaped his father by staging his own death, for a ghost.

king defrauds the congregation, was a 'disgusting thing' that 'won't *bear* illustrating'.[3] Twain's publisher, Charles L. Webster, narrowly averted an early disaster when he learned that an engraver had tampered with one of the illustrations, creating an obscene image in the sample copies that the company's agents were already showing to potential customers. The illustration depicts Huck Finn standing before the aunt and uncle of his more respectable companion, Tom Sawyer. Uncle Silas Phelps's hips are thrust forward assertively, and his penis appears to protrude from his trousers. Silas's wardrobe malfunction delayed the release of the US edition until after Christmas.[4]

Twain's self-censorship was not sufficient for some of his contemporaries. His friend Richard Watson Gilder made further cuts when publishing advance excerpts of the novel in the *Century Magazine*. While Gilder attempted to economize, not simply censor, he tended to omit or reduce the more pungent details of the text: sweat, nudity, a human corpse, dead cats, spoiled eggs, and anything that made the sacred rub shoulders with the profane.[5] When *Huck Finn* was finally published as a book, it elicited both praise and offence. Robert Bridges, the American writer rather than the British poet, wrote a sarcastic review that attacked some of the grittier scenes, which included

> A very refined and delicate piece of narration by Huck Finn, describing his venerable and dilapidated 'pap' as afflicted with delirium tremens, rolling over and over, 'kicking things every which way', and 'saying there was devils ahold of him'. This chapter is especially suited to amuse the children on long, rainy afternoons.[6]

The book was first banned in March 1885, when the board of the Concord Public Library in Massachusetts deemed it unfit for their shelves. It was 'rough, coarse, and inelegant, dealing with a series of experiences not elevating, the whole book being more suited to the slums than to intelligent, respectable people'.[7] There was also a public library ban in Clinton, Massachusetts that year.[8] In contrast, the social scientist Franklin Sanborn thought that the novel should be held in the New York State Reformatory reference library, recommending that it 'form the subject of a debate in your Practical Morality Class'.[9] Twain responded to the Concord ban with good humour, claiming impishly that it would provoke people to read *Huck Finn* 'instead of merely intending to', at which point 'they will discover, to my great advantage and their own indignant disappointment, that there is nothing objectionable in the book after all'.[10] Read they did. Webster sold fifty-one thousand copies by May 1886.[11]

The early objections to *Huck Finn* focused on its suitability for children or 'respectable people', which continued to be in question into the twentieth century. The Denver Public Library attempted to ban the book in 1902, though Twain claimed that this was the result of a personal vendetta, and that the book was back on the shelves days later. He also claimed that the original Concord library ban was an attempt 'to curry favour with a personage'.[12] When the Omaha Public Library removed the book from its children's section later that year, Twain quipped that 'this noise is doing much harm' by driving 'a number of hitherto spotless people to reading Huck Finn, out of natural human curiosity to learn what this is all about—people who had not heard of him before; people whose morals will go to wreck and ruin now'.[13] In 1905 the Brooklyn Public Library moved the book from the children's into the adult collection.[14]

A different debate, however, erupted among literary critics by the mid-twentieth century, a debate hinging not on the respectability of Twain's writing, but on its artistry. Since the earliest reviews, critics had objected to the novel's haphazard plotting, especially its peculiar ending. In the emotional climax, while Jim is held captive at the Phelps farm, Huck drafts a letter betraying him to Miss Watson. Having been 'sivilized' in slave-holding Missouri, Huck considers Jim to be Miss Watson's property, and believes that returning him to her is a moral duty. When Huck thinks about his time with Jim on their journey, however, compassion overcomes him, and he destroys the letter. He is fully convinced that, in doing so, he is committing a grave sin, but says to himself, 'All right, then, I'll *go* to hell.'[15] It is a powerful scene, but Twain soon reintroduces Tom Sawyer, who hijacks the plot, imitating adventure fiction in a quixotic plan to liberate Jim that subjects him to a number of indignities, such as sleeping among spiders and vermin. Only after the plan goes awry, Tom is shot in the leg, and Jim allows himself to be retaken to help save him, does Tom reveal that Jim has already been free for two months—the recently deceased Miss Watson having released him in her will. These concluding chapters strike many readers as incongruous. They undercut the emotional stakes of Huck's decision to go to hell and Jim's flight from enslavement, reducing Huck to Tom's sidekick and Jim to a compliant dupe.

Lionel Trilling and T. S. Eliot launched defences of *Huck Finn* as a work of serious literature in their 1948 and 1950 introductions to the novel. Trilling called it 'one of the world's great books and one of the central documents of American culture',[16] while Eliot praised Huck as 'one of the permanent symbolic figures of fiction; not unworthy to take a place with Ulysses, Faust, Don Quixote, Don Juan, Hamlet and other great discoveries that man has made about himself'.[17] Both critics acknowledged, and then swiftly dispensed with, the problem of the ending. Responding in 1953, Leo Marx claimed that 'Everyone now agrees that *Huckleberry Finn* is a masterpiece', but did not let the ending slide, identifying it not only as an artistic flaw but also as a 'glaring lapse of moral imagination'. For Marx, Tom's antics obscure the novel's tragic vision—that, despite moments of freedom on the raft, Huck and Jim are powerless to escape a corrupt society that considers Jim to be property and condemns Huck for doing the right thing.[18]

This debate culminated with another rewriting of the novel in 1970, John Seelye's *The True Adventures of Huckleberry Finn*. A critic himself, Seelye wrote this tongue-in-cheek adaptation to please the critics (or, as his Huck calls them, the 'crickits') so that 'now that they've got *their* book, maybe they'll leave the other one alone'.[19] Seelye's version is a rare example of *un*censorship that follows through where Twain holds back. It restores some of Twain's original, stronger wording, and replaces the maligned ending with a tragic one in which Jim drowns while attempting to escape from the Phelps farm. This Huck swears freely, smokes weed, excretes, masturbates, and dates a girl (an abolitionist's daughter, like Olivia Langdon Clemens). Out of respect for the dead, he blacks out a 'FUK YOU' on the wall of the floating house in which he finds, but doesn't recognize, the corpse of his father. Most of the new material never would have made it past the Clemenses, let alone the board of the Concord Public Library. In a different sort of revision, Seelye also makes Jim slightly less of a caricature. Twain's Tom hangs Jim's hat on a tree while he's asleep, and Jim thinks witches have visited him. In Seelye's version, Tom is mistaken about Jim, and nothing comes of the prank. Jim and Huck even have a brief argument about the ethics of abolitionism, though Jim's view is mostly lost on this Huck, who is more explicitly entrenched in his racism.

By rewriting Jim into a rounder, more intelligent character, Seelye targeted Twain's handling of race, which was, by then, the focus of renewed controversy. Charges of racism against *Huck Finn* generally rest on three points. First, the ending appears to make the novel's plot a joke and Jim the butt of it. As the scholar Bernard Bell puts it, 'Twain—nostalgically and metaphorically—sells Jim's soul down the river for laughs at the end of *Adventures of Huckleberry Finn*.'[20] Second, as the novelist Ralph Ellison remarks, 'Twain fitted Jim into the outlines of the minstrel tradition, and it is from behind this stereotype mask that we see Jim's dignity and human capacity—and Twain's complexity—emerge.'[21] The stereotypes used in blackface minstrel shows, with which Twain was well acquainted, are not all negative: Jim is self-sacrificing as well as gullible. They are racist stereotypes nonetheless, and make 'Huck, with his street-sparrow sophistication, seem more adult' than Jim.[22] Third, Twain's narrator and characters, sympathetic and unsympathetic, repeatedly use the epithet 'nigger'— over two hundred times. It is not anachronistic to be bothered by this word in *Huckleberry Finn*. Twain knew well how demeaning it was, and around the time he courted Olivia Langdon he began to use the word with a greater sense of ironic distance, reserving it for capturing other people's views rather than expressing his own. By the 1880s, there was a distinct difference in usage between the older slur and what was, at the time, the more respectful term 'Negro'.[23] So what is the slur doing in *Huckleberry Finn*? Some have argued that Twain needed to use it to convey the target of his satire, a society in which White people do not consider Black people to be human. When Huck concocts a story about a steamboat accident, Sally Phelps asks him if anyone was hurt. 'No'm. Killed a nigger,' Huck fibs. She replies, 'Well, it's lucky; because sometimes people do get hurt.'[24] Twain is certainly looking down at his characters' racism here, but does he escape it himself?

The question of whether a novel published in 1885 is racist, like the question of its aesthetic merit, may seem rather academic. After Trilling's introduction to *Huck Finn* cemented its status as the great American novel, however, it soon became a fixture of school curricula in the United

States. This canonization occurred during the Civil Rights Movement, around 1954, when the Supreme Court declared the racial segregation of schools unconstitutional in *Brown* v. *Board of Education*.[25] By the 1990s, *Huck Finn* was required reading in three-quarters of US high schools, and was taught more frequently than the work of any other writer except Shakespeare.[26] Those who objected to *Huck Finn* in the second half of the twentieth century were no longer genteel readers turning up their noses at its vulgar subject matter: they were now parents, students, and educators concerned about the book's effects on children required to read it in schools, especially Black students in racially mixed groups.

In this context, what became most contentious about *Huck Finn* was the recurrence of the slur. Regardless of Twain's intent in using the word, students were being asked to encounter it, again and again, in their reading and in class. As we discuss in the introduction to this book, speech involves action. A White person who refers to a Black person with a racist slur turns centuries of oppression into a verbal weapon, urging the target of the slur to submit to the name. Can quotation marks and the boundaries of fiction adequately protect young readers from the force of a powerful slur? Can teachers contextualize the word sufficiently, and do they? Is good teaching enough to prevent White students from using it against Black students, or to prevent Black students from feeling degraded by it? These were the questions underlying the *Huckleberry Finn* controversy in the second half of the twentieth century. They are complex questions. On the one hand, as the philosopher Judith Butler argues, even slurs do not inevitably cause harm wherever they appear. For instance, though hurtful language never loses its 'traumatic residue', people who are targeted by terms of abuse can sometimes turn those terms to new purposes, so that 'The word that wounds becomes an instrument of resistance'.[27] On the other hand, the force of a potent slur should not be understated or treated lightly, and requiring Black students to confront *Huckleberry Finn* in the context of group readings and discussions places a burden on them that other students are not made to carry.

The first challenge to the book in schools is sometimes said to have occurred in 1957, when the New York City Board of Education removed it from a list of approved textbooks for elementary and junior high schools, though it is not clear that protests about the novel were actually what prompted this decision.[28] The book was removed from a required reading list at Miami–Dade Junior College in Miami, Florida, in 1969 and from required courses at New Trier High School in Winnetka, Illinois, around 1976. In 1982 John H. Wallace, who had been an administrator at the Mark Twain Intermediate School in Virginia, led a campaign to have the Fairfax County School Board remove the novel from reading lists, which the superintendent of schools prevented.[29] Wallace would become *Huck Finn*'s most out-spoken public opponent, calling it 'the most grotesque example of racist trash ever written'.[30] Cases soon proliferated: the American Library Association lists forty-eight further challenges or removals between 1981 and 2008. In the twenty-first century, a new strategy for responding to challenges emerged. Some schools began to man-date special training for teachers on how to approach material dealing with race.[31] A challenge in Arizona in 1998 led to a judicial ruling. In *Monteiro* v. *Tempe Union High School District*, a parent complained that the school district was subjecting her daughter and other Black students to discrimination by requiring them to read *Huck Finn* and William Faulkner's 'A Rose for Emily'. She claimed that studying these works had psychologically injured Black students and increased the racist harassment of Black students by White students. While acknowledging 'that words can hurt, particularly in the case of chil-dren, and that words of a racist nature can hurt especially severely', the Court of Appeals for the Ninth Circuit asserted the authority of educators to make curricular decisions and the right of students to receive information: 'when a school board identifies information that it believes to be a useful part of a student's education, that stu-dent has the right to receive the information.'[32] (In a concurring opinion, Judge Boochever noted that the adoption of 'books with overt messages of racial hatred, such as those promoting the views of the Aryan Nation, the Ku Klux Klan, or similar hate groups' would potentially raise 'different issues which we need not consider in this case'.[33]) There would be further proceedings in the case to deter-mine whether the alleged harassment and hostile environment at the school constituted discrimination, but the school board would not be forced to remove the books.[34] In November 2016, in response to a parent complaint, a school board in Accomack County, Virginia, temporarily suspended the use of *Huck Finn* and Harper Lee's *To Kill a Mockingbird* in classrooms before deciding to retain the books.[35]

In 2011 NewSouth Publishing issued a combined, expurgated edition of *The Adventures of Tom Sawyer* and its more mature sequel, *Adventures of Huckleberry Finn*. Twain scholar Alan Gribben eliminated 228 instances of what he called 'the most inflammatory word in the English language', replacing it with 'slave'. He also expunged the word 'Injun' and changed 'half-breed' to 'half-blood'.[36] The media response to Gribben's edition was energetic and largely negative. In the *New York Times*, Michiko Kakutani defended the original texts as 'sacrosanct intellectual property', while, on Ta-Nehisi Coates's blog for the *Atlantic*, Jamelle Bouie argued that the censored edition served only to 'feed the American aversion to history and reflection'.[37] Few commentators were sympathetic to Gribben's stated aim, which was to 'introduce both books to a wider readership than they can currently enjoy' rather than to limit access to the originals.[38]

It is not unheard of, however, for schools to teach censored versions of *Huck Finn*. Harper and Brothers published an expurgated teaching edition as early as 1931, and the edition taken off textbook lists in New York City in 1957 appears to have been an expurgated one.[39] Puffin Books published a simplified and condensed version for young readers in 1953, which was reissued as a Penguin Reader in 2000. In 1963 the Philadelphia Board of Education used a text that omitted racist slurs, removed violence, and simplified dialect.[40] Wallace produced his own expurgated text in 1983 and advocated its use during his campaign against the novel.[41] After Gribben's NewSouth *Huck Finn* continued this tradition in 2011, comedians Gabriel Diani and Etta Devine published *Adventures of Huckleberry Finn: Robotic Edition*, in which the offending slur is replaced with 'robot' and Jim is rendered as a robot in the illustrations. Their version ridicules Gribben's by pushing verbal substitution to the point of absurdity, using language that makes Jim inhuman while stripping away the historical context in which his humanity would have been at stake. Expurgated texts of *Huckleberry Finn* are a distortion of the past that insulates readers from troubling aspects of the novel and the history it depicts. Given the many different forms the book has taken, however, claims for the sanctity of the original text are perhaps untenable.

Adventures of Huckleberry Finn is now charged with such cultural significance in the United States that it is unlikely to disappear from curricula in the near future, or to be studied only in universities, where students are better equipped to grapple with historical context. The question of when and how to teach *Huck Finn* to young readers, and in what version, will undoubtedly continue to be asked in schools.

Notes

1. Harold Beaver, *Huckleberry Finn* (London: Allen & Unwin, 1987), pp. 29, 77.

2. Susy Clemens, *Papa: An Intimate Biography of Mark Twain*, ed. Charles Neider (Garden City, NY: Doubleday, 1985), p. 189.

3. *Mark Twain, Business Man*, ed. Samuel Charles Webster (Boston: Little, Brown, 1946), p. 261.

4. Walter Blair, *Mark Twain and 'Huck Finn'* (Berkeley: University of California Press, 1960), pp. 364–68.

5. Arthur L. Scott, 'The *Century Magazine* Edits *Huckleberry Finn*, 1884–1885', *American Literature*, 27.3 (1955), 356–62 (pp. 358–61).

6. [Robert Bridges], review of *Adventures of Huckleberry Finn*, *Life*, 26 February 1885, in *Mark Twain: The Critical Heritage*, ed. Frederick Anderson (London: Routledge, 1971; repr. 1997), pp. 126–27 (p. 126).

7. *Boston Transcript*, 17 March 1885, quoted in James S. Leonard and Thomas A. Tenney, 'Introduction: The Controversy over *Huckleberry Finn*', in *Satire or Evasion? Black Perspectives on 'Huckleberry Finn'*, ed. Leonard and others (Durham, NC: Duke University Press, 1992), pp. 1–11 (p. 2).

8. R. Kent Rasmussen, 'Introduction', in Mark Twain, *Adventures of Huckleberry Finn* (London: Penguin, 2014), pp. xiii–xxxv (p. xviii).

9. Franklin Sanborn to Zebulon Brockway, *Critic*, n.s., 3 (1885), 264, quoted in Steven Mailloux, 'The Rhetorical Use and Abuse of Fiction: Eating Books in Late Nineteenth-Century America', in *Revisionary Interventions into the Americanist Canon*, ed. Donald E. Pease (Durham, NC: Duke University Press, 1994), pp. 133–57 (p. 151).

10. Mark Twain to Frank A. Nichols (28 March 1885), in 'Mark Twain and Massachusetts', *Daily Alta California*, 14 April 1885, p. 5.

11. Blair, p. 370.

12. 'Mark Twain on "Huck Finn"', *New York Tribune*, 22 August 1902, p. 9.

13. Mark Twain, letter to *Omaha World-[Herald]* (23 August 1902), quoted in Rasmussen, p. xviii.

14. Blair, p. 3.

15. Twain, *Adventures of Huckleberry Finn* (London: Penguin, 2014), p. 215 (emphasis original).

16. Lionel Trilling, 'Introduction', in Mark Twain, *Adventures of Huckleberry Finn*, ed. Trilling (New York: Holt, Rinehart, and Winston, 1963), p. vi.

17. T. S. Eliot, 'An Introduction to *Huckleberry Finn*', in *Huck Finn*, ed. Harold Bloom (Philadelphia: Chelsea House, 2004), pp. 17–24 (p. 18).

18. Leo Marx, 'Mr Eliot, Mr Trilling, and "Huckleberry Finn"', *American Scholar*, 22.4 (1953), 423–40 (pp. 423, 435).

19. John Seelye, *The True Adventures of Huckleberry Finn* (Evanston, IL: Northwestern University Press, 1970), p. xii (emphasis original).

20. Bernard Bell, 'Twain's "Nigger" Jim', in *Satire or Evasion?*, pp. 124–40 (p. 138).

21. Ralph Ellison, 'Change the Joke and Slip the Yoke', in *Shadow and Act* (London: Secker & Warburg, 1967), pp. 45–59 (p. 50).

22. Ellison, p. 50. See also Frederick Woodard and Donnarae MacCann, 'Minstrel Shackles and Nineteenth-Century "Liberality" in *Huckleberry Finn*', in *Satire or Evasion?*, pp. 141–53.

23. Leonard and Tenney, pp. 7–8. See also Jonathan Arac, *'Huckleberry Finn' as Idol and Target: The Functions of Criticism in our Time* (Madison: University of Wisconsin Press, 1997), pp. 78–80.

24. Twain, *Adventures of Huckleberry Finn* (London: Penguin, 2014), p. 222.

25. Peaches Henry, 'The Struggle for Tolerance: Race and Censorship in *Huckleberry Finn*', in *Satire or Evasion?*, pp. 25–48 (p. 25).

26. Arac, p. 7.

27. Judith Butler, *Excitable Speech: A Politics of the Performative* (New York: Routledge, 1997), pp. 38, 163.

28. Arac, pp. 63–66.

29. Henry, pp. 26–27.

30. John H. Wallace, 'The Case against *Huck Finn*', in *Satire or Evasion?*, pp. 16–24 (p. 16).

31. Robert P. Doyle, *Banned Books: Challenging our Freedom to Read* (Chicago: American Library Association, 2014), pp. 315–16.

32. Monteiro v. Tempe Union High Sch. Dist., 158 F.3d 1022, 1026–27, 1028 (9th Cir. 1998).

33. *Monteiro*, 158 F.3d at 1035 (Boochever, J., concurring).

34. *Monteiro*, 158 F.3d at 1035.

35. Jessica Chasmar, '"Huckleberry Finn", "To Kill a Mockingbird" Return to Virginia Classrooms after Vote', *Washington Times*, 7 December 2016, http://www.washingtontimes.com/news/2016/dec/7/huckleberry-finn-to-kill-a-mockingbird-return-to-v,

accessed 20 February 2017; Danuta Kean, 'To Kill a Mockingbird Removed from Virginia Schools for Racist Language', *Guardian*, 5 December 2016, https://www.theguardian.com/books/2016/ dec/05/to-kill-a-mockingbird-removed-virginia-schools-racist-language-harper-lee, accessed 4 January 2017.

36. Alan Gribben, 'Editor's Introduction: Reuniting Two Companion Books', in Mark Twain, *Adventures of Tom Sawyer and Huckleberry Finn: The NewSouth Edition*, ed. Gribben (Montgomery, AL: NewSouth, 2011), pp. 7–28 (pp. 13–14).

37. Jamelle Bouie, 'Taking the History Out of "Huck Finn"', *Atlantic*, 4 January 2011, http://www.theatlantic.com/entertainment/archive/ 2011/01/taking-the-history-out-of-huck-finn/68870, accessed 15 December 2016; Michiko Kakutani, 'Light Out, Huck, They Still Want to Sivilize You', *New York Times*, 6 January 2011, http://www. nytimes.com/2011/01/07/books/07huck.html?pagewanted=all&_ r=0, accessed 31 January 2017.

38. Gribben, p. 9.

39. Arac, pp. 64, 66.

40. Henry, p. 26.

41. Thomas A. Tenney, 'For Further Reading', in *Satire or Evasion?*, pp. 239–69 (p. 242).

8

The Soil
Émile Zola

Everyone agreed that the English translation of Émile Zola's *La Terre* would have to be expurgated. His English publishers, Vizetelly & Company, recognized his reputation for candour, and advertised their translations of his Rougon-Macquart novels under the series title 'Zola's Powerful Realistic Novels'. But, as the editor Ernest Vizetelly recalled, the seventeenth novel in the series 'seemed to surpass in outspokenness any of the novelist's previous works'.[1] In the English advertisement for the novel, Zola described *La Terre* as 'the story of the French peasant, his love of land, his struggle to acquire it, his crushing toil, his brief delights, and his great misery'.[2] The French peasant's delights and misery involved content that would not appeal to English tastes: unrestrained sexuality; sexual violence; childbirth; bawdy, scatological humour; a flatulent poacher called 'Jesus Christ'; and a scene where a girl helps to guide a bull's penis into a cow. Vizetelly & Company published their translation, entitled *The Soil*, in heavily expurgated form. While Zola's fiction was controversial, it was generally accepted to be literature, and therefore not the kind of material that the law was likely to treat as obscene. The publishers had no reason to anticipate criminal charges. The prosecution of Henry Vizetelly marked the beginning of an era in which modern literature could be suppressed under English obscenity law.

Émile Zola writing *Fécondité* while in hiding in Walton-upon-Thames during the Dreyfus Affair. Photograph by Ernest Vizetelly's son, Victor René.

Founded in 1880 by Henry Vizetelly, Vizetelly & Company was a short-lived but influential publishing house that attempted to change the way books were marketed and distributed. Since the mid nineteenth century the market had been dominated by circulating libraries—private companies that lent out the latest fiction, poetry, and non-fiction to their subscribers. The most important libraries, in terms of their buying power and influence, were Mudie's Select Library and W. H. Smith's. Smith's, which ran lending libraries from railway bookstalls, favoured cheap reprints of classic and popular fiction in single volumes that were convenient for train reading, while Mudie's circulated larger and more leisurely three-volume novels. Most readers could not afford to buy three-volume novels, which usually cost thirty-one shillings and six pence, so the libraries had a virtual monopoly on the market for new literary fiction. Few publishers could take on novels that would not appeal to the libraries and their customers.[3] Smith's bookstalls refused anything that they deemed to be 'indecent, immoral or seditious',[4] while Mudie described his selection policy as a 'barrier' between his subscribers and 'the lower floods of literature'.[5] Novels by George Meredith, Charles Reade, and George Moore were refused because they did not meet the libraries' moral standards.[6] Other writers padded, cut, and expurgated their fiction to satisfy the libraries.[7] The circulating libraries were, therefore, one of the most widespread and effective agents of censorship in the Victorian period. Moore, who in his early career was a disciple of Zola, attempted to break the system, with Vizetelly's help.[8] In 1884 Vizetelly published Moore's *A Mummer's Wife*, a tale of adultery and alcoholism, bypassing the libraries by offering the novel for sale directly to the public in one volume at just six shillings.[9] It was a commercial success.

In addition to helping Moore, Vizetelly & Company was also pioneering in its publication of major modern European writers in translation, including Flaubert, Tolstoy, and Dostoevsky, as well as scholarly unexpurgated editions of Restoration drama, at prices many readers could afford.[10] By 1888, the company's diverse catalogue offered readers avant-garde European fiction and realist English fiction, classic English drama, popular sensation and crime fiction, and the Rougon-Macquart novels of Zola.[11] French editions of Zola circulated freely

in the United Kingdom, and had long been available to the relatively
small group of readers who could read them. Vizetelly's cheap translations, which were priced between two shillings and six pence and six
shillings, became the focus of a moral panic precisely because they
were targeted at the non-elite readers that the Education Acts 1870
and 1880 had created by expanding access to education and making
school compulsory. This newly literate demographic was a concern
for social purity reformers like the National Vigilance Association
(NVA), formed in 1885, which was dedicated to 'the enforcement and
improvement of the laws for the repression of criminal vice and public immorality'.[12] The NVA lobbied hard to introduce laws to protect
children and women from sexual exploitation, but they were equally
energetic in their efforts to suppress, for instance, a poster featuring
a scantily clad acrobat, a collection of anatomical waxworks, and an
exhibition of modern French illustrations from Rabelais.[13] (The waxworks and illustrations were returned to their owners on the understanding that they would not be displayed in England again.[14]) The
NVA also agitated against the unchecked circulation of 'pernicious
literature',[15] a term that embraced obscene advertisements and pamphlets, and—unfortunately for Vizetelly—indecent French novels.[16]

Vizetelly & Company had not intended to publish an indecent
book. They warned Zola that, though they would be as faithful to
his text as possible, they would have to make changes.[17] In Ernest
Vizetelly's euphemistic phrase, *La Terre* 'needed "toning" for the English reader'. Ernest and his father, Henry, cut and modified the text,
particularly its depiction of women's bodies and sexual experiences.[18]
'N'en-a-pas' Berthe, whose lack of pubic hair is the subject of village
gossip in the French text, loses her nickname in the Vizetelly translation, and a ribald conversation about her legendary hairlessness is
reduced, cryptically, to 'he went on saying some very improper things
about Berthe'.[19] The first description of rape places less emphasis on
the victim's thoughts. In the French original, the narrative registers
Françoise's pain, confusion, and fear of pregnancy. She begs her attacker
to withdraw, and he ejaculates on the earth. In the Vizetelly translation, Françoise loses consciousness, and the deliberate prevention of
pregnancy is omitted.[20] An extended, graphic depiction of childbirth
is cut almost entirely. In the original, Françoise is fascinated by every

detail of her sister's body in labour—the rippling and stretching of flesh, the size of her belly and vagina, the baby's head appearing and disappearing, as if in a perpetual game of hide-and-seek; but in the demure English translation, the messy work of childbirth is reduced to a mysterious 'kind of billow'.[21] And Françoise's one experience of orgasm, an overpowering spasm of pleasure experienced after a second rape, is reduced to an indefinite 'sensation'.[22] The total effect of these alterations is to make Zola's depiction of sexual brutality less explicit. Even so, the Vizetellys preserved the novel's plot and most of the controversial content: there is still an incestuous relationship between siblings, and all the instances of violence, including sexual violence, are retained. Françoise helps a bull inseminate a cow, as she does in the original, though there is no longer any reference to her hand touching its penis. Her sister has an abortion, though the technique used is deleted. The flatulent poacher is still flatulent, though somewhat deflated: he loses his nickname, becoming Hyacinthe, and the outrageous phrase 'Jesus Christ was windy' becomes 'Hyacinthe was a very windy individual'.[23] *The Soil* was more reticent than *La Terre*, but it still contained plenty of material for social purity reformers to condemn.

The NVA's principal voice in the House of Commons was Samuel Smith, a philanthropist, activist against cruelty to children, and Liberal member of parliament for Flintshire.[24] Addressing the House in 1888, Smith proposed a motion to enforce and, if necessary, strengthen the laws against obscene publications and indecent pictures. He quoted liberally from a recent article by Henry in the *Pall Mall Gazette*, a newspaper edited by W. T. Stead, one of the NVA's most prominent figures. Vizetelly had given the *Gazette* a statement about his success in publishing translations of French literature, including Zola.[25] 'After much hesitation,' Vizetelly wrote, 'we determined to issue an unabridged translation of "Nana", suppressing nothing and merely throwing a slight veil over those passages to which exception was likely to be taken.' By using the term 'unabridged' to describe *Nana*, a novel about the career of a courtesan, Vizetelly had given his critics ammunition. He was also incautious to boast of his sales figures. The total sales of *Nana* were, he claimed, 'little short of a hundred thousand. We reckon it a bad week when the sale of our Zola translations falls below a thousand volumes.'[26] As far as Smith was concerned, this statement amounted to the 'public confession' of the 'chief culprit in the spread of this pernicious literature'. Zola's novels were 'only fit for swine', and reading them must 'turn the mind into something akin to a sty'. He quoted at length from a hostile article in the *Sentinel* that claimed (on the evidence of two pages spotted in a bookseller's window) that a young man who had not learned 'the Divine secret of self-control' would be bound to commit 'some form of outward sin within twenty-four hours' of reading a Zola novel. For good measure, Smith read from an essay that dismissed *La Terre* as 'inartistic garbage', 'dirt and horror'. Such literature was a threat not only to the individual, Smith argued, but even to the integrity of the nation. In France, 'its poison was destroying the whole national life'. Would the House 'wait till this deadly poison spread itself over English soil and killed the life of this great and noble people?'[27]

The Soil was a convenient target for paternalism and xenophobia. It was marketed to the lower classes, it depicted sex and birth control, it was French, and its publisher had a foreign name. (The Vizetellys had come to England in the age of Elizabeth I, but during the Zola controversy Henry Vizetelly was treated by his critics as an invasive foreign body.[28]) Responding to Smith's motion, the Home Secretary, Henry Matthews, declined to urge the Director of Public Prosecutions to act, but he dropped a strong hint that a private prosecution would be regarded favourably by the government, because it would express the judgement of the public. He agreed that modern French literature, which had reached an unprecedented 'depth of immorality' and was being openly sold in cheap editions, threatened 'great harm to the moral health of the country'. He was sure that Smith and those of 'honest convictions' would not 'shrink from the slight personal inconvenience of putting the law in motion in any case of real public mischief'.[29] Smith's motion was passed. The debate left the law unchanged, but the NVA heard the Home Secretary's hint. The organization would use *The Soil* and its un-English publisher to test the limits of obscenity law.

The NVA could have made a complaint under the Obscene Publications Act 1857, which allowed magistrates to issue warrants for police to seize material suspected of being obscene. This strategy would not have led to criminal proceedings, but would have allowed the police to destroy Vizetelly's stock. Instead, the NVA brought a private criminal prosecution, alleging that Vizetelly had published an obscene libel, an offence cemented in English common law in 1727, when the bookseller Edmund Curll was convicted for publishing *Venus in the Cloister* (see Chapter 2). On 10 August 1888, Henry Vizetelly appeared at Bow Street Magistrates' Court to answer a summons for having published three obscene libels: *Nana*, *The Soil*, and *Piping Hot!*, the Vizetelly translation of Zola's *Pot-bouille*. The counsel for the prosecution was Herbert Henry Asquith, future Home Secretary and Prime Minister. The presiding magistrate directed Asquith to begin by reading from 'the worst of the three books'—*The Soil*.[30] Asquith was prepared for this. In his memoirs, he recalled that he had spent 'the best part of a fortnight in the Long Vacation, with scissors and a pot of paste at hand, in a diligent quest for the most objectionable passages in M. Zola's voluminous works'.[31] Asquith's anthology of objectionables persuaded the magistrate to commit Vizetelly for trial at the Old Bailey. At this point, the government took over the prosecution from the NVA. Ernest Vizetelly recognized this as a pivotal moment: 'the question was no longer one of fighting a band of fanatics, but of contending against the law-officers of the Crown.'[32]

The Vizetellys attempted to raise public awareness of the threat the prosecution posed to English literature. The company compiled an anthology of potentially obscene passages by canonical authors, entitled *Extracts Principally from English Classics: Showing that the Legal Suppression of M. Zola's Novels Would Logically Involve the Bowdlerizing of Some of the Greatest Works in English Literature*. The word 'bowdlerize' derives from the editors of *The Family Shakespeare*, Henrietta Bowdler and her brother the Reverend Thomas Bowdler, whose expurgated editions of Shakespeare excluded anything 'which cannot with propriety be read aloud in a family'—a common practice of reading in the nineteenth century.[33] Shakespearean bawdy, including passages expurgated by the Bowdlers, features prominently in Vizetelly's anthology. So do other Elizabethan dramatists, eighteenth-century novelists, Lord Byron and Percy Bysshe Shelley, and contemporary poets such as Algernon Charles Swinburne, whose first collection was withdrawn from sale by its publisher.[34] Vizetelly knew full well that both old and modern literature had long been vulnerable to mild bowdlerizing and more oppressive forms of censorship, but his anthology demonstrates how yesterday's obscenity can become today's classic. He portrayed Zola's novels as modern classics by including excerpts from essays on Zola's style and moral purpose, and a brief outline of the Rougon-Macquart series by Zola himself. He advertised his anthology in an open letter to Sir Augustus Stephenson, the Solicitor to the Treasury and Director of Public Prosecutions, asking whether publishers would be allowed to continue publishing Shakespeare and other established writers if Zola's novels were found obscene.[35] 'What about Shakespeare?' is a popular rhetorical strategy in anti-censorship arguments, but is rarely effective in persuading censors. The courts, for their part, only consider the books in front of them. In the 1878 prosecution of Annie Besant and Charles Bradlaugh for publishing a pamphlet about birth control, Chief Justice Cockburn had refused to allow Besant to use Laurence Sterne's *Tristram Shandy*, a novel full of childbirth humour, as evidence for her defence.[36] Vizetelly's anthology was no more effective than Besant's argument.

On 31 October 1888, Henry Vizetelly appeared at the Old Bailey to answer a charge of obscene libel.[37] The indictment stated that Vizetelly had published 'a certain lewd wicked bawdy and obscene libel in the form of a book entitled "The Soil"', and that, 'being a person of a wicked and depraved mind and disposition', he intended to 'vitiate and corrupt the morals of all the subjects of our present Sovereign Lady the Queen and to debauch poison and infect the minds of the youth of this Kingdom'. The indictment listed the objectionable passages identified by Asquith, beginning with pages 11 through 13 of *The Soil*, the scene in which Françoise assists the bull.[38] (Though the original charge had mentioned three novels, only *The Soil* was discussed at the trial.) The first lawyer Vizetelly approached declined to defend him on the grounds that he would have to read books that contained 'passages which my conscience would not excuse me for reading'.[39] In the end, Vizetelly's counsel was Francis Williams, Recorder of Cardiff. Sir Edward Clarke, who would go on to defend Oscar Wilde, was Crown prosecutor (see Chapter 9).[40]

Clarke opened by setting out the test of obscenity from *R v. Hicklin*, a case that would become the scourge of literature in the Anglo-American legal tradition, thanks in part to its use against Vizetelly.[41] The Hicklin

test was developed to suppress an anti-Catholic pamphlet that had provoked rioting and sectarian violence in urban centres across England.
Hicklin was not a criminal prosecution like the Vizetelly case. It was a
proceeding under the Obscene Publications Act 1857, which empow-
ered magistrates to issue warrants to seize and destroy obscene articles.
In 1868 Chief Justice Cockburn and the other judges sitting on the
Queen's Bench heard an appeal against the decision of Benjamin Hicklin, a magistrate. The judges were asked to authorize the destruction of
The Confessional Unmasked, an anthology of racy passages excerpted from
Catholic writings on the confession of sexual sins. It had been distributed by Henry Scott, a member of the Protestant Electoral Union, to
stir up hatred against Catholics. Sectarian tensions were rising throughout 1867 and into 1868: there were riots, acts of vandalism, attacks on
Catholics and Protestants, and fourteen deaths.[42] Fears of public disorder
had been the driving force behind obscenity law since the eighteenth
century, and now those fears would motivate an expansive interpretation
of the law. Circulating anti-Catholic propaganda was not a crime, but
the sexual content in *The Confessional Unmasked* provided a pretext to
suppress it. The judges held, unanimously, that *The Confessional Unmasked*
was obscene and should be destroyed. Scott's intention in distributing
the pamphlet was irrelevant. According to Cockburn, 'the test of obscenity is this, whether the tendency of the matter charged as obscenity is
to deprave and corrupt those whose minds are open to such immoral
influences, and into whose hands a publication of this sort may fall'.[43]
The pamphlet was duly suppressed, and a legal time bomb was now
ticking for literature. It was perfectly true, Cockburn said, that 'there
are a great many publications of high repute in the literary productions
of this country the tendency of which is immodest, and, if you please,
immoral'.[44] By Cockburn's standard of obscenity, any 'matter', even literary matter, could be found obscene if the judge thought it might deprave
and corrupt some hypothetical, particularly impressionable person who
might, perhaps, read the text. This set a low threshold for obscenity. *The
Soil* certainly could not withstand the Hicklin test.

After summarizing *Hicklin* for the jury in Vizetelly's case, Clarke
demolished Vizetelly's 'What about Shakespeare?' defence. He
acknowledged that there were 'in our own classics, especially in those
dating from some centuries ago, passages which conflict with our

ideas', but explained that Cockburn had said in *Hicklin* that this did not prevent other works from being indicted.[45] Vizetelly would not get away with publishing obscene matter simply because others had in the past. English classics were not on trial. *The Soil* would be considered on its own merits.

Clarke described *The Soil* as 'a filthy book from end to end'. Under the Hicklin test, any obscene passage was sufficient to condemn the book, and Clarke presented the jury with 'twenty-one passages, some of them extending over several pages, such as no writer with pure motives ever put into a literary work'. It was 'bestial obscenity' published 'to pander to the worst passions'.[46] For half an hour, he read extracts from *The Soil*, to the evident disgust of the jury. After Clarke read from the passage where Françoise assists the bull, they made their opinion clear.[47] A juror interrupted Clarke and asked the judge whether it was necessary to read all the objectionable passages. As if holding them hostage, Clarke offered the jurors a way to escape their ordeal:

> You will understand that it is at least as unpleasant for me to read as for you to listen to these passages. If you are prepared at any moment to say that they are obscene, I will gladly stop reading them.[48]

Vizetelly's counsel now gave up hope of persuading the hostile jury that *The Soil* was not obscene, and Vizetelly changed his plea to guilty. Williams attempted to prevent a harsh sentence by reminding the judge that Zola was a 'great French writer', but Clarke did not allow this to slip by, responding: 'No, no; a voluminous writer. Don't insult French literature!' In summing up, the judge echoed the language of the NVA's mission statement, declaring that the prosecution had been 'absolutely essential in the interests of public morality'.[49] Vizetelly was fined one hundred pounds and undertook to 'keep the peace and behave properly' for twelve months.[50] Vizetelly & Company were to cease circulating their editions of *The Soil*, *Nana*, and *Piping Hot!*, and Clarke warned that prosecutions would be brought against any other parties who published them.[51] The Home Office wrote to mayors to encourage them to initiate similar prosecutions.[52]

In early 1889 Vizetelly & Company, now at risk of bankruptcy because booksellers were reluctant to work with them, returned to their Zola back catalogue. They believed that they were permitted to do so. Only three novels had been found to be obscene, and they thought the undertaking not to publish 'any other of the works which M. Zola has produced [. . .] which are at least as objectionable as those which are indicted' meant that they were free to publish expurgated versions. Ernest Vizetelly embarked upon a marathon expurgation project, working through all the firm's editions of Zola, except for the three indicted novels. The firm had used stereotype plates to print their Zola editions, so the text could not easily be changed. Ernest had to identify passages to cut out of the plates and then write new text of the same length to fill the gap. He took two months to work through fifteen volumes, amending or deleting 325 pages. His alterations, he thought, 'were sufficient to satisfy everybody except fanatical Puritans'.[53]

The NVA was not satisfied. On 1 and 2 May 1889, five booksellers answered summonses for publishing obscene libels, most of which were English translations of French literature. Once again, Vizetelly and Zola were the principal scapegoats. Twelve of the twenty summonses were issued to Vizetelly, and seven of these were for translations of Zola novels. The other five were also for French literature in translation, including Gustave Flaubert's *Madame Bovary* and works by Guy de Maupassant.[54] Henry Vizetelly appeared at the Old Bailey on 30 May 1889. The trial was brief, and the extent of his expurgations was never acknowledged. Vizetelly's counsel insisted he plead guilty. Ernest's account implies that Henry, now penniless and seriously ill, did not fully understand the proceedings and was coerced into pleading guilty:

> He was in a condition little short of actual physical collapse. In a dreamy way, as it were, he gave, or seemed to give, a feeble assent to everything. [. . .] Vizetelly took his stand at the foot of the solicitor's table, his son who sat there, and who at every moment feared to see him fall, holding his hand the while. For an instant, when challenged, he hesitated, then ejaculated the word 'guilty', much as if he were expectorating.[55]

Ernest attempted to testify to the severity of his father's illness, but no clemency was shown on account of Henry Vizetelly's age, poverty, or ill health. His previous promise to maintain good behaviour was counted against him. The punishment was severe: three months in prison.[56] Despite a public appeal for Vizetelly's release supported by eminent authors, critics, and dramatists, the Home Secretary declined to intervene, and the publisher served his full sentence.[57] The government had signalled its approval of the NVA's action, and allowed Vizetelly's imprisonment to stand as a warning to other publishers. Booksellers began to seek the NVA's opinion of their stock to reduce their liability.[58] In 1891 Thomas Henry Thompson, a Vizetelly employee, was charged after he sold prints and a pamphlet he called 'Vizetelly's Defence' to an agent of the NVA.[59]

After his release, Henry Vizetelly wrote his memoir, which reveals that, during a long and varied career, he had succeeded in challenging different forms of censorship. As an apprentice wood-engraver, he eagerly read 'forbidden books' such as Thomas Paine's *Rights of Man* and *Age of Reason*, Robert Southey's *Wat Tyler*, Lord Byron's 'Vision of Judgment', and a report of the trial of a young man transported overseas for lending a book by Paine. The forbidden book that fascinated Vizetelly most was Shelley's *Queen Mab*, which he read not for its poetry, but for its bold expression of 'agnostic and republican ideas' (see Chapter 4). As a journalist, Vizetelly agitated against the last of the 'taxes on knowledge', the tax on paper, which inhibited the circulation of cheap newspapers, periodicals, and books. As the Paris correspondent for the *Illustrated London News*, he negotiated with the French press bureau, which had seized copies of the English newspaper because of two lines reporting on rumours of a plot against the French emperor. Vizetelly offered to cut out the objectionable lines (the bureau refused), then to black them out (the bureau refused again, angrily, because this was a 'Russian' practice). He retrieved the seized copies by pledging to substitute the offending page with a new 'cancel-page'. His memoir is almost silent, however, on the rise and fall of Vizetelly & Company, apart from a brief comment that his translations gave English readers access to writings that had been 'sealed books to the multitude', until 'the persecution of a band of fanatics' brought about his ruin. The last lines turn from his own tragedy to

Zola's recent visit to England, noting the cheers with which he was welcomed by the Attorney General and the Institute of Journalists.[60] Vizetelly did not mistake this enthusiasm for the defeat of censorship. He disagreed with the critic A. T. Quiller-Couch, who thought Zola's popularity demonstrated that 'the public conscience will not permit a repetition of the Vizetelly trial'.[61] Vizetelly predicted that 'in the event of a new prosecution the press would again remain silent until the "National Vigilants" had secured a verdict, when it would once more join in approving the "vindication of the law"'. Three and a half years after his imprisonment, and three months after Zola's visit to England, Henry Vizetelly died.[62]

Ernest Vizetelly resolved to avenge the 'ruin of his family' by 'outflanking' the NVA and promoting Zola in England.[63] *La Débâcle*, a novel about the Franco-Prussian war that could not easily be misrepresented as obscene, was an excellent candidate for translation. Vizetelly's translation was published serially as *The Downfall* in the *Weekly Times and Echo*, and then in a one-volume edition with Chatto & Windus in 1892. It was a commercial success, and new translations of Zola's works were produced, many translated or edited by Ernest. He continued to censor the texts to meet English standards of taste, with Zola's assent. The author wrote to Ernest that *Le Docteur Pascal* contained nothing that would 'offend the prudery of your compatriots', but gave him 'full authority to modify any passages which may seem to you to be *inquiétants*'.[64] Ernest also helped Zola go into hiding in England in 1898, following the French judiciary's attempt to prevent the author from denouncing the conspiracy against Alfred Dreyfus, the Jewish military officer falsely imprisoned to protect high-ranking military officials.[65]

Zola's works, in the end, had not been suppressed for long. But the prosecutions of Henry Vizetelly had a lasting impact on English authors and publishers, and set a dangerous example. An organized group of offendees could turn a good-faith publisher into a criminal. The publication of literature could be a misdemeanour. Literature could be assessed for obscenity using the Hicklin test, which meant that even a single passage, if judged to have the tendency to corrupt vulnerable readers, could condemn a whole work. And, by extension, literature could be seized and destroyed under the Obscene Publications Act 1857. The

Vizetelly trials inaugurated a series of moral crusades and legal proceedings against retailers, publishers, authors, and books, including *The Well of Loneliness*, *Ulysses*, and *Lady Chatterley's Lover*, throughout the first half of the twentieth century (see Chapters 10, 11, and 12).

Notes

1. Ernest Vizetelly, *Émile Zola, Novelist and Reformer: An Account of his Life & Work. Illustrated by Portraits, Views, & Fac-similes* (London: Lane, 1904), p. 254.

2. Dorothy E. Speirs, 'Émile Zola's Novels', in Marie Elena Korey, with Yannick Portebois and others, *Vizetelly & Compan(ies): A Complex Tale of Victorian Printing and Publishing: An Exhibition with Essays* (Toronto: University of Toronto Press, 2003), pp. 79–105 (p. 95).

3. Guinevere L. Griest, *Mudie's Circulating Library and the Victorian Novel* (Newton Abbot: David & Charles, 1970), pp. 35–40, 46–52, 88–101; Mary Hammond, *Reading, Publishing and the Formation of Literary Taste in England, 1880–1914* (Aldershot: Ashgate, 2006), pp. 74–78; Charles Wilson, *First with the News: The History of W. H. Smith 1792–1972* (London: Cape, 1985), pp. 357–64.

4. Hammond, p. 67.

5. Griest, p. 145.

6. Griest, pp. 140–49; Wilson, pp. 365–68.

7. Griest, pp. 47–51, 55–56, 89–119.

8. Griest, pp. 148–49, 209.

9. Simon Curtis, 'Vizetelly & Co', *Poetry Nation Review*, 9.6 (1983), 28–31 (pp. 28–29); Richard Landon, 'A Man under Fire: Henry Vizetelly and the Question of Obscenity in Victorian England', in Korey and others, pp. 108–23 (p. 110).

10. Curtis, p. 28; Brendan Fleming, 'The First English Translation of *La Terre* (1888): An Assessment of the Letters from Vizetelly & Co. to Émile Zola', *Publishing History*, 50 (2001), 47–59 (p. 48); Yannick Portebois, 'A Publisher and his Books: The Catalogue of Vizetelly & Co., 1880–1890', in Korey and others, pp. 39–78.

11. Portebois, p. 58; Speirs, pp. 85–89.

12. William Alexander Coote, *A Romance of Philanthropy: Being a Record of Some of the Principal Incidents Connected with the Exceptionally Successful Thirty Years' Work of the National Vigilance Association* (London: National Vigilance Association, 1916), p. 5. See also Anthony Cummins, 'Émile

Zola's Cheap English Dress: The Vizetelly Translations, Late-Victorian Print Culture, and the Crisis of Literary Value', *Review of English Studies*, n.s., 60.243 (2008), 108–32 (pp. 109–13); Denise Merkle, 'Vizetelly & Company as (Ex)change Agent: Towards the Modernization of the British Publishing Industry', in *Agents of Translation*, ed. John Milton and Paul Bandia, Benjamins Translation Library, 81 (Amsterdam: Benjamins, 2009), 85–105 (pp. 86–87); Katherine Mullin, 'Pernicious Literature: Vigilance in the Age of Zola (1886–1899)', in *Prudes on the Prowl: Fiction and Obscenity in England, 1850 to the Present Day*, ed. David Bradshaw and Rachel Potter (Oxford: Oxford University Press, 2013), pp. 30–51 (pp. 31–32); Speirs, pp. 85–89.

13. Edward J. Bristow, *Vice and Vigilance: Purity Movements in Britain since 1700* (Dublin: Gill & Macmillan, 1977), pp. 106–21, 205–15; Coote, pp. 26, 42–68, 94–107.

14. Coote, pp. 101, 105–06.

15. Mullin, p. 31.

16. Coote, pp. 42–47.

17. Fleming, p. 51.

18. Ernest Vizetelly, *Émile Zola*, pp. 255–56.

19. Émile Zola, *The Soil: A Realistic Novel* (London: Vizetelly, 1888), p. 114 [Internet Archive e-book]; Émile Zola, *La Terre*, in *Œuvres Complètes*, ed. Henri Mitterand, 15 vols (Paris: Cercle du Livre Précieux, 1966–69), v: *Germinal; L'Œuvre; La Terre*, ed. Mitterand (1967), 856–57 (Book II, Chapter 4).

20. Zola, *The Soil*, p. 209; Zola, *La Terre*, p. 940 (Book III, Chapter 4).

21. Zola, *The Soil*, p. 221; Zola, *La Terre*, pp. 953–54 (Book III, Chapter 5).

22. Zola, *The Soil*, p. 399; Zola, *La Terre*, pp. 1089–90 (Book V, Chapter 3).

23. Zola, *The Soil*, p. 272; Zola, *La Terre*, p. 993 (Book IV, Chapter 3).

24. G. Le G. Norgate, 'Smith, Samuel (1836–1906)', rev. H. C. G. Matthew, *Oxford Dictionary of National Biography* (Oxford: Oxford University Press, 2004), http://www.oxforddnb.com/view/article/36157, accessed 2 January 2017.

25. HC Deb 8 May 1888, vol 325, col 1708.

26. Edward Vizetelly [Henry Vizetelly], 'My Life and Publications', *Pall Mall Gazette*, 24 March 1888, pp. 2–3 (p. 2).

27. HC Deb 8 May 1888, vol 325, cols 1708–10.

28. Deana Heath, *Purifying Empire: Obscenity and the Politics of Moral Regulation in Britain, India and Australia* (Cambridge: Cambridge University Press, 2010), pp. 65–92 (pp. 66–67); Anthony Patterson, *Mrs Grundy's*

Enemies: Censorship, Realist Fiction and the Politics of Sexual Representation (Oxford: Peter Lang, 2013), pp. 34–35; Ernest Vizetelly, *Émile Zola*, p. 244.

29. HC Deb 8 May 1888, vol 325, cols 1719–21.

30. Ernest Vizetelly, *Émile Zola*, p. 268.

31. Herbert Henry Asquith, *Memories & Reflections, 1852–1927*, 2 vols (London: Cassell, 1928), I, 89.

32. Ernest Vizetelly, *Émile Zola*, p. 270.

33. Colin Franklin, 'The Bowdlers and their *Family Shakespeare*', *Book Collector*, 49.2 (2000), 227–43 (p. 232). Thomas Bowdler, *The Family Shakespeare: In Which Nothing Is Added to the Original Text, but Those Words and Expressions Are Omitted Which Cannot with Propriety Be Read in a Family*, 6 vols (London: Longman, Brown, Green and Longmans, 1853).

34. [Henry Vizetelly], *Extracts Principally from English Classics: Showing that the Legal Suppression of M. Zola's Novels Would Logically Involve the Bowdlerizing of Some of the Greatest Works in English Literature* (London: [Vizetelly], 1888), pp. 11–15, 84–87.

35. Henry Vizetelly to Sir A. K. Stephenson, quoted in [Henry Vizetelly], *Extracts*, p. 1. See also J. Ll. J. Edwards, *The Law Officers of the Crown: A Study of the Offices of Attorney-General and Solicitor-General of England with an Account of the Office of the Director of Public Prosecutions of England* (London: Sweet & Maxwell, 1964), p. 376.

36. Norman St John-Stevas, *Obscenity and the Law* (London: Secker & Warburg, 1956), p. 155.

37. 'No More Translations from Zola', *Pall Mall Gazette*, 31 October 1888, p. 10; 'Trial of Henry Vizitelli [*sic*]', 31 October 1888, t18881022-990, The Proceedings of the Old Bailey, https://www.oldbaileyonline.org/browse.jsp?id=def1-990-18881022&div=t18881022-990#highlight, accessed 26 December 2016.

38. Central Criminal Court Records, Crim. 4, 1036, pt. 1, quoted in Landon, pp. 114–15.

39. George Moore, *A Communication to my Friends* (London: Nonesuch, 1933), p. 69.

40. Ernest Vizetelly, *Émile Zola*, pp. 275–77.

41. 'No More Translations from Zola', p. 10. See also Geoffrey Robertson, *Obscenity: An Account of Censorship Laws and their Enforcement in England and Wales* (London: Weidenfeld & Nicolson, 1979), pp. 30–32.

42. Kevin Birmingham, *The Most Dangerous Book: The Battle for James Joyce's 'Ulysses'* (London: Head of Zeus, 2015), pp. 174–77.

43. *R v Hicklin* (1868) LR 3 QB 360, 371.

44. *R v Hicklin* (1868) LR 3 QB 360, 371.
45. 'No More Translations from Zola', p. 10.
46. 'No More Translations from Zola', p. 10.
47. Ernest Vizetelly, *Émile Zola*, p. 278.
48. 'No More Translations from Zola', p. 10.
49. 'No More Translations from Zola', p. 10.
50. 'Trial of Henry Vizitelli [*sic*]'.
51. 'No More Translations from Zola', p. 10.
52. Heath, p. 69.
53. Ernest Vizetelly, *Émile Zola*, pp. 282, 284–85, 290.
54. Coote, pp. 42–43.
55. Ernest Vizetelly, *Émile Zola*, pp. 291–92.
56. 'Trial of Henry Vizetelly', 30 May 1889, t18890527-524, The Proceedings of the Old Bailey, https://www.oldbaileyonline.org/browse. jsp?id=def1-524-18890527&div=t18890527-524#highlight, accessed 26 December 2016.
57. Ernest Vizetelly, *Émile Zola*, pp. 295–98.
58. 'Holywell Street Panicstricken', *Pall Mall Gazette*, 1 June 1889, p. 6.
59. 'The Charge of Selling Indecent Prints', *The Times*, 28 February 1890, p. 10.
60. Henry Vizetelly, *Glances Back through Seventy Years: Autobiographical and Other Reminiscences*, 2 vols (London: Kegan Paul, Trench, Trübner, 1893), I, 121; II, 41–45, 53–60, 204–7, 432.
61. A.T.Q.C. [Arthur Quiller-Couch], 'A Literary Causerie', *Speaker: The Liberal Review*, 14 October 1893, p. 412.
62. Ernest Vizetelly, *Émile Zola*, p. 340. See further p. 299.
63. Ernest Vizetelly, *Émile Zola*, pp. 314–15.
64. Ernest Vizetelly, *Émile Zola*, pp. 318–19. See further pp. 314–19, 543–46.
65. Ernest Vizetelly, *With Zola in England: A Story of Exile* (London: Chatto & Windus, 1899).

9

The Picture of Dorian Gray
Oscar Wilde

Oscar Wilde spent his career playing with the boundary between life and art. When challenging Victorian moralism, he treated art as if it were not answerable to life: art existed for art's sake. In the Preface to *The Picture of Dorian Gray* he famously insists, '*There is no such thing as a moral or an immoral book. Books are well written, or badly written. That is all.*'[1] At the same time, when defending the importance of art, Wilde sometimes extended its domain until it seemed to swallow up life altogether. As he writes in 'Phrases and Philosophies for the Use of the Young', 'One should either be a work of art, or wear a work of art.'[2] Though Wilde's epigrams are usually tongue-in-cheek, this one describes his own public persona. An author, critic, editor, and public speaker, Wilde was also a dandy whose dress, wit, and cross-class socializing made him into living theatre. His conduct was as much of a threat to Victorian values, especially to Victorian masculinity, as his writing was.[3]

Though two of Wilde's plays, *Vera* and *Salomé*, were barred from the British stage, the short novel *Dorian Gray*, first published in 1890, was his most controversial work. Dorian is a beautiful and wealthy young man who forms intimate friendships with two older men. Lord Henry Wotton, who speaks in epigrams and paradoxes, initiates Dorian into the pursuit of pleasure, while Basil Hallward, infatuated with Dorian, paints his portrait. Dorian is struck by the permanence of the portrait

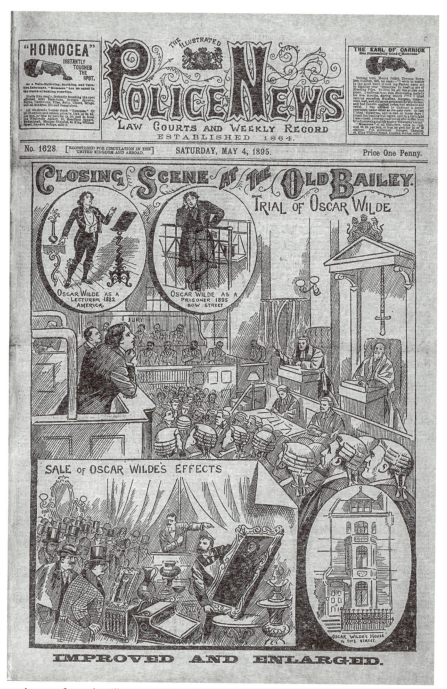

A page from the *Illustrated Police News* depicting the final day of Oscar Wilde's first gross indecency trial and the sale of the insolvent author's property.

in contrast to his own fleeting perfection, and wishes that the artwork would grow old while he remains eternally young. His wish comes true, though he has effectively sold his soul: over the course of the narrative, as he descends into nebulous evil that includes driving an actress to suicide, frequenting East London opium dens, ruining young men in unspecified ways, and murdering his friend, Dorian remains outwardly unchanged, while his portrait ages and becomes 'hideous'.[4] When Dorian attempts to destroy the painting, which he now sees as evidence of his sins, he succeeds only in killing himself, transforming in death into the wretched old man that the portrait had come to depict.

Before the novel appeared in *Lippincott's Monthly Magazine* in the United Kingdom and the United States, the editor J. M. Stoddart and his associates made a number of changes, apparently without Wilde's knowledge. Stoddart reduced intimations of sexual conduct that the public would consider transgressive, including erotic relationships between men, extramarital sex, and prostitution.[5] Despite these changes, the British press was both outraged and contemptuous, and W. H. Smith & Son withdrew the issue of *Lippincott's* from its bookstalls.[6] A review in the *St James's Gazette* wondered if the National Vigilance Association would prosecute the author or publisher (as it had Henry Vizetelly for his translations of Émile Zola—see Chapter 8). The review compared *Dorian Gray* to W. T. Stead's sensational exposé of child prostitution, 'The Maiden Tribute of Modern Babylon', finding them both to be 'corrupt but not dangerous' and 'incurably silly'. They were 'catchpenny revelations of the non-existent' that 'ought to be chucked into the fire'.[7] Other reviewers came closer to spelling out the novel's illicit sexual content. The *Daily Chronicle* called *Dorian Gray* a 'poisonous book, the atmosphere of which is heavy with the mephitic odours of moral and spiritual putrefaction' and listed, among many other faults, 'its effeminate frivolity'.[8] The *Scots Observer* said Wilde had 'again been writing stuff that were better unwritten', and accused him of appealing to 'none but outlawed noblemen and perverted telegraph-boys', a reference to the male prostitutes and clients exposed in the Cleveland Street scandal of 1889.[9] Clearly, readers had picked up on the erotic charge in Dorian's associations with men.

Wilde replied to these reviews with letters to the editors, which expanded into public exchanges in which he defended both the novel and his philosophy of aestheticism. He argued that immorality was a suitable subject for art: 'Good people, belonging as they do to the normal, and so, commonplace, type, are artistically uninteresting. Bad people are, from the point of view of art, fascinating studies.' While insisting on an essential separation between art and ethics, he explained that *Dorian Gray* did in fact have a moral—'All excess, as well as all renunciation, brings its own punishment.'[10] He also attempted to counter the insinuation that Dorian has sex with men, claiming that 'Each man sees his own sin in Dorian Gray. What Dorian Gray's sins are no one knows. He who finds them has brought them.'[11] Wilde thought the novel was sufficiently ambiguous for this claim to be true, but the author and critic Walter Pater convinced him to change a passage that seemed to make the nature of Basil's love for Dorian too clear.[12] The author made several such changes for the single-volume edition of 1891, while also adding six new chapters and a preface. The revisions notwithstanding, Macmillan and Company declined to publish this edition because of its content, and it was published with Ward Lock & Company.[13]

Wilde's greatest ordeal was still to come. The unfavourable reviews of *Dorian Gray*, his letters to the press, and his subsequent revisions would become evidence in 1895 when the author found himself defending his work at the Old Bailey. Wilde was not initially the one on trial, but he had walked into what his lover's father described as a 'booby trap'.[14] For over a year, the Marquess of Queensberry had been trying to stop his son, Lord Alfred Douglas, from seeing Wilde. The Marquess wrote to Douglas in 1894 after observing the two men dining together,

> I am not going to try to analyse this intimacy, and I make no charge; but to my mind to pose as a thing is as bad as to be it. With my own eyes I saw you both in the most loathsome and disgusting relationship as expressed by your manner and your expression. Never in my experience have I ever seen such a sight as that in your horrible features.[15]

After a threatening visit to Wilde's residence and a failed attempt to disrupt the opening night of his play *The Importance of Being Earnest* with some vegetables, Queensberry left an unsealed calling card for Wilde with a porter at the Albemarle Club. It read, 'For Oscar Wilde posing as somdomite.' (This was silently amended in court to 'For Oscar Wilde posing as sodomite'.)[16]

During the late nineteenth century, the term 'homosexual' was not yet current in Britain. The word 'sodomy', derived from the city of Sodom in the Old Testament, referred to specific illegal sex acts, namely bestiality and anal penetration of men or women. Sodomy laws based on the Buggery Act of 1533 were used to prosecute a variety of sex acts between men as sodomy, attempted sodomy, or indecent assault.[17] By saying that Wilde was 'posing', Queensberry was getting at something more elusive, not necessarily a specific act, but a way of acting. He did not know for certain what Wilde and Douglas were doing in private, but what he saw in public was two men displaying the 'manner and expression' of sexual partners. Wilde and his circle, on the other hand, defined their identity for themselves with reference to the ancient Greek tradition of pederasty, in which older men were both mentors and lovers to younger men. (The name 'Dorian' is an allusion to the Dorian tribesmen, who practiced pederasty.[18]) Love between men was also known as 'Uranian' love. Because British society considered this form of sexuality criminal and immoral, Douglas dubbed it 'the love that dare not speak its name'. Queensberry had not accused Wilde of doing anything illegal, but he had accused Wilde of *acting like* he was doing something illegal, and by giving the unsealed card to a porter the Marquess had effectively published it. Wilde responded with a private prosecution for criminal libel.

Prosecuting Queensberry for libel was foolhardy, because it challenged the Marquess to justify the libel, which meant proving that it was true and that publishing it was for the public benefit. Queensberry's phrase 'posing as' meant that not only Wilde's sexual history, but also the way he presented himself in his life and his art, could be evidence of the truth of the libel. The Marquess's plea alleged that Wilde had 'incited and solicited' over twelve young men to 'commit sodomy and other acts of gross indecency and immorality with him', that he had in fact committed 'other acts of gross indecency and immorality' with them, that he had taken 'indecent liberties' with another, that he had 'corrupted and debauched the morals' of seven of the men, and that his works 'Phrases and Philosophies for the Use of the Young' and *The Picture of Dorian Gray* were 'calculated to subvert morality and to encourage unnatural vice'.[19] Queensberry was the one on trial, but Wilde and his work would be exposed to merciless scrutiny in order to determine whether the Queensberry libel was justified.

Queensberry's counsel, Edward Carson, launched a sustained attack on Wilde's writing. Referring to the 1891 *Dorian Gray* as the 'purged' edition, the barrister quoted passages from the 1890 text, including lines describing Basil's first encounter with Dorian:[20]

> I knew that I had come face to face with some one whose mere personality was so fascinating that, if I allowed it to do so, it would absorb my whole nature, my whole soul, my very art itself. [. . .] I knew that if I spoke to Dorian I would become absolutely devoted to him, and that I ought not to speak to him.[21]

Carson asked Wilde if his 'description of the feeling of one man towards a youth, just grown up, was a proper or an improper feeling'. Wilde replied that it was 'the most perfect description possible of what an artist would feel on meeting a beautiful personality that he felt some way was necessary to his art and life'.[22] The author repeatedly tried to counter suggestions of indecency by appealing to the purity of art. He even claimed that an affectionate letter to Douglas, which blackmailers had tried to use against him, was a prose poem. When Carson asked him to discuss the letter 'apart from art', Wilde said, 'I cannot answer any question apart from art' and quipped, to the amusement of the gallery, 'A man who was not an artist could never have written that letter.'[23]

Though Wilde's statements about his work were characteristically audacious, they challenged Carson's logic in several important ways. Wilde objected strenuously to the barrister's use of the phrases 'sodomitical novel' or 'sodomitical book' in reference to *Dorian Gray* and a French novel by Joris-Karl Huysmans entitled *À rebours*, saying, 'I don't know what you mean by a sodomitical novel.' There was indeed a crucial ambiguity in this term. Did it designate a book that, in Carson's words, merely 'dealt with sodomitical incidents', or one 'which would lead to and teach sodomitical practices'?[24] Carson seemed to think these meanings were interchangeable—much like opponents of crime fiction and comic books from the nineteenth century into the twentieth, who feared that young readers would imitate what they read (see Chapter 15). Wilde denied both implications. He claimed that he had never revealed Dorian Gray's sin to be sodomy, and, in response to Carson's question whether a 'well written book putting forth sodomitical views might be a good book', he asserted, 'No work of art ever puts forward views of any kind.'[25]

Similarly, Wilde denied that 'any book or work of art ever produces any effect on conduct at all'.[26] This is a bold statement that strikes at the root of moral censorship, which usually imagines impressionable readers, often young, who will imitate or otherwise be corrupted by what they read. At this point in the trial, Carson was cross-examining Wilde on his short collection of epigrams, 'Phrases and Philosophies for the Use of the Young'. These epigrams are ironic and express an attitude of mischievous amorality ('If one tells the truth, one is sure, sooner or later, to be found out'[27]). Wilde made clear in court that he had not intended the 'Phrases and Philosophies' to be taken at face value, nor for them to have 'any effect but that of literature'. He claimed, 'I rarely think that anything I write is true', and said that his writing was meant instead 'to represent wilful moods of paradox, of fun, nonsense, of anything at all'. When Carson asked whether the epigram about telling the truth and being found out constituted a 'good educational axiom for youth', Wilde retorted, 'Anything that stimulates thought in people of any age is good for them.' Judging by the gallery's laughter at this reply and at the epigrams Carson quoted, some observers in the Old Bailey got the jokes.[28]

Unfortunately for Wilde, his 'Phrases' had appeared in the first and only issue of the Oxford undergraduate magazine the *Chameleon* along with a story called 'The Priest and the Acolyte' by John Francis Bloxam, which depicted an erotic relationship between a young priest and a boy of fourteen. Douglas's 'Two Loves', a poem defending 'the love that dare not speak its name', also appeared in the issue. Wilde tried to distance himself from 'The Priest and the Acolyte', but, adhering to his principle that art is amoral, he refused to call it blasphemous. He admitted that the conjunction of the story and his 'Phrases' might make his epigrams appear more serious than they were intended to be.[29]

Piqued by Carson's questioning, Wilde also allowed artistic elitism to get the better of him. Having said 'You cannot ask me what mis-interpretation of my work the ignorant, the illiterate, the foolish may put on it', he then assented to Carson's suggestion that the 'majority of people would come within your definition of Philistines and illiterate'. If Wilde had given the public more credit, he could have claimed that his readers were sufficiently critical not to be influenced by Dorian Gray's sins, whatever they were, nor to take the 'Phrases' as rules to live by. Instead, by suggesting that few readers were sophisticated enough to understand him, Wilde opened himself up to the argument that the general public, who 'do not understand the artistic bearing of the language', would interpret his work as Carson had done.[30]

In his opening statement for the defence, Carson told the jury that he could have rested his case on Wilde's literature alone. *Dorian Gray* and Wilde's letters to Douglas contained 'exactly the same idea' as 'The Priest and the Acolyte', that 'of a man using towards a man the language which men sometimes use, and perhaps legitimately use, towards women'. The defence had more damaging evidence, how-ever, still to introduce. Carson had already cross-examined Wilde on his public association with various young working-class men, and observed that the author contradicted himself when he dismissed the average person's ideas about art while professing to enjoy the con-versation of men beneath his station. If Wilde was so disdainful of the ordinary man's opinion, why did he appear in public with these young men? The barrister now announced his intention to call several of them as witnesses, along with staff of the Savoy Hotel. The hotel staff would testify to finding 'disgusting filth' on Wilde's sheets and, on one occasion, a boy in his bed. The young men would testify that the author had committed sex acts with them. Wilde's counsel, Sir Edward Clarke, interrupted Carson. He had decided to concede the case.[31]

Clarke did not want to proceed further in 'an investigation of mat-ters of the most appalling character'. He attempted to limit the damage to Wilde's reputation, requesting that the jury find Queensberry not guilty based on Wilde's literature and letters alone. Clarke argued that the writing was enough to justify the libel, because it showed what Wilde was 'posing as'. This was wishful thinking. If Queensberry's libel was justified, it was true and was published for the public benefit. That was all. Without leaving the courtroom, the jury returned a verdict of not guilty, exculpating the Marquess.[32] His solicitor sent the witness statements and the shorthand notes of the trial to the Director of Public Prosecutions, who initiated proceedings against Wilde.[33]

Wilde was charged with conspiracy and gross indecency, an offence that had been created in 1885 as part of the Criminal Law Amendment Act, which was otherwise concerned with sexual offences against women. A new, broader category of sexual offence, gross indecency covered any sexual activity between men, and had a maximum sentence of two years, while sodomy had a minimum sentence of ten.[34] Wilde was tried with his accused co-conspirator Alfred Taylor, who was alleged to have procured young men, to whom Wilde would offer food, drink, clothing, gifts, and money in exchange for sex. The new prosecutor quoted Carson's cross-examination of Wilde from the libel trial, but Clarke now argued more successfully that the literature should not be used against the man—especially other people's literature—an argument with which the judge concurred in his instructions to the jury. Clarke also managed to expose several of the witnesses who testified against Wilde as professional blackmailers. The prosecution withdrew the conspiracy charges. One witness perjured himself. The trial ended in a hung jury.[35] The matter could have rested there, but the Solicitor General was determined to pursue the case because of rumours about the Prime Minister, Lord Rosebery, whose name had arisen incidentally in the libel trial. Letting Wilde off the hook might look like an official cover-up.[36] The Solicitor General himself, Sir Frank Lockwood, was the prosecutor in the third trial. Wilde was convicted of gross indecency, and given the maximum sentence of two years' imprisonment with hard labour.[37]

The trials bankrupted the forty-one-year-old author.[38] Public opinion turned sharply against him. After the libel trial, the *Echo* wrote sarcastically, 'He appears to have illustrated in his life the beauty and truthfulness of his teachings. He said, in cross-examination, that he considered there was no such thing as morality, and he seems to have harmonized his practice with his theory.'[39] Publishers stopped listing Wilde's books, *An Ideal Husband* was pulled from the stage, and *The Importance of Being Earnest* continued its run with Wilde's name removed from the advertising bills.[40] The biographer Richard Ellmann writes, 'It was as if he had never written any of those plays, dialogues, stories, and poems.'[41] Wilde wrote little after his conviction, with the notable exceptions of a long letter to Douglas called *De Profundis*, which was published in expurgated form after Wilde's death, and *The Ballad of Reading Gaol*, in which he meditates on his own incarceration while telling the story of a man sentenced to death for murder. This poem includes the lines that became Wilde's epitaph:

> And alien tears will fill for him
> > Pity's long-broken urn,
> For his mourners will be outcast men,
> > And outcasts always mourn.[42]

On his release, Wilde spent the remaining three years of his life in self-imposed exile on the Continent, and was buried in Paris. The law had never officially condemned his art, but it had condemned his life, which silenced him all the more effectively. Though *The Ballad of Reading Gaol* sold well in England,[43] Wilde wrote to his friend Robert Ross in August 1898, 'I don't think I shall ever really write again. Something is killed in me. I feel no desire to write. I am unconscious of power. Of course my first year in prison destroyed me body and soul. It could not be otherwise.'[44]

Notes

1. Oscar Wilde, 'The 1891 Preface to *The Picture of Dorian Gray*', in *The Picture of Dorian Gray: An Annotated, Uncensored Edition*, ed. Nicholas Frankel (Cambridge, MA: Belknap Press, 2011), p. 273 (emphasis original).
2. Oscar Wilde, 'Phrases and Philosophies for the Use of the Young', in *Complete Works of Oscar Wilde*, intro. Merlin Holland (Glasgow: HarperCollins, 2003), pp. 1244–45 (p. 1245).
3. James Eli Adams, 'Dandyism and Late Victorian Masculinity', in *Oscar Wilde in Context*, ed. Kerry Powell and Peter Raby (Cambridge: Cambridge University Press, 2013), pp. 220–29 (pp. 220–21).
4. Oscar Wilde, *The Picture of Dorian Gray* (1890), in *The Complete Works of Oscar Wilde*, III: '*The Picture of Dorian Gray*': *The 1890 and 1891 Texts*, ed. Joseph Bristow (2005), 1–164 (p. 118).

5. Nicholas Frankel, 'Textual Introduction', in *The Picture of Dorian Gray*, ed. Frankel, pp. 38–64 (pp. 40–42). See also Joseph Bristow, 'Introduction', in *The Complete Works of Oscar Wilde*, III, xi–lx (pp. xxxviii–xli).

6. Nicholas Frankel, 'General Introduction', in *The Picture of Dorian Gray*, ed. Frankel, pp. 1–37 (pp. 7–8). See also Merlin Holland, *The Real Trial of Oscar Wilde* (New York: Perennial, 2004), p. 63 note 113.

7. 'A Study in Puppydom', *St James's Gazette*, 24 June 1890, in Stuart Mason, *Oscar Wilde: Art and Morality: A Record of the Discussion Which Followed the Publication of 'Dorian Gray'*, rev. edn (London: Palmer, 1912), pp. 27–34 (pp. 28, 34).

8. Edward Thomas, *Daily Chronicle*, 30 June 1890, in Mason, pp. 65–69 (pp. 65–66).

9. 'Reviews and Magazines', *Scots Observer*, 5 July 1890, in Mason, pp. 75–82 (pp. 75–76).

10. Oscar Wilde, 'Mr Oscar Wilde Again', letter to editor, *St James's Gazette*, 27 June 1890, in Mason, pp. 39–44 (pp. 42, 43).

11. Oscar Wilde, 'Mr Wilde's Rejoinder', letter to editor, *Scots Observer*, 12 July 1890, in Mason, pp. 78–81 (p. 81).

12. Richard Ellmann, *Oscar Wilde* (London: Penguin, 1988), p. 304; Holland, p. 78 and note 131, p. 79.

13. Ellmann, pp. 304–5.

14. Holland, p. xx.

15. John Sholto Douglas, 9th Marquess of Queensberry, to Lord Alfred Douglas (1 April 1894), in Ellmann, p. 394.

16. Holland, pp. xiv, 26. See further pp. xviii–xix.

17. Sean Brady, *Masculinity and Male Homosexuality in Britain, 1861–1913* (Basingstoke: Palgrave Macmillan, 2005), pp. 10–12, 27, 96–98.

18. Brady, pp. 180–81.

19. Holland, pp. 286–91.

20. Holland, p. 85.

21. Wilde, *The Picture of Dorian Gray* (1890), p. 8.

22. Holland, p. 85.

23. Holland, p. 105.

24. Holland, pp. 81, 97, 99, 100.

25. Holland, p. 80.

26. Holland, p. 74.

27. Wilde, 'Phrases and Philosophies for the Use of the Young', p. 1244.

28. Holland, pp. 73, 74, 75.

29. Holland, pp. 70, 77.

30. Holland, pp. 81, 261.
31. Holland, p. 256. See further pp. 253–54, 277.
32. Holland, p. 281. See further pp. 280–83.
33. Ellmann, pp. 427–28.
34. Brady, pp. 91–93, 96–97.
35. H. Montgomery Hyde, *The Trials of Oscar Wilde* (New York: Dover, 1962), pp. 166–219.
36. Ellmann, pp. 423–24, 437.
37. Hyde, p. 272.
38. Ellmann, p. 431.
39. *Echo*, 5 April 1895, quoted in Hyde, p. 155.
40. Hyde, pp. 164–65.
41. Ellmann, p. 454.
42. Oscar Wilde, *The Ballad of Reading Gaol*, in *Complete Works of Oscar Wilde*, intro. Holland, pp. 883–99 (p. 896).
43. Ellmann, pp. 525–26.
44. Oscar Wilde to Robert Ross ([16] August 1898), in *The Complete Letters of Oscar Wilde*, ed. Merlin Holland and Rupert Hart-Davis (London: Fourth Estate, 2000), p. 1095.

10

The Well of Loneliness
Radclyffe Hall

Radclyffe Hall's *The Well of Loneliness*, first published in 1928, is a novel about a young girl named Stephen who gradually realizes that she is attracted to women. When her mother discovers her love for a married woman and casts her out, Stephen moves to London and then Paris, where she joins an expatriate community of lesbians and gay men. During the First World War she works in an all-women ambulance unit, and, for the first time, meets someone who returns her affection. She and her lover Mary try to build a life together after the war ends, but Stephen cannot bear to see Mary stigmatized because of their relationship, and drives her into the arms of a man. The novel ends with Stephen's plea, 'Acknowledge us, oh God, before the whole world. Give us also the right to our existence!'[1] In writing *The Well of Loneliness*, Hall dared to defend love between women and condemn those whose hatred made this love so perilous. The book fell victim to the prejudices it was attempting to challenge, and was treated as obscenity purely for its sympathetic depiction of lesbians. In the United Kingdom, the Home Secretary, Sir William Joynson-Hicks, personally mobilized the law against the book. It fared better in the United States, where the archaic Victorian test of obscenity was beginning to give way and where the civil liberties lawyer Morris Ernst took charge of the defence. The judgments that liberated *The*

Una Troubridge (left) and Radclyffe Hall (right) photographed at home in 1927.

Well of Loneliness in US courts stressed that there was 'not one word' of obscenity in the book. In the United Kingdom, the courts noted that there was 'not one word' condemning the 'vice' of lesbianism, and ruled the book obscene.

Radclyffe Hall, known to her friends as John, was a popular and acclaimed author, winner of the James Tait Black and the Femina Vie Heureuse prizes for her novel *Adam's Breed* (1926). She lived with Una Troubridge, who had, in a minor scandal, left her husband for Hall. Hall recognized that social hostility and the lack of civil and religious recognition meant that few lesbians felt able to live openly as she did. She hoped to change social attitudes by writing *The Well of Loneliness*. A devout Christian, she described the novel as 'a cry for better understanding, for a wider and more merciful toleration, for acceptance of these people as God has made them'.[2] 'So far as I know,' she wrote, 'nothing of the kind has ever been attempted before in fiction.'[3]

Publishers were not eager to help Hall make the attempt. In 1898 a bookseller named Bedborough had been prosecuted for selling Havelock Ellis's *Sexual Inversion*, an early study of sexual identity that Hall drew on when writing *The Well of Loneliness*.[4] By 1928, *Sexual Inversion* circulated freely, but publishers were wary of dealing with the same subject in fiction. The publishers Cassell, Heinemann, and Secker all turned Hall's novel down. Jonathan Cape recognized the danger but also the commercial possibilities. He offered a large advance, with a catch: if there were legal proceedings against the book, he and Hall would share any costs.[5] But Cape's marketing strategy reassured Hall. With a plain cover and high price, *The Well of Loneliness* would be a highbrow, serious novel, not a cheap, mass-market book designed to appeal to the prurient.[6] Hall's literary prizes were listed opposite the title page, and a preface by Havelock Ellis endorsed the book's literary merits and 'psychological and sociological significance', it being 'the first English novel which presents, in a completely faithful and uncompromising form, various aspects of sexual inversion as it exists among us today'. Perhaps nervous of Ellis's matter-of-fact language, Cape edited the preface to remove any explicit reference to 'inversion'.[7] In the printed first edition, Ellis's preface refers obliquely to 'one particular aspect of sexual life', but readers would have to read the entire novel to find out what that was.[8]

The first readers of *The Well of Loneliness* received it as a ground-breaking novel in which a lesbian discovers her sexual identity and defends her right to love. As such, the book has been of great importance to later generations of lesbian readers. But Stephen Gordon's identity does not perfectly correspond to the modern understanding of gender and sexuality. Hall uses the historical term 'invert', which she had discovered in the work of Ellis and other sexologists, a concept that contains several aspects of identity that are now recognized as distinct, such as sexual orientation and gender presentation. In Ellis's work, 'actively inverted' women are exclusively attracted to women and have a 'more or less distinct trace of masculinity', which they might express by dressing, speaking, and behaving in a masculine way.[9] Stephen Gordon is an invert. She is attracted only to women and is repulsed by the thought of having romantic relationships with men. She has a muscular, masculine physique, and excels at riding and hunting. She has the fashion sense of a dapper squire. She values honour above all virtues, and her desire to protect women finds its full expression in her last act of self-sacrifice for her lover. In short, she is Hall's ideal country gentleman. Her masculinity and her inversion are inextricable. As our understanding of gender and sexuality has developed since Hall's time, readers have used new terms to describe Stephen: butch, transsexual, transgender.[10] Though the novel's importance as a landmark work of lesbian and transgender writing should not be understated, the historical term 'invert' does not have the same meaning as 'lesbian' or 'transgender man'. The novel emphasizes Stephen's masculinity, while using feminine pronouns to refer to her. When Hall offered the book to publishers, she presented it as the 'life of a woman who is a born invert', and both terms—woman and invert—are used to describe Stephen throughout.[11] Both as a woman who loves women and as an invert, Stephen was a pioneer.

Early reviews praised the book for its serious treatment of a difficult subject. Some reviewers faulted the style, finding the prose clumsy, the structure baggy, and the tone unrelentingly tragic.[12] Most agreed with Hall that inversion should not be a taboo topic, given that it was a fact of life. *The Well of Loneliness* was an unspectacular success.[13] The novel's fortunes changed when a copy reached James Douglas of the *Sunday Express*, a notoriously reactionary columnist famous for manufacturing outrage against literature. Fulminating against D. H. Lawrence's *The Rainbow* in 1915, in remarks that were read in court when the book was declared obscene, he called for the 'sanitary inspector of literature' to quarantine diseased art.[14] Anti-feminist and homophobic, convinced that the artistic output of his age was expediting the fall of Christian civilization, Douglas found in Hall's novel the epitome of all that he hated and feared. Inversion was an 'utterly inadmissible' subject for a novel, he wrote, 'because the novel is read by people of all ages'. He was particularly critical of the idea that inverts were born inverted, because this conflicted with 'the Christian doctrine of free-will'. Inverts, he insisted, were 'damned because they choose to be damned, not because they are doomed from the beginning'. Descending into the register for which he was known, Douglas described inversion as 'pestilence', 'plague', 'putrefaction', 'contagion', and 'leprosy'. Bringing this list of horrors to a boldface climax, he declared: '*I would rather give a healthy boy or a healthy girl a phial of prussic acid than this novel. Poison kills the body, but moral poison kills the soul*'.[15] (The writer Aldous Huxley responded with a 'sporting offer'. He would provide the healthy boy, phial of acid, and a copy of *The Well of Loneliness*. If Douglas kept his word, Huxley would pay for his defence and a monument to his memory after he was hanged.[16]) Douglas concluded by appealing to the Home Secretary to set the law in motion.[17]

Every age has its Douglases demanding that the government protect the children from a flow of literary filth. In 1928 the Home Secretary, William Joynson-Hicks (nicknamed Jix) was ready to listen.[18] Censorship was one of his hobby-horses. He was in favour of using and extending his already considerable powers, but he could act against the novel only if someone brought it to his notice.[19] Douglas, for all his sound and fury, had not made a formal complaint against the book. To Hall's astonishment, Jonathan Cape gave Joynson-Hicks his opening. He sent Joynson-Hicks a copy of the novel with a selection of glowing reviews, and promised to withdraw the book from circulation if the Home Secretary said it was in the best interests of the public to do so. Joynson-Hicks moved swiftly, forwarding the book to Sir George Stephenson, deputy of the Director of Public Prosecutions (DPP), asking for his opinion on whether a jury would convict Cape of obscene libel.[20] This question served two purposes: it established whether a criminal prosecution might be successful, and also whether the book could meet the standard for obscenity under the Obscene Publications Act 1857, which allowed magistrates to order the seizure and destruction of books.[21] Stephenson affirmed that in his view the book would 'corrupt the minds of young persons if it fell into their hands' and therefore met the test for obscenity. There would be a reasonable prospect of conviction in a criminal prosecution, and Chief Magistrate Sir Chartres Biron, who had read the book, had confirmed that he was willing to proceed against it.[22] Joynson-Hicks informed Cape that the book was 'inherently obscene' and could be suppressed by criminal proceedings, and asked him to withdraw it.[23] The Home Secretary's letter did not contain an order to cease production, nor did it constitute a ban, but the message was clear. If Cape did not withdraw the novel, he would be prosecuted. Cape telegraphed his printers to tell them to cease production immediately, and announced in *The Times* that the firm had discontinued publication of *The Well of Loneliness* in accordance with the wishes of the Home Office.[24]

Douglas was triumphant. Writers were alarmed and wrote letters protesting against government censorship of unpopular topics.[25] The writers' protests, Douglas's editorials, and the whiff of scandal increased demand for the book, which Cape exploited. The novel was not banned, so booksellers could sell their remaining stock, and production could continue under a different imprint. When Cape ordered his printers to cease production, he also ordered them to make moulds of the type, which he sent to Pegasus Press in Paris, to whom he had leased the rights to the book. With the moulds, Pegasus was able to produce editions identical to Cape's within a month. Pegasus supplied Cape's unfilled orders by post, sold editions in Paris to British tourists, and reached new customers in Britain via Leopold Hill, a London bookseller who acted as the firm's agent. Business was brisk.[26] When news of the book's continued free circulation reached Joynson-Hicks, he instructed the Post Office to intercept mail sent to Pegasus Press, and ordered Customs to seize all copies sent as goods or found in passengers' baggage. But the Board of Customs and Excise, after reading the book, decided it was neither indecent nor obscene. With the backing of Winston Churchill, then Chancellor of the Exchequer, they released the copies they had seized. The Home

Office and DPP arranged for the books released by Customs, and some of the intercepted mail, to be allowed to reach their destinations. When copies of the books reached the offices of Cape and Hill, the police were ready.[27]

On 19 October 1928 Chief Inspector John Protheroe notified Sir Chartres Biron at Bow Street Magistrates' Court that he had reason to believe that copies of an obscene book, *The Well of Loneliness*, were being kept at the premises of Leopold Hill of Great Russell Street and Jonathan Cape of Bedford Square. Biron issued warrants under the Obscene Publications Act 1857, and on the same day Protheroe seized 247 copies from Hill and six copies from Cape.[28] Cape and Hill were summonsed to appear at Bow Street to show cause why the books should not be destroyed. The stakes in the proceedings were relatively low: at risk were fewer than three hundred copies of *The Well of Loneliness* and legal costs, for which Hall was partly liable because of her contract with Cape. But the political and cultural significance of the proceedings was apparent to all, and both sides prepared with the diligence appropriate to a major trial. The solicitor Harold Rubinstein asked 160 expert witnesses to testify to the book's decency and merit.[29] Many were reluctant to support a novel that openly discussed love between women, and refused to help, pleading 'the weak heart of a father, or a cousin who is about to have twins', as Virginia Woolf put it.[30] In contrast, the National Union of Railwaymen and the South Wales Miners' Federation sent supportive testimonials to Hall.[31] On 9 November, the hearing at Bow Street Magistrates' Court was packed with interested parties: a group of spectators, mostly women; forty expert witnesses, including the Woolfs and E. M. Forster; the author herself, a striking figure in a riding hat and motor-coat; and a silent observer, the DPP, Sir Archibald Bodkin.[32]

Cape's counsel, Norman Birkett, attempted to argue that the book dealt not with 'perversion', by which he meant sexual relations between women, but only with 'inversion', which he characterized as a disability. The magistrate was unconvinced, and Hall was horrified.[33] She challenged Birkett in recess and made him retract his misleading account.[34] Birkett's plan to use expert witnesses to demonstrate that the book was not obscene was also flawed. The Chief Magistrate disallowed all the expert testimony because the question of literary merit, and the witnesses' opinion of the book, were irrelevant under the court's test of obscenity.[35] Biron reminded Birkett of the legal test of obscenity, which was established in 1868, in the case of R v. Hicklin (see Chapter 8): 'whether the tendency of the matter charged as obscenity is to deprave and corrupt those whose minds are open to such immoral influences, and into whose hands a publication of this sort may fall'.[36] The Hicklin test did not take into account the book's literary merits or the author's intention. The only question that mattered was 'whether its tendency might be to corrupt'. And that was not a question for witnesses to answer; it was a question for the court, in the form of Sir Chartres Biron.[37]

The magistrate delivered his decision a week later. He now argued that the novel's literary merits made it *more* likely to deprave and corrupt. In the spirit of Douglas, he declared 'the more palatable the poison the more insidious'.[38] Hall's novel was obscene because 'there is not a single word from beginning to end of this book which suggests that anyone with these horrible tendencies is in the least degree blameworthy'. If the book had made inversion seem like an evil that the characters were struggling to overcome, then, Biron said, 'it might have a strong moral influence'. Instead, 'the actual physical acts of these women indulging in unnatural vices are described in the most alluring terms' and were shown to produce 'rest, contentment, and pleasure'.[39]

The Well of Loneliness does not blame its characters for their orientation, or pretend that gay sex is unsatisfying. Though Hall presents the invert's lot as a difficult one, she gives Stephen bold speeches in defence of her right to love, such as her defiant declaration that her love was 'good, good, *good*',[40] to which Biron took particular exception.[41] Had Stephen tried to resist her sexuality, or been treated less sympathetically, the book might have circulated freely. Compton Mackenzie's *Extraordinary Women,* a comic novel dealing with lesbianism, was published at the same time as *The Well of Loneliness*, but the DPP decided not to act against it because it painted a 'most distasteful and detestable picture' of lesbians and their 'degraded condition'.[42] In contrast, Biron decided that *The Well of Loneliness* was obscene.[43]

Hall had not been invited to address the court. According to the Hicklin test, the author's intent was irrelevant, and under the Obscene

Publications Act the author was not an interested party. She had to listen in silence as her work was traduced and lesbians characterized as perverts. One of Biron's jibes, however, provoked her to interrupt. Reflecting on Stephen's work in the all-women ambulance unit, Biron described the women as 'addicted' to the 'vice' of lesbianism. 'I protest,' Hall shouted. Biron warned her, 'If you cannot behave yourself in Court I shall have to have you removed.' Hall responded, 'It is a shame', and was silent.[44] Thirty years later, Norman Birkett, now a member of the House of Lords, remembered this moment in a speech supporting reform of the Obscene Publications Act. Hall 'had no voice whatever', he recalled, which was emblematic of the wider silencing of authors and expert witnesses in obscenity cases.[45] In 1959 Birkett had the satisfaction of seeing the 1857 Act repealed and replaced with a new Obscene Publications Act that created a public good defence and ensured the admission of expert testimony. In 1960 this public good defence would be used to liberate D. H. Lawrence's *Lady Chatterley's Lover* (see Chapter 12). In 1928 Cape and Hill had no recourse except appeal.

On 14 December 1928 the County of London Sessions heard their case. The government was represented by the Attorney General, Sir Thomas Inskip. He described *The Well of Loneliness* as 'propaganda for the practice which has long been known as Lesbianism'.[46] There was 'not a word from start to finish' to say that lesbians were 'a pest to society'.[47] While Inskip spoke, the bench of magistrates passed around copies of the novel.[48] This was their first and last reading of the book. Inskip directed their attention to particular passages—not passages containing sexually explicit descriptions or language, of which there were none—but passages that he claimed would inspire libidinous thoughts in that peculiar individual described in the Hicklin test, the person whose mind is open to immoral influences. At one point, Stephen's lover asks her, 'Could you marry me?'[49] Inskip invited the bench to imagine a 'young person' reading that sentence: 'His mind revolves around libidinous thoughts and it depraves and corrupts him as he conjures up the picture which the writer of this book intends.'[50] The single, discreet line that indicates when Stephen and Mary have sex—'and that night they were not divided'[51]—would also 'conjure' pictures.[52] J. B. Melville, representing Hill, attempted to cast doubt on

the reality of this imaginary libidinous young person and to convey a
more accurate impression of the book.[53] One magistrate, the chairman
of the court, interrupted to ask for the meaning of the 'gift' that Mary
gives to Stephen. Melville and the chairman engaged in a delicate
circumlocution of the word 'sex'.

CHAIRMAN	What is the gift?
MELVILLE	I suppose her love.
CHAIRMAN	Not much more than that? I want to see what you are really going to say. You know what my question means without me putting it into words.
MELVILLE	It means what your Lordship is suggesting to me undoubtedly.
CHAIRMAN	I only want to know. You are being quite frank.[54]

Melville argued that *The Well of Loneliness* was not 'pornographic',[55]
but Inskip replied that the key word in the 1857 Act was 'obscene', not
'pornographic'.[56] After a five-minute discussion, the court affirmed
Biron's decision. *The Well of Loneliness* was 'prejudicial to the morals of
the community', 'disgusting', and 'obscene'.[57] Scotland Yard kept three
of the seized copies for future reference, and destroyed the rest.[58]

Hall had to cover her share of the legal fees, and a deal with the
American publisher Knopf fell through.[59] But news of the suppression of *The Well of Loneliness* reached an enterprising new publishing
house in New York that was in search of a bestseller and prepared to
fight the censors. The firm's founders, Pascal Covici and Donald Friede,
had been arrested before, Covici for publishing Ben Hecht's *Fantazius
Mallare* and Friede for selling a copy of Theodore Dreiser's *An American
Tragedy* to an officer of the Boston Vice and Narcotics squad. Covici,
Friede secured the rights to Hall's novel by giving Cape 20 per cent
royalties and a ten thousand dollar advance, the advance to be paid even
if they were prevented from publishing, and they retained Morris Ernst,
who would later go on to defend the Random House edition of James
Joyce's *Ulysses* (see Chapter 11). Ernst would be paid twenty-five cents
for every copy they sold. Following Ernst's plan, the publishers steered
The Well of Loneliness through a series of legal proceedings, moving from
the lowest courts to a federal customs court, eventually securing the
book's free circulation in the United States.[60]

Their edition incorporated Havelock Ellis's preface, so that if a copy were seized, the preface would have to be submitted in evidence, and they moved production and distribution to New Jersey, so that legal proceedings in New York could not impede sales. On Ernst's advice, when the first copies were printed, Friede contacted John S. Sumner of the New York Society for the Suppression of Vice, successor of Anthony Comstock (see Chapter 6), to inform him that they 'would be publishing in a few days and wanted to make sure of the fact that he would not go around arresting innocent clerks in the book stores'.[61] The publishers took full responsibility for publishing the book, and would co-operate with any prosecution.[62] Sumner bought a copy of the novel from Friede, who was arrested and charged with selling an obscene book.[63]

'With my arrest,' Friede recalled, 'one of the most effective legal campaigns I have ever witnessed began to function.'[64] Ernst developed arguments and strategies that had failed in England but were gaining traction in US case law. Foremost was the rejection of the Hicklin test, which had become part of US law in the nineteenth century. The English test, Ernst argued, was 'unfair, unreasonable and unsound', and increasingly alien to US jurisprudence, which rejected the role of a censor of literature.[65] He also argued that the novel's high price, length, lack of illustrations, acquisition by reputable booksellers, and critical reputation were relevant.[66] He compared *The Well of Loneliness* to a nineteenth-century French novel recently liberated by the US courts, Théophile Gautier's *Mademoiselle de Maupin*. Gautier's novel describes a love triangle between a man, a woman, and Maupin, who has a fluid gender identity and sexuality. According to Ernst, Hall's novel was restrained, serious, and inexplicit, where Gautier's was frivolous, pagan, and indecent. If the highest court in the state had vindicated even *Mademoiselle de Maupin*, Ernst argued, surely *The Well of Loneliness* could not be suppressed? 'The sole possible objection' was to Hall's theme, which raised a significant question for the court: '*Will the law condemn a book otherwise unobjectionable because of its theme?*'[67]

Ernst's arguments met one minor obstacle in the form of a magistrate who still believed in the Hicklin test. Hyman Bushel argued that 'those whose minds are open to such immoral influences' meant 'those who are subject to perverted influences, and in whom that abnormality may be called into activity'.[68] ('Justice Cockburn Rides Again,' Ernst noted, invoking the judge who first formulated the Hicklin test.[69]) Bushel referred the case for trial at the New York Court of Special Sessions, and from that point on the fortunes of *The Well of Loneliness* turned. The court issued a unanimous opinion on 19 April 1929. (Friede had to rush back from Boston, where he had been found guilty in the *American Tragedy* case the previous day.[70]) The court noted, briefly, that *The Well of Loneliness* 'deals with a delicate social problem which in itself cannot be said is in violation of the law unless it is written in such a manner as to make it obscene'. The book was not obscene.[71] For Ernst, the decision established that 'no theme, as a theme,' could be the pretext for censorship of literature.[72]

Ernst oversaw one last legal proceeding to secure the book's free circulation throughout the United States. A copy was posted to Ernst from Paris, and seized by US Customs on 26 December 1928. Ernst sought a review of the customs decision in the US Customs Court, where Meyer Stein, representing Ernst, pointed out that a customs decision against the book would be meaningless, given that another court had just ruled it could be sold freely in New York.[73] On 26 July 1929 the court issued a written decision: 'We confess that we have not found one word, phrase, sentence or paragraph' that could be held obscene and, though the theme was 'unusual', it was handled in 'faultless literary style'. The book was released.[74]

Under two related but diverging legal systems, *The Well of Loneliness* had been declared obscene and not obscene. Ultimately censorship brought Hall success. By the end of 1929, Covici, Friede had sold over one hundred thousand copies, and Hall received a royalty cheque for sixty-four thousand dollars.[75] *The Well of Loneliness* became the iconic lesbian novel of the period, and inspired many writers, particularly in the United States, to write lesbian fiction, though subject to the chilling effect caused by continued obscenity proceedings against literature.[76] Ernst would successfully defend *Ulysses* in 1933. In the United Kingdom, in the aftermath of the Hall case, obscenity law was used to suppress *Sleeveless Errand* (1929) by Norah James, *Boy* (1931) by James Hanley, and *Bessie Cotter* (1935) by Wallace Smith. In 1932 Count Geoffrey Wladislas Vaile Potocki de Montalk was imprisoned for 'publishing' an obscene libel, a short collection of parodies entitled

Here Lies John Penis.[77] He had only handed the manuscript to a printer, but this was publication enough. The prosecution of Montalk led to future cases in which authors were indicted for obscene libel alongside their books' publishers.[78] Such proceedings against literature exerted a chilling effect that discouraged writers and publishers from representing gay love. *The Well of Loneliness* was not republished until 1949, and even then the Public Morality Council, a vigilance society, attempted to suppress it.[79] E. M. Forster, who had tried to defend Hall, refrained from publishing his own novel about gay men, entitled *Maurice*. Finished in 1914, and dedicated to 'a Happier Year', *Maurice* would not be published until 1971, after Forster's death.[80]

Notes

1. Radclyffe Hall, *The Well of Loneliness* (London: Cape, 1928), p. 512.
2. Radclyffe Hall to Havelock Ellis (2 December 1928), quoted in Elizabeth English, *Lesbian Modernism: Censorship, Sexuality and Genre Fiction* (Edinburgh: Edinburgh University Press, 2015), p. 3.
3. Radclyffe Hall to Newman Flower (17 April 1928), quoted in Michael Baker, *Our Three Selves: The Life of Radclyffe Hall* (London: Hamish Hamilton, 1985), p. 202.
4. Geoffrey Robertson, *Obscenity: An Account of Censorship Laws and their Enforcement in England and Wales* (London: Weidenfeld & Nicolson, 1979), p. 32; Norman St John-Stevas, *Obscenity and the Law* (London: Secker & Warburg, 1956), pp. 83–85.
5. Baker, pp. 202–5; Diana Souhami, *The Trials of Radclyffe Hall* (London: Weidenfeld & Nicolson, 1998), p. 168.
6. Michael S. Howard, *Jonathan Cape, Publisher: Herbert Jonathan Cape, G. Wren Howard* (London: Cape, 1971), p. 103.
7. Baker, p. 205.
8. Havelock Ellis, 'Commentary', in Hall, *The Well of Loneliness*, p. 7.
9. Havelock Ellis, *Studies in the Psychology of Sex* (Philadelphia: Davis), II: *Sexual Inversion*, 2nd edn (1901), 133–34, 140–43 [HathiTrust e-book].
10. Laura Green, 'Hall of Mirrors: Radclyffe Hall's *The Well of Loneliness* and Modernist Fictions of Identity', *Twentieth Century Literature*, 49.3 (2003), 277–97 (p. 281). See also [Jack Halberstam as] Judith Halberstam, '"A Writer of Misfits": "John" Radclyffe Hall and the Discourse of Inversion', in *Palatable Poison: Critical Perspectives on 'The Well of Loneliness'*, ed. Laura Doan and Jay Prosser (New York: Columbia University Press,

2001), pp. 145–61; Jay Prosser, '"Some Primitive Thing Conceived in a Turbulent Age of Transition": The Transsexual Emerging from *The Well*', in *Palatable Poison*, pp. 129–44.

11. Radclyffe Hall to Newman Flower (17 April 1928), quoted in Baker, p. 202.

12. 'A Selection of Early Reviews', in *Palatable Poison*, pp. 50–73.

13. Laura Doan and Jay Prosser, 'Introduction: Critical Perspectives Past and Present', in *Palatable Poison*, pp. 1–31 (pp. 4–5); Howard, p. 103; Souhami, pp. 173–75.

14. James Douglas, 'The Rainbow', *Star*, 22 October 1915, p. 4, quoted in David Bradshaw, 'James Douglas: The Sanitary Inspector of Literature', in *Prudes on the Prowl: Fiction and Obscenity in England, 1850 to the Present Day*, ed. Bradshaw and Rachel Potter (Oxford: Oxford University Press, 2013), pp. 90–110 (p. 95).

15. James Douglas, 'A Book that Must Be Suppressed', *Sunday Express*, 19 August 1928, p. 10, in *Palatable Poison*, pp. 36–38 (emphasis original).

16. Aldous Huxley, 'In Praise of Intolerance', *Vanity Fair*, 31 (February 1929), quoted in Bradshaw, p. 103.

17. Douglas, 'A Book that Must Be Suppressed', p. 10.

18. F. M. L. Thompson, 'Hicks, William Joynson-, first Viscount Brentford (1865–1932)', in *Oxford Dictionary of National Biography* (Oxford: Oxford University Press, 2004; online edn 2010), http://www.oxforddnb.com/view/article/33858, accessed 28 December 2016.

19. Viscount Brentford [William Joynson-Hicks], *Do We Need a Censor?*, Criterion Miscellany, 6 (London: Faber & Faber, 1929) [Harvard e-book].

20. Souhami, pp. 178–80.

21. Colin Manchester, 'Lord Campbell's Act: England's First Obscenity Statute', *Journal of Legal History*, 9.2 (1988), 223–41 (p. 230).

22. Sir George Stephenson to Sir William Joynson-Hicks (20 August 1928), quoted in Souhami, pp. 180–81.

23. Sir William Joynson-Hicks to Sir George Stephenson (21 August 1928), quoted in Souhami, p. 181.

24. Baker, p. 227; Souhami, p. 181.

25. Rachel Potter, 'Censorship and Sovereignty (1916–1929)', in *Prudes on the Prowl*, pp. 71–89 (pp. 84–85).

26. Howard, pp. 106–7.

27. Souhami, pp. 189–91; Alan Travis, *Bound and Gagged: A Secret History of Obscenity in Britain* (London: Profile Books, 2000), pp. 56–61.

28. Transcript of *DPP v Cape* (County of London Sessions, 14 Dec 1928) 31–32, in Ottawa, Library and Archives Canada (LAC), R3608-0-3-E,

MG30-D237, imgs. 1007–83, http://heritage.canadiana.ca/view/oocihm.lac_reel_h1198, accessed 26 December 2016.

29. Baker, pp. 233–34; Howard, pp. 107–8; Souhami, p. 194.

30. Virginia Woolf to Quentin Bell (1 November 1928), in *The Letters of Virginia Woolf*, ed. Nigel Nicolson and Joanne Trautmann, 6 vols (London: Hogarth Press, 1975–80), III, ed. Nicolson and Trautmann (1977), 554–56 (p. 555). See also Baker, pp. 234–37; Howard, pp. 107–8.

31. Baker, p. 237.

32. Baker, pp. 239–40; Howard, p. 108.

33. 'Alleged Obscene Novel', *The Times*, 10 November 1928, p. 9. See also Baker, pp. 240–41; Vera Brittain, *Radclyffe Hall: A Case of Obscenity?* (South Brunswick: Barnes, 1969), p. 89; Robertson, pp. 35–36.

34. Baker, p. 241; Souhami, pp. 207–8.

35. St John-Stevas, pp. 101–2. See also Souhami, pp. 205–6.

36. *R v Hicklin* (1868) LR 3 QB 360, 371. See also Brittain, p. 89; Souhami, p. 205; St John-Stevas, p. 101.

37. Brittain, p. 91. See also 'Alleged Obscene Novel', p. 9; Brittain, pp. 89–92; Souhami, pp. 205–6; St John-Stevas, pp. 101–2.

38. Transcript of *DPP v Cape* (Bow Street Police Court, 16 November 1928) 5, in LAC, R3608-0-3-E, MG30-D237, imgs. 987–1004, http://heritage.canadiana.ca/view/oocihm.lac_reel_h1198, accessed 26 December 2016.

39. Transcript of *DPP v Cape* (Bow Street Police Court, 16 November 1928) 6–7.

40. Hall, *The Well of Loneliness*, p. 239.

41. Transcript of *DPP v Cape* (Bow Street Police Court, 16 November 1928) 9.

42. London, The National Archives, HO 45/15727, quoted in English, pp. 7–8.

43. Transcript of *DPP v Cape* (Bow Street Police Court, 16 November 1928) 16.

44. Transcript of *DPP v Cape* (Bow Street Police Court, 16 November 1928) 10. See also 'Novel Condemned as Obscene', *The Times*, 17 November 1928, p. 5.

45. HL Deb 2 June 1959, vol 216, col 499.

46. Transcript of *DPP v Cape* (County of London Sessions, 14 Dec 1928) 30.

47. Transcript of *DPP v Cape* (County of London Sessions, 14 Dec 1928) 71.

48. Transcript of *DPP v Cape* (County of London Sessions, 14 Dec 1928) 13.

49. Hall, *The Well of Loneliness*, p. 177.

50. Transcript of *DPP v Cape* (County of London Sessions, 14 Dec 1928) 14–15.

51. Hall, *The Well of Loneliness*, p. 365.

52. Transcript of *DPP v Cape* (County of London Sessions, 14 Dec 1928) 21.

53. Transcript of *DPP v Cape* (County of London Sessions, 14 Dec 1928) 41.

54. Transcript of *DPP v Cape* (County of London Sessions, 14 Dec 1928) 61.

55. Transcript of *DPP v Cape* (County of London Sessions, 14 Dec 1928) 34, 37–38, 42.

56. Transcript of *DPP v Cape* (County of London Sessions, 14 Dec 1928) 70.

57. Transcript of *DPP v Cape* (County of London Sessions, 14 Dec 1928) 73–74.

58. Travis, p. 89.

59. Souhami, pp. 188–89, 213.

60. Donald Friede, *The Mechanical Angel: His Adventures and Enterprises in the Glittering 1920's* (New York: Knopf, 1948), pp. 81, 91, 93, 137.

61. Friede, p. 139. See further pp. 93–94, 138–39.

62. Friede, p. 139.

63. Leslie A. Taylor, "'I Made Up my Mind to Get It': The American Trial of *The Well of Loneliness*, New York City, 1928–1929', *Journal of the History of Sexuality*, 10.2 (2001), 250–86 (p. 270).

64. Friede, p. 139.

65. Brief for the Defendants at 4, People v. Friede, 133 Misc. 611 (N.Y. Magis. Ct. 1929), in LAC, R3608-0-3-E, MG30-D237, imgs. 1227–69, http://heritage.canadiana.ca/view/oocihm.lac_reel_h1198, accessed 26 December 2016. See further pp. 3–8.

66. Brief for the Defendants at 19–32.

67. Brief for the Defendants at 9 (emphasis original). See further pp. 17–18.

68. *Friede*, 133 Misc. at 614 (N.Y. Magis. Ct. 1929).

69. Morris Ernst and Alan U. Schwartz, *Censorship: The Search for the Obscene* (New York: Macmillan, 1964), p. 76.

70. Friede, p. 148.

71. People v. Friede, slip op. at 2 (N.Y. Ct. Spec. Sess. April 19, 1929), in LAC, R3608-0-3-E, MG30-D237, img. 1107, http://heritage.canadiana.ca/view/oocihm.lac_reel_h1198, accessed 2 December 2016.

72. Ernst and Schwartz, p. 79.

73. P. Sheehy, Acting Deputy Collector, Customs Bureau, New York Post Office, to Morris Ernst (26 December 1928), in LAC, R3608-0-3-E, MG30-D237, img. 1087, http://heritage.canadiana.ca/view/oocihm.lac_reel_h1198, accessed 26 December 2016; Stenographic Minutes at 2, 4–5, Ernst v. United States, No. 336438-G (Cust. Ct. May 13, 1929), in LAC, R3608-0-3-E, MG30-D237, imgs. 1111–19, http://heritage.canadiana.ca/view/oocihm.lac_reel_h1198, accessed 26 December 2016.

74. Ernst v. United States, No. 336438-G-10410-29, slip op. at 2 (Cust. Ct. July 26, 1929), in LAC, R3608-0-3-E, MG30-D237, imgs. 1161–63, http://heritage.canadiana.ca/view/oocihm.lac_reel_h1198, accessed 26 December 2016.

75. Edward de Grazia, *Girls Lean Back Everywhere: The Law of Obscenity and the Assault on Genius* (New York: Vintage, 1993), p. 202.

76. Taylor, pp. 284–85.

77. Robertson, pp. 36–37.

78. Colin Manchester, 'A History of the Crime of Obscene Libel', *Journal of Legal History*, 12.1 (1991), 36–57 (p. 46).

79. David Bradshaw, 'American Beastliness, the Great Purge and its After-math (1946–1959)', in *Prudes on the Prowl*, pp. 138–58 (pp. 142–44).

80. E. M. Forster, *Maurice*, ed. P. N. Furbank (London: Penguin, 2005), p. 2.

11

Ulysses
James Joyce

Now that *Ulysses* is the stuff of 'great books' lists, advanced literature seminars, and Bloomsday re-enactments, it is hard to appreciate how politically charged its publication was. In 1926 *Ulysses* was so far from being enshrined in the ivory tower that the literary critic F. R. Leavis, just embarking on his career, could not teach the book in his undergraduate course at Cambridge University. In fact, he couldn't acquire the book at all. When he petitioned the Home Office to allow him a copy, the Assistant Under Secretary of State observed that he 'must be a dangerous crank' to want to teach it in a 'mixed class of undergraduates'—'mixed' meaning that there were women in the class.[1] Police investigated Leavis, and the Director of Public Prosecutions, Sir Archibald Bodkin, requested assurances from the vice chancellor of the university that the book would not be taught, threatening prosecution if it were circulated. The vice chancellor acquiesced. Leavis lectured on an excerpt of Joyce's writing anyway, but believed that he had fallen into 'disfavour' among his more conventional colleagues.[2]

Ulysses could not have existed without a radical culture not only of artists and editors, but also of anarchists, suffragists, and sex educators. Against this culture, a new generation of moral reformers was holding the line, including John S. Sumner, who had succeeded Anthony Comstock as secretary of the New York Society for the Suppression of Vice (NYSSV) (see Chapter 6).[3] James Joyce provoked the moral reformers by shedding

James Joyce (left) meets with *Ulysses* publisher Sylvia Beach (centre) and Adrienne Monnier (right) at Beach's bookshop Shakespeare and Company in 1938.

light on a sexual reality, sometimes sordid, that they attempted to keep in the dark. He was the standard-bearer the radicals needed: an artist whose writing became more offensive the more that censors tried to tame it.

Joyce's long battle with censorship began when publishers and printers in the United Kingdom baulked at his earlier works *Dubliners* and *A Portrait of the Artist as a Young Man*. Publishers, printers, and booksellers were all legally responsible for bringing books to the public. Each could be prosecuted under English common law for the offence of obscene libel. Each, therefore, might refuse a book on the grounds that it might be prosecuted. In the early twentieth century, the spectre of Henry Vizetelly, convicted in 1888 and 1889 for publishing English translations of Émile Zola, still haunted the print industry, and Joyce imagined he might become the Irish Zola (see Chapter 8).[4] Neither of Joyce's early works was as bold as *Ulysses* would become, but they portrayed the seedy side of life in Ireland, the home Joyce left for Continental Europe. A story about a 'gallant' mooching money off a woman he has picked up, a visit to a prostitute in the red-light district, mild vulgarity ('bloody', 'fart', 'ballocks'), a description of a woman's thighs, Dublin pubs appearing under their real names, and slights against Victoria and Edward VII were sticking points.[5]

Joyce's early difficulty publishing his work established two patterns that would hold throughout his career: his reluctance to expurgate, and his reliance on sympathetic patrons, many of them women, who put themselves at risk for him. First submitted for publication in 1905, *Dubliners* did not circulate until 1914. Two publishers in succession accepted the manuscript, made escalating demands for expurgation, and finally backed out after a prolonged tug-of-war with the author. In the second case, the printer destroyed the sheets rather than sell them to Joyce to publish himself.[6] The author pilloried the publisher and the printer in a poem entitled 'Gas from a Burner', of which the following lines are a sample:

Who was it said: Resist not evil?
I'll burn that book, so help me devil.
I'll sing a psalm as I watch it burn
And the ashes I'll keep in a one-handled urn.
I'll penance do with farts and groans
Kneeling upon my marrowbones.[7]

A Portrait emerged intact in the United Kingdom only because the editor Harriet Shaw Weaver, one of Joyce's patrons, who had battled printers' censorship to publish a version in her magazine the *Egoist*, undertook to publish the novel herself. When over seven different printers refused the job or attempted to make revisions, she helped arrange its publication in New York, then imported the sheets for her own edition.[8]

Portions of *Ulysses* began to appear in the United States in 1918 thanks to Margaret Anderson and Jane Heap, the editors of the *Little Review*, an avant-garde literary magazine with anarchist roots. The editors were desperate to publish the best modern literature, and *Ulysses* was exactly what they were searching for: 'This is the most beautiful thing we'll ever have,' Anderson said. 'We'll print it if it's the last effort of our lives.'[9]

This 'beautiful thing' is a novel with little plot and immense scope: it centres on two characters, an ad canvasser named Leopold Bloom and a young writer named Stephen Dedalus, whose paths intersect over the course of one day: 16 June 1904. Bloom shops, eats, drinks, attends a funeral, does some work, ogles women, endures ridicule and anti-Semitic abuse, and tries not to bump into the man he knows is going to have sex with his wife. Dedalus teaches a class, collects his pay, does a favour for his employer, and talks with friends and scholars. The incidents correspond loosely to episodes in Homer's *Odyssey*, Bloom being a sort of Ulysses on an epic journey around Dublin and back to his wife's bed. What makes the novel so distinctive, however—and so long—is that Joyce opens his imagination to every half-formed impression that crosses his characters' minds, to the crowded life that seethes around them, and to the mythic significance lurking in seaside rambles and bar-room disputes. Late in the novel and the day, Bloom and Dedalus visit a brothel in Nighttown, and the book closes by shifting perspective to Leopold's wife, Molly, whose thoughts dwell on the mundane and the sexual with equal freedom:

> whats the idea making us like that with a big hole in the middle of us like a Stallion driving it up into you because thats all they want out of you with that determined vicious look in his eye I had to halfshut my eyes still he hasnt such a tremendous amount of spunk in him when I made him pull it out and do it on me considering how big it is so much the better in case any of it wasnt washed out properly [...][10]

The final episodes are the most vulnerable to accusations of obscenity—but they did not exist yet in 1918, when the novel began to appear in the *Little Review*.

The foreign editor of the magazine was the poet Ezra Pound. Under the pretence of improving the novel's artistry, he expurgated some passages, including one in which Bloom enjoys a leisurely bowel movement while reading the newspaper in a backyard jakes. Among other changes, Pound transmuted the Dead Sea from 'the grey sunken cunt of the world' into its 'grey sunken belly'.[11] Nevertheless, in the four years that the *Little Review* serialized *Ulysses*, four issues were confiscated and destroyed by the US Post Office. An issue of the *Little Review* had already been seized in 1917 for publishing Wyndham Lewis's short story 'Cantleman's Spring-Mate'. This censorship ostensibly occurred under the Comstock Act, which prohibited the mailing of obscene publications, but the Post Office's powers had grown as a result of the Espionage Act of 1917, a wartime measure, and there is evidence that the *Little Review* was targeted as an anarchist publication. Lewis's story may have been censored for its unflattering depiction of a British soldier, not just its sex scene.[12]

The Post Office did not inform the editors exactly what material was objectionable, politically or morally, in *Ulysses*, but scholar Paul Vanderham has speculated that the January 1919 issue may have been seized for Bloom's memory of kissing Molly on Howth Head: 'Wildly I lay on her, kissed her: eyes, her lips, her stretched neck beating, woman's breasts full in her blouse of nun's veiling, fat nipples upright. Hot I tongued her.' The *lèse majesté* of 'Lozenge and comfit manufacturer to His Majesty the King. God. Save. Our. Sitting on his throne, sucking jujubes' might also have been relevant.[13] The January 1920 issue took a few more shots at the royal family: 'haven't we had enough of those sausageeating bastards on the throne from George the elector down to the flatulent old bitch that's dead?' And about Edward: 'There's a bloody sight more pox than pax about that boyo.'[14] The July–August 1920 issue was a crowning achievement: Bloom masturbating in his trousers on the beach while Gerty MacDowell flashes her knickers at him. ('It pollutes one to speak of it, even to cry out against it,' wrote one reader to Anderson. 'I hate, I loathe, I detest the whole thing and everything connected with it. It has done something tragic to my illusions about America. How could you?'[15])

After the first confiscation, the editors began censoring bits of *Ulysses*, indicating the omissions with ellipses, and apologizing in a footnote to the May 1919 issue for having 'ruined Mr. Joyce's story by cutting certain passages in which he mentions natural facts known to everyone'. This issue was still seized. A note to the November 1919 issue explained that 'A passage of some twenty lines has been omitted to avoid the censor's possible suppression'. The missing passage contained a discussion of erections caused by asphyxiation during hanging.[16] The editors had no desire to see their magazine destroyed, as Anderson later recalled:

> It was like a burning at the stake as far as I was concerned. The care we had taken to preserve Joyce's text intact; the worry over the bills that accumulated when we had no advance funds; the technique I used on printer, bookbinders, paper houses—tears, prayers, hysterics or rages— to make them push ahead without a guarantee of money; the addressing, wrapping, stamping, mailing; the excitement of anticipating the world's response to the literary masterpiece of our generation ... and then a notice from the Post Office: BURNED.[17]

The Gerty incident, part of the episode known as 'Nausicaa' in Joyce's grand Homeric scheme, would turn out to have even worse consequences for Anderson and Heap.

An unsolicited copy of the July–August issue ended up in the possession of a teenaged girl, who showed it to her father, who showed it to the New York District Attorney, who showed it to John Sumner, secretary of the NYSSV. It was the nightmare scenario around which the entire edifice of Anglo-American obscenity law had been constructed. Introduced into English common law in 1868, the Hicklin test designated a work obscene if the 'tendency of the matter [...] is to deprave and corrupt those who are open to such immoral influences, and into whose hands a publication of this sort may fall'.[18] Here was *Ulysses*, fallen into the hands of an innocent young woman—exactly the sort of reader that the law and the NYSSV were designed to save from corruption. Worse, the issue contained an example of a corrupted young woman.[19]

Pound had made the version of 'Nausicaa' in the *Little Review* a little more vague than Joyce intended, leaving a bit of doubt as to what

Bloom is doing while MacDowell, enjoying his gaze, leans back to watch fireworks explode overhead ('he could see her other things too, nainsook knickers, four and eleven, on account of being white and she let him and she saw that he saw').[20] Joyce himself clothes the climactic moment in metaphor:

> O! then the Roman candle burst and it was like a sigh of O! and every-
> one cried O! O! and it gushed out of it a stream of rain gold hair threads
> and they shed and ah! they were all greeny dewy stars falling with golden,
> O so lovely! O so soft, sweet, soft![21]

Enough naughtiness remained, however, including the singing of a nearby church choir, which lent the scene a soupçon of blasphemy. (Though there was plenty of blasphemy in Joyce and other modernists' work, obscenity law had been the authorities' tool of choice for suppressing literature since the conviction of Vizetelly.[22]) Sumner purchased the issue from the Washington Square Book Shop, and had one of its owners, Josephine Bell Arens, summoned before a magistrate. Arens had already fallen foul of the Espionage Act in 1917 for her poem celebrating the anarchist Emma Goldman, published in the *Masses*.[23] Acting for Anderson and Heap, the attorney John Quinn, who was also the financial backer of the magazine, had the charges transferred to them.[24]

Though Quinn did his best to defend 'Nausicaa' in court, the law was stacked against him. He called experts to the stand—but this was not the usual practice under the Hicklin test, and the judges cut the procession short when they became fed up with the Freudian jargon the second witness was using. Quinn argued that the book was no worse than the Bible or works by Swift, Rabelais, or Shakespeare—but the Hicklin test did not yield to the 'What about Shakespeare?' argument. Other books were irrelevant, and all that mattered was whether the work in question had the tendency to deprave or corrupt. Quinn argued that the law should be concerned with the novel's effect on an average reader, not an especially vulnerable one—but the Hicklin test was concerned with the vulnerable reader, not the average one. Most ingeniously of all, Quinn claimed that *Ulysses* was not comprehensible enough to be obscene.[25]

In response, the prosecution read passages of the book aloud, despite one judge's objection that there was a woman in the room. (When Quinn pointed out that this woman, Anderson, was the publisher, the judge said she could not have understood what she had published.) Though the judges showed some interest in Quinn's argument from unintelligibility, they convicted Anderson and Heap, and fined them fifty dollars each. This was the end of *Ulysses'* run in the *Little Review*.[26]

The conviction was not, however, the end of *Ulysses*. Typically intractable, Joyce revised 'Nausicaa' to make it even bolder, and proceeded with his novel, which was growing despite the agonizing attacks of iritis that reduced him to scribbling phrases in notebooks and on stray scraps of paper when he was well enough to see them.[27] The US obscenity conviction would make publishing a complete edition difficult, and Joyce now turned to Sylvia Beach, who owned the private lending library Shakespeare and Company in Paris, where Joyce lived. Beach offered to publish *Ulysses* privately. Although Joyce's typists kept quitting, and one typist's chivalrous husband burned part of his manuscript, the Shakespeare and Company *Ulysses* was published in 1922, and Weaver's Egoist edition followed shortly thereafter.[28] After struggling to find an English printer, Weaver hired Beach's printer in Dijon, Maurice Darantière.[29]

Copies of these editions were smuggled into the United States in ingenious ways: Ernest Hemingway's radical friend Barnet Braverman, editor of a magazine called the *Progressive Woman*, gradually smuggled copies, at first carried openly, then hidden in his trousers, into Detroit from Canada, where the book was not yet banned.[30] (It would be, from January 1923 to 1949.[31]) John Quinn's fourteen personal copies were secreted in a box with Picassos and a Cézanne. The pages of Weaver's edition, printed in Paris, were hidden inside newspapers and reassembled in the United States.[32] The publisher Samuel Roth, whose 1957 Supreme Court case would give his name to the Roth test of obscenity (see Chapter 2), published expurgated extracts of *Ulysses* in his magazine *Two Worlds* without Joyce's permission, an act which 167 supporters of Joyce, including Albert Einstein, D. H. Lawrence, and Hemingway, condemned in an 'International Protest'.[33]

In the United Kingdom, Weaver personally carried copies to London bookshops. The police were watching her, however, and reviews of the novel in the *Observer* and *Quarterly Review* had come to the attention of the Home Office. James Douglas of the *Sunday Express*, who stoked opposition to *Lady Chatterley's Lover* and *The Well of Loneliness*, was among those condemning *Ulysses* (see Chapters 10 and 12). The Home Office took note of which booksellers were stocking the novel in March 1922, and then ordered it seized from the post in November. Customs confiscated a copy at Croydon Airport in December. Sir Archibald Bodkin, after reading only forty-two pages, advised the Home Office that the book was obscene—just in time for customs to destroy Weaver's latest print run of five hundred copies, which were arriving from France to be smuggled into the United States. About five hundred copies seized in Boston and New York had already been burned.[34]

Ten years later, *Ulysses* was still in a peculiar limbo. Enough people had managed to read it that it had gained widespread critical recognition, and it had become a central influence on the modernist movement in literature, but distribution and importation were still illegal in the United States and the United Kingdom. It would take more than a rebellious author and his radical supporters to beat the Hicklin test of obscenity.

Cracks had begun to show in the test, however, and a few progressive judges and attorneys in the United States had begun prying them open. When the October 1917 issue of the *Little Review* was banned for publishing 'Cantleman's Spring-Mate', the editors appealed the Post Office's decision to the courts. Judge Augustus Hand heard the case, and, though he decided against Anderson and Heap, he alluded to the breadth of the obscenity test, which, he thought, many great works had escaped only because they were already considered 'classics'. A few years earlier, in 1913, Augustus Hand's cousin Judge Learned Hand had questioned the Hicklin test while applying it to the novel *Hagar Revelly* by Daniel Carson Goodman. In 1922 a bookseller named Raymond Halsey, prosecuted by the NYSSV for selling a translation of Théophile Gautier's *Mademoiselle de Maupin*, was not only acquitted by a jury, but successfully sued the Society for malicious prosecution. The New York Supreme Court departed from Hicklin in deciding that a literary work should not be judged in parts, but as a whole.[35] The *Mademoiselle de Maupin* case was important in the liberation of Radclyffe Hall's *The Well of Loneliness*.

The biggest breakthroughs occurred in cases dealing with, of all things, sexual education manuals. Augustus Hand wrote the decision acquitting Mary Dennett, charged with mailing her book *The Sex Side of Life*, and Judge John M. Woolsey dismissed obscenity proceedings against Marie Stopes's *Married Love* and a book she had imported entitled *Contraception*. Woolsey turned to the *Oxford English Dictionary*, ignoring the Hicklin standard of obscenity altogether, and found that the word 'obscene' did not apply to these books. Sexual education may seem a far cry from literature, but their defences against obscenity law are closely related. In the Dennett case, the court found that *The Sex Side of Life*, a book designed for young people, had educational value that outweighed the risk of moral depravity. Similarly, one can argue for the social value of art that deals frankly with sex. The attorney who represented Dennett and Stopes, Morris Ernst of the American Civil Liberties Union, also fought against literary censorship. He successfully defended the US edition of *The Well of Loneliness* in 1929.[36] He would go on to defend *Ulysses*.

That defence occurred in 1933, when Bennett Cerf of Random House resolved to bring out an edition of the novel in the United States. Doing so would require provoking a legal case against *Ulysses* that could be won. Ernst gathered evidence of *Ulysses'* wide acceptance in a community of critics, librarians, and distinguished readers that extended across the country.[37] Knowing that expert witnesses were not usually allowed in obscenity cases, Ernst arranged to have documents testifying to the work's literary merit pasted inside a copy of *Ulysses*, so that they would be entered into evidence along with the book. He had the copy imported and seized at the border so that he could challenge its confiscation.[38] Ernst also had a second copy imported and seized, and arranged for an exemption from the Treasury on the grounds that it was a 'classic': remarkably, this exemption was granted.[39] The fact that the US Treasury recognized the book's literary merit would make it difficult for the government to argue in the customs case that it ought to be prohibited.

Ernst prepared a brief that argued for the book's value as a 'modern classic'. Because the Hicklin test made no allowances for literary merit, however, Ernst needed to attack the test directly. Using the same language he had used in *The Well of Loneliness* case, he called the test

> patently unfair, unreasonable and unsound, because it sought to gauge the mental and moral capacity of the community by that of its dullest-witted and most fallible members, and because it sought to withhold from society any material which might conceivably injure its lowest and most impressionable element.[40]

He cited Woolsey's dictionary definition of obscenity from the case of Stopes's *Married Love* ('offensive to modesty or decency, or expressing or suggesting unchaste or lustful ideas') and Learned Hand's formulation from *United States* v. *Kennerley* ('the *present critical point* in the compromise between candor and shame at which the community may have arrived *here and now*').[41] Ernst constructed a case history that included notable departures from the Hicklin standard. He argued that the test of obscenity was a 'living standard'—that it needed to change with the times.[42]

With some legal manoeuvring and a dose of good luck, Ernst scored a sympathetic judge: Woolsey. The judge was, once again, receptive. He was a man of letters, and postponed the case so that he could read *Ulysses* carefully.[43] At the trial, the government's attorney, Sam Coleman, intended to rely on the vulgar language in the novel. In an echo of the *Little Review* trial, however, Coleman refused to read the words out loud because a woman—Ernst's wife, Margaret—was in the room. Ernst was less inhibited, and walked Woolsey through a spirited defence of Anglo-Saxon terminology, which Margaret had, in fact, helped him prepare. The word 'fuck', he said, 'had strength and integrity' and 'more honesty than phrases that modern authors use to connote the same experience'. (Regarding the phrase 'they slept together', Woolsey joked, 'That isn't even usually the truth.') Ernst demonstrated Joyce's stream of consciousness technique by saying, 'while pleading before you, I've also been thinking about that ring around your tie, how your gown does not fit too well on your shoulders, and the picture of George Washington back of your bench.' The judge was on exactly the same page: 'I have listened as intently as I know how but I must confess that while listening to you I've also been thinking about the Heppelwhite chair behind you.'[44]

Unsurprisingly, Woolsey delivered a succinct but eloquent decision in favour of *Ulysses*, which was published in the Random House edition of the novel as ammunition against future challenges.[45] Woolsey discarded the Hicklin test, judging the book's effect not on the most impressionable readers, but on 'l'homme moyen sensuel'—the 'person with average sex instincts'. (He asked two such men, friends of his, whether *Ulysses* aroused them. It didn't.) He wrote:

> It is only with the normal person that the law is concerned. Such a test as I have described, therefore, is the only proper test of obscenity in the case of a book like 'Ulysses' which is a sincere and serious attempt to devise a new literary method for the observation and description of mankind.

Woolsey concluded, 'whilst in many places the effect of "Ulysses" on the reader is somewhat emetic, nowhere does it tend to be an aphrodisiac.'[46] The book was not obscene.

The new District Attorney, Martin Conboy, a man with links to the NYSSV, appealed Woolsey's decision in 1934. His brief claimed that 'the rule of *Regina* v. *Hicklin* is established as the yardstick by which books are to be measured in the Federal Courts'.[47] Bolder than Coleman had been, he read out fifty-three passages from *Ulysses* in court.[48] At the judges' bench, however, were sitting Learned Hand and Augustus Hand. With Judge Manton dissenting, the Judges Hand delivered what scholar Kevin Birmingham describes as a more 'unquotable' decision than the 'literary' Woolsey's.[49] They cleared *Ulysses*, and in doing so they finished what they had helped begin, setting out new standards of obscenity that would rob the Hicklin test of much of its force. The 'dominant effect' of a work would need to be considered. The 'relevancy of the objectionable parts to the theme' would need to be assessed. And literary merit would matter, with 'the estimation of approved critics, if the book is modern, and the verdict of the past if it is ancient' counting as evidence.[50]

After *Ulysses*, works of literature would still be subject to obscenity prosecutions in the United States, and judges would continue to differ in how rigidly they applied the law. The case was, however, a significant step towards protecting literature from moral censorship.[51] The next steps would not occur until the Supreme Court finally renounced the Hicklin test in *Roth* v. *United States* in 1957, which created the Roth test of obscenity, in which the social value of the publication became a significant factor. The Roth test enabled the eighteenth-century erotic novel *Memoirs of a Woman of Pleasure* to be published freely (see Chapter 2). In the United Kingdom, the publisher John Lane announced an edition of *Ulysses* in 1936, and officials quietly determined not to proceed against it. Though the Attorney General called the Hicklin test 'inadequate' behind closed doors, the *Ulysses* controversy had not affected the law.[52] In 1950 the Public Morality Council, a moral purity society, brought the Bodley Head edition of *Ulysses* to the consideration of the Director of Public Prosecutions, Sir Theobald Mathew, who did not believe a court was likely to find the book obscene, and declined to prosecute.[53] The Hicklin test would live on in the United Kingdom until 1959, when Parliament set the new standards against which *Lady Chatterley's Lover* would be tried (see Chapters 12 and 16).

Notes

1. London, The National Archives, HO 144/20071, quoted in Kevin Birmingham, *The Most Dangerous Book: The Battle for James Joyce's 'Ulysses'* (London: Head of Zeus, 2015), p. 264.

2. F. R. Leavis, 'Freedom to Read', *Times Literary Supplement*, 3 May 1963, p. 325. See also Alan Travis, *Bound and Gagged: A Secret History of Obscenity in Britain* (London: Profile Books, 2000), pp. 26–36.

3. Birmingham, *The Most Dangerous Book*, pp. 157–70.

4. Birmingham, *The Most Dangerous Book*, pp. 65–66.

5. Birmingham, *The Most Dangerous Book*, pp. 59–62.

6. Richard Ellmann, *James Joyce*, rev. edn (Oxford: Oxford University Press, 1959; rev. and corrected 1983), pp. 219–22, 231, 282, 310–11, 314–15, 328–38, 353.

7. James Joyce, 'Gas from a Burner' (Trieste, 1912), British Library, https://www.bl.uk/collection-items/gas-from-a-burner-by-james-joyce, accessed 14 March 2017.

8. Ellmann, pp. 400–1, 404–5, 414.

9. Margaret Anderson, *My Thirty Years' War: An Autobiography* (London: Knopf, 1930), p. 175.

10. James Joyce, *Ulysses* (Oxford: Oxford University Press, 1998; repr. 2008), p. 694.

11. Joyce, *Ulysses* (Oxford), p. 59; James Joyce, *Ulysses*, Episode IV, in *Little Review*, June 1918, p. 44 [Modernist Journals Project e-book]. See also Vanderham, *James Joyce and Censorship: The Trials of 'Ulysses'* (Basingstoke: Macmillan, 1998), pp. 18–26.

12. Birmingham, *The Most Dangerous Book*, p. 115; Vanderham, pp. 17–18, 28–29. See also Mark Gaipa and others, 'General Introduction', in James Joyce, *The Little Review 'Ulysses'*, ed. Gaipa and others (New Haven: Yale University Press, 2015), pp. xi–xix (p. xvii).

13. James Joyce, *Ulysses*, Episode VIII, in *Little Review* (January 1919), pp. 27, 47 [Modernist Journals Project e-book]. See also Vanderham, pp. 30–31.

14. James Joyce, *Ulysses*, Episode XII (Continued), in *Little Review* (January 1920), p. 55 [Modernist Journals Project e-book]. See also Vanderham, p. 34.

15. Anderson, p. 213.

16. James Joyce, *Ulysses*, Episode IX, in *Little Review* (May 1919), p. 21 note [Modernist Journals Project e-book]; James Joyce, *Ulysses*, Episode XII, in *Little Review* (November 1919), p. 49 [Modernist Journals Project e-book]. See also Vanderham, pp. 32–34.

17. Anderson, p. 175 (ellipsis original).

18. *R v Hicklin* (1868) LR 3 QB 360, 371.

19. Vanderham, p. 39.

20. James Joyce, *Ulysses*, Episode XIII concluded, in *Little Review* (July–August 1920), p. 43 [Modernist Journals Project e-book]. See also Birmingham, p. 197.

21. Joyce, *Ulysses*, Episode XIII concluded, pp. 43–44.

22. Steve Pinkerton, *Blasphemous Modernism: The Twentieth-Century Word Made Flesh* (Oxford: Oxford University Press, 2017), p. 4 and note 18.

23. Birmingham, *The Most Dangerous Book*, p. 161. See also Vanderham, p. 41.

24. Vanderham, p. 42.

25. Vanderham, pp. 48–49.

26. Vanderham, pp. 52–53.

27. Birmingham, *The Most Dangerous Book*, pp. 9–10, 99, 198, 210–11.

28. Ellmann, pp. 504–8.

29. Ellmann, pp. 497, 505 and note. See also Birmingham, *The Most Dangerous Book*, pp. 244–45.

30. Birmingham, *The Most Dangerous Book*, pp. 235–40.

31. Bruce Ryder, 'Undercover Censorship: Exploring the History of the Regulation of Publications in Canada', in *Interpreting Censorship in Canada*, ed. Klaus Petersen and Allan C. Hutchinson (Toronto: University of Toronto Press, 1999), pp. 129–56 (p. 132).

32. Birmingham, *The Most Dangerous Book*, pp. 244–48, 262.

33. Jay A. Gertzman, *Samuel Roth, Infamous Modernist* (Gainesville: University Press of Florida, 2013), p. 81 [Florida Scholarship Online e-book].

34. Birmingham, *The Most Dangerous Book*, pp. 219–20, 248–53. See also Ellmann, p. 505 note; Travis, pp. 22–26.

35. Marisa Anne Pagnattaro, 'Carving a Literary Exception: The Obscenity Standard and *Ulysses*', *Twentieth Century Literature*, 47.2 (2001), 217–40 (pp. 220–24).

36. Pagnattaro, pp. 224–25.

37. 'Preliminary Memorandum Submitted on Behalf of Claimant, with Exhibits', in *The United States of America v. One Book Entitled Ulysses by James Joyce: Documents and Commentary—A 50-Year Retrospective*, ed. Michael Moscato and Leslie LeBlanc (Frederick, MD: University Publications of America, 1984), pp. 227–29 (p. 229).

38. Morris L. Ernst, 'Reflections on the *Ulysses* Trial and Censorship', in *The United States of America v. One Book Entitled Ulysses by James Joyce: Documents and Commentary*, pp. 44–53 (p. 47).

39. 'Claimant's Memorandum in Support of Motion to Dismiss Libel', in *The United States of America v. One Book Entitled Ulysses by James Joyce: Documents and Commentary*, pp. 235–72 (p. 255).

40. 'Claimant's Memorandum in Support of Motion to Dismiss Libel', pp. 249–50, 255.

41. 'Claimant's Memorandum in Support of Motion to Dismiss Libel', p. 249; United States v. Kennerley, 209 F. 119, 121 (S.D.N.Y. 1913), quoted in 'Claimant's Memorandum in Support of Motion to Dismiss Libel', p. 244 (emphasis original).

42. 'Claimant's Memorandum in Support of Motion to Dismiss Libel', p. 244.

43. Birmingham, *The Most Dangerous Book*, pp. 310–11, 314–15.

44. Morris L. Ernst, 'The Censor Marches On', in *The United States of America v. One Book Entitled Ulysses by James Joyce: Documents and Commentary*, pp. 19–24 (pp. 22, 23). See also Ernst, 'Reflections on the *Ulysses* Trial and Censorship', pp. 45–49.

45. Birmingham, *The Most Dangerous Book*, p. 330.

46. United States v. One Book Called "Ulysses", 5 F. Supp. 182, 184, 185 (S.D.N.Y. 1933).

47. 'Brief for Libellant-Appellant', in *The United States of America v. One Book Entitled Ulysses by James Joyce: Documents and Commentary*, pp. 369–76 (p. 374).

48. Birmingham, *The Most Dangerous Book*, p. 333.

49. Kevin Birmingham, 'The Prestige of the Law: Revisiting Obscenity Law and Judge Woolsey's *Ulysses* Decision', *James Joyce Quarterly*, 50.4 (2013), 991–1009 (pp. 991, 998).

50. United States v. One Book Entitled Ulysses by James Joyce, 72 F.2d 705, 708 (2d Cir. 1934).

51. Pagnattaro, pp. 233–37.

52. London, The National Archives, HO 144/20071, quoted in Birmingham, *The Most Dangerous Book*, p. 336.

53. David Bradshaw, 'American Beastliness, the Great Purge and its Aftermath (1946–1959)', in *Prudes on the Prowl: Fiction and Obscenity in England, 1850 to the Present Day*, ed. Bradshaw and Rachel Potter (Oxford: Oxford University Press, 2013), pp. 138–58 (pp. 142–44).

12

Lady Chatterley's Lover
D. H. Lawrence

When D. H. Lawrence first tried to publish *Lady Chatterley's Lover* in 1928, he knew what to expect. He had already been bruised by previous encounters with censorship, including the destruction of copies of *The Rainbow* under the Obscene Publications Act 1857. Nervous publishers initially refused *Women in Love*, and then required cuts so that the novel would be suitable for the circulating libraries,[1] which, though less central to book distribution than they had been in the nineteenth century, had formed the Circulating Library Association, with its own censorship policy, in 1909 (see Chapter 8).[2] Lawrence's latest novel, which featured detailed sex scenes and a heavy dose of four-letter words, and which told the story of a married woman who finds sexual fulfilment with the gamekeeper of her estate, was not likely to fare any better than his previous work. The first sign of trouble was that the typist he had hired quit at chapter five.[3]

With the help of his friend Pino Orioli, Lawrence had the novel printed privately in Florence, where they both lived, by typesetters who could not read English. Lawrence advertised the novel to acquaintances, provided no review copies, handled all the finances himself, and posted copies directly to subscribers.[4] Concerned about his copyright, which his clandestine Florentine *Lady Chatterley* would be insufficient to defend, Lawrence also attempted to publish an above-board, expurgated edition, but could not bring himself to slash the sexual content, which

Readers outside a London bookshop peek inside *Lady Chatterley's Lover* after Penguin's successful court battle in 1960.

he considered integral to the book.[5] ('I might as well try to clip my own nose into shape with scissors. The book bleeds,' he complained.[6]) The novel was swiftly pirated.[7] Officers in the United Kingdom began to seize imported copies of *Lady Chatterley* and to call at the homes of Lawrence's acquaintances. The manuscript of his poetry collection *Pansies* was taken from the post and held under the authority of the high-handed Home Secretary, Sir William Joynson-Hicks, who similarly interfered with correspondence to the publisher of *The Well of Loneliness* (see Chapter 10). In 1929 the police raided an exhibition of Lawrence's watercolour nudes at the Warren Gallery in London, seizing several of them.[8] Lawrence, who had been suffering from tuberculosis, died the following year, and the publishers Secker and Knopf brought out authorized expurgated editions of *Lady Chatterley's Lover* in the United Kingdom and the United States in 1932. In the United States, Dial Press published an edition of an early version of the novel under the title *The First Lady Chatterley* in 1944. This book was found obscene in New York, then cleared on appeal.[9] The court cases that finally permitted the unexpurgated final version of the novel to circulate freely did not occur until about thirty years after the author's death.

In 1959 Grove Press published an unexpurgated *Lady Chatterley's Lover*. When the United States Post Office moved against the publisher by seizing twenty-four cartons of copies from the mail, the attorney Charles Rembar prepared to challenge the ban at a Post Office Department trial.[10] Between Morris Ernst's successful defences of *The Well of Loneliness* and *Ulysses* and the case that Rembar now faced, something important had changed (see Chapter 11 for *Ulysses*). In the 1957 case *Roth* v. *United States*, the Supreme Court of the United States weighed in, for the first time, on the question of obscenity. Holding that the First Amendment of the Constitution did not protect obscene speech, the court defined a new test of obscenity, which became known as the Roth test. Unlike Ernst, Rembar could explicitly present his case as a constitutional one: unless *Lady Chatterley's Lover* were obscene under the Roth test, it was protected by the First Amendment, and the Post Office had no right to interfere with it.

Compared to the Hicklin test of obscenity, derived from the 1868 English case *R* v. *Hicklin* and now officially defunct, the Roth test was much less strict. Courts would need to assess 'whether to the average person, applying contemporary community standards, the dominant theme of the material taken as a whole appeals to prurient interest'.[11] From the point of view of a lawyer defending a work of literature, there were several important gains here. Because works needed to be judged as wholes, and their 'dominant theme' needed to be considered, judges and juries could not condemn books simply by taking passages out of context. The references to 'the average person' and 'contemporary community standards' acknowledged that obscenity was variable, that it changed over time and from place to place, and that the standards of a whole community needed to be considered, not just those of the most conservative or most impressionable members. On the other hand, there was still a great deal of ambiguity in the *Roth* decision, and considerable danger for literature. The concept of 'community standards' seemed to make obscenity a matter of sheer majority rule. Wasn't the First Amendment supposed to protect minority rights—to allow people to express ideas, even unpopular ones? Though millions of copies of *Lady Chatterley's Lover* were sold, Rembar did not believe the average person in the United States would actually *approve* of the book. He wrote, 'the First Amendment is a cheap thing if all it provides is the assurance that one may say what a current majority is willing to hear.'[12]

Rembar had a different idea of what the crucial component of the Roth test was. From other language in the decision, he had concluded that a publication could not be obscene unless it were utterly without redeeming social value. He would eventually have some success with this argument, notably in his defence of John Cleland's erotic novel *Memoirs of a Woman of Pleasure* (see Chapter 2). Though Rembar tried out the social value argument in the later stages of the *Lady Chatterley* case, it was not yet decisive, and the liberation of the novel ultimately hinged on the phrase 'prurient interest'.[13] At the one-day Post Office trial, Rembar called critics Malcolm Cowley and Alfred Kazin as expert witnesses, and attempted to show that the book neither appealed to prurient interest nor fell outside contemporary community standards. Kazin testified:

> Lawrence was a deeply and naturally religious writer who was concerned wholly with giving man in our industrial and mechanical period a new sense of consecration for his life. For him, sex, far from being an obsession in the clinical sense, was a symbol of this path toward imaginative freedom.[14]

The judicial officer hearing the case declined to make a decision, and simply passed the case on to the Postmaster General, Arthur E. Summerfield, who, without having been present at the trial, ruled the book to be obscene: 'Any literary merit the book may have is far outweighed by the pornographic and smutty passages and words, so that the book, taken as a whole, is an obscene and filthy work.'[15]

Grove Press appealed to the courts for a judicial review of the Post Office decision, and was successful. The federal district judge, Frederick van Pelt Bryan, appreciated the distinction Rembar was drawing between 'sexual interest' and 'prurient interest'.[16] The attorney had argued that contemporary community standards in the United States permitted a great deal of appeal to sexual interest, including sexy advertising in mainstream media such as *Life* magazine, issues of which he had attempted to enter into evidence. 'Prurient' suggested something else—a 'dirty', 'morbid', 'unwholesome' approach to sexual content.[17] The judge decided that *Lady Chatterley's Lover* was not obscene under the Roth test, and a court of appeals affirmed his decision. The Post Office did not appeal further, and no action was taken against the book in any other state. *Lady Chatterley's Lover* was free in the United States.[18]

In the United Kingdom, Customs routinely seized imported copies of *Lady Chatterley's Lover*, and a bookseller in Soho was convicted of selling it in 1955.[19] Penguin Books had been reprinting the works of Lawrence since 1950, but had not ventured to publish *Lady Chatterley*. While the Hicklin test had lost ground in the United States even before *Roth*, English obscenity law had not changed since the nineteenth century. The common law offence of obscene libel, established in the eighteenth century, could be used to prosecute authors, publishers, retailers, or anybody else involved in the publication and circulation of a work. The Obscene Publications Act 1857 permitted books to be seized and destroyed wholesale without anyone being charged with an offence. In prosecutions and seize-and-destroy proceedings, the 1868 *Hicklin* case still provided the test of obscenity. In short, Penguin was no less likely to face conviction for publishing Lawrence than Henry Vizetelly had been for publishing the works of Émile Zola in 1888 and 1889 (see Chapter 8).

Spurred on by the prosecution of five reputable publishers in 1954, members of parliament pushed for legislative reform (see Chapter 16). The resulting Obscene Publications Act 1959 created

an opening for Penguin. While conceding greater powers of search
and seizure to the police, the new Act introduced several changes
designed to protect literature. The standard of obscenity was softened so that it would take into account the entirety of a text, the
circumstances of its publication, and the likelihood of its reaching vulnerable readers. A work had previously been obscene if 'the
tendency of the matter charged as obscenity is to deprave and corrupt those whose minds are open to such immoral influences, and
into whose hands a publication of this sort may fall'.[20] A work was
now obscene if, 'taken as a whole', its effect was 'such as to tend
to deprave and corrupt persons who are likely, having regard to all
relevant circumstances, to read, see or hear the matter contained or
embodied in it'. Most importantly for Penguin, there would now
be a public good defence whereby an obscene work's publication
could be justified if it was 'in the interests of science, literature, art
or learning, or of other objects of general concern'. Expert testimony on a publication's contribution to the public good would be
admissible.[21] Though Penguin might simply have escaped prosecution, as Weidenfeld & Nicolson did in publishing *Lolita*, Customs
and Excise officials were confused about how the new legislation
would affect their established practice of confiscating other editions
of *Lady Chatterley's Lover*. The Director of Public Prosecutions, Sir
Theobald Mathew, decided to prosecute. Penguin's edition would
be a test case for the new statute.[22]

On 16 August 1960 Detective Inspector Charles Monahan called
at the London office of Penguin Books to collect twelve copies of
Lady Chatterley's Lover. By giving copies to the police, Penguin took
sole responsibility for circulating the book, protecting third parties,
such as booksellers, from criminal liability.[23] The trial of Penguin
Books Ltd for publishing an obscene article was held at the Old
Bailey between 20 October and 2 November 1960. The prosecution
attempted to establish, beyond a reasonable doubt, that the book was
obscene. The defence attempted to refute the prosecution's argument
and prove that the book had been published for the public good.
Unlike the US proceedings, this was a criminal trial, and a jury would
decide the result.

Crown prosecutor Mervyn Griffith-Jones emphasized to the jury the novel's sexual content and 'bawdy conversation'. In his opening remarks, he noted that there were thirteen episodes of sexual intercourse in the novel, that twelve were described in detail, that the only variation between them was where they took place, and that 'The emphasis is always on the pleasure, the satisfaction and the sensuality of the episode'. The rest of the plot was 'little more than padding'. With apologies for his Anglo-Saxon, he itemized the expletives in the novel: 'The word "fuck" or "fucking" occurs no less than thirty times. [. . .] "Cunt" fourteen times; "balls" thirteen times; "shit" and "arse" six times apiece; "cock" four times; "piss" three times, and so on.'[24] Even if this enumeration of sex scenes and strong words had persuaded the jury of the obscenity of particular passages from the novel, the strategy was insufficient under the new law, which obliged the jury to consider the examples in the context of the whole work. Gerald Gardiner, acting for the defence, objected to the prosecution directing the jury's attention to any passages before they had read the entire novel, and Griffith-Jones deferred his discussion of instances.[25] Once Gardiner had made his opening speech for the defence, the jurors would retire to comfortable armchairs to read the book—as though they had 'bought it at a bookstall', in the judge's words—over three days.[26] Griffith-Jones would then present his evidence that the book had the tendency to deprave and corrupt.

In his opening remarks, Griffith-Jones had invited the jury to consider the book's impact on particularly vulnerable minds, using terms that might have persuaded a jury in 1928, but which are reported to have amused the jury in 1960:

> ask yourselves the question, when you have read it through, would you approve of your young sons, young daughters—because girls can read as well as boys—reading this book. Is it a book that you would have lying around in your own house? Is it a book that you would even wish your wife or your servants to read?[27]

The jurors, some of whom were women, were unlikely to have been surprised to learn that girls can read, or concerned about their wives and servants running off to have sex with their gamekeepers. Gardiner

cast more fundamental doubts on the figure of the corruptible reader
in his opening remarks:

> In a case like this one is perhaps permitted to reflect that nobody sug-
> gests that the Director of Public Prosecutions becomes depraved or
> corrupted; counsel read the book, they do not become depraved or
> corrupted; witnesses read the book, they do not become depraved
> or corrupted; nobody suggests the judge or the jury become depraved
> or corrupted. It is always somebody else; it is never ourselves.[28]

Who, then, was the somebody else whose potential depravity proved
the obscenity of the book? For the prosecution, the cheapness and
wide distribution of Penguin paperbacks increased the likelihood that
Lady Chatterley's Lover would find such a person.

Over the course of the trial, it became apparent that the real concern was not wives and servants but sons and daughters—young readers who lacked the capacity to understand Lawrence. Lawrence had
not written *Lady Chatterley's Lover* for children, but at the price of
three shillings and six pence, the novel could be purchased for pocket
money. Under cross-examination, scholar Joan Bennett volunteered
the question of how a child would understand the book, though her
answer was not the one Griffith-Jones might have wanted. When the
prosecutor asked if she thought 'the average reader' would 'see anything in this book about marriage other than the picture of the wife
going and having adulterous sexual intercourse', Bennett protested, 'I
do not know what you mean by an average reader. If by an "average
reader" you mean an intelligent child . . .?' This being an advantageous
definition of 'average reader', Griffith-Jones encouraged Bennett to
go on. 'Well then, I don't think that is all they would get', she said.[29]

Reflecting on Bennett's testimony in his summing up, Justice Byrne
appeared to share the prosecution's concern for the reader's capacity,
suggesting that the jury consider the novel's impact on people without
a literary education. If, as Bennett had said, 'a reader who is capable
of understanding' Lawrence would learn about the author's ideas by
reading *Lady Chatterley*, 'Well, who are the people who are capable
of understanding him?' The book might well 'present a very different picture' to 'an authority on English literature' than it would 'to a
person with no literary background, no learning or little learning, and

no knowledge or little knowledge of Lawrence'.[30] Was the book really only comprehensible to Lawrence scholars and academics? Would the book deprave and corrupt the average reader of Penguin paperbacks, or the person of 'no learning or little learning', or the 'intelligent child'?

These questions were, ultimately, for the jury to decide. The defence's expert witnesses were there, in theory, not to give their opinion of the book's obscenity, but to support the public good defence. Penguin's counsel called a parade of academics, theologians, educators, politicians, and literary reviewers, who testified to the novel's literary, ethical, and pedagogical value. (The Crown attempted in vain to find experts to testify against the book.[31]) Unusually, Roy Jenkins MP appeared on the stand and, before he was cut off, began to express his belief that *Lady Chatterley's Lover* was the kind of book the literary defence in the law was designed to protect.[32] For Rembar, who had used two experts and a precise constitutional argument to free the book, the British process was moralistic and legally unfocused:

> the trial became a contest between a prosecution saying the ideas and the principal character in the book were immoral, and a defense saying the book was a righteous one and look at all these respectable and/or famous people who think that *Lady Chatterley* is good for you.[33]

Gardiner's witnesses recast the allegedly obscene novel as a serious analysis of the condition of England in the aftermath of the Great War, and showed the novel's depiction of sexual relationships to be inseparable from its larger social significance. The critic Vivian de Sola Pinto argued that the book

> has a double theme: a very broad one, the condemnation of the mechanization of humanity in an industrial society, and a more particular one, the necessity for human happiness to find adequate sexual relationship based on tenderness and affection, mutual affection.[34]

Where the prosecution saw a poorly written, monotonous mass of sex and swearing, the defence's witnesses found a purposeful study of interpersonal relationships in the industrial age.

It is, in fact, hard to miss the argument that Lawrence is making about sex in *Lady Chatterley*. His heroine, Connie Chatterley, moves

steadily towards the sort of sexual relationship that he himself recom-
mends. Connie takes refuge from her false and unhealthy marriage
in an affair with a playwright named Michaelis, but their affection
for each other is self-serving and therefore doomed. Connie's next
relationship, with her husband's gamekeeper, Oliver Mellors, saves her
life. Over the course of their affair, she regains her health, cultivating
self-knowledge as well as disgust with every aspect of modern society.
This movement away from the modern age towards the philosophy of
D. H. Lawrence is mirrored in Connie's sexuality. She turns against the
intellectual life of her husband, and celebrates the life of the body. The
crucial moment is an act of anal sex near the end of the novel (a scene
which did not feature as prominently in the trial as one might expect,
perhaps because it is one of the less explicit incidents). In the final
scenes, Lawrence would like us to believe, Connie and Mellors achieve
a perfect union, then resolve to divorce their spouses, marry, and raise a
child together. The novel closes with a letter from Mellors to Connie:

> So I love chastity now, because it is the peace that comes of fucking. I
> love being chaste now. I love it as snowdrops love the snow. I love this
> chastity, which is the pause of peace of our fucking, between us now
> like a snowdrop of forked white fire.[35]

The critic Helen Gardner observed in court that the language in
Mellors's letter is justified in the context of the book. It characterizes Mellors, and it serves Lawrence's larger purpose, which was to
purify sexual acts and sexual language. The meaning of words, Gardner
explained, is contextual: no words are 'brutal and disgusting in themselves'. Lawrence changes the meaning of the word 'fuck', so that, by
the last page of the novel, the word 'has become related to natural
processes', and can be used, quite seriously, to celebrate chastity.[36] The
defence argued that Lawrence's language was part of an artistic whole
that displayed literary and other merits, and was therefore in the public
good.

On 2 November the foreman of the jury returned a verdict of not
guilty.[37] Either *Lady Chatterley's Lover* was justified for the public good,
or it was not obscene in the first place. The Obscene Publications Act
1959 had done what it was designed to do, at least by those, such as

Roy Jenkins MP, who were trying to create protections for literature. Both the obscenity and the merits of a controversial but serious work of literature had been tested in a court of law, and the publishers had been acquitted. The same statute that cleared *Lady Chatterley*, however, would soon condemn, repeatedly, an erotic novel from the eighteenth century: John Cleland's *Memoirs of a Woman of Pleasure*. Authors, publishers, and retailers now had a way to defend themselves, but the courts would continue to be the arbiters of decency in art. Lawrence himself would not necessarily have objected in principle. Though he did not consider his work obscene, he had his own definition of obscenity: whatever treats sex as shameful, dirty, and excremental. He wrote in 1930:

> But even I would censor genuine pornography, rigorously. It would not be very difficult. In the first place, genuine pornography is almost always underworld, it doesn't come into the open. In the second, you can recognize it by the insult it offers, invariably, to sex, and to the human spirit.[38]

Notes

1. Damian Grant, 'D. H. Lawrence: A Suitable Case for Censorship', in *Writing and Censorship in Britain*, ed. Paul Hyland and Neil Sammells (London: Routledge, 1992), pp. 200–18 (pp. 204–6).

2. Nicola Wilson, 'Circulating Morals (1900–1915)', in *Prudes on the Prowl: Fiction and Obscenity in England, 1850 to the Present Day*, ed. David Bradshaw and Rachel Potter (Oxford: Oxford University Press, 2013), pp. 52–70 (pp. 58–59).

3. Michael Squires, 'Introduction', in D. H. Lawrence, *'Lady Chatterley's Lover' and 'A Propos of "Lady Chatterley's Lover"'*, ed. Michael Squires (Cambridge: Cambridge University Press, 2002), pp. xix–lx (p. xxiv).

4. Derek Britton, *Lady Chatterley: The Making of the Novel* (London: Hyman, 1988), pp. 262–67.

5. Squires, pp. xxxiv–xxxv.

6. D. H. Lawrence, *A Propos of 'Lady Chatterley's Lover'*, in *'Lady Chatterley's Lover' and 'A Propos of "Lady Chatterley's Lover"'*, pp. 303–35 (p. 307).

7. Britton, pp. 261–62.

8. Grant, pp. 209–14.

9. Squires, p. xxxv.

10. Charles Rembar, *The End of Obscenity: The Trials of 'Lady Chatterley', 'Tropic of Cancer', and 'Fanny Hill'* (London: Deutsch, 1969), pp. 59–63.

11. Roth v. United States, 354 U.S. 476, 488 (1957).

12. Rembar, pp. 120–23.

13. Rembar, p. 141. See further pp. 55–58, 141–43.

14. Rembar, p. 100.

15. Rembar, p. 117. See further pp. 114, 134.

16. Rembar, p. 99. See further pp. 141–43.

17. Rembar, p. 124. See further pp. 98–99.

18. Rembar, pp. 141, 147–51.

19. Alan Travis, *Bound and Gagged: A Secret History of Obscenity in Britain* (London: Profile Books, 2000), p. 147.

20. *R v Hicklin* (1868) LR 3 QB 360, 371.

21. Obscene Publications Act 1959, ss 1(1), 4(1) and (3).

22. Travis, pp. 140–46.

23. *The Trial of Lady Chatterley: Regina v. Penguin Books Limited*, ed. C. H. Rolph (London: Penguin, 1961), pp. 1–2, 22–23.

24. *The Lady Chatterley's Lover Trial: Regina v. Penguin Books Limited*, ed. H. Montgomery Hyde (London: Bodley Head, 1990), pp. 63–64.

25. *The Lady Chatterley's Lover Trial*, ed. Hyde, pp. 68–70.

26. *The Lady Chatterley's Lover Trial*, ed. Hyde, p. 86. See also *The Trial of Lady Chatterley*, ed. Rolph, p. 39.

27. *The Lady Chatterley's Lover Trial*, ed. Hyde, pp. 61–62. See further p. 17.

28. *The Lady Chatterley's Lover Trial*, ed. Hyde, p. 82.

29. *The Trial of Lady Chatterley*, ed. Rolph, p. 64.

30. *The Lady Chatterley's Lover Trial*, ed. Hyde, p. 312.

31. Travis, pp. 138, 148–54.

32. *The Trial of Lady Chatterley*, ed. Rolph, pp. 113–14.

33. Rembar, p. 157.

34. *The Trial of Lady Chatterley*, ed. Rolph, p. 74.

35. D. H. Lawrence, *Lady Chatterley's Lover*, in *'Lady Chatterley's Lover' and 'A Propos of "Lady Chatterley's Lover"'*, pp. 1–302 (p. 301).

36. *The Lady Chatterley's Lover Trial*, ed. Hyde, p. 118.

37. *The Lady Chatterley's Lover Trial*, ed. Hyde, p. 332.

38. D. H. Lawrence, *Pornography and Obscenity* (New York: Knopf, 1930), p. 12.

13

The Land of Spices
Kate O'Brien

Legend has it that *The Land of Spices*, by Irish novelist Kate O'Brien, was banned for a single clause: 'she saw *Etienne* and her father, in the embrace of love.'[1] 'She' is the novel's protagonist, Helen Archer, who, as a teenager in Belgium, witnessed an intimate encounter between Henry Archer and his male student. Turning against her humanist father, Helen became a nun. At the opening of the novel, she is introduced as the English-born, European-educated Reverend Mother of a convent school in Ireland, where she butts heads with nationalist priests and authoritarian nuns, nurtures a precocious young girl, and reflects on her vocation. *The Land of Spices* was a casualty of Ireland's stringent literary censorship, which was so extensive that the list of prohibited books became known as the 'Everyman's Guide to the Modern Classics'.[2]

The Constitution of the Irish Free State (1922) guaranteed the right to 'free expression of opinion', but only when 'not opposed to public morality'. In the state's early years the Cumann na nGaedheal government passed powerful censorship legislation designed to protect the public from malign influences. These influences were largely perceived as foreign—an influx of degraded works, mostly English newspapers, contaminating the Irish market. The Oireachtas, the legislature of Ireland, enacted the Censorship of Films Act in 1923, and

A broadside advertisement for the *Standard* calls for censorship in Ireland.

by the end of the decade had turned its attention to print.[3] In response to pressure from the Catholic Truth Society of Ireland and the Irish Vigilance Association, Minister for Justice Kevin O'Higgins created a Committee on Evil Literature in 1926 to study the threat posed by indecent publications. Many of the witnesses that gave evidence before the committee were representatives of Catholic organizations, such as the Catholic Writers' Guild, the Marian Sodalities of Ireland, and the Irish Christian Brothers. Religion was the impetus behind the Irish censorship, which was designed to consolidate the identity of the newly formed state.[4]

Though existing UK law already prohibited the sale, distribution, importation, and sending by post of obscene publications, the committee concluded that the law was insufficient to address 'the widespread complaints regarding the circulation of objectionable reading matter in Ireland'. The report identified two particular problems. First, interpretation of the terms 'indecent' and 'obscene' had become too 'narrow', and judges tended to 'give the person indicted the benefit of the doubt', leading to relatively few convictions. Second, most publishers were located outside of Ireland, where they could not be prosecuted. The report recommended a system of direct state censorship by a government-appointed body.[5]

What was this 'evil literature', and how did it threaten the Irish public? The committee worried above all about newspapers dealing with 'sensational crimes, divorce cases and prosecutions for sex offences', which, while not perhaps obscene in particular instances, would over time 'present wholly distorted pictures of social life' and 'excite in morbid minds the impulse to imitation'.[6] Also of concern was 'the widely disseminated and increasing propaganda in favour of the limitation of families by the unnatural prevention of conception'.[7] In contrast to these 'fugitive publications', indecent books were considered less dangerous 'owing to their more limited sale'.[8] The committee acknowledged that literature would raise particular challenges for a censorship system, which would have to distinguish between 'books of an immoral tendency' and 'those having a purely literary aim in view but which, as part of their reflection of the world, admit representation of the vices or the passions that exist'.[9] While

recognizing the need to protect 'the classics' and other genuine literary works from censorship, the committee ominously declared that
many of the books that had attracted complaints 'have no literary
merit whatever' and are 'frankly pornographic'.[10] In practice, it would
be easy enough for censors to deny the literary merit of whatever
they considered indecent, especially works by modern writers like
O'Brien, who did not have the protective reputation of a Rabelais,
Shakespeare, or Balzac.

In 1928, on the recommendation of the committee, the new Minister for Justice, James Fitzgerald-Kenney, introduced the Censorship
of Publications Bill, which sparked resistance in the press and among
Irish writers, including G. B. Shaw and W. B. Yeats.[11] There was broad
consensus in the Dáil, Ireland's lower house, that greater powers were
needed to deal with sensationalist periodicals and works by birth control activists. Several deputies, however, argued that books should be left
alone. They foresaw that the proposed Censorship Board would have
to make difficult judgement calls, that it could abuse its powers, and
that it would be accused of sectarian bias. Professor Michael Tierney
of University College Dublin wondered how the board would know
where to draw the line when censoring books, and warned, 'I am
very much afraid that the result of this section will be that under
the authority of this Dáil a list of prohibited books will be produced
which will make a laughingstock of this country.'[12] In response to
such concerns, the minister narrowed the definition of indecency
and introduced additional factors that the board would be permitted to consider, including literary merit, the language of publication,
the probable readership, and the intended circulation of publications.[13]
The bill did not specify precisely how these factors might be weighed,
and left much to the discretion of the board.

In the Seanad the bill met its staunchest political opponent, the
baronet and war veteran Sir John Keane, who proved to be the most
committed defender of intellectual freedom in the Oireachtas debates.
Acknowledging that his opinion was unpopular, Keane observed drily
that if the proposed censorship were to prove an innovation in 'mental
betterment, then we shall have achieved a wonderful victory over all
past history in this new State of ours'. He asserted the liberty of the
writer in strong terms:

I imagine a writer of any influence is a writer who writes with his whole being, a writer who cannot help writing—a writer who must write of the world as he finds it with all his faculties, and he must deal with realism as he sees it, with squalor as he sees it, and other things as he finds them.[14]

Though eloquent, Keane was also incautious. He argued that there were two ways of 'disciplining the mind and character', the 'method of repression and control and the method of selection and liberty of choice', associating the former with Catholicism and the latter with Protestantism. He insisted he was not saying that the Protestant way was better, but claimed that the bill was designed to impose the Catholic method.[15] The other senators scrambled to distance themselves from his views, one pointing to the Puritans as evidence that Catholics did not have a monopoly on repression. After further quarrelling over amendments in both houses—Should the board have five or nine members? Perhaps seven?—the bill passed, and the Censorship of Publications Board was born.

Within four years, on the advice of the (five-member) board and under the authority of the Minister for Justice, 320 items had been added to the Register of Prohibited Publications, including *The Well of Loneliness* (see Chapter 10), *Lady Chatterley's Lover* (see Chapter 12), and works by Sherwood Anderson, Theodore Dreiser, Daphne Du Maurier, William Faulkner, Aldous Huxley, Wyndham Lewis, W. Somerset Maugham, Claude McKay, George Moore, Liam O'Flaherty, Seán Ó Faoláin, G. B. Shaw, H. G. Wells, and the birth control educators Marie Stopes and Margaret Sanger.[16] By 1936, the total was over six hundred, and new additions included Boccaccio, Ernest Hemingway, the Marquis de Sade, Vladimir Nabokov (in English translation), and Mae West.[17] Books on the register could not be sold or distributed, and could not be kept, imported, or advertised for sale or distribution, except by special permit from the minister.

The censorship legislation was not actually very effective at preventing the circulation of books, since they were often available for months or years before the board issued a decision on them, but it did socially stigmatize banned authors and affected booksellers' willingness to carry their work.[18] In this oppressive climate the

Limerick-born Kate O'Brien was emerging as a writer, winning the Hawthornden and James Tait Black prizes for her first novel, *Without my Cloak*, in 1932.[19] The scholar Ailbhe Smyth writes that O'Brien, herself a lesbian, 'search[ed] for ways of naming experiences which women had not (yet) dared to name, even to themselves, and which swerve close to, if not right into, the "wild zone" of a space beyond the rigid boundaries of convention'.[20] O'Brien's third novel, *Mary Lavelle*, fell foul of the Censorship Board in 1936. We do not know exactly on what grounds the novel was banned, since the board met behind closed doors and used a set form of words to report its recommendations to the minister. The Act of 1929 defines 'indecent' as 'suggestive of, or inciting to sexual immorality or unnatural vice or likely in any other similar way to corrupt or deprave', where the phrase 'unnatural vice' is code for homosexuality. *Mary Lavelle* tells the story of a twenty-four-year-old Irish woman who defers her wedding in order to work in Spain as a governess. There, she is caught in a love triangle involving her employer and his married son. Mary, a virgin, has rather unpleasant sex with the son ('He took her quickly and bravely. The pain made her cry out and writhe in shock, but he held her hard against him and in great love compelled her to endure it'), and she bonds with a gay woman, who confesses, 'I like you the way a man would, you see. I never can see you without—without wanting to touch you. I could look at your face for ever.'[21] Such passages might have provoked the ban, though, crucially, the board was not supposed to ban a book based only on instances of ostensible indecency. The Act states that a book can be prohibited only if it is 'in its general tendency indecent or obscene', and a periodical only if recent issues have 'usually or frequently been indecent or obscene'. Fitzgerald-Kenney repeatedly assured the Oireachtas that the legislation was intended to deal with publications that were professedly, not incidentally, indecent. Were the members of the board respecting the law, or, having been sent books with objectionable passages already underlined by the Catholic Truth Society or customs officials, were they simply banning books based on portions taken out of context?[22]

This question brought *The Land of Spices* into the new Seanad of the Republic of Ireland. O'Brien's fifth novel was added to the Register of

Prohibited Publications on 6 May 1941.[23] By the following year, 1,552 books had been banned, and opposition to the board was at a peak.[24] Fellow victim of censorship Seán Ó Faoláin had founded a literary magazine called the *Bell*, which published criticism of the institution. He singled out the prohibition of *The Land of Spices* as a clear case of injustice.[25] Once again taking up the cause of the suppressed writer, Keane introduced a motion alleging that the Censorship Board had lost public confidence and calling for it to be reconstituted. His argument revolved around three books: Eric Cross's *The Tailor and Ansty*, Halliday Sutherland's *The Laws of Life*, and *The Land of Spices*. Characteristically forceful, Keane accused the Censorship of Publications Board of being a 'literary Gestapo'—this in 1942.[26] In the ensuing four-day debate, Keane and his nemesis, Professor William Magennis, read extracts from the books, which created a dilemma for the Seanad, since prohibited material was going to be entered into the official reports. The chairman had all quotations redacted, with the result that we do not know precisely which passages were read out, only that several raised expressions of shock and disgust from various senators. It is obvious, however, which passage Keane read from *The Land of Spices*, because he continued, 'For that phrase and that phrase alone that book is censored.'[27] The phrase, of course, was '*Etienne* and her father, in the embrace of love'. But was Keane correct?

William Magennis was chair of the Censorship Board, on which he had sat for over eight years. He had been involved with the 'evil literature' question since 1925, when he sat on a subcommittee created by the Catholic Truth Society, and he had also been the first chair of the Censorship of Films Appeal Board.[28] In the 1942 debate he was relentless, delivering a marathon speech in which he belaboured every infelicity in Keane's reasoning, played on the baronet's English roots and Protestant faith, took the Gestapo remark very personally ('I am not exactly Heinrich Himmler'), and mired the discussion in minutiae. Accused of Victorian prudery, Magennis said, 'My standards do not date back to Queen Victoria's days; they date back to Moses.'[29] He denied Keane's allegation that *The Land of Spices* was censored for one phrase alone, which would have been a gross misapplication of the law. He argued that the 'central interest' of the novel 'is sodomy', and that 'from the first few pages of the book up to that passage, it is dominated by the influence of the terrible theme'. He claimed that, while reading the novel,

> All the time your interest and curiosity are excited in a mounting degree as to what it was that happened. It is only now, when the woman has remorse for having hated her father to such a degree of enormity that she broke away from his house and took refuge in an Order, that you learn what it was.[30]

Magennis evidently thought that tantalizing the reader by slowly revealing the crucial event in Helen's life was, in the language of the Act, 'suggestive of, or inciting to [...] unnatural vice'. He also mentioned, without specifying, 'a great deal of matter [...] in other passages in the book that makes it evil reading'.[31] Keane's interpretation of the novel was more convincing: that its theme is religious vocation, and the 'suggestion of homosexuality' is instrumental to the story of Helen Archer's development as a nun.[32] Magennis did, however, make a case that the Censorship Board could have based its decision on what it understood to be the 'general tendency' of the novel, not just a single passage.

Keane's protest motion was never going to pass. The balance of parliamentary opinion was still strongly in favour of censorship, and the senators did not believe that the board really had lost public confidence. Seán O'Donovan forced the motion to a vote rather than allow Keane to withdraw it, so that its decisive defeat—thirty-four to two—would go on the record. In the course of the debate, however, Michael Tierney and James Green Douglas both suggested an appeals process to check the Censorship Board's powers. Keane had succeeded in reopening the controversy and raising the possibility of reforming the Act. In 1944 he would also challenge the wartime censorship of books, post, and official records, and he prepared an amending Censorship of Publications Bill, which he withdrew on assurances that Éamon de Valera's Fianna Fáil government would reform the legislation itself.[33] It did so, and the Censorship of Publications Act 1946 was passed, which permitted either five members of the Oireachtas or the author, editor, or publisher of a work to appeal its prohibition through an appeals board. At the personal urging of Keane, O'Brien successfully appealed the ban of *The Land of Spices*.[34] She was the only author to appeal the prohibition of her own work. An appeal of the *Mary Lavelle* ban was denied.[35]

In the 1960s continued censorship of Irish writers, including Edna O'Brien and John McGahern, led to further reform.[36] A third Censorship of Publications Act was passed in 1967, which introduced an expiration period to certain prohibitions. Prohibition orders issued against books on the grounds of indecency or obscenity would expire after twelve years. Because *Mary Lavelle* had been published more than twelve years earlier, its ban was automatically lifted when the Act came into effect.

In recent years, the Censorship Board has fallen into disuse, though as of 2012 the Register of Prohibited Publications still listed eight books banned for abortion advocacy (including *How to Drive your Man Wild in Bed*) and about two hundred and forty periodical titles, including *Playgirl* magazine, the English edition of *News of the World*, and a large assortment of true crime and detective magazines.[37] In 2011, when the members of the Censorship Board completed their terms, they were not replaced. In late 2013 Niall Collins of Fianna Fáil, TD for Limerick, introduced a private member's bill to abolish the Censorship Board, which he described as an 'aging monolith', a 'bygone reminder of a bygone time'. While the opinion prevailed in the house that literary censorship was obsolete, and that legislation on child pornography and incitement to hatred now provided the necessary restrictions on publications, the Fine Gael–Labour coalition government defeated the bill. Pat Rabbitte, Minister for Communications, Energy and Natural Resources, assured the Dáil that the government intended to address the censorship issue, but needed to consider all three of the Acts together rather than repeal them piecemeal. Moreover, the board would need to be reconstituted at least once more to deal with a complaint about *Laura: A Novel You Will Never Forget* by Alan Shatter, then Minister for Justice and Equality.[38] The board cleared *Laura* in 2014,[39] but in March 2016 it banned a novel entitled *The Raped Little Runaway*, the first book it had censored in eighteen years. The chair of the board, Shane McCarthy, told the *Irish Examiner*, 'The collective view of the board was that it was a vile publication as it contained graphic descriptions of the rape of a minor.' In December 2016, a man charged with the sexual assault of a boy under ten was also charged for possession of the book under child pornography laws.[40]

Notes

1. Kate O'Brien, *The Land of Spices* (London: Virago, 2000), p. 165.
2. Donal Ó Drisceoil, 'A Dark Chapter: Censorship and the Irish Writer', in *The Oxford History of the Irish Book*, ed. Robert Welch and Brian Walker (Oxford: Oxford University Press, 2006–), v: *The Irish Book in English, 1891–2000*, ed. Clare Hutton and Patrick Walsh (2011), 285–303 (p. 285).
3. Michael Adams, *Censorship: The Irish Experience* (Dublin: Scepter Books, 1968), pp. 16–17.
4. Committee on Evil Literature, *Report of the Committee on Evil Literature* (Dublin, 1927), p. 4, http://opac.oireachtas.ie/AWData/Library3/Library2/DL068551.pdf, accessed 20 December 2016; Ó Drisceoil, p. 288.
5. Committee on Evil Literature, pp. 6–11.
6. Committee on Evil Literature, pp. 9, 10.
7. Committee on Evil Literature, p. 13.
8. Committee on Evil Literature, p. 16.
9. Committee on Evil Literature, p. 18.
10. Committee on Evil Literature, pp. 16, 18.
11. Adams, pp. 38–40, 48–49.
12. 26 *Dáil Debates* col. 645 (18 October 1928).
13. 28 *Dáil Debates* cols. 1528–30 (20 March 1929).
14. 12 *Seanad Debates* cols. 56, 63 (11 April 1929).
15. 12 *Seanad Debates* cols. 68, 68–69 (11 April 1929).
16. *Books Prohibited in the Irish Free State under the Censorship of Publications Act, 1929* (Dublin: Eason & Son, 1933).
17. *Books Prohibited in the Irish Free State under the Censorship of Publications Act, 1929 (as on 30 April, 1936)* (Dublin: Eason & Son, 1936).
18. Ó Drisceoil, pp. 293–94.
19. Eibhear Walshe, *Kate O'Brien: A Writing Life* (Dublin: Irish Academic Press, 2006), p. 51.
20. Ailbhe Smyth, 'Counterpoints: A Note (or Two) on Feminism and Kate O'Brien', in *Ordinary People Dancing: Essays on Kate O'Brien*, ed. Eibhear Walshe (Cork: Cork University Press, 1993), pp. 24–35 (p. 30).
21. Kate O'Brien, *Mary Lavelle* (London: Virago, 1984; repr. 2006), pp. 248, 269.
22. Ó Drisceoil, pp. 290–91.
23. Walshe, p. 89.
24. 27 *Seanad Debates* cols. 157–58 (2 December 1942); Adams, p. 98.
25. Adams, pp. 81–82.

26. 27 *Seanad Debates* col. 21 (18 November 1942).

27. 27 *Seanad Debates* col. 25 (18 November 1942).

28. Adams, p. 19 and note.

29. 27 *Seanad Debates* cols. 126, 159 (2 December 1942).

30. 27 *Seanad Debates* cols. 70, 71 (18 November 1942).

31. 27 *Seanad Debates* cols. 71, 77 (18 November 1942).

32. 27 *Seanad Debates* col. 318 (9 December 1942).

33. 28 *Seanad Debates* cols. 710–64 (27 January 1944); 28 *Seanad Debates* cols. 851–68, 885–935 (24 February 1944); 28 *Seanad Debates* cols. 1422–28 (20 June 1944); 29 *Seanad Debates* cols. 711–14 (6 December 1944).

34. Walshe, p. 90.

35. Ó Drisceoil, p. 298.

36. Ó Drisceoil, pp. 299–300.

37. Censorship of Publications Board, *Register of Prohibited Publications* (Dublin, 2012), http://www.justice.ie/en/JELR/Pages/WP15000099, accessed 23 December 2016.

38. 827 *Dáil Debates* No. 4 (24 January 2014).

39. Kevin Doyle, 'Shatter's Novel Is Cleared by the Censor', *Irish Independent*, 9 May 2014, http://www.independent.ie/irish-news/politics/shatters-novel-is-cleared-by-the-censor-30258684.html, accessed 23 December 2016.

40. Gordon Deegan, 'Charged for Having First Book Banned in Decades', *Irish Examiner*, 21 December 2016, http://www.irishexaminer.com/ireland/charged-for-having-first-book-banned-in-decades-436096.html, accessed 1 January 2017. See also Michael Barry, 'Censorship Board Bans Book for the First Time since 1998', *Irish Times*, 12 March 2016, http://www.irishtimes.com/news/ireland/irish-news/censorship-board-bans-book-for-the-first-time-since-1998-1.2571029, accessed 23 December 2016.

14

Black Boy
Richard Wright

Richard Wright's *Black Boy* tells the story of his youth in the Southern United States, where he was born in 1908 on a Mississippi plantation, the grandson of men and women who had been enslaved. He describes his father's absence, his mother's illness, and the arbitrary authority of Black adults who beat him and attempted to control his mind. He describes the violence of the streets of Memphis, Tennessee, into which his mother sent him, a child, with a stick as a weapon and the warning 'If you come back into this house without those groceries, I'll whip you!' He describes the oppression that undergirded these conditions of life: the official racism of Jim Crow, the aggressions big and small through which White people kept Black people in subjection, and the 'white death'—death by Whites—'the threat of which hung over every male black in the South'. He describes the hunger of his body, and he describes the hunger of his mind—how, shuttled from one home and school to another, browbeaten with a religion in which he did not believe, he longed 'for a kind of consciousness, a mode of being that the way of life about me had said could not be, must not be, and upon which the penalty of death had been placed'.[1]

Wright first sensed intellectual satisfaction in Jackson, Mississippi, where a young schoolteacher named Ella boarded with his grandmother. When Wright asked her what she was reading, Ella told him

Richard Wright, photographed in Harlem by Gordon Parks in 1943.

the story of the villainous Bluebeard, who murders his wives. Wright recalls:

> The tale made the world around me be, throb, live. As she spoke, reality changed, the look of things altered, and the world became peopled with magical presences. My sense of life deepened and the feel of things was different, somehow.

Wright's grandmother cut the story short, calling it the 'Devil's work'.[2] Years later, she would burn the books Wright brought home to read. But fiction had sparked something in him: 'I had tasted what to me was life, and I would have more of it, somehow, someway.' Wright read what he could get his hands on ('tattered, secondhand copies of *Flynn's Detective Weekly* or the *Argosy All-Story Magazine*') and began to write, publishing a tale called 'The Voodoo of Hell's Half-Acre' in a local Black newspaper, to the baffled disapproval of his family and school-mates.[3] In 1925 he moved back to Memphis, where he would buy and resell used books and magazines so that he could read them. Because Jim Crow laws barred him from using the public library, Wright prevailed on an Irish Catholic, himself a target of hatred in the South, to lend him a library card, with which he would borrow books under the pretence of running errands. In this way Wright discovered realist and naturalist fiction, including Theodore Dreiser's novels, which gave him a 'sense of life itself', and laid the foundation for his own career as an author.[4]

Wright wrote in his journal that the central question of his life was 'How can I live freely?'[5] His struggle did not end when his career began. In 1938, living in Harlem and now free to read, he wondered to what extent he was free to write. He had conceived a novel that readers would not 'read and weep over and feel good about', but which would 'be so hard and deep that they would have to face it without the consolation of tears'.[6] This novel was called *Native Son*, and featured a Black antihero named Bigger Thomas. Out of fear of being caught in a White woman's bedroom, Bigger accidentally suffocates his employer's daughter, Mary Dalton. He later rapes and murders his Black girlfriend, Bessie Mears, before being sentenced to death. In planning this novel, Wright struggled with self-censorship, a sense that he could not get away with writing what he wanted to. In 'How Big-ger Was Born' he describes the internalized voice of his White readers, a censor 'draped in white' like a member of the Ku Klux Klan:

> Like Bigger himself, I felt a mental censor—product of the fears which a Negro feels from living in America—standing over me, draped in white, warning me not to write. This censor's warnings were translated into my own thought processes thus: 'What will white people think if I draw the picture of such a Negro boy? Will they not at once say: "See, didn't we tell you all along that niggers are like that? Now, look, one of their own kind has come along and drawn the picture for us!"'[7]

Wright worried, too, about fellow Black members of the Communist Party who might find his politics suspect and middle-class Black people who were 'ashamed of Bigger and what he meant'. Wright overcame these fears and wrote Bigger's story 'because', he explained,

> I felt with all of my being that he was more important than what any person, white or black, would say or try to make of him, more impor-tant than any political analysis designed to explain or deny him, more important, even, than my own sense of fear, shame, and diffidence.[8]

Wright wrote the novel, secured a publishing contract with Harper & Brothers, and won a Guggenheim fellowship.[9]

Native Son next encountered pre-publication censorship, though of a kind that required the author's participation. Wright's publisher had sent a copy of the novel to the influential Book-of-the-Month Club, whose judges expressed interest in making it one of their selec-tions, provided Wright agreed to make some changes. Bigger and his friend would no longer masturbate in a cinema, Mary Dalton would no longer have sex with her boyfriend while Bigger is chauffeuring them, and she would no longer grind her hip against Bigger when, taking advantage of her intoxication, he kisses and gropes her while helping her to bed. This last change would leave unclear whether Mary is conscious, making Bigger seem even more predatory. Wright made the changes, and when it appeared in 1940 *Native Son* enjoyed the enhanced distribution and publicity of a Book-of-the-Month.

His initial fears were borne out in a few of the critical responses, including Lillian Johnson's and Langston Hughes's, but the book was a tremendous success, selling 215,000 copies in the first three weeks.[10] The revisions also convinced the publisher Gollancz, who had initially turned down the book, to publish it in the United Kingdom.[11] Wright's negotiation with the judges is an example of how marketing decisions can blend into censorship. Wright was free to reject the judges' demands, but they were powerful cultural gatekeepers, and it was in his best interest to appease them.

In 1944 Wright planned to publish his autobiography, originally entitled *American Hunger*. Once again the Book-of-the-Month Club was interested, but once again he needed to revise the text to meet their expectations. At his publisher's suggestion, Wright altered some dialogue in which his White employer asks him about the size of his penis.[12] More drastically, he cut the final third of the book, which covered his time in Chicago and his involvement with the Communist Party. The new version, *Black Boy*, would end when the young man, living in Memphis, had finally saved enough money to move to the Northern United States. This ending is artistically effective, since it leaves Wright on the verge of an unknown future opening up before him. But it also gives the impression that his troubles might be over— that the North might prove to be an anti-racist utopia, which was not, of course, the case. Evidence suggests that the judges were pushing this optimistic interpretation, and hoped to spare some aspect of the country from Wright's scathing depiction. Dorothy Canfield Fisher asked Wright if he could mention 'hope' in the book's new ending, and if he could credit America for making him 'conscious of possibilities'. She wondered if he might acknowledge the work White people had done in combating racism.[13] Wright went as far as using the word 'hope' and listing the (White and male) American authors who had influenced him, but he refused to compromise his critical vision of the nation any further: he wrote back, 'I do not think that Negroes will be treated any better in this country until whites themselves realize that there is something dead wrong with the American way of life.'[14] Fisher was satisfied: 'You have *not* said a word beyond what you really felt and feel—I might have known you'd be incapable of that—the ending is a beautiful piece of writing and deeply full of meaning.'[15] Published in

March 1945, the book sold more than five hundred thousand copies by the end of the year.[16]

Wright believed that the Communist Party had put pressure on the Book-of-the-Month Club to cut the Chicago section of his autobiography.[17] He had been involved with the party, but denounced it in 1944 in an essay extracted from *American Hunger*. This split prompted the FBI, which had begun monitoring Wright in the early 1940s because of his book *12 Million Black Voices*, to recommend his inclusion on the Security Index, a list of national security risks. Evidently rebelling against the Communist Party over its handling of racial politics was even more dangerous than being a communist.[18] The FBI file on Wright grew to 254 pages between 1942 and 1963. The bureau's extensive surveillance of African American writers under director J. Edgar Hoover was itself a diffuse form of censorship likely to create a chilling effect. Wright knew that he was being watched, and the author Amiri Baraka thought that Wright had toned down his revolutionary politics because of it. On the other hand, Wright and other Black authors who were aware of their surveillance also explicitly addressed it in their work. Wright records his experience with humour in his 1949 poem 'The FB Eye Blues':

> That old FB eye
> Tied a bell to my bed stall
> Said old FB eye
> Tied a bell to my bed stall
> Each time I love my baby, gover'ment knows it all.[19]

Wright died in Paris in 1960. He would not live to see his work challenged in US schools. The American Library Association lists nine challenges to *Black Boy* between 1972 and 2007, and eight to *Native Son* between 1978 and 1998, some of which resulted in the books being removed from schools.[20] The most notable of these incidents, in Long Island, New York, sparked a court case that made it to the Supreme Court of the United States. In 1975 members of the Island Trees Union Free School District Board of Education attended a conference in Watkins Glen, New York, held by a conservative parents' organization called People of New York United (PONYU). There the board saw a list of 'objectionable' books, with titles, excerpts, and commentary.[21]

Two passages from *Black Boy* appeared on the list.[22] The first consisted of slurs that Wright and fellow Black children in West Helena, Arkansas, ('seven, eight, and nine years of age') used to chant at a Jewish grocer's shop:

> *Bloody Christ killers*
>   *Never trust a Jew*
> *Bloody Christ killers*
>   *What won't a Jew do?*[23]

and

> *Red, white, and blue*
>   *Your pa was a Jew*
> *Your ma a dirty Dago*
>   *What the hell is you?*[24]

The second excerpt was a string of abuse that White men directed at Wright himself and the Black man whom they had paid him to fight:

> 'Crush that nigger's nuts, nigger!'
> 'Hit that nigger!'
> 'Aw, fight, you goddamn niggers!'
> 'Sock 'im in his f–k–g piece!'
> 'Make 'im bleed!'[25]

The PONYU list removes these passages from their context, making it impossible to judge their purpose in the book. In the first excerpt, Wright is not endorsing his childish ignorance. Rather, his anti-Semitism illustrates his flawed education: 'To hold an attitude of antagonism or distrust toward Jews was bred in us from childhood; it was not merely racial prejudice, it was a part of our cultural heritage.'[26] The second excerpt, meanwhile, is one of the most powerful examples in the book of Wright's degradation at the hands of White men. When Wright is employed as an assistant at a spectacles factory in Memphis, his White foreman tries to turn him against a young Black man named Harrison working at a different spectacles factory. The foreman tells each of the men that the other is waiting for him with a knife. The plan almost works: Wright and Harrison know they are being manipulated, but still become suspicious of each other. Finally, the foreman and his White associates offer to give Wright and Harrison five dollars each if they will fight. Wright doesn't want to, but Harrison needs the money. Their disagreement escalates the manufactured hostility between them, they agree to the match, and, egged on by the White men, they thrash each other. Afterwards, Wright records, 'I felt that I had done something unclean, something for which I could never properly atone.'[27]

On their return from the conference, the Island Trees board members had a janitor let them into the high school library, where they found nine of the listed books in the card catalogue. (They performed this search after hours at an event called 'Winter School Night', to the amusement of the *New York Daily News*, which printed a cartoon portraying 'two members of the Board as a pair of shady hoods who surreptitiously sneak into school buildings under cover of darkness to snatch library books'.[28]) The board requested that these nine books, plus two more from the junior high school, be removed for review. The offending titles were *Black Boy*, *Slaughterhouse-Five* by Kurt Vonnegut, *The Naked Ape* by Desmond Morris, *Down These Mean Streets* by Piri Thomas, *Best Short Stories by Negro Writers*, edited by Langston Hughes, *Laughing Boy* by Oliver LaFarge, *A Hero Ain't Nothing but a Sandwich* by Alice Childress, *Soul on Ice* by Eldridge Cleaver, *A Reader for Writers*, edited by Jerome Archer, *The Fixer* by Bernard Malamud, and the anonymous *Go Ask Alice*, now generally understood to be the work of Beatrice Sparks.[29] It is worth noting that nearly half of the authors on this list—Thomas, Hughes, Childress, Cleaver, and Wright, were Black. *A Reader for Writers* appeared on the PONYU list because of content that 'equates Malcolm X, considered by many to be a traitor to this country, with the founding fathers of our country', though members of the school board claimed to have banned it for Jonathan Swift's satire *A Modest Proposal* instead.[30]

The school district superintendent, Richard Morrow, wrote to the board, advising them to follow their existing policy, which required the superintendent to appoint a committee to examine challenged books. Morrow warned that 'unilateral banning by the Board, without inputs from the staff, would surely create a furious uproar—not only in the staff, but across the community, Long Island and the state'.[31] He objected to banning books on the basis of a list compiled by a third party, and, in a later meeting, he argued that it was wrong to judge books based on excerpts taken out of context. The board continued to withhold the books, but appointed its own committee to review them. This committee, consisting of parents and staff, recommended that six of the books be returned to the shelves, two of them with restricted access. The board overruled this recommendation, and returned only *Laughing Boy* and *Black Boy* to the shelves, placing restrictions on access to *Black Boy*.[32]

Morrow was right, in part, about the uproar. Newspapers took against the board of education, which forced it to issue a press release defending its actions. The press release, which accused the teachers' union of attacking the board, claimed that the banned books 'contain material which is offensive to Christians, Jews, Blacks, and Americans in general', as well as 'obscenities, blasphemies, brutality, and perversion beyond description'. The board portrayed itself as parents' 'faithful Watchdogs', the defenders of community values, and this may well have been the case.[33] An informal poll of 4,979 local residences by the board's legal counsel found that 59 per cent of the 866 respondents supported the board, and the two board members who were running for re-election retained their positions.[34]

The board did have opponents, however. Several students and parents were troubled by the ban, including seventeen-year-old Steven Pico, who 'had been told about how books were banned in communist countries and burned in Nazi Germany' and 'could not believe that it was happening in the United States in the 1970s'.[35] Pico believed that his rights had been infringed, and resolved to fight the board. He would later estimate that most of his fellow students opposed his actions or did not care: 'High school students and their families', he recalled, 'are preoccupied with getting into colleges, and most people fear involvement in controversial issues. Teachers were worried about tenure and their jobs, since the Board of Education was also their employer.'[36] One teacher whispered to him that he was doing the right thing, and he was troubled 'that she felt the need to whisper'.[37]

With the support of a group of like-minded students—Jacqueline Gold, Russell Rieger, Glenn Yarris, and Paul Sochinski—Pico sought 'the best attorneys'. The American Civil Liberties Union agreed to take on the case, and Pico sought an injunction against the school board.[38] The decision of the district judge was a summary judgment, arrived at without a trial. The judge found agreement among all parties about the facts of the case:

> the board acted not on religious principles but on its conservative educational philosophy, and on its belief that the nine books removed from the school library and curriculum were irrelevant, vulgar, immoral, and in bad taste, making them educationally unsuitable for the district's junior and senior high school students.

Given these facts, he ruled in favour of the school board, finding that its actions were 'within the broad range of discretion constitutionally afforded to educational officials who are elected by the community'.[39]

On the students' appeal, the Court of Appeals for the Second Circuit overturned the initial ruling. Two of the three judges thought that the facts of the case were not sufficiently established: the board's 'erratic, arbitrary, and free-wheeling' approach to the ban called its motives into question. Had the books been removed from the library merely because of vulgarity, or had they been banned in order to establish certain 'views as the correct and orthodox ones for all purposes in the particular community'? The two judges were especially worried that the board's arbitrary decision could create a chilling effect on speech. They remanded the case for a trial so that the motives and actions of the board could be examined fully.[40] The board appealed to the US Supreme Court.

At this time judicial opinion about First Amendment cases in schools was deeply divided. Legal precedents had established that students had rights to the freedoms of speech and religion under the First Amendment of the US Constitution, but also that those rights were subject to limitations in schools. School boards had the responsibility to inculcate community values in students and to make decisions about library books and curricula. Some judges wanted to ensure that school boards did not overstep their authority and infringe students' rights by suppressing unorthodox ideas and opinions. Others thought that the courts had better leave the school boards alone, lest the courts become, in the words of Chief Justice Burger, a '"super censor" of school board library decisions'.[41] The Supreme Court, which Pico called 'the most conservative court in sixty years', reflected this rift.[42] The only thing that a majority of five could agree on was that the case should indeed go to trial to determine the board's motivations. A plurality of three justices ventured the constitutional theory behind this decision, which involved the concept of the 'right to receive information and ideas', a corollary of the freedom of expression protected by the First Amendment. If, in removing books from the library, the board members had exercised their discretion in a 'narrowly partisan or political manner', then they had violated the students' rights to receive ideas.[43] Rather than face a trial, the board returned the books to the shelves.[44]

The balance of future court decisions would continue to sway between protecting students' First Amendment rights and recognizing the power of school officials to limit those rights.[45] The plurality opinion in *Pico* is not a binding precedent, but it has been used as guidance in other cases, especially those involving censorship in school libraries. In 1995 a district court concurred with the *Pico* plurality when preventing a Kansas school board from removing Nancy Garden's *Annie on my Mind* from libraries because, as one board member put it, the book 'glorified homosexuality as a lifestyle'.[46] The Island Trees case was fundamentally about whether the state's educational institutions could impose on students the values of the majority by suppressing access to other perspectives. Pico himself was convinced that 'racism was a factor' in the case. He asked, 'Why were so many books discussing the experiences of minority groups in the U.S. on that original list?'[47] His introduction to censorship was only a small brush with the forces that Richard Wright fought throughout his life, and Pico would remember it as the moment when his 'education had in many ways finally begun'.[48]

Notes

1. Richard Wright, *Black Boy: A Record of Childhood and Youth* (London: Vintage, 2000), pp. 16, 170, 173.
2. Wright, *Black Boy*, p. 37.
3. Wright, *Black Boy*, pp. 38, 132, 168. See further p. 128.

4. Wright, *Black Boy*, p. 252. See further p. 246–47.

5. Richard Wright, journal, quoted in Jennifer Jensen Wallach, *Richard Wright: From Black Boy to World Citizen* (Chicago: Dee, 2010), p. 6.

6. Richard Wright, 'How Bigger Was Born', in Wright, *Early Works: Lawd Today!, Uncle Tom's Children, Native Son*, ed. Arnold Rampersad (New York: Library of America, 1991), pp. 851–81 (p. 874).

7. Wright, 'How Bigger Was Born', p. 867.

8. Wright, 'How Bigger Was Born', pp. 869–70.

9. Hazel Rowley, *Richard Wright: The Life and Times* (Chicago: University of Chicago Press, 2008), pp. 156–57, 164.

10. Rowley, pp. 182–84, 191–93.

11. Arnold Rampersad, 'Note on the Texts', in Wright, *Early Works*, pp. 909–14 (pp. 912–13).

12. Arnold Rampersad, 'Note on the Texts', in Richard Wright, *Later Works: Black Boy (American Hunger), The Outsider*, ed. Rampersad (New York: Library of America, 1991), pp. 868–74 (p. 868).

13. Rowley, pp. 286–91.

14. Richard Wright to Dorothy Canfield Fisher (20 July 1944), Canfield Fisher papers, quoted in Rowley, p. 289.

15. Dorothy Canfield Fisher to Richard Wright (23 July [1944]), in *Keeping Fires Night and Day: Selected Letters of Dorothy Canfield Fisher*, ed. Mark J. Madigan (Columbia: University of Missouri Press, 1993), p. 236.

16. Rowley, pp. 290, 321.

17. Rampersad, 'Note on the Texts', in Wright, *Later Works*, p. 869.

18. Wallach, pp. 112–15. See also Rowley, pp. 275–76, 295.

19. Richard Wright, 'The FB Eye Blues', quoted in William J. Maxwell, *F.B. Eyes: How J. Edgar Hoover's Ghostreaders Framed African American Literature* (Princeton: Princeton University Press, 2015), p. 216. See also Maxwell, pp. 119–21, 284.

20. Robert P. Doyle, *Banned Books: Challenging our Freedom to Read* (Chicago: American Library Association, 2014), pp. 331–32.

21. Bd. of Educ., Island Trees Union Free Sch. Dist. No. 26 v. Pico, 457 U.S. 853, 856 (1982).

22. Pico v. Bd. of Educ., Island Trees Union Free Sch. Dist. No. 26, 638 F.2d 404, 421 (2d Cir. 1980) (Mansfield, J., dissenting).

23. Wright, *Black Boy*, p. 59 (emphasis original).

24. Wright, *Black Boy*, p. 59 (emphasis original).

25. Wright, *Black Boy*, p. 245.

26. Wright, *Black Boy*, p. 60.

27. Wright, *Black Boy*, p. 245. See further pp. 237–45.

28. Board of Education, Island Trees Union Free School District No. 26, 'Press Release', 19 March 1976, quoted in Pico v. Bd. of Educ., Island Trees Union Free Sch. Dist., 474 F. Supp. 387, 390 (E.D.N.Y. 1979).

29. *Pico*, 638 F.2d at 407 n. 2.

30. *Pico*, 638 F.2d at 407, 408. See further p. 412.

31. Richard Morrow to Board of Education, Re: 'List of Books to Be Banned', 27 February 1972, quoted in *Pico*, 638 F.2d at 409.

32. *Pico*, 638 F.2d at 409–11; *Pico*, 638 F.2d at 423 (Mansfield, J., dissenting).

33. Board of Education, Island Trees Union Free School District No. 26, 'Press Release', quoted in *Pico* 474 F. Supp. at 390, 391.

34. *Pico*, 638 F.2d at 411–12.

35. Steven Pico, 'An Introduction to Censorship', *School Library Media Quarterly* 18.2 (1990), 84–87 (p. 85).

36. Debra Lau Whelan, 'NCAC Talks to the Man Behind Pico v Board of Ed', Blogging Censorship, National Coalition Against Censorship, 9 July 2013, https://ncacblog.wordpress.com/2013/07/09/ncac-talks-to-the-man-behind-pico-v-board-of-ed, accessed 23 December 2016.

37. Pico, p. 87.

38. Pico, p. 85. See also *Pico*, 638 F.2d at 404.

39. *Pico*, 474 F. Supp. at 392, 398.

40. *Pico*, 638 F.2d at 416, 417.

41. *Pico*, 457 U.S. at 885 (Burger, C.J., dissenting).

42. Pico, p. 86.

43. *Pico*, 457 U.S. at 854, 867 (plurality opinion).

44. Pico, p. 86.

45. Herbert N. Foerstel, *Banned in the U.S.A.: A Reference Guide to Book Censorship in Schools and Public Libraries* (Westport, CT: Greenwood Press, 1994), pp. 90–97.

46. Case v. Unified Sch. Dist. No. 233, 908 F. Supp. 864, 871, 874–76 (D. Kan. 1995). See also Office for Intellectual Freedom of the American Library Association, *Intellectual Freedom Manual*, 8th edn (Chicago: American Library Association, 2010), p. 341.

47. Whelan.

48. Pico, p. 85.

15

'The Orphan', *Shock SuspenStories* No. 14

Bill Gaines, Al Feldstein, and Jack Kamen

In the decade after the Second World War, so many people feared that American-style comic books depicting crime, violence, horror, and sex were luring children into delinquency that a vigorous movement emerged in response. This movement spanned the political spectrum in several countries, including the United States, the United Kingdom, and Canada, and fuelled extensive censorship that no single case can encapsulate. Students burned books, including issues of *Superman* and *Batman*, in school bonfires. Municipalities and states in the United States used various measures to classify comics and keep objectionable ones out of children's hands. Canada's federal government prohibited crime comics, with the consequence that a retailer in Manitoba was convicted for stocking *Dick Tracy Monthly* No. 62. The United Kingdom similarly outlawed crime and horror comics. In 1954, under scrutiny from the Senate Subcommittee on Juvenile Delinquency, US comic book publishers submitted to a rigid code of content that changed the course of the entire medium.

One of the most frequent and least repentant offenders during the comic book scare was Bill Gaines of Entertaining Comics (EC), whose titles *Tales from the Crypt*, *The Vault of Horror*, and *The Haunt of Fear* epitomized the horror genre. A story from Gaines's *Shock Suspen-Stories* called 'The Orphan', edited by Al Feldstein and drawn by Jack

The first page of Entertaining Comics' 'The Orphan', in which Lucy kills her father and frames her mother.

Kamen, features a little girl who shoots her abusive father, framing her adulterous mother and the mother's lover, who are both executed in the electric chair. For those who believed that children were likely to imitate what they read, this story was a prime example of the danger of comic books, and it became a key piece of evidence in the campaign against the comics.[1]

New media provoke new fears. Radio, film, television, and video games have each appeared threatening in their turn. The comic book scare had its roots in the rise of mass literacy in the nineteenth century, when an expanded reading public, which now included the working classes and the young, seemed ripe for corruption by literature about crime. In 1840 a valet named François Benjamin Courvoisier slit the throat of his employer and claimed he got the idea from Harrison Ainsworth's Newgate novel *Jack Sheppard*, which he had read and seen adapted in the theatre.[2] Authors of Newgate novels selected their protagonists from the ranks of famous outlaws, and were criticized for portraying them sympathetically.[3] While the British worried about Newgate novels, penny dreadfuls, shilling shockers, and sensation fiction, Americans fretted over half-dime novels, dime novels, and illustrated crime-story papers. The moral crusader Anthony Comstock, secretary of the New York Society for the Suppression of Vice, told stories of young men whose reading allegedly drove them to violence.[4] Under the influence of Comstock and other moral reformers, several states prohibited written and pictorial representations of crime.[5]

Since their beginnings in daily newspaper strips, comics had been somewhat disreputable. Though some publishers forged defensive alliances with educators, academics, and medical professionals, criticism of the comics gathered momentum during the Second World War and snowballed into moral panic after it. Comics were fascist. Comics were communist. Worst of all, comics caused crimes.[6] Juvenile delinquency appeared to be on the rise in the United States throughout the 1940s and 1950s, both in frequency and in severity, though it is difficult to know how much of this increase was a function of public perception and changes to law enforcement practices.[7] At the same time, comic book publishers were branching out into new genres. In 1942 the first crime comic appeared: Charles Biro's *Crime Does Not Pay*. Unlike detective and superhero comics, *Crime Does Not Pay* was modelled on true crime stories and focused on the perpetrators rather than the heroes. As the title suggests, the series ensured that the villains were caught and punished, and moralized about the evils of lawlessness, but its images were brutal. Knock-offs soon followed, and the genre pro-liferated.[8] While the content of radio and film was tightly regulated, comic book publishers enjoyed the liberty of the press, and could test the limits of good taste. A notorious image from Jack Cole's 'Murder Morphine and Me' in *True Crime Comics* No. 2, published in the late 1940s, depicts a man about to stab a woman in the eye with a hypo-dermic syringe. (The scene turns out to be a nightmare from which the woman awakens.) Research conducted at the time suggested that over 90 per cent of children and 80 per cent of teenagers were reading comic books.[9] The idea that some of these books were psychologically damaging children became the bedrock of the anti-comics movement.

In the United States, where crime comics originated, the movement included the Catholic Church's National Organization for Decent Literature, the American Legion, law enforcement, politicians, retailers, Scouting troops, women's clubs, parent–teacher associations (PTAs), librarians, educators, and students.[10] From 1945, schools began holding scattered book burnings. In 1948, at St Patrick's Academy in Bingham-ton, New York, a student led a campaign to boycott local retailers until they pledged to drop comic books. Students gathered up cartons of comics, which they immolated in a school-wide spectacle as they sang 'The Catholic Action Song'. After another 1948 bonfire, this one at Spencer Elementary in West Virginia, an alarmed editor of the *Charleston Daily Mail* drew parallels with the student book burnings in Nazi Germany.[11] The purges also call to mind fifteenth-century Florence, where the religious reformer Girolamo Savonarola inspired boys to gather up the worldly possessions of the Florentines, including books and artwork, to be destroyed in Bonfires of the Vanities. In 1955, during another wave of burnings in which Scouting groups and the Legion Auxiliary joined the schools, a Girl Scout troop in Pennsylvania named their comic book pyre the 'Bonfire of the Future'.[12]

One of the leading figures of the anti-comics movement was Dr Fredric Wertham, and some called him 'Savonarola', though he was a progressive psychiatrist, not a spiritual leader.[13] In collaboration with Richard Wright (author of *Black Boy*—see Chapter 14), Wertham founded the Lafargue Clinic in Harlem, which provided affordable mental health care to the under-served, largely Black population.[14] Wertham gave expert testimony against racial segregation in schools, and opposed censorship of adult media, defending books in censorship cases. In contrast to the popular views of the time, Wertham saw crime as an effect with social causes rather than a purely individual problem.[15] He wrote:

> To understand a delinquent child one has to know the social soil in which he developed and became delinquent or troubled. And, equally important, one should know the child's inner life history, the way in which his experiences are reflected in his wishes, fantasies and rationalizations.[16]

At the Lafargue Clinic, Wertham began to study the effects of comic book reading, and became convinced that it was a factor in juvenile delinquency. While he maintained that there were many such factors, he made comics into a personal hobby-horse, and lent his professional clout to the anti-comics movement.

In 1948 Wertham organized a symposium in New York entitled 'The Psychopathology of Comic Books', which he subsequently published in the *American Journal of Psychotherapy*. Wertham's associates argued that comic books encourage children to identify with aggressors, whether villains or heroes, thereby stimulating their own aggression. The folklorist Gershon Legman claimed:

> The effect—and there are those who think it has been a conscious intention—has been to raise up an entire generation of adolescents who have felt, thousands upon thousands of times, all the sensations and emotions of committing murder, except pulling the trigger. And toy guns—advertised in the back pages of the comics—have supplied that.[17]

Wertham popularized his research in the *Saturday Review of Literature*, *Reader's Digest*, the *Ladies' Home Journal*, and eventually his 1954 book *Seduction of the Innocent*. His condemnation of crime comics, which he defined broadly enough to include superhero comics and any other genres that depict violence, extended well beyond the supposed correlation between comic reading and crime. He attacked *Wonder Woman* and *Batman* for lesbian and gay undertones, and even descended into a hunt for sexually suggestive shapes hidden in the lines of drawings. More plausibly, he also criticized the comics' racism and exploitation of violence against women.[18] One of his most important rhetorical tools was the anecdote, which he used to illustrate the consequences he believed might follow when children identified with aggressive characters. With stories of children committing theft, torture, and murder, Wertham stirred up fears of copycat violence.[19] Comic books were the new *Jack Sheppard*, and there were plenty of Courvoisiers to go around.

Other experts have questioned Wertham's research, both in his own time and now. Having examined his manuscript archive, which became accessible in 2010, Carol Tilley claims that *Seduction of the Innocent* 'included numerous falsifications and distortions'. She shows how the psychiatrist played fast and loose with his evidence, changing patients' words, combining statements from different people, and relating second-hand incidents as if he had witnessed them himself.[20] Wertham's contemporaries did not have the benefit of this information, but, in a 1949 essay that appeared as evidence in the US Senate juvenile delinquency hearings, the criminologist and education professor Frederic M. Thrasher challenged Wertham's methods, including his reliance on 'a few selected and extreme cases of children's deviate behaviour'.[21] Carl H. Rush Jr., executive assistant for the American Psychological Association, stressed the need for longitudinal studies, which would track children's development over time. He described the idea that comic books might catalyze antisocial behaviour as 'high speculation on which there is very little empirical evidence'.[22]

Wertham's narrative proved compelling. The public was largely on his side, and wanted action.[23] In 1948 Canada led the way. Backed by the British Columbia PTA, E. Davie Fulton, Conservative MP, proposed legislation. While he initially met resistance, a pair of Courvoisiers soon supplied him with a fresh anecdote. Two boys in Dawson Creek, aged eleven and thirteen, had fired a stolen rifle into a car on the highway, killing the driver. When it came out that the boys read up to fifty comics a week, the coroner, the prosecutor, and the magistrate all denounced the books.[24] Fulton read from 'The Psychopathology

of Comic Books' in the House of Commons.[25] The Fulton Bill was
a bipartisan measure, introduced as a private member's bill by a Conservative backbencher with the support of the Liberal government.
Enacted in 1949, it extended the obscenity provisions in the Criminal
Code, making it illegal to create, print, publish, distribute, or sell a
crime comic, or to possess one for these purposes. A crime comic was
defined as 'a magazine, periodical or book that exclusively or substantially comprises matter depicting pictorially [...] the commission of
crimes, real or fictitious'.[26]

There were only a handful of cases under this law, one of them
sparked by the detective comic *Dick Tracy*, which had originated in
American daily newspapers and which appeared censored in Canadian
papers.[27] The monthly version of *Dick Tracy*, published as a comic book,
was not a 'crime comic' in the strict sense, since it centred on the detective, not the perpetrators. Fulton himself wrote that, in retrospect, 'the
crime comics we were concerned about were not the relatively innocent
things of the "Dick Tracy" or "Li'l Abner" type'.[28] Nevertheless, in 1953
an officer of the Winnipeg Police Morality Squad purchased *Dick Tracy*
No. 62 from a shop, and arrested the proprietor, Abe Roher. Roher was
convicted, appealed, lost, and was fined five dollars plus costs.[29] Crime
comics dwindled in Canada after the passage of the Fulton Bill, and 'love
and sex and girlie comics' filled the void, prompting the Senate to establish a committee on 'salacious literature'. In the absence of widespread
enforcement of Fulton's prohibition, crime comics soon returned, along
with horror comics, which set a new standard for violent and gruesome
images.[30]

In the United Kingdom, the anti-comics campaign was still building, and it fastened on what were at first called 'American-style comics',
later horror comics. Comic books had entered the country in the
hands of US infantry during the Second World War, which made
them targets of national and class prejudices. Groups involved in the
campaign included PTAs, the Association of Assistant Mistresses, the
Authors' World Peace Appeal, the National Council for the Defence
of Children (later the Council for Children's Welfare), the Comics
Campaign Council, the Child Care Committee of the International
Women's Day Committee, magistrates, and the National Union of
Teachers. Members of the Communist Party, who were key players in

the campaign, rejected comics as racist, fascist, pro-war propaganda—a tool of American cultural imperialism.[31] In 1954 the Archbishop of Canterbury led a deputation to the government from the Church of England Council for Education, which called for legislation to deal with comics, and the National Union of Teachers curated an exhibition of offensive comics at Westminster and around the United Kingdom.[32] By 1955, Winston Churchill's government was prepared to legislate.

The Children and Young Persons (Harmful Publications) Act criminalized printing, publishing, selling, letting, hiring, or possessing for these purposes

> any book, magazine or other like work which is of a kind likely to fall into the hands of children or young persons and consists wholly or mainly of stories told in pictures (with or without the addition of written matter), being stories portraying—
> (a) the commission of crimes; or
> (b) acts of violence or cruelty; or
> (c) incidents of a repulsive or horrible nature;
> in such a way that the work as a whole would tend to corrupt a child or young person into whose hands it might fall.[33]

This intricate wording reflects how hard it was to pin down exactly what the law was banning: a variety of comic book genres that ranged from classic crime stories to tales of horror populated with ghouls and monsters. At the heart of the Act is language adapted directly from Chief Justice Cockburn's 1868 test of obscenity, the Hicklin test, which imagined that books might fall into vulnerable readers' hands and corrupt them.

The British debates unfolded more dramatically than the Canadian ones. There were the usual arguments about delinquency, with stories of copycat violence and an anecdote about a group of several hundred Glaswegian children who had run amok in a cemetery in pursuit of the 'Gorbals vampire'.[34] But the bill had several vocal opponents in the Commons, including Roy Jenkins, Labour MP and future Home Secretary, who was pushing for a total overhaul of obscenity legislation, and wanted to fold violence into a new definition of obscenity.

He objected in particular to using language from the Hicklin test: 'unfortunate words—which have already done more than their fair share of harm'. He reminded the House that Hicklin had been used to convict Henry Vizetelly for publishing the novels of Émile Zola in translation and had been the basis of legal challenges to serious literature in the twentieth century (see Chapter 8). On comics and crime, he warned, 'We should not jump too quickly to the conclusion that because two things happen one necessarily happens as a result of the other.'[35] Conservative MP and future UK publisher of *Lolita*, Nigel Nicolson, complained that publishers would not be able to tell from the legislation whether they were breaking the law. Future Labour leader Michael Foot and Ronald Bell of the Tories found themselves united by different principles that converged against the bill. Foot warned that the proposed legislation would lead to prosecutions of innocent people and to chilling effect: 'In an atmosphere of suppression, it is not the individual cases that come before the courts which matter so much as the general effect produced on what booksellers are prepared to sell or libraries are prepared to stock.' Bell, for his part, thought that children needed to be 'gradually inoculated through wise parents and wise teachers and given an opportunity of judgment between good and evil in increasingly difficult doses' in order to develop mature judgement.[36]

These speakers and other opponents of the bill were spitting into the wind, and much of the debate was concerned with making sure the ban would be enforceable. When Foot wanted to remove the prohibition on depicting crimes because it was too broad, Sir H. Lucas-Tooth described Gaines's 'The Orphan', without mentioning it by name, as an example of a comic that might slip through the cracks. Because the illustrations do not show the moment when the little girl, Lucy, shoots her father, the violence prohibition alone would not suffice.[37] Notwithstanding protests over principles and wrangling over details, it was clear that the bill would pass, and Charles Leslie Hale MP waxed sarcastic about the efforts being expended on comic books in the age of the nuclear bomb. He imagined how, 'when London has disappeared and is being rebuilt Phoenix-like on the ashes of the old, an historian of the future will pay tribute to our modest labours today'. This tribute, Hale said, would appear in the epitaph of a nuclear apocalypse victim, which would conclude with the following lines:

> Yet need we not deplore too readily
> The tragedy of his final fate atomic,
> From one contamination he lived free,
> Parliament saved him from the horror comic.[38]

Did Parliament save future generations from the horror comic? There were no prosecutions under the statute until 1970, when there were two convictions.[39] According to the Bishop of Ripon, mere discussion of the bill drove horror comics from the shelves.[40] The legislation was also, however, belated. By the time the House of Commons got around to debating them, American-style comics had already changed at the source.

In the United States, action against comics had risen from the grass roots up through municipal police forces and city councils, state committees and legislatures, to the Senate. At first, states attacked comics using Comstock-era laws against crime publications. In March 1948 the US Supreme Court ruled in *Winters* v. *New York* that the New York State law was unconstitutional because of its vague wording, which meant that similar laws in other states were also unconstitutional. This decision did not halt the campaign. According to the American Municipal Association, by September 1948 almost fifty municipalities had banned comics in some form, and, by March 1949, fourteen state legislatures had anti-comics legislation in the works.[41] The campaign reached the federal level in 1954, when the US Senate Subcommittee on Juvenile Delinquency, chaired by Senator Robert C. Hendrickson, held three days of televised hearings to determine if comic books were a delinquency risk.

Wertham and Fulton both appeared at the hearings—Wertham to make his usual arguments, and Fulton to complain that the Canadian legislation had failed as a result of inadequate enforcement by the provinces. Retailers accused wholesalers of requiring them to circulate objectionable comics, wholesalers accused distributors of doing the same, and respectable comic artists and publishers, such as the newspaper cartoonists and Dell Publishing, distanced themselves from the horror and crime mongers. National Comics, precursor of DC, was revealed to have a strict code already in place, an editorial policy so repressive that it partially banned women: 'The inclusion of females in stories is specifically discouraged. Women, when used in plot structure, should be secondary in importance, and should be drawn realistically, without exaggeration of feminine physical qualities.'[42] Monroe Froehlich Jr., manager of the company that published Marvel Comics, put up moderate resistance, though he conceded, 'If there is sufficient evidence to prove that anything that we might publish might be injurious to a child who is in the pattern of becoming delinquent, we would stop, we would be the first ones to stop.'[43] Here was, as always, the crux: did comics actually harm children? The subcommittee received evidence on both sides of this question, none conclusive and much of it flawed. Some experts who supported the comics had served as paid educational advisers to publishers, which compromised their impartiality, while their opponents continued to rely on speculation and moral outrage rather than sound evidence.

By the time of the hearings, Bill Gaines had established himself as the *enfant terrible* of the comic book industry. He had joined with Lev Gleason and several other publishers to create the Association of Comics Magazine Publishers in 1948, which attempted to establish a code of content, but the association was small, enforcement was poor, and Gaines, having largely flouted the code, left the group.[44] Aside from his crime and horror material, Gaines published lampoon comics, such as *Mad* and *Panic*, which parodied 'The Night before Christmas' in its first issue. In Massachusetts officials intimidated newsagents into pulling the magazine off their shelves because it 'desecrated Christmas'. An EC receptionist in New York, Shirley Norris, was arrested under an indecency statute for selling the same issue, ostensibly because of a mildly risqué drawing of a man in drag. A judge threw out the case.[45] In a cartoon entitled 'Are You a Red Dupe?' Gaines played the 'Red Scare' off the comics scare, claiming 'The group most anxious to destroy comics are the communists!'[46]

Gaines asked the subcommittee to hear his testimony, which he gave on 21 April in a room where comic books, including some of his own, were displayed as examples of the phenomenon the Senate was investigating.[47] Senators Hendrickson, Thomas C. Hennings Jr., and Estes Kefauver were present. The spokesman of crime and horror, who testified immediately after Wertham, was defiant: 'It would be just as difficult to explain the harmless thrill of a horror story to a

Dr. Wertham as it would be to explain the sublimity of love to a frigid old maid.' Rejecting the principle that publications needed to be censored to protect the most vulnerable readers, Gaines quoted from Judge Woolsey's *Ulysses* decision: 'It is only with the normal person that the law is concerned' (see Chapter 11). Gaines suggested that anti-comics campaigners were unduly concerned with 'dirty, sneaky, perverted monsters who use the comics as a blueprint for action.' In fact, he claimed, 'Perverted little monsters are few and far between. They don't read comics. The chances are most of them are in schools for retarded children.' Despite his incautious wording, Gaines did not believe criminal behaviour was innate. Like Wertham, he claimed that environmental factors were to blame for crime. Gaines simply denied that fiction was one of these factors. The 'problems' children face, he said, 'are economic and social and they are complex'. Defending one of his stories from Wertham's accusations of racism, Gaines claimed that it was 'one of a series of stories designed to show the evils of race prejudice and mob violence, in this case against Mexican Catholics'.[48]

The subcommittee examined Gaines on other stories, which he struggled to justify on the senators' terms. He emphasized the surprise ending of 'The Orphan', which reveals only in the final panel that Lucy is the one who shot her father, but he did not succeed in articulating why this matters. His logic appeared to be that children would not identify with Lucy's criminal actions when reading the story because they would not know until the very end what she has actually done. While his reasoning was murky, Gaines's convictions were clearer. His goal was to entertain children. Senator Kefauver grilled him on the cover of *Crime SuspenStories* No. 22, which depicted a man holding a bloody axe in one hand and a woman's severed head in the other, her lower body visible on the floor in the background. Gaines insisted the image was in good taste, 'for the cover of a horror comic':

> A cover in bad taste, for example, might be defined as holding the head a little higher so that the neck could be seen dripping blood from it and moving the body over a little further so that the neck of the body could be seen to be bloody.

The senator was unconvinced.[49]

The hearings were, on the whole, bad press for the comics industry, which took defensive action. In September 1954, five months before the UK parliamentary debates, publishers formed the Comics Magazine Association of America (CMAA), which would be subject to strict regulation by the Comics Code Authority. The CMAA considered appointing Wertham as the first 'czar' of the Comics Code Authority, but the position went to the magistrate Charles F. Murphy.[50] The rules he enforced were extensive, restricting sex, horror, crime, profanity, violence, subversion of authority, racism, religious discrimination, and general 'violations of good taste or decency'. Supernatural monsters such as vampires and werewolves were banned, and the words 'horror' and 'terror' could not appear in comic book titles. 'Crime' could be used, but not alone and not in larger print than the other words on the cover. The good guys would have to be portrayed as good, the bad guys as bad. Good would always win, and crime would always be punished.[51] Though this new regime forestalled federal legislation and reshaped the comic book medium, it was not enough to appease all opponents. Burning, campaigning, and state-level legislating continued, while prohibitions in Washington and California were declared unconstitutional by state supreme courts.[52]

Gaines himself had initiated the meetings in which the CMAA was born, but he bailed out when he saw where the group was heading, and independently announced the discontinuation of EC's crime and horror comics. Finding that wholesalers refused to take even his new, tamer titles, he reluctantly joined the association. His experience illustrates how arbitrary the application of the code could be. In 1955, after Murphy had turned down a story in *Incredible Science Fiction* because it contained mutants, Gaines attempted to replace it with a reprint of his *Weird Fantasy* No. 18 story 'Judgment Day!', written with Al Feldstein and drawn by Joe Orlando.[53] At the end of this anti-racist parable involving blue and orange robots, the protagonist Tarlton removes his spacesuit helmet, revealing that he is Black.[54] Murphy told Gaines and Feldstein, 'You can't have a Negro.' After Gaines threatened to denounce the Comics Code Authority for racism, Murphy permitted the Black protagonist, as long as Gaines removed the beads of sweat from his face. With a parting 'Fuck you', Gaines published the original story—Black man, sweat, and all. This was his last comic book.[55]

Losing money on all of his titles, Gaines discontinued every one of them except *Mad*, which he converted to its current magazine format.[56] The industry was declining sharply, for several reasons: censorship, anti-comics opinion, the loss of the distributor American News Company, and the rise of television.[57] By 1956, the number of comic book titles published in the United States had dwindled by over half, and artists sought work elsewhere.[58] Though sales soon picked up again, the code continued to regulate mainstream comic books, while more edgy material emerged in the underground press of the 1960s, some of it running into censorship troubles of its own (see Chapter 17). Revisions in 1971 and 1989 introduced more nuance to the code, loosening some of the old provisions and adding new ones, such as a requirement to portray gay characters positively, but maintaining a general respect for authority. In the 1980s, independent publishers began to operate outside the CMAA, and mainstream publishers began to create titles that did not bear the Code Authority's seal.[59] Marvel left the association in 2001, and the remaining publishers, DC and Archie, left in 2011, ending the censorship regime that the Senate subcommittee hearings had precipitated.[60] In 2017 the Canadian government proposed to eliminate the crime comics prohibition. The UK anti-comics statute is still on the books.

Notes

1. Martin Barker, *A Haunt of Fears: The Strange History of the British Horror Comics Campaign* (London: Pluto Press, 1984), pp. 15, 91–92.

2. *Supplement to the Times*, 25 June 1840, p. 14.

3. Lyn Pykett, 'The Newgate Novel and Sensation Fiction, 1830–1868', in *The Cambridge Companion to Crime Fiction*, ed. Martin Priestman (Cambridge: Cambridge University Press, 2003), pp. 19–39 (pp. 20–21, 29–32).

4. Anthony Comstock, *Traps for the Young*, ed. Robert Bremner (Cambridge, MA: Belknap Press, 1967), pp. 26–41.

5. David Hajdu, *Ten-Cent Plague: The Great Comic-Book Scare and How It Changed America* (New York: Farrar, Straus and Giroux, 2008), pp. 94–95.

6. Hajdu, pp. 11–12, 40–42, 44–46, 79–83, 92–93. See also Bart Beaty, *Fredric Wertham and the Critique of Mass Culture* (Jackson: University Press of Mississippi, 2005), pp. 106–16.

7. James Gilbert, *A Cycle of Outrage: America's Reaction to the Juvenile Delinquent in the 1950s* (New York: Oxford University Press, 1986), pp. 11–14, 63–71. See also Hajdu, pp. 83–86.

8. Hajdu, pp. 59–70, 110.

9. Carol L. Tilley, 'Seducing the Innocent: Fredric Wertham and the Falsifications that Helped Condemn Comics', *Information & Culture*, 47.4 (2012), 383–413 (p. 387).

10. Paul Lopes, *Demanding Respect: The Evolution of the American Comic Book* (Philadelphia: Temple University Press, 2009), pp. 37–46.

11. Hajdu, pp. 115–27. See also Beaty, p. 116.

12. Hajdu, p. 303. See further pp. 296–304.

13. Fredric Wertham, *Seduction of the Innocent* (Laurel, NY: Main Road Books, 2004), p. 15.

14. Tilley, p. 391. See also Beaty, p. 17.

15. Beaty, pp. 17, 133, 143–44. See also *Hearings Before the Subcomm. to Investigate Juvenile Delinquency of the S. Comm. on the Judiciary*, 83rd Cong. 91–92 (1954) (testimony of Dr Frederic [*sic*] Wertham, Psychiatrist, Director, Lafargue Clinic, New York, N.Y.) [Internet Archive e-book].

16. Wertham, *Seduction of the Innocent*, p. 3.

17. Fredric Wertham and others, 'The Psychopathology of Comic Books', *American Journal of Psychotherapy*, 50.4 (1996), 417–34 (p. 418).

18. Wertham, *Seduction of the Innocent*, pp. 91, 95, 96, 98, 101–5, 107, 110, 113, 189–93, and insert.

19. Fredric Wertham, 'The Comics ... Very Funny!', *Saturday Review of Literature*, 31.22 (1948), 6–7, 26–29.

20. Tilley, pp. 386, 393–401.

21. *Hearings Before the Subcomm. to Investigate Juvenile Delinquency*, 17 (exhibit no. 3, Frederic M. Thrasher, 'The Comics and Delinquency: Cause or Scapegoat').

22. *Hearings Before the Subcomm. to Investigate Juvenile Delinquency*, 163 (exhibit no. 22, Carl H. Rush Jr. to Richard Clendenen).

23. Amy Kiste Nyberg, *Seal of Approval: The History of the Comics Code* (Jackson: University Press of Mississippi, 1998), pp. 20–21.

24. John Burchill, 'Dick Tracy Gets Smacked Down: Crime Comics in Manitoba', *Manitoba History*, 77 (2015), 28–35 (p. 30). See also Canada, *House of Commons Debates*, 4 October 1949, p. 514, http://parl.canadiana.ca/view/oop.debates_HOC2101_01/1?r=0&s=1, accessed 23 December 2016; Wertham, *Seduction of the Innocent*, pp. 274–76.

25. Canada, *House of Commons Debates*, 4 October 1949, pp. 512–13, http://parl.canadiana.ca/view/oop.debates_HOC2101_01/1?r=0&s=1, accessed 23 December 2016.

26. Criminal Code, RSC 1985, c C-46, s 163 (7).

27. Janice Dickin McGinnis, 'Bogeymen and the Law: Crime Comics and Pornography', *Ottawa Law Review*, 20.1 (1988), 3–23 (p. 4 and notes 4, 5).

28. E. D. Fulton, 'Comment on Crime Comics and Pornography', *Ottawa Law Review*, 20.1 (1988), 25–31 (p. 28).

29. *R. v. Roher* (1953), 107 C.C.C. 103, 10 W.W.R. (N.S.) 309 (Man. C.A.). See also Burchill, pp. 32–33.

30. *Hearings Before the Subcomm. to Investigate Juvenile Delinquency*, 260 (statement of Hon. E. D. Fulton, Member, House of Commons, Canada).

31. Barker, pp. 8–35.

32. Barker, pp. 50–55; HC Deb 22 February 1955, vol 537, cols 1072–73.

33. Children and Young Persons (Harmful Publications) Act 1955, s 1.

34. Barker, p. 34; HC Deb 22 February 1955, vol 537, col 1149.

35. HC Deb 22 February 1955, vol 537, cols 1092, 1097.

36. HC Deb 22 February 1955, vol 537, cols 1107, 1114. See further col 1122.

37. HC Deb 24 March 1955, vol 538, col 2371.

38. HC Deb 28 March 1955, vol 539, col 104.

39. HC Deb 5 December 1974, vol 882, cols 588–9W; HC Deb 22 December 1982, vol 34, cols 549–50W.

40. HL Deb 28 April 1955, vol 192, col 627.

41. Hajdu, pp. 92–97, 108, 150.

42. *Hearings Before the Subcomm. to Investigate Juvenile Delinquency*, 139 (exhibit no. 21, National Comics Publications, Inc., Editorial Policy for Superman D–C Publications).

43. *Hearings Before the Subcomm. to Investigate Juvenile Delinquency*, 181 (testimony of Monroe Froehlich, Jr., Business Manager, Magazine Management Co., New York, N.Y.).

44. Hajdu, pp. 128–31, 142; *Hearings Before the Subcomm. to Investigate Juvenile Delinquency*, 71 (testimony of Henry Edward Schultz, General Counsel, Association of Comics Magazine Publishers, Inc., New York, N.Y.).

45. Hajdu, pp. 218–23.

46. *Hearings Before the Subcomm. to Investigate Juvenile Delinquency*, 62 (exhibit no. 8b, 'Are You a Red Dupe?').

47. Hajdu, pp. 254–56.

48. *Hearings Before the Subcomm. to Investigate Juvenile Delinquency*, 98, 99 (testimony of William Gaines, Publisher, Entertaining Comics Group, New York, N.Y.).

49.   *Hearings Before the Subcomm. to Investigate Juvenile Delinquency*, 101–2, 103 (testimony of Gaines).

50.   Hajdu, pp. 285–86. See also Nyberg, pp. 110–12.

51.   Comics Magazine Association of America, 'Comics Code, 1954', in Nyberg, pp. 166–69.

52.   Hajdu, pp. 293–304, 310–18; Nyberg, pp. 132–36.

53.   Hajdu, pp. 286–90, 320–21.

54.   Bill Gaines and Al Feldstein, 'Judgment Day!', illustrated by Joe Orlando, *Weird Fantasy*, March–April 1953, in Grant Geissman, *Foul Play! The Art and Artists of the Notorious 1950s E.C. Comics!* (New York: Harper Design, 2005), pp. 147–53 (p. 153).

55.   Hajdu, pp. 322–23.

56.   Hajdu, pp. 321, 323.

57.   Nyberg, pp. x–xii, 124–26.

58.   Hajdu, pp. 326–29.

59.   Comics Magazine Association of America, 'Comics Code, 1971', in Nyberg, pp. 170–74; Comics Magazine Association of America, 'Comics Code, 1989', in Nyberg, pp. 175–79; Nyberg, pp. xii, 136–38, 145–46, 153.

60.   Douglas Wolk, 'R.I.P.: The Comics Code Authority', *Time*, 24 January 2011, http://techland.time.com/2011/01/24/r-i-p-the-comics-code-authority, accessed 23 December 2016.

16

Lolita
Vladimir Nabokov

U nable to find anyone daring enough to publish his third novel written in English, the Russian writer Vladimir Nabokov, now living in the United States and teaching at Cornell University, turned to his agent in France. Nabokov unwittingly placed the manuscript with an eccentric and largely pornographic French publishing house that was fuelling moral panic in England. The resulting drama played out on a transatlantic stage.

Lolita was a dangerous novel. In 1950, 'beset with technical difficulties and doubts', Nabokov almost burned a draft of it in his garden incinerator before his wife, Véra Nabokov, stopped him.[1] His doubts may have been chiefly artistic, but, as he later wrote, he knew that 'we have here all sorts of Watch and Ward Societies, Catholic Legions of Decency, etc., and that, moreover, every post master in the country can start censorship trouble.'[2] He hesitated to send the manuscript to his American agent by post, and resolved to publish it pseudonymously. He was worried that he might lose his teaching career, and that a careless reading public would confuse him with his fictional narrator, the eloquent and depraved Humbert Humbert.[3]

Humbert is a paedophile who describes the girls he lusts after as 'nymphets'. He lodges with and then marries a woman named Charlotte Haze so that he can groom her daughter, Dolores, whom he calls 'Lolita'. Charlotte dies in an accident shortly after discovering Humbert's

Maurice Girodias, whose Olympia Press published *Lolita* in France.

intentions, leaving him to rape his twelve-year-old stepdaughter in kitschy motels while they drive around the United States in a tragic parody of a family road trip. He later murders another sexual predator, Clare Quilty, into whose company Dolores had fled. Addressing an imaginary jury, Humbert frames his narrative as a prisoner's confession. Sometimes, especially at the end of the novel, he expresses remorse and acknowledges a measure of the harm he has done to Dolores, but at other times he attempts to charm and mollify his audience.

Though Humbert's euphemistic style spares the reader much of the detail of his sexual crimes, the book's subject was shocking enough to deter American publishers. Nabokov wrote:

> there are at least three themes which are utterly taboo as far as most American publishers are concerned. The two others are: a Negro–White marriage which is a complete and glorious success resulting in lots of children and grandchildren; and the total atheist who lives a happy and useful life, and dies in his sleep at the age of 106.[4]

These other 'taboos' being digs at American prejudices, Nabokov implies that he chose the only theme he could find that was absolutely beyond the pale.

Viking, Simon & Schuster, New Directions, Doubleday, and Farrar, Straus and Young all rejected *Lolita*. According to Nabokov, Pascal Covici of Viking Press 'said we should all go to jail if the thing were published'.[5] This fear was only slightly exaggerated. Several literary works had already led to successful prosecutions in the United States, including the 'Nausicaa' episode of *Ulysses* in the *Little Review*, Theodore Dreiser's *An American Tragedy*, and Lillian Smith's *Strange Fruit* (see Chapter 11 for *Ulysses*). In 1948 the case of *Memoirs of Hecate County*, by Nabokov's acquaintance Edmund Wilson, reached the Supreme Court, where one justice recused himself and the other eight were evenly split.[6] The lower court's fine of one thousand dollars was affirmed.[7]

Nabokov looked to Europe for a less repressive market, and his French agent arranged publication with Maurice Girodias's Olympia Press. Girodias had evidently got the wrong end of the stick, and initially thought *Lolita* was a defence of paedophilia.[8] He issued it in two volumes as part of his Traveller's Companion Series, which was a mixed bag of literature and erotica, including the vintage erotic novel *Fanny Hill* and newer titles, such as *The Loins of Amon, Thongs,*

The Whip Angels, and *The Enormous Bed* (see Chapter 2 for *Fanny Hill*).[9] The series was aimed at English-speaking tourists, and Girodias rushed to print the novel before the end of the summer of 1955.[10] Nabokov later claimed that he had not known about Olympia's catalogue, but admitted that he probably would have gone ahead with the contract even if he did, 'though less cheerfully'.[11] The London Sunday papers saved *Lolita* from the fate of entertaining—and probably disappointing—travelling consumers of erotic novels in perpetuity. In the *Sunday Times* Graham Greene numbered the book among the best of the year, while in the *Sunday Express* John Gordon denounced it as pornography. Now the subject of a proper critical controversy, *Lolita* achieved fame. Despite his initial reservations, Nabokov's name was on the cover.[12]

Nabokov's decision to publish his novel with a 'Pornologist on Olympus', as Girodias styled himself in *Playboy*, was not without consequences. The discreet green volumes of the Traveller's Companions Series were being smuggled out of Paris, past English customs officials charged with confiscating obscene publications. In London, booksellers in Soho would rent them out, usually for five pounds (two refundable on return of the book). The Director of Public Prosecutions considered this new, expensive, 'rather filthier' type of pornography even worse than the cheap kind, which had previously caused concern because of its greater availability to working-class and young readers.[13] The nation's moral guardians, including the Public Morality Council and the Metropolitan Police, were anxious to stem the tide of pornography, and there was general dissatisfaction with the current state of English obscenity law. While failing to quash the trade in pornography, the law did censor literature, and several people, including the Society of Authors and Roy Jenkins MP were working to reform it. In 1954 five books published by reputable publishers had been targeted for prosecution—*Julia* by 'Margot Bland' (Kathryn Dyson Taylor), *September in Quinze* by Vivian Connell, *The Image and the Search* by Walter Baxter, *The Man in Control* by Hugh McGraw, and *The Philanderer* by Stanley Kauffmann. Hutchinson, the publisher of *September in Quinze*, was convicted, and T. Werner Laurie, the publisher of *Julia*, pleaded guilty rather than face the expense of fighting the case.[14] Taylor and Baxter were both charged along with their publishers.[15] Magistrates in

Swindon had also ordered the destruction of Boccaccio's *Decameron* among about one hundred and thirty-five other books, although the decision was allegedly due to the illustrations in this particular edition rather than the text, and was overturned on appeal.[16] Two years later, in 1956, a bookseller was convicted, twice, for selling *Lolita*.[17]

The incident went something like this. Acting on information from the Public Morality Council, a police officer visited a shop in Soho, and purchased the first volume of *Lolita* from the bookseller. The officer could then swear that the shop had sold at least one copy of an obscene publication, and could request a warrant from a magistrate under the Obscene Publications Act 1857 to seize other publications found on the premises. The officer submitted the purchased copy of *Lolita* to the Director of Public Prosecutions, who considered *Lolita* obscene enough on the face of it to initiate a prosecution under the common law for obscene libel. The bookseller was tried, convicted, and conditionally discharged at Bow Street Magistrates' Court. Under the 1857 Act, the bookseller would also be summoned before a magistrate to show cause why *Lolita* and any other seized books should not be destroyed. A few months later, the same merchant was convicted and fined for selling the second volume of *Lolita*, which was similarly subject to destruction proceedings. The Commissioner of Police of the Metropolis, Sir John Nott-Bower, admitted that, if *Lolita* had not been an Olympia book, the police officer would have been much more likely to leave it alone.[18]

The courts kept the Home Office apprised of convictions and destruction orders, and the Home Office issued a confidential blacklist of destroyed books, an official Blue Book, to the police. In 1954 the Blue Book contained four thousand titles, including classics such as Daniel Defoe's *Moll Flanders* and Gustave Flaubert's *Madame Bovary*, as well as pulp fiction, such as Hans Vogel's *Love from Las Vegas*, which was subject to seventy-seven destruction orders between 1950 and 1954. Customs and Excise kept their own, more selective blacklist. The 1954 version included the works of Jean Genet, John Cleland's *The Memoirs of Fanny Hill*, Continental editions of D. H. Lawrence's *Lady Chatterley's Lover*, the Marquis de Sade's *Justine*, Henry Miller's *Tropic of Cancer* and *Tropic of Capricorn*, and a French edition of the *Kama Sutra*.[19] The Home Office also had responsibilities to other nations under international treaties, including the Convention for the Suppression of the Circulation of and Traffic in Obscene Publications. Under the auspices of this treaty, the Home Office periodically contacted the French Ministry of the Interior about obscene books that originated in France. One communication, dated 3 September 1953, mentioned 'books of a highly obscene character' published by Olympia Press and enclosed a list of 'the kind of works in question'.[20] The Permanent Under-Secretary of State denied in 1957 that *Lolita* was ever mentioned by name in the correspondence with France and that it was subject to a French ban.[21] In December 1956, however, the Ministry of the Interior had in fact prohibited the circulation of twenty-five Olympia books, including *Lolita*, using legislation designed to censor foreign political publications.[22] At the same time, the publisher Gallimard was preparing to publish a French translation of *Lolita*, which would not be subject to the ban.[23]

Girodias sued the French government, and attempted to enlist Nabokov in the fight, but the author declined to participate in what he called the 'lolitigation', citing concern for his teaching position and claiming, 'My moral defense of the book is the book itself.'[24] He did, however, contribute an essay to Girodias's pamphlet *L'Affaire 'Lolita'*, which was designed to establish the novel's literary merit and drum up outrage at the censorship. Singling out *Lolita* among the banned books, and comparing it to James Joyce's *Ulysses*, Girodias gave a version of the case in which the English had roped the French into a bourgeois crusade against avant-garde authors, such as Samuel Beckett, Henry Miller, and Nabokov.[25] It is probable, however, that *Lolita* was considered not the main target but an acceptable casualty in the censorship of the Traveller's Companions. The poet T. S. Eliot advised the Select Committee on Obscene Publications in 1958 that it was difficult to draw a firm line between pornography and literature:

> I do not think in these matters you can construct any net which will catch the fish you want and let the others go through: you either catch too many fish and do injustice to some, or you will not catch enough and do harm to the public.[26]

Véra Nabokov resented Girodias for his 'pronouncements in favor of pornography' and for his use of *Lolita* 'as a kind of shield for his list of publications some of which are absolutely devoid of any artistic value and extremely repulsive'.[27] Girodias eventually succeeded in lifting the French ban on *Lolita*.[28]

It did not cost Nabokov much effort to send Girodias the essay 'On a Book Entitled *Lolita*', because he had already prepared it as part of his US publication strategy. Given the success of the novel, which was now translated into Danish and Swedish,[29] the chill was thawing, and American publishers were expressing interest.[30] Girodias's steep contractual terms made negotiations complicated, however, and there remained the danger of prosecution.[31] Nabokov looked for a publisher with the means to defend the book as far as the Supreme Court.[32] For a while he had a tentative arrangement with Doubleday, who printed his essay and excerpts of the book in the *Anchor Review* to prevent future obscenity trouble.[33]

In 'On a Book Entitled *Lolita*', Nabokov roundly mocks pornography, in which, he says, 'action has to be limited to the copulation of clichés. Style, structure, imagery should never distract the reader from his tepid lust.' With respect to *Lolita* itself, he takes a stance reminiscent of Oscar Wilde's (see Chapter 9), shrugging off morality in favour of aesthetics:

> I am neither a reader nor a writer of didactic fiction, and [. . .] *Lolita* has no moral in tow. For me a work of fiction exists only insofar as it affords me what I shall bluntly call aesthetic bliss, that is a sense of being somehow, somewhere, connected with other states of being where art (curiosity, tenderness, kindness, ecstasy) is the norm.

He calls the fine details of the novel, such as a description of Dolores playing tennis and a list of students' names, its 'nerves' and 'secret points, the subliminal co-ordinates by means of which the book is plotted'.[34]

Of course, the author could have aimed for 'aesthetic bliss' without choosing such a provocative subject, and the word 'bliss', with its hint of sexual climax, suggests that Nabokov had his tongue in his cheek. Designed as it was for the specific purpose of warding off prosecution, his essay is not a satisfying explanation of *Lolita*. The book has engaged and continues to engage readers on an ethical level. *Lolita* offers, among other things, an ethical 'challenge', as critic Susan Mooney puts it. How well can one resist Humbert's rhetoric, see through the fantasy he has created of 'Lolita' the alluring 'nymphet', and perceive the abuse of a little girl? Some have fallen for Humbert's version of the story. When his first attempt to drug and rape Dolores fails, she initiates sex, and there are readers who have used this fact to lay responsibility on her.[35] Yet even Humbert has flashes of moral sense, however self-serving:

> Unless it can be proven to me—to me as I am now, today, with my heart and my beard, and my putrefaction—that in the infinite run it does not matter a jot that a North American girl-child named Dolores Haze had been deprived of her childhood by a maniac, unless this can be proven (and if it can, then life is a joke), I see nothing for the treatment of my misery but the melancholy and very local palliative of articulate art.[36]

Hidden in this tangle of words is the admission that, if Humbert's abuse of Dolores doesn't matter, then life is a joke. Nigel Nicolson, Conservative MP and one of the partners of the publishing house that would eventually publish *Lolita* in Britain, claimed that '*Lolita* has a built-in condemnation of what it describes'. If he thought it had depicted child abuse in a positive light, he would not have agreed to publish it.[37]

In the United States, the complex negotiations had finally resulted in a contract with G. P. Putnam's Sons. Customs had examined the Olympia edition in 1957 and judged it not to be obscene.[38] In 1958 the Putnam edition appeared, and no legal action was taken against it, though there were bans in public libraries.[39] *Lolita* could still not be published in Britain, however. Weidenfeld & Nicolson accepted the manuscript, but would not issue the book until the obscenity law reform was complete.[40] Nicolson's political efforts in this cause reflected his professional interests. On several occasions he complained that he had no way of telling if a new edition of *Lolita* was likely to be prosecuted:

> The advice to 'Publish and be damned' is very bad advice. I do not in the very least want to be damned. But I feel that this particular work is one of such outstanding merit, and has been so widely acclaimed all over the world, that a publisher must have the courage to make it available to British readers.[41]

In July 1959 the new Obscene Publications Act became law. It was a compromise designed to consolidate, strengthen, and clarify existing obscenity legislation. Superseding both the 1857 Act and the common law offence of obscene libel, the new Act provided for seize-and-destroy proceedings against obscene books as well as criminal prosecutions of people involved in publishing them. It gave greater powers to police to search the premises where obscene publications were sold, while providing mechanisms for literary authors to defend their work. A book would need to be judged as a whole, not in part; expert witnesses would be permitted to give evidence; and a public good defence would be available for works that were in the 'interests of science, literature, art or learning, or of other objects of general concern'. The Act also softened, at last, the Hicklin test of obscenity, which had governed obscenity proceedings since 1868. Now a work would be obscene only if it tended to 'deprave and corrupt' readers who were *likely* to read it, not anyone open to immoral influences and into whose hands it might happen to fall.[42] The test case for the new legislation would be D. H. Lawrence's *Lady Chatterley's Lover* (see Chapter 12).

Weidenfeld & Nicolson had approached over thirty printers before finding one who would risk the legal consequences of printing *Lolita*. Nicolson's reputation had been injured by his association with the book, as well as his opposition to Conservative government policy in the Suez Crisis, and he had lost his seat in Parliament. The Attorney General believed that the book would be prosecuted, obscenity reform or no. Once the new law had passed, the publishers sent a copy of *Lolita* to the Director of Public Prosecutions for inspection. At an optimistic publication party the evening before the book's release, an anonymous phone call from the government, apparently unofficial, conveyed good news to George Weidenfeld. *Lolita* would not be prosecuted.[43] Now, four years after its publication in Paris, the book was legally available in the United Kingdom. Probably with some help from the Streisand effect, Nabokov came out rather well, earning enough from sales of *Lolita* to resign his teaching position and write full-time, and selling the film rights to Stanley Kubrick. Asked in a 1967 interview how he was dealing with fame, he said, '*Lolita* is famous, not I. I am an obscure, doubly obscure, novelist with an unpronounceable name.'[44]

Notes

1. Herbert Gold, 'Interview with Vladimir Nabokov', in *Vladimir Nabokov's 'Lolita': A Casebook*, ed. Ellen Pifer (Oxford: Oxford University Press, 2003), pp. 195–206 (p. 205).

2. [Vladimir Nabokov] to Maurice Girodias (14 May 1957), in Vladimir Nabokov, *Selected Letters 1940–1977*, ed. Dmitri Nabokov and Matthew J. Bruccoli (London: Vintage, 1991), p. 218.

3. [Véra Nabokov?] to Katharine White (23 December 1953), in Nabokov, *Selected Letters 1940–1977*, p. 142.

4. Vladimir Nabokov, 'On a Book Entitled *Lolita*', in Nabokov, *Lolita* (London: Penguin, 1995; repr. 2000), pp. 311–17 (p. 314).

5. Vladimir Nabokov to Edmund Wilson (30 July 1954), in *Dear Bunny, Dear Volodya: The Nabokov–Wilson Letters, 1940–1971*, ed. Simon Karlinsky, rev. and expanded edn (Berkeley: University of California Press, 2001), p. 317.

6. Edward de Grazia, *Girls Lean Back Everywhere: The Law of Obscenity and the Assault on Genius* (New York: Vintage, 1993), pp. 227–28.

7. George H. Douglas, *Edmund Wilson's America* (Kentucky: University Press of Kentucky, 1983), p. 125.

8. Ann Feeney, '*Lolita* and Censorship: A Case Study', *Reference Services Review*, 21.4 (1993), 67–74, 90 (p. 69). See also Elisabeth Ladenson, *Dirt for Art's Sake: Books on Trial from 'Madame Bovary' to 'Lolita'* (Ithaca, NY: Cornell University Press, 2007), pp. 207–8.

9. Select Committee on the Obscene Publications Bill, *Minutes of Evidence Taken Before the Select Committee on the Obscene Publications Bill and Appendices* (HC 1956–57, 122), 73.

10. Vladimir Nabokov to Philip Rahv (13 July 1955), in Nabokov, *Selected Letters 1940–1977*, p. 172.

11. Vladimir Nabokov, '*Lolita* and Mr. Girodias', *Evergreen Review*, 100 (Summer/Fall 1998), http://evergreenreview.com/read/lolita-and-mr-girodias, accessed 20 December 2016.

12. Feeney, p. 69.

13. Select Committee on the Obscene Publications Bill, 28. See further pp. 70, 73.

14. David Bradshaw, 'American Beastliness, the Great Purge and its Aftermath (1946–1959)', in *Prudes on the Prowl: Fiction and Obscenity in England, 1850 to the Present Day*, ed. Bradshaw and Rachel Potter (Oxford: Oxford University Press, 2013), pp. 138–58 (pp. 146–50).

15. Colin Manchester, 'A History of the Crime of Obscene Libel', *Journal of Legal History*, 12.1 (1991), 36–57 (p. 46).

16. HC Deb 29 March 1957, vol 567, cols 1508, 1524; Select Committee on the Obscene Publications Bill, 29–30, 43.

17. Select Committee on the Obscene Publications Bill, 28.

18. Select Committee on the Obscene Publications Bill, 28, 79, 82, 84–85.

19. Alan Travis, *Bound and Gagged: A Secret History of Obscenity in Britain* (London: Profile Books, 2000), pp. 97–100, 116–22. See also Select Committee on the Obscene Publications Bill, 53.

20. Home Office to Ministry of the Interior (3 September 1953), in *L'Affaire 'Lolita': défense de l'écrivain*, [ed. Maurice Girodias] (Paris: Olympia Press, 1957), p. 86 (our translation). See also Bradshaw, p. 153; Select Committee on the Obscene Publications Bill, 1, 6, 11, 14, 15.

21. Select Committee on the Obscene Publications Bill, 11, 15.

22. Maurice Girodias, 'L'Affaire *Lolita*', in *L'Affaire 'Lolita': défense de l'écrivain*, pp. 51–64 (pp. 53–54). See also Brian Boyd, *Vladimir Nabokov: The American Years* (London: Vintage, 1993), p. 301; Feeney, p. 70.

23. Feeney, p. 70.

24. Vladimir Nabokov to Maurice Girodias (10 March 1957), in Nabokov, *Selected Letters 1940–1977*, p. 210.

25. Girodias, 'L'Affaire *Lolita*', pp. 51–53, 56.

26. Select Committee on Obscene Publications, *Report from the Select Committee on Obscene Publications Together with the Proceedings of the Committee, Minutes of Evidence and Appendices* (HC 1957–58 123-I), 17.

27. Mrs [Véra] Vladimir Nabokov to George Weidenfeld (18 March 1961), in Nabokov, *Selected Letters 1940–1977*, p. 328.

28. Maurice Girodias, 'Pornologist on Olympus', *Playboy*, April 1961, p. 145. See also Feeney, p. 70.

29. V. [Vladimir Nabokov] to Elena Sikorski (14 September 1957), in Nabokov, *Selected Letters 1940–1977*, p. 227.

30. Vladimir Nabokov to Walter J. Minton (29 November 1957), in Nabokov, *Selected Letters 1940–1977*, pp. 236–37.

31. Mrs [Véra] Vladimir Nabokov to Walter J. Minton (19 September 1957), in Nabokov, *Selected Letters 1940–1977*, p. 227.

32. Vladimir Nabokov to Minton (29 November 1957), p. 237.

33. Vladimir Nabokov to Jason Epstein (1 October 1956), in Nabokov, *Selected Letters 1940–1977*, p. 191 and editors' notes 2, 3. See also Vladimir Nabokov to Maurice Girodias (14 December 1956), in Nabokov, *Selected Letters 1940–1977*, pp. 196–97.

34. Nabokov, 'On a Book Entitled *Lolita*', pp. 313, 314–15, 316.

35. Susan Mooney, *The Artistic Censoring of Sexuality: Fantasy and Judgment in the Twentieth-Century Novel* (Columbus: Ohio State University Press, 2008), p. 153. See further pp. 112–14, 117–18, 122 note 10, 129 and note 17, 130, 160.

36. Nabokov, *Lolita*, p. 283.

37. HC Deb 16 December 1958, vol 597, col 1048.

38. Robert W. Dill to The Olympia Press (8 February 1957), in *L'Affaire 'Lolita': défense de l'écrivain*, p. 66.

39. Feeney, p. 70. See also Andrea Pitzer, *The Secret History of Vladimir Nabokov* (New York: Pegasus Books, 2013), p. 248; Stacy Schiff, *Véra (Mrs. Vladimir Nabokov)* (London: Picador, 2000), p. 246.

40. George Weidenfeld to Vladimir Nabokov (28 January 1959), in Nabokov, *Selected Letters 1940–1977*, pp. 278–79.

41. HC Deb 16 December 1958, vol 597, col 1050.

42. Obscene Publications Act 1959.

43. Schiff, pp. 246–47, 248, 256–57, 258. See also Bradshaw, p. 158.

44. Gold, p. 206.

17

OZ 28: Schoolkids Edition

Richard Neville, Felix Dennis, Jim Anderson, and Guest Editors

At first glance, the 1960s look like an auspicious decade for press freedom in the United Kingdom. The Obscene Publications Act 1959 had created a public good defence designed to protect works of literary merit, and Vladimir Nabokov's *Lolita* was published that year without incident (see Chapter 16). In 1960 D. H. Lawrence's *Lady Chatterley's Lover* was cleared in a test case for the new legislation (see Chapter 12). Other works did not initially fare so well, but eventually escaped official censorship, such as Hubert Selby Jr.'s *Last Exit to Brooklyn*, which was cleared on appeal in 1968, and John Cleland's erotic novel *Memoirs of a Woman of Pleasure*, which circulated freely by 1970 (see Chapter 2). Denmark decriminalized pornography in the late 1960s, and the 1970 American Presidential Commission on Obscenity and Pornography recommended similar action, citing Denmark's example.[1] President Nixon rejected the report, but there was a sexual revolution underway. Did Britain still need obscenity laws to protect the nation from being 'depraved and corrupted' by sex?

In fact, the emerging counterculture posed a new threat, against which the forces of state censorship rallied. The concept of obscenity, previously restricted to sex, began to encompass material about drugs and violence.[2] The Obscene Publications Act 1959 granted the police greater powers of search and seizure, and the follow-up in 1964

The front cover of *OZ* 28, with strategically placed photograph of guest editor
Robb Douglas.

criminalized the possession of an obscene publication with intent to distribute it, where previously only distribution was illegal. Scotland Yard formed an Obscene Publications Squad, which turned out to be a protection racket that took bribes from Soho pornographers while harassing targets of political convenience, such as the underground press and other mouthpieces of alternative culture.[3] Targets of a rash of prosecutions in the late 1960s and early 1970s included a progressive education manual entitled *The Little Red Schoolbook*, Paul Ableman's *The Mouth and Oral Sex*, Bill Butler of the Unicorn Bookshop in Brighton, the underground magazines *International Times* (*IT*) and *OZ*, and the underground comic book *Nasty Tales*.[4] The 1971 *OZ* trial became emblematic of the conflict between the hippies and the man. (Though, as Alan Travis has revealed, at least one man was 'rooting for the hippies'—Labour Home Secretary Roy Jenkins, who had led the progressive side of the obscenity law reform in the 1950s, and was infuriated by Obscene Publications Squad raids on *IT* and art galleries.[5])

OZ's trouble with the law began much earlier, in Australia, which had its own strict censorship regime that included state-level Obscene Publications Acts and an extensive customs blacklist overseen by a censorship board. *The Well of Loneliness*, *Ulysses*, and *Memoirs of a Woman of Pleasure* had all been on the list. Customs had also banned crime and horror comic books by incorporating violence and horror into the definition of obscenity. Several books that circulated freely in the United States and the United Kingdom, such as *Lolita* and *Lady Chatterley's Lover*, were still on the Australian list of prohibited publications in 1963.[6] In that year, Richard Neville, who had struggled against censorship as editor of the student magazine *Tharunka* at the University of New South Wales, created a new 'magazine of dissent' with some fellow students. Neville claims the title was simply a nonsense syllable, though the allusion to Australia's nickname now seems obvious. *OZ* had not yet adopted the trippy aesthetic that would characterize its London run, but it was anti-authoritarian from the start. Its first issue contained anonymous interviews with women who had had abortions and a doctor who performed them. In New South Wales, where abortion was illegal and carried a sentence of ten years for the patient as well as for those who performed the procedure, the subject was taboo. As a result largely of the abortion article and another on chastity belts, Neville, Richard Walsh, and Peter Grose were charged with obscenity. They pleaded guilty and were fined. Their printer decided *OZ* was not worth the risk.[7]

The magazine continued with a new printer, taking aim at police beatings of gay men, state censorship, 'White Australia' immigration policy, and the Rupert Murdoch press. Copies of issue 6 were seized by police and, according to Neville, issue 8 was banned from State Rail stalls.[8] Neville, Walsh, and the cartoonist Martin Sharp were charged with obscenity for issue 6, the cover of which depicted Neville and two other men, their backs to the camera, pretending to use a public sculpture as a urinal. The definition of obscenity in New South Wales was similar to that used in the United Kingdom, and in the trial the defendants called expert witnesses to testify to the issue's literary merit. Points of contention included: the cover, the pun 'get folked', a satire about violent teenage behaviour involving a gang rape, and a bit by the comedian Lenny Bruce about an ex-marine who entertains a church congregation with dirty stories. The conviction was overturned on appeal in 1965 by Justice Aaron Levine.[9]

The Australian obscenity cases were a hint of what was to come when *OZ* launched in 1967 in London, where Neville and Sharp now lived. After a shaky start in January and an emergency injection of funds from Louise Ferrier, by May *OZ* had begun to find its new look.[10] Infusing the boyish irreverence of the Australian magazine with a psychedelic groove, London *OZ* 3 ushered in the Summer of Love on eye-searing waves of fuchsia and blue. Left-wing politics continued to be evident in the content—an interview with the Black Power activist Michael X, opposition to the Vietnam War, articles by the second-wave feminist Germaine Greer, issues on women's liberation and gay liberation, criticism of drug and abortion laws. The magazine's overriding commitments, however, were to hippie hedonism and a provocative visual style. In Neville's words,

> OZ has relentlessly promoted scorching elements of the new culture—dope, rock'n'roll and fucking in the streets; it is the only magazine in this country to consistently and constructively analyse the tension between the freak/dropout community and the militant left and to struggle to develop a theory from such antagonism.[11]

Though the London magazine repeatedly had trouble with printers, distributors, and the Obscene Publications Squad, especially over issue 23, the 'homosexual *OZ*' special issue, it was *OZ* 28, the Schoolkids Edition, that landed the editors in court.[12] In *OZ* 26 they had advertised for volunteers: 'Some of us at OZ are feeling old and boring, so we invite any of our readers who are under eighteen to come and edit the April issue.'[13] Around twenty teenagers, aged fifteen to eighteen, were selected, and converged on London, where they took editorial control of the magazine, except for the ads.[14] The resulting issue reflected the concerns of young people for whom authority took the form of parents, schoolmasters, exam boards, and the police. One article recounts the adventures of student activists who criticized school discipline by staging guerrilla theatre in schoolyards, rarely finishing their performances before being chased off by teachers or police officers. *OZ* often printed letters that were critical of the magazine, but this tendency is heightened in issue 28. A letters section entitled 'OZ Sucks' conveys the disaffection of people who want change but don't find the underground a sufficiently serious or authentic alternative to the mainstream. One letter-writer complains about the use of sex for shock value in the magazine: 'You (OZ) are VITAL. And don't you ever (how could you) OZ, as I feel you do, slacken on that responsibility.'[15]

Nevertheless, the schoolkids entered into the *OZ* spirit, and the issue offered plenty of risqué material, much of which would be scrutinized in court. The blue cover is adorned, front and back, with stylized drawings of nude Black women: one is licking another's breast, one is using a dildo, one is wearing a strap-on, a fifth is holding something rope-like between her legs—perhaps a whip? (It was suggested in court that this was a rat's tail.) An image of oral sex has prudently been concealed with an inset photograph of one of the guest editors, Robb Douglas, wearing a headband and staring pensively into the camera. Inside the covers, one article argues for the right to have sex in public, one reveals the social dynamics of a group of girls as they become sexually active, and another, by the emerging music journalist Charles Shaar Murray, discusses 'fuck music'. Sketches illustrate articles about school abuses: a headmaster masturbates while groping a vomiting boy, and teachers stimulate each other with switches. There are advertisements for Swedish pornography

('Excellent for masturbation and Fuckstimulation!!'), a vibrator, and a virility enhancer called 'Magnaphall'. A small ad reads 'Teenage male models wanted'. In an ad for the magazine *Suck*, a woman describes fellatio, including a permutation involving an ice cube. A Fabulous Furry Freak Brothers comic by American underground artist Gilbert Shelton plays out a gag in which groups of men in search of drugs attack each other with escalating degrees of violence, like fish eaten by progressively larger fish. A comic by Robert Crumb, also of the American underground, parodies the 'Pud' strips from packs of Double Bubble gum, and depicts the boy named Pud forcing a girl to give him oral sex. There are cartoons by the French artist Siné, one of which consists of a man penetrating a dismembered woman's abdomen, and another of a woman urinating on a penis-shaped cactus. A full-page photograph of one of the students, fifteen-year-old Bertie, in her school uniform is captioned 'Jailbait of the Week'.[16] This was a reference to another cartoon character by Crumb, thirteen-year-old Honeybunch Kaminski, who had appeared in a poster in *OZ* 24, topless and with the same caption, as a flippant response to an anti-*OZ* advertisement in *People* magazine.[17]

The most notorious image in issue 28 was a collage by one of the students, Vivian Berger, entitled 'Rupert the Bear Finds Gipsy Granny'. Berger superimposed Rupert's head onto a Crumb comic in which a man with an outsized penis, taking a running start, breaks the hymen of a woman on her back. Rhyming captions narrate what is going on. Most descriptions of this image misidentify 'Gipsy Granny' as a Crumb character. She actually belongs to Rupert's family-friendly setting, where she is the grandmother of Rupert's friend Rollo.[18] In the original Crumb comic the supine woman is a 'vulture demoness', a creature with the head of a bird and the body of a woman. A band of demonesses has captured the protagonist, Eggs Ackley. In the sequence that appears in *OZ*, Eggs has knocked one demoness unconscious, and is attempting to rape her.[19] Berger's collage transplants the Rupert characters underground and into the world of Crumb, a world of exaggerated proportions and graphic misogynistic violence.

On 8 June 1970 the obscenity squad raided the *OZ* offices, confiscating copies of issue 28 along with other documents.[20] The general editors, Neville, Felix Dennis, and Jim Anderson, were charged with three counts under the Obscene Publications Acts, one count of sending indecent material through the post, and one count of conspiring with

Vivian and 'certain other young persons to produce a magazine containing divers obscene, lewd, indecent and sexually perverted articles, cartoons, drawings and illustrations with intent thereby to debauch and corrupt the morals of children and young persons within the realm'.[21]

Conspiracy to corrupt public morals was the most dangerous charge. It was an old offence that had been dug up out of the common law and that carried no maximum penalty. The editors faced the theoretical possibility of life imprisonment and, in Neville's case, the less theoretical likelihood of deportation. Like the blasphemy charge that would be brought against *Gay News* six years after the *OZ* trial (see Chapter 19), conspiracy to corrupt public morals offered prosecutors a tool that was independent of the hard-won political compromises of the Obscene Publications Acts. The first precedent for corruption of public morals in England was the case of Sir Charles Sedley, who, in 1663, 'excrementiz'd' in Covent Garden and then delivered a blasphemous sermon, naked, from a balcony. In another account, he threw vessels of urine on the people below. The peace was, naturally, disturbed, which gave the secular courts reason to prosecute.[22] Nearly three hundred years later, in 1961, conspiracy to corrupt public morals was deployed against the publisher of *The Ladies Directory*, a directory of prostitutes. At the time of the *OZ* trial, the offence had just been used again, successfully, against the underground magazine *IT* for publishing gay contact ads. The concern, the Law Lords clarified, was that the ads were soliciting underage men for gay sex, which in 1971 meant men under twenty-one.[23] The 'teenage male models' ad in *OZ* raised similar suspicions.

The human rights barrister Geoffrey Robertson, also of Australia, who was a Rhodes Scholar at Oxford at the time, launched his legal career by assisting with the defence. After struggling to find a Queen's Counsel, the team secured John Mortimer, who was also defending *The Little Red Schoolbook*. Mortimer represented Dennis and Anderson. Determined to expose the trial as a political one and unwilling to be confined to a lawyer's script, Neville represented himself. It was one of several gestures of protest during the proceedings. In another, Neville, Dennis, and Anderson appeared at the preliminary hearing wearing schoolboy uniforms.[24]

In an interview with *Index on Censorship* late in his life, Mortimer said, 'I think the idea of being depraved and corrupted by a book is ... nobody's ever said what that really meant.'[25] It was a good point.

Since the R v. *Hicklin* decision in 1868, obscenity law in England and Wales had required judges and juries to determine whether a publication tended to deprave and corrupt readers, but this judgment was treated as a matter of common sense, and the law did not spell out how such a judgment could be reached. As the Court of Appeals later confirmed, obscenity was not a matter of expert knowledge, and expert witnesses were not supposed to comment on a publication's tendency to corrupt and deprave. The Obscene Publications Act 1959 permitted expert witnesses to testify in obscenity cases, but only to offer evidence for the public good defence. A literary critic could say that *Lady Chatterley's Lover* was a work of literary merit, but a psychologist could not say what effect it might have on readers—that was for the jury to decide. The *OZ* trial was a peculiar exception, possibly because of the conspiracy charge, which also alleged the intent to corrupt.[26] Judge Michael Argyle allowed expert witnesses to speak both to the merit of *OZ* and to its likely effects on readers. The long list of experts included the artist Feliks Topolski, author and children's rights activist Leila Berg, Caroline Coon of the drug user advocacy organization Release, several psychologists, writer and musician George Melly, law professor Ronald Dworkin, DJ John Peel, novelist Mervyn Jones, Edward de Bono (author of *The Use of Lateral Thinking*), and comedian Marty Feldman, who angered the judge by declining to swear on the Bible and claiming that parts of it were more obscene than *OZ*.[27]

The meaning of obscenity, usually assumed to be self-evident, was now open to examination, leading to a six-week-long trial that was both revealing and absurd. It became clear that to 'corrupt and deprave' meant, above all, to encourage people to take drugs and have any kind of sex other than straight, vaginal intercourse within marriage. The moral standards of the judge and the prosecution frequently clashed with those of the witnesses. The prosecutor, Brian Leary, asked Melly whether it was right to depict oral sex in a positive way. Melly replied, 'I don't think cunnilingus could do actual harm if you believe that sexuality is a wide thing in which one can do a large number of things as long as they don't hurt the opposite partner.' Argyle, lacking 'a classical education', asked what cunnilingus was, and Melly offered a series of euphemisms, including '*yodelling in the canyon*'.[28] There were several such moments of cross-cultural dissonance, as when Dennis explained

the phrase 'Right on!' to Argyle by throwing up his fist in a Black Pan-
ther salute.[29] When John Peel, who had once had a sexually transmit-
ted infection, suggested that it was a common affliction and that many
people in the courtroom might have had one, Argyle took umbrage at
the 'very great accusation' and later had Peel's water glass destroyed.[30]
Cross-examining Anderson about the cover image of a woman wearing a strap-on dildo, Leary asked him, 'do you find the erect male
organ nice?' Anderson, who was gay, remained silent. What could he
say? Leary rephrased, asking if Anderson found penises indecent. He
did not. This reply launched one of the trial's several forays into the
meaning of indecency and obscenity. Anderson was certain that it
would be indecent for someone to urinate in the courtroom, but not
certain that, in every circumstance, it would be indecent for parents to
masturbate in front of their children. Leary was incredulous.[31]

Appearing as a prosecution witness, but rooting for the defence,
Vivian Berger testified about his Rupert cartoon, which Anderson
and Topolski both defended on the grounds that the juxtaposition of
Rupert and Crumb was clever. ('MAKING RUPERT BEAR FUCK?' Leary
shouted at Anderson.[32]) Berger insisted that his strip was typical of
the kind of material students passed around at school, and took an
unorthodox angle on the obscenity question: that he was portraying
obscenity, not being obscene. He thought that obscenity was the content, not the depiction of it—if war was obscene, it did not mean that
the reporting of war was obscene.[33] (Vivian's mother, Grace Berger,
happened to be chair of the National Council for Civil Liberties, and
appeared for the defence.[34]) Neville ran with Vivian's idea in his closing arguments. Depiction was not the same as action. The act of urinating in court would be indecent, but a drawing of the act would
not be. Rupert's penis was not really 'being thrust in our face', and
readers were not 'in the firing line' of the drawing of a masturbating
schoolmaster.[35]

In a move similar to that made by Judge Woolsey, who found *Ulysses*
'emetic' rather than arousing, Mortimer attacked the premise that *OZ*
would deprave and corrupt readers by encouraging them to imitate
the actions depicted (see Chapter 11). Rather, he argued, much of the
content would elicit either laughter or disgust. Nobody was 'going to
be lured into a homosexual relationship with an elderly schoolmaster

by that nasty cartoon'.[36] On the other hand, as Lord Chief Justice John Widgery would observe in the Court of Appeals, the image on the back cover of women 'indulging in lesbian activities' was 'extremely attractively drawn'.[37] Mortimer challenged the corrupting effect of this more appealing material by gesturing to the ancient history of erotic art, the sexual content of Shakespeare, and the general pervasiveness of sex in modern culture:

> But consider how a young person today is bombarded from all sides by 'invitations to free love'. Sex rears from every hoarding, beckons from every advertisement, shouts and murmurs at him from every television commercial. If you want to advertise bath salts, for instance, you suggest that having a bath in a certain sort of bath foam will immediately produce a naked lady riding up to your door on a white charger.[38]

Importantly for the conspiracy charge, which specified an intent to corrupt the morals of children, the defence argued that *OZ* 28, despite being called 'Schoolkids *OZ*', was not likely to appeal to children and was aimed at the usual, older readership.[39] Neville pleaded ignorance about the teenage male models ad, which he claimed not to have suspected to be a solicitation for illegal sex—and if it might be, why did the police not investigate the ones who had taken out the ad?[40]

Because so much rested on the gap between what the counterculture and the establishment considered to be corrupt behaviour, Mortimer and Neville appealed to the jurors' tolerance of different values. At this time, jurors were still required to own property, and the *OZ* editors had ended up with 'ten men and two women, all lower-middle-class artisans of average age about sixty', a very different demographic from the long-haired young men in the dock and their even younger alleged co-conspirators.[41] Mortimer implored the jurors to recognize the freedom of expression and to extend the principle to young people:

> The importance is for us all to be able to say what we feel. And if, in putting forth their feelings, however mistakenly, however clumsily, children find that our reaction is to trundle out the law, to attack and suppress and censor, then there is a danger that they will shrug their shoulders and smile and turn away from us. Then, we shall indeed be a lonely generation, because we shall have lost them forever.[42]

After insisting on the centrality of love, not just sex, to the counterculture, Neville wrapped up his closing speech by quoting a verse from Bob Dylan's 'The Times They Are a-Changin'', extending a hand to the jury: 'Will you lend a hand?' he asked them.[43]

In his summing-up, Argyle called Vivian Berger a 'police informant', demolished several of the 'so-called' expert witnesses, wondered if the jury had ever heard of fellatio and cunnilingus before the trial, and read out the *Suck* advertisement word for word.[44] (A sample: 'By that time, he's pumping and it's so great to be looking straight at his pelvis and seeing it drive his prick into me. And I love the taste—that sharp, salty taste with a bit of chlorox in it.'[45]) Argyle suggested that, if *OZ* were a window on the hippie world, 'well, windows sometimes need cleaning, don't they?' It was clear where he stood.[46] The jury, reduced to eleven by a dismissal, decided that the editors were innocent of the conspiracy charge. By a ten to one majority, however, they found the defendants guilty of the charges under the Obscene Publications Acts and the Post Office Act.[47] Argyle had a reputation for ferocious sentences, and would later become president of an organization dedicated to bringing back the death penalty. Before sentencing, he remanded the editors to prison for three weeks to undergo psychiatric evaluation.[48] The men were forced to have their hair cut, an indignity which garnered them some sympathy in a mainstream press that had largely been against them.[49] Several members of parliament, including Michael Foot and Tony Benn, protested the editors' imprisonment in early-day motions in the House of Commons. After the evaluation, Argyle sentenced Dennis to nine months, Anderson to twelve, and Neville to fifteen, and fined the company one thousand pounds plus a quarter of the prosecution's costs. Neville was recommended for deportation. The judge claimed that Dennis's lesser sentence was due to a lack of intelligence. (When he later repeated this claim among other allegations in the *Spectator* in 1995, Dennis successfully obtained a settlement from the magazine.)[50] Outside the Old Bailey, the moral campaigner Mary Whitehouse, president of the National Viewers' and Listeners' Association, held signs reading, 'THANK YOU JUDGE AND JURY' and 'LONG LIVE BRITISH RULE OF LAW'.[51] *OZ* supporters burned Argyle in effigy.[52]

Throughout the trial a fundraising and publicity campaign had been thriving under the banner 'Friends of *OZ*'. John Lennon and Yoko Ono spearheaded the recording of a pop anthem, performed by Bill Elliot and the Elastic OZ Band, entitled 'God Save *OZ*', or perhaps 'God Save Us'. ('Let us fight for children's rights | Let us fight for freedom.') The B-side was called 'Do the *OZ*'. There was a parade in which a gigantic papier-mâché model of the topless young Honeybunch was transported on the back of a truck, and Crumb's cartoon became a mascot of the trial, sold on badges and T-shirts.[53] Neville wore the T-shirt in court. Clearly this image was meant to rile up the establishment and assert the freedom of speech, but it is also a reminder that the exercise of this freedom is not necessarily benign. While the magazine provided a platform for radical causes that were fighting oppression, it also indulged in exploitation. In addition to Honeybunch, the T-shirt designs that the magazine advertised for the OZ Defence Fund included 'Three Virgins', a nude photograph of three schoolgirls that had featured in the magazine as a double-page spread. Several 1972 issues contained advertisements for nude photographs of children under the heading 'Exciting Sex Offers'. OZ 43, despite printing a reader's complaint that the magazine was advertising child pornography, still reprinted the ad. 'Whatever else you defeat', the reader wrote, 'with your present attitude you will also defeat yourself, the counter culture you support and any worthwhile principles it encompasses'.[54] The sexual liberation had a dangerous streak of sexual irresponsibility.

The Court of Appeals determined that Argyle had misdirected the jury in several significant ways. He had given the impression of a bias against expert witnesses. More importantly, instead of sticking to the precise test of obscenity in the Obscene Publications Act 1959, he had relied on the word's etymology and its dictionary definition, offering the terms 'repulsive', 'filthy', 'loathsome', and 'lewd' as synonyms. He had implied that the public good defence was only meant to protect great works of art. And he had misrepresented the aversion defence, the idea that *OZ*'s content might repulse its readers rather than corrupt or deprave them.[55] Less favourably for *OZ*, the court also decided that Argyle and the prosecution had been mistaken to consider *OZ* 28 as a whole, rather than on an item-by-item basis. The Obscene Publications

Act 1959 required works to be considered as wholes in order to prevent prosecutors from cherry-picking raunchy episodes out of a larger book. The Act left unclear, however, how magazines, anthologies, and other publications containing multiple smaller works were to be judged. The Court of Appeals established that, in these publications, each individual item was to be assessed as a whole, and any obscene item was enough to render the entire publication obscene.[56] This meant one final hurdle for *OZ*. Although Argyle's misdirection had invalidated the jury's verdict, the Court of Appeals still had the power to rule that no miscarriage of justice had occurred, and Lord Widgery had become fixated on the advertisement for *Suck* magazine. This was not aversive: it made oral sex look good. Was it corrupting? According to Robertson, a story circulated among lawyers that the other judges brought in some Soho pornography to give Lord Widgery a crash course in modern sexual practices.[57] At any rate, the court overturned the Obscene Publications Act convictions, preserving only the convictions under the Post Office Act, which had a much lower bar for indecency and obscenity, but also lower penalties. The editors were each given a six-month sentence, suspended for two years, and the company's liability for the prosecution's costs was reduced to fifty pounds. Neville was not deported.[58] It could have been worse.

After the *OZ* case and the Law Lords' decision in the *IT* case, the conspiracy to corrupt public morals offence was rarely charged, and its use became restricted to advertisements in aid of sex crimes, such as publications by the Paedophile Information Exchange.[59] *Gay News*, founded in 1972, successfully printed gay contact ads without being prosecuted for conspiracy to corrupt public morals. *OZ* wound down in 1973, publishing in its final issue a post-mortem of the underground press, entitled 'What Went Wrong?', by the left-wing commentator David Widgery. While looking forward to the future of revolutionary politics, Widgery sharply criticized the counterculture's limitations: 'Because the underground remained so utterly dominated by men, sexual liberation was framed in terms saturated with male assumptions, right down to the rape fantasy of "Dope, rock and roll and fucking in the streets".'[60] The corruption of the Obscene Publications Squad was exposed in 1977, and twelve officers were imprisoned.[61] Conflicts between social conservatives and 'the permissive society' continued, however, including Mary Whitehouse's campaign to clean up television, radio, film, and occasionally print. In 1976 Mortimer and Robertson successfully defended *Inside Linda Lovelace*, the autobiography of pornographic performer Linda Boreman, from obscenity charges—a victory for the freedom of the press.[62] In 1977 the conviction of Denis Lemon and Gay News Ltd for blasphemy would be a landmark defeat.

Notes

1. Geoffrey Robertson, *Obscenity: An Account of Censorship Laws and their Enforcement in England and Wales* (London: Weidenfeld & Nicolson, 1979), pp. 3–4.
2. Robertson, *Obscenity*, p. 3.
3. Robertson, *Obscenity*, pp. 4–5; See also Geoffrey Robertson, *The Justice Game* (London: Vintage, 1999), pp. 44–45.
4. 'Mr Ripper's Dirty Books', *OZ* (London), September 1968 [University of Wollongong e-book].
5. Alan Travis, *Bound and Gagged: A Secret History of Obscenity in Britain* (London: Profile Books, 2000), pp. 166, 197–212.
6. Nicole Moore, *The Censor's Library: Uncovering the History of Australia's Banned Books* (St Lucia: University of Queensland Press, 2012), pp. 17, 28, 32–36, 38, 110–17, 137–42, 214, 225, 237, 250, 258.
7. Richard Neville, *Hippie Hippie Shake: The Dreams, the Trips, the Trials, the Love-Ins, the Screw-Ups . . . the Sixties* (London: Bloomsbury, 1995), pp. 20, 24, 26–31. See also 'Abortion', *OZ* (Sydney), April 1963, pp. 4–5 [University of Wollongong e-book]; 'The Maiden's Key to Chastity', *OZ* (Sydney), April 1963, pp. 8–9.
8. Neville, *Hippie Hippie Shake*, pp. 33–35, 39–40. See also Moore, p. 258.
9. Neville, *Hippie Hippie Shake*, pp. 40–46, 49–50, 52–53. See also Moore, pp. 258–60; *OZ* (Sydney), February 1964 [University of Wollongong e-book].
10. Neville, *Hippie Hippie Shake*, pp. 76–78.
11. Richard Neville, 'What Really Happened at Scotland Yards [*sic*] Christmas Party: Now! It Can Be Told', *OZ* (London), January 1971, p. 24 [University of Wollongong e-book].
12. 'The Men Who Ban *OZ*', *OZ* (London), March 1968, pp. 9–10, 13 [University of Wollongong e-book]; Neville, *Hippie Hippie Shake*, pp. 104–5, 127–28, 153–54, 172–73; Neville, 'What Really Happened at Scotland Yards Christmas Party', p. 22.
13. *OZ* (London), February 1970, p. 46 [University of Wollongong e-book].

14. Charles Shaar Murray, 'I Was an *Oz* Schoolkid', *Guardian*, 2 August 2001, https://www.theguardian.com/media/2001/aug/02/pressandpublishing. g2, accessed 26 December 2016; Tony Palmer, *The Trials of OZ* (London: Blond & Briggs, 1971), p. 101.

15. *OZ* (London), May 1970, p. 30 [University of Wollongong e-book]. See further pp. 6, 8–9.

16. *OZ* (London), May 1970.

17. Neville, *Hippie Hippie Shake*, pp. 172–73.

18. 'Rupert and Rollo', in *Rupert in More Adventures* ([n.p.]: Daily Express, 1944; repr. Exeter: Pedigree Books, 1996), p. 7.

19. Robert Crumb, 'Eggs Ackley among the Vulture Demonesses', in *The Complete Crumb Comics*, ed. Gary Groth and others (Seattle: Fantagraphics Books, 1991), VI: *On the Crest of a Wave*, 8–22 (p. 18).

20. Neville, *Hippie Hippie Shake*, pp. 211–12.

21. *R v Anderson* [1972] 1 QB 304 (CA) 308.

22. Robertson, *Obscenity*, p. 21 and note 16.

23. Geoffrey Robertson and Andrew Nicol, *Media Law*, 5th edn (London: Penguin, 2008), pp. 247–48.

24. Neville, *Hippie Hippie Shake*, pp. 224–25.

25. 'Return to Oz', *Index on Censorship*, 37.3 (2008), 32–41 (p. 34, ellipsis original), https://www.indexoncensorship.org/2014/06/archive, accessed 26 December.

26. *R v Anderson* [1972] 1 QB 304 (CA) 313.

27. Robertson, *The Justice Game*, p. 33.

28. Robertson, *The Justice Game*, p. 28 (emphasis original).

29. Neville, *Hippie Hippie Shake*, pp. 314–15. See also Palmer, pp. 108–9.

30. Robertson, *The Justice Game*, p. 30. See further pp. 28, 29–30.

31. Neville, *Hippie Hippie Shake*, p. 313. See further pp. 313–14.

32. Robertson, *The Justice Game*, p. 25.

33. Palmer, pp. 71–72.

34. Neville, *Hippie Hippie Shake*, pp. 316–17.

35. Neville, *Hippie Hippie Shake*, p. 324. See also Palmer, p. 232.

36. Palmer, p. 207. See also Robertson, *The Justice Game*, p. 35.

37. *R v Anderson* [1972] 1 QB 304 (CA) 311.

38. Palmer, p. 205. See further pp. 206, 209.

39. Neville, *Hippie Hippie Shake*, p. 286; Palmer, pp. 211–12.

40. Palmer, pp. 230–31.

41. Robertson, *The Justice Game*, p. 23.

42. Palmer, p. 216.

43. Neville, *Hippie Hippie Shake*, p. 327.

44. Neville, *Hippie Hippie Shake*, p. 330.

45. *OZ* (London), May 1970, p. 28.

46. Robertson, *The Justice Game*, pp. 38–39.

47. Palmer, pp. 261–62.

48. Robertson, *The Justice Game*, pp. 22–23, 39, 46.

49. Neville, *Hippie Hippie Shake*, pp. 335–36. See also Robertson, *The Justice Game*, pp. 39–40.

50. Robertson, *The Justice Game*, pp. 40, 46. See also Palmer, pp. 274–75.

51. 'The Oz Obscenity Trial, Mary Whitehouse 1971', Reportdigital, http://www.reportdigital.co.uk/gallery/1970s/1900/1916/1044/the-oz-obscenity-trial-mary-whitehouse-1971.html, accessed 26 December 2016.

52. Robertson, *The Justice Game*, p. 41.

53. Neville, *Hippie Hippie Shake*, pp. 273–74, 282–83, 312.

54. *OZ* (London), July 1972, pp. 8, 13 [University of Wollongong e-book].

55. *R v Anderson* [1972] 1 QB 304 (CA) 314. See further pp. 313–16.

56. *R v Anderson* [1972] 1 QB 304 (CA) 312.

57. Robertson, *The Justice Game*, pp. 43–44.

58. *R v Anderson* [1972] 1 QB 304 (CA) 317–18.

59. Robertson and Nicol, pp. 246–47.

60. David Widgery, 'What Went Wrong?', *OZ* (London), November 1973, p. 66 [University of Wollongong e-book].

61. Robertson, *Obscenity*, p. 5.

62. Robertson, *The Justice Game*, p. 46.

18

Black Voices from Prison
Etheridge Knight and Incarcerated Men at
Indiana State Prison

E theridge Knight's poem 'Cell Song' ends with a question:

> can there anything
> good come out of
> prison

First published in 1968 in *Poems from Prison*, these lines express an incarcerated poet's fear that his nocturnal labour will amount to nothing.[1] Knight was wounded in the Korean War, in which he had served as a medical technician. He became addicted to narcotics and, after his honourable discharge, was arrested several times for drug-related offences before being imprisoned in 1960, and then transferred from Indiana State Reformatory to Indiana State Prison.[2] Knight clearly hoped that something good could come out of prison: later in 1968, shortly before making parole, he co-authored and edited *Black Voices from Prison*, an anthology of verse and prose, fiction and non-fiction, by inmates at Indiana State, most of them Black. With the help of Knight's correspondent Roberto Giammanco, a translation was published in Italy that year. Giammanco could not find a publisher for an American edition in English until 1970.[3] The book was banned from a Texas prison in 1999.

The cover of the 1970 paperback edition of *Black Voices from Prison*, published by Pathfinder Press.

In the early 1960s members of the Black Muslim movement had begun seeking judicial protection of religious freedom in prisons, which opened the door to other court battles for prisoners' rights, battles that were subsequently fought as part of the Civil Rights Movement. Later in the decade, inmates began to organize protests and rebellions, and demanded various reforms, including better living conditions and medical treatment, a minimum wage, the right to organize, an end to inhumane punishment, improved educational opportunities, political and religious liberties, and limits to the censorship of publications and correspondence. Some inmates were informed by radical politics, especially those of the Black Power movement, through which they criticized the penal system as a mechanism of racial oppression.[4] Outside the prisons, there was public support for reform, and when New York state troopers put down the 1971 Attica Correctional Facility uprising with deadly force, killing twenty-nine inmates and ten hostages, sympathy was expressed for the prisoners in the *New York Times*. The mayor of Newark linked the state violence at Attica, where 63 per cent of the inmates were Black or Puerto Rican, to the violence used to quell civil disturbances in ghettoes.[5] Knight's collection enabled the voices of Black men in Indiana State Prison to join a nationwide conversation about race and the future of incarceration.

Black Voices from Prison draws on the Black Power movement. While attempting to capture the subjective reality of incarcerated men, including 'the feeling a man has of being swallowed up by the earth', the book challenges the systemic racism of White American society and the resulting injustices both outside and inside the penal system.[6] In an interview recorded in *Black Voices from Prison*, Charles W. Baker aligns himself with Malcolm X and revolution against Martin Luther King Jr. and the Civil Rights Movement's more reformist approach. Unless 'the black man' can 'bring about a change in this system', Baker says, 'He will never be judged by his qualities, he will never be judged as an individual. He will always be judged as black—the white man's conception of black: nonhuman.'[7]

While a desire for radical change pervades the collection, its diverse genres and perspectives create a vigorous dialogue. This dialogue is visible most clearly in 'The Day the Young Blacks Came', a section containing excerpts of Knight's correspondence with three of a group of fifty-five young Black men who had been transferred from the Indiana State Reformatory to the State Prison in August 1968. According to one of these men, the group was transferred because of a peaceful protest against institutional racism, during which 'We uttered not one word of violence. (How could we even breathe with fifteen to twenty shotguns pointed directly at us?) We had no weapons—although a few of us were armed with Bibles and Coca Colas'.[8] After the transfer, protests continued at the Reformatory, culminating in a sit-in held by 208 inmates, 207 of them Black. Prison guards shot at the group, killing James Durr, fatally wounding Robert Clancy, and injuring forty-five others. Eleven former inmates successfully sued guards and prison officials over the use of undue force.[9]

Knight deliberately includes 'the most argumentative' of his exchanges with the three 'young blacks', to whom he gives the aliases 'Slim', 'Water', and 'Bucky'. These men accuse Knight of being too passive in the cause of Black liberation. Water and Bucky call him 'tommish' or an 'Uncle Tom', terms that signify a Black man who is subservient to White people.[10] When Knight chastises Water for resisting incautiously, Water explains that he wants to join the Black Panthers after his release, and asserts his willingness to fight oppression with violence: 'Since I did my in depth study of our problem in this country, I could easily kill any hunky in the world if it would aid in freedom.'[11] Bucky, a fellow poet, takes offence at Knight's suggestion that he try to write more legibly: 'I think you want to be accepted by the general public, and brother, that's W-H-I-T-E. The revolution is B-L-A-C-K. Dig that?'[12]

Throughout this dialogue, it is clear that Knight, Slim, Water, and Bucky are trading more than their own words. The letters are punctuated with requests for, offers of, and questions about books, articles, and poems. The texts that circulated among these four included poems by Sonia Sanchez, the Black American magazine *Ebony*, the essay collection *William Styron's Nat Turner: Ten Black Writers Respond*, *Black Power: The Politics of Liberation* by Stokely Carmichael (later Kwame Ture) and Charles V. Hamilton, *Dark Ghetto* by Kenneth B. Clark, an issue of a periodical called *Liberator*, and the *Journal of Black Poetry*.

Bucky writes to Knight, 'Black Power is on its way. Don't panic! I only mean the book. Ha!'[13]

These references to authors and titles make clear that the lively debate between Knight and his radical friends did not exist in a vacuum, but was part of a larger cultural context that the inmates kept abreast of through reading. In fact, one of the grievances leading to the Indiana State Reformatory protests was censorship. A letter to the *Pittsburgh Courier* and the *Indianapolis Recorder* claimed that four men 'were placed in isolation for reading literature written by black authors' and 'unsparingly harassed'.[14] By collecting and publishing their writing, Knight, his co-editor, and his co-authors contributed in turn to a wider intellectual culture.

These voices having emerged from prison, can they now reach back inside? US courts have ruled that incarcerated people do not have full First Amendment rights. Prison regulations control, within certain limits, what books can be sent to inmates or held in prison libraries, while forms of chilling effect and 'informal censorship' further constrain the reading material available to incarcerated people.[15] In Texas, *Black Voices from Prison* was denied to an inmate in 1999 because of 'RCL' (racial) content on pages 30 and 47, and an appeal of the decision was unsuccessful.[16]

On page 30 of *Black Voices from Prison*, we find the 'Testament' of twenty-four-year-old David Flournoy, who recounts his youth in a 'little town where the Mississippi and Ohio rivers meet':

> As I said before, I've been fighting all my life. When me and my buddies weren't fighting somebody from our end of town, we would go peckerwood hunting, hoping to find some white boys our age to beat up. We won most of the time, but sometimes we lost. But until we left home we had never had the nerve to fight any grown-up white man. After the first time it was easy. Our specialty was bopping the whiteys that came to the colored sections of towns looking for women. We fought and robbed and balled for six months and all the time it was like I was outside of me or like I was saying no, no to myself.[17]

On page 47, in another 'Testament', Clarence Harris reflects on his youth in Memphis, Tennessee, where he 'discovered that men were different because of their skin color' on the day a White man ran over his dog: 'The white man told my father: "Nigger, it should have been that little nigger there instead of the dog. You should've kept them both out of the street. And don't you ask me nothing about that dog!"' Harris writes, 'from that time on I was taught that the white man was king and was to be treated as such; I learned that they were to be idolized, feared, catered to, and also to be emulated as much as possible without stepping out of your place.' Later, he continues:

> I became a part of the black environment in the North that had a smattering of white middle-class bourgeois values, but I couldn't handle the unreality of trying to be white. And I took to the streets. There, we had our own thing, our own language, our own special walks, our hipness and our soul, which we attributed to heart and toughness, and the ability to survive. We wanted to be kings, too, but not kings of rats. By now, I had quit school, and I knew what was happening with whitey.[18]

The citation of these two pages as the reason for denying the book is arbitrary, since *Black Voices from Prison* deals with racism and interracial violence elsewhere. Other material could also theoretically have triggered a denial. For instance, there are discussions of sexual violence in the book, such as Knight's description of gang rape, which he disturbingly calls 'not a rape' but 'a ceremony, a ritual', or his analysis of prison rape—the imperative for a young man 'to ride or to be ridden'.[19] Unlike obscenity law, however, prison censorship does not require that a work be assessed as a whole. Even one instance of prohibited content is sufficient to prevent a publication from entering the institution. Why were these two instances of 'RCL' content prohibited? We cannot know for certain. The Texas Department of Criminal Justice (TDCJ) preserves records of book denials only for four years, and the policy document under which the 1999 decision was made was destroyed in 2004. Reference to the denial of the book and the offending pages survive in a list of books that have been denied to Texas inmates, which was entered into evidence in *Prison Legal News* v. *Livingston*. Despite the absence of records, we can draw some conclusions from the court decisions that govern prison censorship.

Incarcerated people have First Amendment rights, but these rights are limited by the penal system. (Similarly, the First Amendment rights of students are limited by school boards—see Chapters 14, 24, and 25.) In the 1987 case *Turner* v. *Safley*, the Supreme Court held: 'when a prison regulation impinges on inmates' constitutional rights, the regulation is valid if it is reasonably related to legitimate penological interests.'[20] Subsequent cases have applied this principle to the censorship of publications in prisons, 'with some courts allowing censorship of strongly expressed views or allegations that the censors find distasteful or threatening, while others hold that there must actually be some advocacy or concrete risk of violent or other unlawful action to justify censorship'.[21] In one recent case, the human rights organization Prison Legal News (PLN) took civil action against the executive director of the Texas Department of Criminal Justice because of the censorship of several books about incarceration that PLN had mailed to Texas inmates: *The Perpetual Prison Machine: How America Profits from Crime*, *Lockdown America: Police and Prisons in the Age of Crisis*, *Soledad Brother: The Prison Letters of George Jackson*, and *Women behind Bars: The Crisis of Women in the U.S. Prison System*. In 2012 the Court of Appeals for the Fifth Circuit ruled in favour of the department, noting that other books critical of prisons had been allowed into the system. Prison Legal News, the court found, had failed to demonstrate 'that TDCJ's practices and exclusion decisions bear no reasonable relation to valid penological objectives'. In effect, PLN faced the nearly impossible task of demonstrating that, contrary to the TDCJ's claims, 'depictions of prison rape' would 'pose no threat to safety or rehabilitation' and material 'describing racial tensions' would not 'present a threat of violence'. The court expressed 'deference to the judgment of prison administrators' in censorship decisions, unless the administrators' judgement is proven to be irrational.[22]

In the United Kingdom, similarly, a prison governor can ban material 'if he or she considers that the content presents a threat to good order or discipline, or that possession of the material is likely to have an adverse effect on the prisoner's physical or mental condition'.[23] From late 2013 to late 2014, people in British prisons could access publications temporarily through prison libraries and interlibrary loan services, but no one could send reading material directly to incarcerated people. Inmates could purchase publications only through prison shops, and they needed to make up the cost with their earnings and the limited allowances from friends and family that the Incentives and Earned Privileges scheme permitted. Exceptions were possible in theory, but the standard practice made it difficult for incarcerated people to own certain books, especially rare titles not obtainable through Amazon, the retailer that the prison shops used. In December 2014 the High Court of England and Wales ruled that books should be excluded from the Incentives and Earned Privileges policy. Justice Collins wrote that, since the Secretary of State for Justice had acknowledged the importance of access to books in prison, 'to refer to them as a privilege is strange'. After this decision, books could be sent to inmates from one of several approved retailers.[24] In 2015 Secretary of State for Justice Michael Gove further reduced these restrictions. Friends and family can send books directly to inmates, who can now have more than twelve at a time, subject to caps on the total volume of the possessions in their cells.[25]

Current policy in Texas, where *Black Voices from Prison* was banned, reflects US law. The TDCJ correspondence rules no longer explicitly mention race, but do forbid 'material that a reasonable person would construe as written solely for the purpose of communicating information designed to achieve the breakdown of prisons through offender disruption such as strikes or riots, or STG [i.e., gang] activity'. Other restrictions include 'material on the setting up and operation of criminal schemes or how to avoid detection of criminal schemes', 'information regarding the manufacture of explosives, weapons, or drugs', 'graphic presentations of sexual behavior that is in violation of the law, such as rape, incest, sex with a minor, bestiality, necrophilia, or bondage', and, with some exceptions, 'sexually explicit images'. Books can now be sent to inmates only from a publisher or retailer.[26]

It is likely, then, that in 1999 the treatment of race in *Black Voices from Prison* was deemed in some way to threaten the security of the institution where the book was denied, even though the cited pages do not advocate racial hatred or violence and, being accounts of Flournoy's and Harris's life experiences, are patently not 'written solely for the purpose of communicating information designed to achieve the breakdown of prisons'. The censorship of *Black Voices from*

Prison raises questions about where prison officials, whose power of discretion the courts have confirmed, draw the line between expressing radical political ideas and actively inciting disorder. The banning of the book in the Texas prison system constituted an interruption that prevented *Black Voices from Prison* from informing further dialogue among incarcerated people in Texas, and at a time when dialogue about prisons was urgently needed.

The prisoners' rights movement declined in the 1970s, along with the Black Power movement which had energized it. Over the following decades, the penal system expanded dramatically, and racial disparities in incarceration rates increased, impelled by a variety of forces, including the war on drugs, 'law-and-order' public policies, neoliberal economics, and an underlying systemic racism.[27] The total incarceration rate increased more than fivefold between 1972 and 2007.[28] Mass incarceration continues to affect Black and Latino/a people disproportionately. In 2015 one in thirty-seven adults in the United States was under correctional supervision, whether incarcerated, on probation, or paroled.[29] The rate at which Black men were imprisoned in state and federal prisons, with sentences greater than one year, was 5.7 times that of non-Hispanic White men; the rate for Black women was almost twice that of non-Hispanic White women; 2.6 per cent of all Black male residents were serving sentences of at least one year, as were 1.0 per cent of Hispanic male residents.[30] In *The New Jim Crow*, legal scholar Michelle Alexander argues that, like slavery and segregation, mass incarceration works to maintain a 'racial undercaste': 'Once released, former prisoners enter a hidden underworld of legalized discrimination and permanent social exclusion.'[31]

Published on the cusp of the current period of mass incarceration, and denied to a Texas inmate in the 1990s, when disparities between the incarceration rates of Black and White people were at their highest,[32] *Black Voices from Prison* contains an important critique of the penal system in the United States, as well as a record of how a group of Black men were affected by it and resisted it. In one story that Knight tells, J. W. 'Icewater' Prewitt, still maintaining his innocence, sacrifices his chances for parole through disobedience. Prewitt, Knight writes, 'has said NO to the whole system'.[33]

Notes

1. Etheridge Knight, 'Cell Song', in Etheridge Knight and other inmates of Indiana State Prison, *Black Voices from Prison* (New York: Pathfinder Press, 1970), p. 141.

2. Michael S. Collins, *Understanding Etheridge Knight* (Columbia: University of South Carolina Press, 2012), pp. 4–6.

3. Collins, p. 51.

4. Mary Bosworth, *Explaining U.S. Imprisonment* (Los Angeles: SAGE, 2010), pp. 98–115; Marie Gottschalk, *The Prison and the Gallows: The Politics of Mass Incarceration in America* (Cambridge: Cambridge University Press, 2006), pp. 165–83.

5. Bosworth, pp. 100, 104. See also Gottschalk, *The Prison and the Gallows*, p. 181.

6. William Healy, 'Another Day Coming', in Knight and others, pp. 49–58 (p. 49).

7. Charles W. Baker, 'Interview of Charles W. Baker', in Knight and others, pp. 37–45 (p. 43).

8. Letter to Civil Rights Division (16 August 1968), in Etheridge Knight, 'The Day the Young Blacks Came', in Knight and others, pp. 161–83 (p. 168).

9. 'Ex-Convicts Win Brutality Suit', *New York Times*, 27 November 1974, http://www.nytimes.com/1974/11/27/archives/exconvicts-win-brutality-suit-9-guards-27-aides-accused-in-69.html?_r=0, accessed 24 February 2017. See also Knight, 'The Day the Young Blacks Came', p. 162.

10. Knight, 'The Day the Young Blacks Came', pp. 164, 169, 171, 182.

11. Knight, 'The Day the Young Blacks Came', p. 173.

12. Knight, 'The Day the Young Blacks Came', p. 182.

13. Knight, 'The Day the Young Blacks Came', p. 180. See further pp. 170, 172, 173, 176, 181, 182.

14. Letter to the editor, *Pittsburgh Courier* and *Indianapolis Recorder*, September 1969, quoted in Knight, 'The Day the Young Blacks Came', p. 161.

15. Tammi Arford, 'Captive Knowledge: Censorship and Control in Prison Libraries' (unpublished doctoral dissertation, Northeastern University, Boston, MA, 2013; full text in Northeastern University Digital Repository Service), p. 130, http://hdl.handle.net/2047/d20003234, accessed 1 January 2017. See further pp. 128–58.

16. Exhibit 8(b) (List of Books Denied by DRC) at 41, Prison Legal News v. Livingston, No. CIV.A. C-09-296 (S.D. Tex. Jan. 4, 2011). See also Maggie Watson and others, 'Banned Books in the Texas Prison System:

How the Texas Department of Criminal Justice Censors Books Sent to Prisoners', Texas Civil Rights Project, 2011, p. 31, https://www.texascivilrightsproject.org/en/wp-content/uploads/2016/04/TCRP_Prison_Books_Report.pdf, accessed 1 January 2017.

17. David Flournoy, 'Testament', in Knight and others, pp. 29–32 (p. 30).

18. Clarence Harris, 'Testament', in Knight and others, pp. 46–48 (p. 47).

19. Etheridge Knight, 'The Innocents', in Knight and others, pp. 95–121 (pp. 99–100, 109).

20. Turner v. Safley, 482 U.S. 78, 89 (1987).

21. John Boston and Daniel E. Manville, *Prisoners' Self-Help Litigation Manual*, 4th edn (New York: Oceana, 2010), p. 198.

22. Prison Legal News v. Livingston, 683 F.3d 201, 216, 218, 221 (5th Cir. 2012).

23. Juliette Jowit, 'Are Books Really Banned in Prisons?', *Guardian*, 26 March 2014, https://www.theguardian.com/news/reality-check/2014/mar/25/books-banned-prisons-justice-secretary, accessed 1 January 2017.

24. *R (Gordon-Jones) v Secretary of State for Justice* [2014] EWHC 3997 [46] (Admin).

25. 'Prisoner Book Restrictions Scrapped by Michael Gove', BBC News, 12 July 2015, http://www.bbc.co.uk/news/uk-33497581, accessed 2 September 2016.

26. Texas Department of Criminal Justice, *Offender Orientation Handbook*, I-202, April 2016, p. 118, http://www.tdcj.state.tx.us/documents/Offender_Orientation_Handbook_English.pdf, accessed 1 January 2017. See further p. 115.

27. Marie Gottschalk, *Caught: The Prison State and the Lockdown of American Politics* (Princeton: Princeton University Press, 2015), pp. 2–16, 145–54. See also *The Growth of Incarceration in the United States: Exploring Causes and Consequences*, ed. Jeremy Travis and others (Washington, DC: National Academies Press, 2014), pp. 104–29 [National Academies Press e-book].

28. *The Growth of Incarceration in the United States*, p. 33.

29. Danielle Kaeble and Lauren Glaze, 'Correctional Populations in the United States, 2015', US Department of Justice, Office of Justice Programs, Bureau of Justice Statistics, December 2016, NCJ 250374, p. 1, https://www.bjs.gov/content/pub/pdf/cpus15.pdf, accessed 30 December 2016.

30. E. Ann Carson and Elizabeth Anderson, 'Prisoners in 2015', US Department of Justice, Office of Justice Programs, Bureau of Justice Statistics,

December 2016, NCJ 250229, p. 30, https://www.bjs.gov/content/pub/pdf/p15.pdf, accessed 30 December 2016.

31. Michelle Alexander, *The New Jim Crow: Mass Incarceration in the Age of Colorblindness*, rev. edn (New York: New Press, 2012), pp. 12–13, 241 [ProQuest e-book].

32. Gottschalk, *Caught*, p. 121.

33. Knight, 'The Innocents', p. 121.

19

'The Love that Dares to Speak its Name' in *Gay News*

James Kirkup

In an interview with the BBC World Service, Salman Rushdie, author of *The Satanic Verses*, said: 'Nobody has the right to not be offended. That right doesn't exist in any declaration I have ever read. If you are offended it is your problem, and frankly lots of things offend lots of people.'[1] This principle, with its ring of hard common sense, has become a cliché of online forums and comment sections, yet it did not hold true in England in 1977, when the editor of *Gay News* was convicted of blasphemy for publishing James Kirkup's poem 'The Love that Dares to Speak its Name'. After the Court of Appeals and the Law Lords upheld the conviction, the European Commission of Human Rights confirmed that blasphemy law protected 'the right of citizens not to be offended in their religious feelings by publications', and was therefore a legitimate restriction on the freedom of speech.[2] The religious feelings being protected were, in the first place, those of Mary Whitehouse, who had brought a private prosecution against *Gay News*.

Formerly a schoolteacher in Shropshire, Whitehouse had resigned in 1964 to campaign against the sex, drugs, and rock and roll culture of the 1960s—the sexually liberated, increasingly secular 'permissive

Protesters assemble outside the Royal Courts of Justice during Denis Lemon's initial appeal of his blasphemy conviction in February 1978.

society'. As a leader of Clean-Up TV, the National Viewers' and Listeners' Association (NVALA), and the Nationwide Festival of Light, she filled a similar role to Anthony Comstock of the New York Society for the Suppression of Vice (see Chapter 6). Better-humoured and less bloodthirsty than Comstock, Whitehouse became the face of a conservative Christian movement that aimed to stem the tide of moral dissolution by ridding the media of objectionable content. She wrote letters of complaint to broadcasting authorities, lobbied government, initiated prosecutions, and mobilized public feeling with speeches and television appearances.[3] In 1976 she achieved a major victory when the NVALA elicited official condemnation of the Danish artist Jens Jørgen Thorsen. Thorsen was attempting to make *The Many Faces of Jesus*, a pornographic film in which Jesus's sexual partners would include John the Baptist and Mary Magdalene, and, having been forbidden to film in Denmark and Sweden, Thorsen was planning to do it in the United Kingdom. In response to the NVALA's campaign, the Archbishop of Canterbury, the Home Secretary, Prime Minister James Callaghan, and Queen Elizabeth II opposed the prospective film. The Archbishop suggested that, were the film to be made, it might be vulnerable to prosecution for blasphemy, and the Prime Minister indicated that Thorsen was not welcome in the country and might be barred from entry by the Home Secretary. The filmmaker did not enter the United Kingdom.[4] The following year, a poem dealing with similar matter to Thorsen's film would appear in *Gay News*, and Whitehouse would try her luck again.

The title of 'The Love that Dares to Speak its Name' alludes to a term used for gay love in the late nineteenth century, coined by Lord Alfred Douglas in his poem 'Two Loves'. When on trial in the Old Bailey for gross indecency in 1895 (see Chapter 9), Oscar Wilde famously said:

> 'The love that dare not speak its name' in this century is such a great affection of an elder for a younger man as there was between David and Jonathan, such as Plato made the very basis of his philosophy, and such as you find in the sonnets of Michelangelo and Shakespeare. It is that deep, spiritual affection that is as pure as it is perfect.[5]

Turning 'dare not' to 'dares', Kirkup invents an episode in which the centurion Longinus has sex with Christ's dead body on Calvary. Longinus performs fellatio on 'that great cock, the instrument | of our salvation, our eternal joy', and ejaculates in Christ's wounds and mouth. 'It was', he says, 'the only way I knew to speak our love's proud name'. Jesus then reciprocates, first spiritually ('I felt him enter into me, and fiercely spend | his spirit's final seed within my hole, my soul') and then, after he is resurrected, physically: 'And took me to him with | the love that now forever dares to speak its name.' Longinus also suggests in the course of his monologue that Christ's lovers included Pontius Pilate, John the Baptist, and the twelve disciples. Christ, he says, 'loved all men, body, soul and spirit.—even me'.[6]

Kirkup was an acclaimed poet, a professor of literature at the University of Foreign Studies in Kyoto who had held various academic posts in the United Kingdom, the United States, Japan, and other countries. Though he later renounced 'The Love that Dares to Speak its Name', his intention in writing it was serious.[7] He was not merely trying to shock readers by injecting explicit sex into the central event of Christian theology. Kirkup identified as bisexual, and his poem reflected on two forms of love between men: the love of men for Christ, and the gay love that mainstream Christianity held to be sinful. Kirkup had been put off in his youth by the violence of the crucifixion story, and attempted in this poem to 'see Christ anew in terms of modern sexual liberation, terms valid for homosexuals, bisexuals, and heterosexuals alike'. He wrote:

> I wanted to portray strong, deep emotion and intense passion (in both senses of the word), to present a human, earthly and imperfect Christ symbolising my own outcast state, and that of all outcasts in our society.
>
> Of course, I knew this would dismay and shock some people—but had I not myself been deeply offended, dismayed and shocked by *their* disgusting version of the Crucifixion?
>
> As for blasphemy—that was never my intention. How could it be?[8]

Denis Lemon, the editor and majority owner of *Gay News*, understood the poem similarly: 'The centurion represents a repressed homosexual, a Christian who is guilt-ridden and cannot reconcile his Christianity with his homosexuality. [. . .] In the end, particularly in the final two stanzas of the poem, the centurion finds salvation.'[9]

The poem seemed to be good material for *Gay News*, which Lemon later described as a 'voice for the opinions and experiences of lesbians and gay men who otherwise would have been largely ignored or vilified'.[10] 'I thought it was a powerful poem,' he said at the time of the trial, 'and I thought that the message it contained was a powerful enough message to take people back, but not in the—not in the sense that Mrs Whitehouse was taken aback by it.'[11] He decided to publish it in the 'Poetry and Classics' section of *Gay News*, issue 96. An illustration by Tony Reeves, reminiscent of Aubrey Beardsley's drawings, depicts a centurion embracing the body of Christ, whose blood drips down a piece of cloth. He is, as the poem suggests, 'beardless, breathless, | but well hung'.[12] A probation officer purchased a copy of the newspaper, claiming to be interested in a front-page article, which reported that the National Association of Probation Officers was in favour of equalizing age of consent laws for gay and straight sex. Months later, having heard about the poem, he read it and contacted an organization called the Responsible Society, which forwarded the poem to Whitehouse.[13] Whitehouse claimed that, when a copy of the poem appeared in her post, there was no accompanying information about where it had been published. (Despite being a professed opponent of those she called the 'Gay-Libbers' and the 'Gay/Humanist lobby', she was anxious to convey that she was motivated by the poem itself and not the venue in which it had appeared.)[14] Although printed literature was outside Whitehouse's usual remit, this poem was more shocking than the occasional racy moment in a BBC Wednesday Play. For her, the images in the poem were not simply imaginative. She believed that Christ himself had been attacked, and that she needed to do something about it:

> I felt, quite simply, deeply ashamed that Christ should be treated in this way. It seemed to me like a kind of re-crucifixion, only this time with twentieth-century weapons. I experienced out of love for Him a great longing to try to make some kind of reparation. It seemed to me that if I did nothing I would be like that Levite priest in Jesus's story of the Good Samaritan, who 'passed by on the other side'.[15]

She resolved to be a good Samaritan, consulted her lawyers, secured permission and an indictment from a judge, and brought a private prosecution for blasphemous libel against Lemon and Gay News Ltd. Kirkup, who was abroad, was not indicted.[16]

Blasphemy law had not been used successfully in England or Wales for fifty-five years, the last conviction having been that of the free-thinker John William Gott, who had described Christ as a circus clown.[17] (In Scotland, where stricter laws had once dealt death to blasphemers,[18] there had not been a prosecution for 150 years.[19]) Like its cousins sedition, defamation, and obscenity, blasphemy had origi-nally been outlawed because it was considered to threaten order in the state. Christianity was part of the laws of the realm, and to blaspheme was not just to attack religion, but to attack the established church[20]— or, by extension, other Christian denominations where their tenets intersected with those of the Church of England.[21] Blasphemy law, first wielded by the secular courts in 1676 against John Taylor, who was fined and pilloried for raving that 'Christ is a whore-master, and religion is a cheat', had by the nineteenth century become a tool for prosecuting freethinkers, like Richard Carlile, who pirated Percy Bysshe Shelley's poem *Queen Mab* (see Chapter 4). In 1883 Lord Chief Justice John Duke Coleridge softened the interpretation of blasphemy law, implying to a jury that it was not blasphemy simply to express opposition to church doctrine in decent language. The manner of expression and the intention mattered: words 'intended to insult the feelings and the deepest religious convictions of the great majority of the persons amongst whom we live' were blasphemous.[22] A blasphemy statute from 1698 was repealed through the Criminal Justice Act 1967, but in 1977 the blasphemous libel offence still lurked in the common law—dormant, moribund, not yet dead.[23]

Its religious content aside, a poem about explicit sex, especially gay sex, was vulnerable to obscenity legislation. But the long series of court battles over literature banned for obscenity in the United Kingdom, starting with Henry Vizetelly's editions of Émile Zola, had sparked legislative debates that eventually produced ground rules designed to protect work with artistic or other social value (see Chapters 8, 12, and 16). Under the Obscene Publications Act 1959, expert witnesses were permitted to testify to a work's value, and the judge or jury would need to decide whether its publication was for the public good, which would be enough to save it. In doing so, they would need to consider the work as a whole. Resuscitating blasphemy was, therefore, an ingenious legal strategy that set the freedom of literary expression back to square one. Every safeguard for literature that freedom of speech reformers had won in Parliament would need to be fought for again in the *Gay News* trial, and success depended on how receptive the judge would be.

Judge Alan King-Hamilton had a general respect for the sacred. Though he was Jewish, he was thoroughly offended by Kirkup's poem. He recalled: 'The impact of the subject matter and the choice of words employed were quite staggering. I was shocked and horrified. One didn't have to be a Christian to be revolted by it.' He considered recusing himself, but 'was convinced that almost every judge would have reacted in the same way', and trusted to his own impartiality.[24] King-Hamilton was not known to be sympathetic to gay people, having once suggested in court that homosexuality was a form of 'decadence and immorality', and that decadence and immorality had caused the fall of the Roman Empire.[25]

Defence counsel John Mortimer and Geoffrey Robertson, veterans of the *OZ* trial (see Chapter 17), tried their best to turn the *Gay News* blasphemy trial into an obscenity one. Robertson represented Gay News Ltd and Mortimer represented Lemon. They argued that the blasphemy offence did not exist, and that obscenity was the appropriate charge.[26] They requested to be able to make opening statements immediately after the prosecutor made his so that the jury would hear each side's interpretation of the poem before reading it. They attempted to present evidence of Kirkup's intention, and to call expert witnesses to analyse the poem's theological and literary qualities. (There were in fact relevant theological questions in the case: a book called *The Myth of God Incarnate* had recently questioned Christ's divinity, and Bishop John Robinson had suggested that Jesus might have been gay.) The judge rejected all of the defence's strategies, evidently impatient with the legal arguments. He said that he had hoped the case would be over by lunchtime and, in one surreal moment, informed the jury of the cricket score.[27] In his autobiography, King-Hamilton wrote that the question of the poem's blasphemy was 'a simple issue which twelve ordinary people ought to be able to decide amongst themselves, without getting bogged down in theological controversy'. He was well aware of what the defence was attempting to do, and wrote that, if the defendants had been charged 'under the Obscene Publications Acts, I think it is very likely that, in the present climate of permissiveness and in the light of recent trials under those Acts, there would have been an acquittal'.[28]

The Crown prosecutor, John Smyth, was therefore permitted to shape the jury's first impression of the poem, which he described as 'so vile it would be hard for the most perverted imagination to conjure up anything worse'. As if the text were a factual assertion rather than a work of fiction, he said, 'It is quite obvious that the poem portrays Jesus Christ as a practising homosexual, and as utterly promiscuous. You will find at least fifteen identifiable individuals with whom Christ is alleged to have performed buggery, as well as with groups.'[29] The jury then, in Robertson's words, had to 'sit in their seats, in full public gaze, while reading the work which the prosecution had just interpreted for them'. In the end, few witnesses were permitted: for the prosecution, the parole officer who had originally received the poem, and, for the defence, the writers and critics Margaret Drabble and Bernard Levin. Forbidden to discuss the artistic value of the poem or illustration, Drabble and Levin could only testify to the good character of *Gay News* itself, a sideline that was technically irrelevant.[30] In closing arguments, Smyth asserted again that depicting Jesus as gay was an attack on Christianity, and asked the jury to consider how they would take such an accusation against worldly royalty, let alone the 'King of Kings', whom the Church of England considered to be without sin. The *Gay News* trial was, he said, 'about whether anything is to remain sacred'. The jury was 'being asked to set the standard for the last quarter of the twentieth century', and they would 'open the floodgates' if they did not find the defendants guilty: 'The privilege of raising a banner against the tiny minority who seek to inflict this sort of thing on us and our children belongs exclusively to you.'[31] In other words, Down with this sort of thing.

Robertson and Mortimer had their only real opportunity to sway the jury in their closing arguments. Robertson pointed out that *Gay News* was not forcing its content on anyone, and argued that 'tolerance' was now the 'fabric of society'.[32] He offered a literary interpretation in which the poem was not literal but figurative. 'The poem was sixty lines long', he recalled, 'and I decided there was nothing for it but to explain, line by line, how it tried to communicate—metaphorically rather than literally, by likening divine love to human love—Christ being the word made flesh.'[33] Robertson drew the jury's attention to the tradition in English poetry of expressing divine love in erotic language. He quoted from one of John Donne's 'holy sonnets', in which the poet, addressing God, concludes:

Take me to you, imprison me, for I
Except y'enthral me never shall be free
Nor ever chaste except you ravish me.[34]

Mortimer then appealed to the jury's sympathy, reminding them that a real person was being tried under the 'antique charge' of blasphemy: 'The Sermon on the Mount tells us to love our neighbours, but Mrs. Mary Whitehouse has put her neighbour in the dock.'[35] He argued that the law of blasphemy was no longer appropriate, attempted to instil reasonable doubt of its applicability, and challenged biblical condemnations of gay sex. Like Robertson, he likened the poem to a respectable example of erotic Christian writing—this time the Song of Songs, which, though it seemed to be about physical love, was usually read allegorically. He urged the jury to see the trial as an attack on artistic expression and to practise Christian forgiveness. As Jesus had said, 'whosoever speaketh a word against the Son of Man it shall be forgiven him.'[36]

Robertson had made a mistake in neglecting to read aloud lines 43 to 48 of the poem, the stanza in which Christ spills his seed into the centurion's soul. King-Hamilton capitalized on this mistake in his instructions to the jury, in which he made overwhelmingly clear what he thought the verdict should be. He asked whether the jurors were surprised that Robertson had been unable to read aloud these lines,

which 'you may think are the ultimate in profanity'.[37] Like the prosecution, he conjured up the spectre of greater permissiveness:

> There is a world of difference between opening a window in a stuffy
> Victorian library and letting in a little fresh air, and on the other hand,
> leaving both windows and doors open so there is a raging draft, bring-
> ing in with it a retinue of attendant dangers with all their consequences.

He left the jury with a series of questions: 'Did it shock you when
you first read it? Could it shock or offend anyone who read it? Could
you read it to an audience of fellow Christians without blushing?'[38]
While Whitehouse and company prayed in the corridors, the jury
eventually reached a guilty verdict by a majority of ten to two, and
the judge praised the ten for their 'moral courage'.[39] Gay News Ltd
was fined one thousand pounds, plus four-fifths of the prosecution's
costs. Lemon was fined five hundred pounds, plus the rest of the prosecution's costs, and given a nine-month suspended prison sentence.[40]
King-Hamilton wrote in his autobiography:

> As for the summing-up itself, I can confidently assert that it was the
> best, by far, that I have ever given. I can say this without blushing
> because, throughout its preparation, and also when delivering it, I
> was half-conscious of being guided by some superhuman inspiration.
> Browning's 'Hand ever above my shoulder' perhaps?[41]

Whitehouse announced, 'It's been a great day for the country—a line
has at last been drawn.' Kirkup told the *Observer* that 'he now considers himself Britain's first dissident poet and will never again return to
this country'.[42]

Even if it were true that, as she insisted, Whitehouse would have
taken action against the poem regardless of the publication in which
it appeared, the homophobic politics of the trial were extreme. A
defender of traditional Christian family values, who saw gay and
lesbian sexuality as a threat to society, had personally attacked a
newspaper aimed primarily at gay readers, pitting her religious feelings against the freedom of speech. Outside the Old Bailey, protesters and other observers had gathered. One said, 'We've come

along, basically, because we see this as a political trial.' Another, who was both gay and Christian, said, 'The whole idea of blasphemy belongs to a previous age where there was a sort of conformity of belief through society.' Radical activists handed out copies of the poem. Protesters held signs and shouted: 'Whitehouse—Out! Out! Out!', 'Press freedom—In! In! In!', 'Gay persecution—Out! Out! Out!' A man with a sign reading 'Jesus Christ, Son of God, Saviour of the World' urged another man to read passages from a Bible, while a woman asked if he had heard of God destroying Sodom and Gomorrah. 'Yes, I have heard that, and it's wrong,' he said. 'Oh, it's wrong?', she replied, banishing him with a wave of her hand. 'You made wrong. Get thee behind me, Satan.'[43]

Lemon and Gay News Ltd appealed the decision, first to the Court of Appeals, and then to the Law Lords. These appeals rested, in the end, on a legal question. King-Hamilton had instructed the jury that the intentions of the author and the publisher did not matter. Were his instructions correct? Because blasphemy law had fallen into disuse, answering this question involved extensive rehashing of old precedents. Robertson and Mortimer argued that the publication could be blasphemous only if there was a 'subjective intent to attack Christianity and the foundations of Christian belief'. According to this reasoning, the defendants had not meant to attack Christianity or provoke Christians, so they hadn't blasphemed. The Court of Appeals interpreted the case history differently, and concluded that only the intent to publish was required. The defendants *had* meant to publish the poem and the drawing. These having been deemed blasphemous by a jury, the defendants had blasphemed. The court judged Lemon's suspended prison sentence to be inappropriate and quashed it, but dismissed the appeals.[44]

While a majority of the Law Lords agreed with the Court of Appeals on the element of intent, Leslie George Scarman, known to be liberal in his politics, took the opportunity to comment on blasphemy law in a manner that considerably raised the stakes of the *Gay News* case. One of the problems with the law was that it applied only to the Church of England and other Christian denominations. Could the law give one religion such special treatment? If the law was unfair,

Lord Scarman argued, it needed to be expanded, not abolished. Blasphemy law was 'shackled by the chains of history', he said:

> I think that there is a case for legislation extending it to protect the
> religious beliefs and feelings of non-Christians. The offence belongs to
> a group of criminal offences designed to safeguard the internal tran-
> quillity of the kingdom. In an increasingly plural society such as that
> of modern Britain it is necessary not only to respect the differing reli-
> gious beliefs, feelings and practices of all but also to protect them from
> scurrility, vilification, ridicule and contempt.[45]

He explained that, while Article 10 of the European Convention for the Protection of Human Rights and Fundamental Freedoms protects the freedom of speech, it allows for this freedom to be limited in order to protect the rights of others. Article 9 guarantees the freedom of religion, which, in Lord Scarman's interpretation, 'imposes a duty on all of us to refrain from insulting or outraging the religious feelings of others'.[46] If, as the Lords had decided, a person could be convicted for committing blasphemy accidentally, then this duty would be a perilous imposition.

Having no further legal recourse in the United Kingdom, Lemon and Gay News Ltd applied to the European Commission of Human Rights, requesting that the Court of Human Rights hear their case. The Commission denied the application, corroborating Lord Scarman's understanding of the relevant human rights. The freedom of expression of Lemon and the publishers of *Gay News* had been 'interfered with', but this interference was justified to protect the rights of Whitehouse, the private prosecutor:

> If it is accepted that the religious feelings of the citizen may deserve
> protection against indecent attacks on the matters held sacred by him,
> then it can also be considered as necessary in a democratic society to
> stipulate that such attacks, if they attain a certain level of severity, shall
> constitute a criminal offence triable at the request of the offended
> person.[47]

The Commission also rejected various other complaints, including that Lemon was the victim of prejudice due to his sexual orientation.

As far as the Commission was concerned, the poem and accompanying drawing would have been found blasphemous regardless of who had published them.[48]

The *Gay News* case had revived blasphemy law, which now threatened to become still more powerful. Whitehouse approved of Lord Scarman's opinion, the words of which were 'written on my heart'.[49] In an interview about the trial she said, 'religious feelings are really the most—are of the essence of people. When you offend against their religious feelings, you offend against, you know, the very deepest thing within the heart and being of a man.'[50] Religious feelings were also, however, the basis for the continued persecution of gay people. When Denis Lemon was convicted of blasphemy, sex between men had only been legal for ten years in England and Wales—and even then, special restrictions applied. The participants needed to be twenty-one or over, and the act had to take place 'in private', which meant that no more than two people could be present. In Scotland and Northern Ireland, sex between men was still illegal.[51] In this context, and in the name of her religion, Whitehouse had attempted to stifle a forum of gay expression that was not even aimed at her, and the law had justified her actions.

Protest followed the *Gay News* case, and 'The Love that Dares to Speak its Name' became a tool of that protest. Lemon recalled in 1992:

> We had *lost* the battle at the Old Bailey, but in the opinion of much of the media, in liberal, artistic and religious circles and, more importantly, in the view of a great many of the general public, we had *won* the war.[52]

The *Socialist Challenge*, the *Socialist Worker*, the Young Liberals' *Liberator*, the *Anarchist Worker*, and the anarchist periodical *Freedom* republished the poem, and the Free Speech Movement distributed it by post.[53] (Because the printers of *Socialist Challenge* declined to print the poem, it appeared as an insert. 'We reprint it', the editors explained, 'as part of the fight for freedom of expression and the press, and civil liberties. We hope that other labour movement papers will do the same.'[54]) William McIlroy, who had edited the *Freethinker*, was fined fifty pounds for sending the poem (an indecent item) by post.[55] About five thousand people demonstrated against the *Gay News* conviction in Trafalgar Square on 11 February 1978.[56] In 1983 the *Penguin Book of Homosexual Verse* acknowledged the continuing force of the *Gay News* decision by printing the title of 'The Love that Dares to Speak its Name' along with a short explanation of why the rest of the text was prohibited.[57] The internet, however, soon provided a medium in which the poem would prove difficult to suppress. From 1996 to 1997, following complaints by two vicars, UK police spent eighteen months investigating the Lesbian and Gay Christian Movement, which had posted on its website a link to the Queer Resources Directory, hosted on a US server, where the poem was displayed. The general secretary of the Lesbian and Gay Christian Movement, Richard Kirker, and the website administrator, Mark Vernon, were interrogated, but no charges were laid.[58] Kirkup's papers indicate that, by 1997, the full text of the poem could be found on several websites.[59] In 2002 the human rights activist Peter Tatchell and others distributed copies of the poem and read it out on the steps of St Martins-in-the-Fields Church, Trafalgar Square. They were not arrested.[60] Police considered action against BBC television presenter Joan Bakewell, who recited some of the poem on her programme *Taboo*.[61]

The final opponent to the poem's circulation was its author. Kirkup considered the work an embarrassing relic of his early career, and its continued life became a thorn in his side. When the poem was read publicly in 2002, he told the *Guardian*: 'They are using it for political ends and I disapprove of all politics and all politicians.'[62] He requested that Penguin remove the title from subsequent editions of the *Penguin Book of Homosexual Verse*, denied permission for the text to be reprinted online, and sought advice on how to prevent its unauthorized spread.[63]

Ten years after the *Gay News* case, Salman Rushdie published *The Satanic Verses*. In the ensuing controversy, which saw Rushdie become a marked man, religious feelings and literary expression would once again collide dramatically, and the question of whether blasphemy law is compatible with a pluralist society would become more pressing than ever (see Chapter 21).

Notes

1. Robin Banerji, 'Sir Salman Rushdie: Pakistan on the Road to Tyranny', BBC News, 18 September 2012, http://www.bbc.co.uk/news/world-asia-india-19624100, accessed 26 December 2016.

2. *Gay News Ltd v UK* (1983) 5 EHRR 123, 130 (Commission Decision).

3. *Ban This Filth! Mary Whitehouse and the Battle to Keep Britain Innocent*, ed. Ben Thompson (London: Faber & Faber, 2012), pp. 4, 7–9, 46.

4. Mary Whitehouse, *Quite Contrary: An Autobiography* (London: Pan Books, 1994), pp. 41–46. See also Leonard W. Levy, *Blasphemy: Verbal Offense against the Sacred, from Moses to Salman Rushdie* (New York: Knopf, 1993), p. 536; *Ban This Filth!*, pp. 296–98; Nicholas Walter, *Blasphemy in Britain: The Practice and Punishment of Blasphemy, and the Trial of 'Gay News'* (London: Rationalist Press Association, 1977), p. 9.

5. H. Montgomery Hyde, *The Trials of Oscar Wilde* (New York: Dover, 1962), p. 201.

6. James Kirkup, 'The Love that Dares to Speak its Name', *Gay News*, 3–16 June 1976, p. 26.

7. 'Rational Record', *New Humanist*, July–August 1976, p. 152.

8. Robin Lustig, '"Sunday School Terrified Me", Says *Gay News* Poet', *Observer*, 17 July 1977, p. 3.

9. 'Blasphemy at the Old Bailey', *Everyman*, BBC1, 1977.

10. Denis Lemon, 'The Love that Dared to Speak its Name: Fifteen Years On, Denis Lemon Reflects on his Trial for Blasphemous Libel', *Gay Times*, July 1992, p. 31.

11. 'Blasphemy at the Old Bailey'.

12. Kirkup, p. 26.

13. Alan King-Hamilton, *And Nothing but the Truth* (London: Weidenfeld & Nicolson, 1982), pp. 172–73; 'Probation Officers Campaign for Gays', *Gay News*, 3–16 June 1976, p. 1.

14. Whitehouse, pp. 49, 55. See further p. 47.

15. Whitehouse, p. 47.

16. Levy, pp. 539–40.

17. Levy, pp. 501–2.

18. Levy, p. 231.

19. Geoffrey Robertson, *The Justice Game* (London: Vintage, 1999), p. 139.

20. Levy, pp. 221–22.

21. Russell Sandberg and Norman Doe, 'The Strange Death of Blasphemy', *Modern Law Review*, 71.6 (2008), 971–86 (pp. 972–73).

22. *R v Bradlaugh* (1883) 15 Cox CC 217, 230. See also Levy, pp. 219–22, 457, 486–88.

23. Levy, p. 536. See also David Nash, *Blasphemy in Modern Britain, 1789 to the Present* (Aldershot: Ashgate, 1999), p. 239.

24. King-Hamilton, pp. 173–74.

25. Walter, p. 10.

26. King-Hamilton, pp. 175, 177.

27. Robertson, pp. 137, 139–41. See also King-Hamilton, pp. 175–79; John Mortimer, *Murderers and Other Friends: Another Part of Life* (London: Penguin, 1995), pp. 85–86.

28. King-Hamilton, pp. 175–76.

29. Walter, p. 11.

30. Robertson, p. 140. See further pp. 140–43.

31. Robertson, p. 143.

32. Walter, p. 14.

33. Robertson, p. 144.

34. John Donne, 'Batter my heart, three-person'd God', ll. 12–14, quoted in Robertson, p. 144.

35. Robertson, p. 147.

36. Robertson, p. 148. See also Walter, pp. 15–16.

37. Robertson, p. 149. See further p. 144.

38. Robertson, p. 150.

39. Walter, p. 16.

40. *R v Lemon* [1979] 1 QB 10 (CA) 12.

41. King-Hamilton, p. 180.

42. Lustig, p. 3.

43. 'Blasphemy at the Old Bailey'.

44. *R v Lemon* [1979] 1 QB 10 (CA) 23. See further pp. 27–30.

45. *Whitehouse v Lemon* [1979] AC 617 (HL) 658.

46. *Whitehouse v Lemon* [1979] AC 617 (HL) 665.

47. *Gay News Ltd v UK* (1983) 5 EHRR 123, 130 (Commission Decision).

48. *Gay News Ltd v UK* (1983) 5 EHRR 123, 131 (Commission Decision).

49. Whitehouse, p. 58.

50. 'Blasphemy at the Old Bailey'.

51. Sebastian Buckle, *The Way Out: A History of Homosexuality in Modern Britain* (London: I. B. Tauris, 2015), p. 17.

52. Lemon, p. 32.

53. Levy, p. 549; Walter, p. 16; Michael Tracey and David Morrison, *Whitehouse* (London: Macmillan, 1979), p. 10.

54. *Socialist Challenge*, 14 July 1977, Supplement.

55. '£50 Fine for Censorship Protest', *Guardian*, 20 September 1977, p. 3. See also Walter, p. 16.

56. Tracey and Morrison, p. 17.

57. *The Penguin Book of Homosexual Verse*, ed. Stephen Coote (Harmondsworth: Penguin, 1983), p. 328.

58. Mark Vernon, 'A Clear Case of Poetic Injustice', *Independent*, 21 July 1997, http://www.independent.co.uk/life-style/a-clear-case-of-poetic-injustice-1251894.html, accessed 26 December 2016; Martin Wroe and Duncan Campbell, 'Police Bid to Stop Blasphemy Poem Fails', *Observer*, 20 July 1997, p. 2.

59. New Haven, Beinecke Library, GEN MSS 773 Box 98 fol. 887.

60. Tania Branigan, 'I Am Being Used, Claims Blasphemy Trial Poet', *Guardian*, 11 July 2002, https://www.theguardian.com/uk/2002/jul/11/books.booksnews, accessed 26 December 2016.

61. Ben Summerskill, 'Police May Act over Joan Bakewell "Blasphemy"', *Observer*, 3 March 2002, p. 13.

62. Branigan.

63. New Haven, Beinecke Library, GEN MSS 773 Box 98 fol. 887.

20

Jenny Lives with Eric and Martin

Susanne Bösche

This is the story of a moral panic about a children's book, and a bad law that stifled discussions about sexuality in schools without ever being enforced. Section 28 of the Local Government Act was enacted in England, Wales, and Scotland in 1988, amid a tabloid storm centred on Susanne Bösche's *Jenny Lives with Eric and Martin*, a picture book about two gay men and their daughter.

Under the heading 'Prohibition on promoting homosexuality by teaching or publishing material', Section 28 amended the Local Government Act of 1986. The new wording stated:

(1) A local authority shall not—
    (a) intentionally promote homosexuality or publish material with the intention of promoting homosexuality;
    (b) promote the teaching in any maintained school of the acceptability of homosexuality as a pretended family relationship.[1]

Local authorities sought legal advice to help them understand what the new law prohibited. London and Manchester authorities were told that 'promote homosexuality' meant encouraging people to become homosexual.[2] Civil liberties advocacy organization Liberty noted that the word 'pretended' added little to the sense of the law, 'except to emphasise Parliament's view that a homosexual family relationship is

The cover of *Jenny Lives with Eric and Martin*, published by Gay Men's Press in 1983.

not a real family relationship'.[3] When Parliament debated the law, homophobic rhetoric ran high. David Wilshire MP, who introduced Section 28, Michael Howard MP, and Jill Knight MP referred to 'homosexual propaganda',[4] 'an apparent endeavour to glamorise homosexuality',[5] and 'propaganda against children'.[6] Knight claimed that children were 'frequently being encouraged into homosexuality and lesbianism', and this was 'being paid for out of rates'.[7]

Gay literature had recently been suppressed wholesale through a Customs and Excise regime called 'Operation Tiger' (after a customs officer's cat). Customs seized books by gay authors, books from publishers blacklisted for publishing gay literature, and even books that happened to have the word 'gay' on the cover—in the author's name, for instance. The primary target of this censorship was the bookshop Gay's the Word in London. In 1985 the directors of Gay's the Word were charged with conspiracy to import indecent material, and appeared at a hearing (which occurred during Gay Pride week). The threshold of indecency and obscenity is lower in the customs statute than it is in domestic obscenity statutes, and no public good exception is available. In the end, the prosecution fell through because of European Union intervention in a similar case. Blow-up sex dolls from Germany had been seized and declared indecent, and the European Court of Justice decided that applying different standards of indecency to domestic and imported goods constituted an arbitrary restriction on trade. If sex dolls were not illegal in the United Kingdom, their importation from Germany could not be prohibited. By implication, gay literature could no longer be barred from the country simply because it was gay literature.[8] This result reflected the demands of European trade, however, rather than a change in the social values or the political climate of the Thatcher era. Three years after the attempted prosecution of Gay's the Word, Parliament approved Section 28. It was another sortie in the same repressive campaign.

The campaign for Section 28 exploited a controversy about the presence in schools of books about gay people. Politicians and tabloid journalists condemned the Inner London Education Authority (ILEA) simply for possessing a copy of *Jenny Lives with Eric and Martin*. The book was cited repeatedly in Parliament as evidence of the promotion of homosexuality in schools and as an example of a 'pretended family relationship'.[9] The *Sun's* front page on 6 May 1986 was headed 'VILE BOOK IN SCHOOL. Pupils see pictures of gay lovers'. An image from the book dominated the front page, captioned 'Perverted ... a page from the book showing Jenny in bed with her gay dad and his naked lover'. The article claimed that the 'shocking schoolbook' was 'being made available by EDUCATION OFFICIALS to junior schools'. The paper quoted an outraged head teacher, Simon Marsh ('Children need protection, not perversion'), and the Campaign for the Improvement of Teaching Standards ('Toleration is one thing. Brainwashing children into believing that homosexuality is the norm is quite another').[10] The *Sun's* claim that the book was being issued to schools was not true, and a complaint to the Press Council about the article was upheld. In fact, ILEA held the book only in a resource centre for teachers, and it was not used in schools.[11] Nevertheless, newspapers, government ministers, and members of parliament implied that *Jenny Lives with Eric and Martin* was used in classrooms and stocked in school libraries. 'It is a picture storybook, aimed at six to eight-year-olds, and is made available by education officials in and for junior schools,' Jill Knight told the House of Commons, and 'anyone who would oppose the Bill should read that book.'[12] The Secretary of State for Education, Kenneth Baker, objected to the book's use in schools and called for it to be withdrawn from the ILEA collection.[13] Haringey Parents' Rights Group were reported to have organized a public burning of copies of the book.[14] The following year, as a result of public protests, ILEA removed the book.[15]

First published in 1981 in Denmark as *Mette bor hos Morten og Erik*, the book was translated in an English edition by Gay Men's Press in 1983. In *Jenny Lives with Eric and Martin*, Jenny does indeed live with Eric and Martin, her two fathers. The book tells the story of a typical weekend: Jenny's delight at a surprise party for Eric, which her mother helps to organize, her rage when compelled to leave her toys to do chores, her bewilderment at arguments over cooking duty, and her indifference to Martin's need for sleep. An unpleasant encounter with Mrs Andrews, whose hatred of 'You gays' terrifies Jenny, interrupts the family's round of household chores. Eric draws a cartoon to answer Jenny's questions about Mrs Andrews, a story within a story about 'Bill and Fred' and grumpy 'Mrs Jones', who learns that her husband lived happily with a man before he fell in love with her. 'There are so many things people think are wrong,' says Mr Jones, but 'it can never be wrong to live with someone you are fond of.'[16] The moral Jenny draws from the cartoon is that Mrs Andrews's cruelty comes from her ignorance. Eric leaves Jenny with the hope that Mrs Andrews will stop being so mean when she is better informed. At the end of the book, Jenny and Eric agree that he is lucky to have her in his life.

The English edition retains Andreas Hansen's black-and-white photographs from the original. Bösche's friends portrayed Eric and Martin, and her own daughter played Jenny.[17] Supporters of Section 28 used the illustrations to stoke moral panic. In Parliament and in the press, opponents of the book objected in particular to certain images, which, they claimed, depicted the little girl in bed with two men, sometimes described as 'naked'.[18] Writer Rachel Tingle commented that *Jenny Lives with Eric and Martin* 'is lavishly illustrated with photographs, one of which shows five-year old Jenny in bed with her naked homosexual father and his lover'.[19] The sequence of photographs in question simply shows Eric and Martin attempting to sleep on a Saturday morning while Jenny reads to her doll next to them, then the three having breakfast in bed. (The men's nudity is implied. Bösche told the BBC, 'in Denmark you don't sleep with the pyjama in the summertime, I guess you do in England'.[20])

Eric imagines that it might be possible to change social attitudes by showing other people that it is normal to live with the person you are fond of. The book's detractors perceived it as a threat because it attempts to do exactly this, depicting Jenny, Eric, and Martin as a family spending the weekend together. To the supporters of Section 28, a book like *Jenny Lives with Eric and Martin* was not simply showing, in a sympathetic light, one way that people live. It was teaching the 'acceptability of homosexuality as a pretended family relationship'. Eric tells Jenny that some people think it is strange for two men to live together 'because it isn't very common'.[21] Uncommon, Bösche's story suggests, is not the same as abnormal.

The passing of Section 28 was marked by dramatic civil protests. The House of Lords debate was interrupted when three lesbian activists abseiled from the public gallery down into the debating chamber.[22] They became known as the 'Abseilers against the Clause', and went on to chain themselves to the railings of Buckingham Palace and invade the studios of the BBC during the live evening news broadcast.[23] While a presenter attempted to stifle one protester by sitting on her and putting his hand over her mouth, the women chained themselves to the newsreader's desk and tried to reach the public over the airwaves. 'BEEB MAN SITS ON LESBIAN', read one headline the next day.[24] There were petitions, attempts to lobby council meetings, and anonymous acts of resistance through political graffiti.[25] A demonstration against the law in April 1988 attracted over twenty thousand people, making it the largest gay and lesbian march in Britain up to that time.[26] Section 28 was, for many, a political awakening, but there seemed no way to move the Conservative government. Frustrated by political inaction, gay and lesbian activists formed Stonewall, a lobby group dedicated to achieving legal equality. Stonewall lobbied effectively to equalize the age of consent for gay and straight sex, to decriminalize sex between men in Jersey and the Isle of Man, and to enable gay men and lesbians to foster and adopt children.[27]

Technically, Section 28 applied only to local authorities, such as city councils—not to teachers, voluntary organizations, artists, or librarians. It was not actually enforced, though in 2000 a nurse initiated legal proceedings against Glasgow City Council, claiming it had violated the prohibition by supporting organizations such as Phace West, the Glasgow Gay and Lesbian Centre, and Bi-G-Les. (The complaint was withdrawn when the council agreed to send a letter to grant recipients stating that the money they received could not be used to promote homosexuality.)[28] The law's indirect effects, however, were much more extensive, as Liberty had predicted.[29] Educators who thought the law applied to them obeyed it, and councils' fears that various forms of expression or education might count as 'promotion' of homosexuality generated a chilling effect. In a survey of 307 schools in 1997, 44 per cent of respondents reported that Section 28 had made it difficult to meet the needs of lesbian and gay pupils.[30] Liberty reported the banning of a directory of voluntary work opportunities by East Sussex County Council, the cancellation by a secondary school head teacher of the Avon Touring Theatre Company's production of *Trapped in Time*, and the banning of lesbian and gay student meetings and activities in college premises in Leeds, Strathclyde, and Essex.[31] 'Lark in the Park', a 'lesbian and gay festival of music, poetry, and drama', was refused financial assistance by the City of Edinburgh District Council because the city received legal advice that funding the festival would contravene Section 28, even though the organizers had specified that their intention was not to 'seek to encourage people who are not lesbian or gay to become lesbian or gay'. The council wanted to support the application, but declined because of its lawyer's opinion that it was possible to promote homosexuality without 'converting' people to homosexuality. The lawyer warned that, because the festival would attract 'large numbers of members of the general public, many of whom are not homosexual, the probability of encouraging homosexuality is increased'. In the lawyer's opinion, it would have been illegal for the council to support the application.[32] Similar incidents were recorded elsewhere. Calderdale Library Services chose not to stock the *Pink Paper*, a gay newspaper, for fear of breaching the law.[33] The Deck Chair Collective's requests for financial support for lesbian events in Edinburgh were refused by three separate Scottish district and city councils. A number of London councils were threatened with legal action for funding gay pride festivals, and Chingford Young Conservatives threatened Waltham Forest London Borough Council with criminal prosecution for encouraging gay people to apply to become foster parents.[34] (Section 28 did not create a criminal offence, so the threat was an idle one.) In every one of these cases, Section 28 was the stated reason for action or inaction. Other acts motivated by the law will have gone unrecorded. For instance, an English district council, which insisted on remaining anonymous, said it had 'dropped or revised' some productions from its annual drama festival after being asked to consider Section 28.[35]

The chilling effect on libraries and arts festivals was not, according to those responsible for promoting Section 28, the aim of the bill. The Earl of Caithness claimed, 'Local authorities have power to provide entertainments. Provided that this, and this only, is what they are intending to do, there is no reason why the clause should inhibit them from staging plays by Joe Orton or Oscar Wilde.'[36] This narrow endorsement of art for art's sake, but *only* for art's sake, did not offer much reassurance, and failed to avert the law's chilling effect.

In late 1988 both the Labour and Liberal Democrat parties committed to repealing Section 28.[37] In 1997 Tony Blair's Labour government came to power and promised to strike the section from the law. But reform came slowly, obstructed by a hostile press, some religious leaders, the House of Lords, and Labour's fear of electoral consequences. During the repeal debates, the rhetoric, misrepresentations, and arguments of the 1980s were dusted off and reused. Dire warnings were made in the press about gay propaganda in schools, and *Jenny Lives with Eric and Martin* was weaponized once again, along with the image of Jenny having breakfast in bed with her parents. The book would be 're-released into school libraries' when Section 28 was repealed, reported *The Times*.[38] Repeating the old claim that local authorities had forced schools to promote homosexuality, the *Daily Mail* reported that repealing Section 28 would allow schools to perform 'banned' plays 'with a homosexual theme' and to use books like *Jenny Lives with Eric and Martin*. The paper described Jenny as 'a little girl with two homosexual male "parents"', the scare quotes signalling that the newspaper did not view Eric and Martin as parents. Section 28 did not, in fact, ban plays with gay themes or books like Bösche's in schools, but the *Daily Mail*'s article expressed the common misconception about the law's scope and effect.[39] When the publisher Neal Cavalier-Smith said that, if Section 28 were to be repealed in Scotland, he would make the book available to any school that wanted it, it was reported that he planned to 'rush the book into Scottish schools', as if he had the power to make library acquisition decisions. Campaigners for Section 28 told newspapers that the publisher's offer 'is exactly what we have been warning of. It underlines the dangers to Scottish schoolchildren and this is why the campaign to keep Clause 28 is so vital to protect our children.'[40] Susanne Bösche expressed her dismay:

> It was absolutely shocking to see the book vilified as homosexual propaganda in the British press back in 1983 [*sic*], and (to a lesser degree) again now. I feel angry that my intentions in writing this book—namely to give children a little more knowledge about the world—have been twisted by grown-up people who choose to use it as a weapon in a political battle.[41]

Speaking to the House of Lords in 2000 in favour of Section 28's repeal, Lord Whitty described the legislation as 'probably one of the worst drafted clauses' on the statute book. He observed that the verb 'promote' is ambiguous and the phrase 'pretended family relation-ship' is 'the kind of terminology used by two middle-aged gentle-men in florid ties who with one breath claim that they have never met a homosexual since they left boarding school and in the other claim that the BBC is absolutely crawling with them'.[42] Section 28 was repealed in Scotland three years before it was repealed in England and Wales. Members of the Scottish Parliament voted to abolish the law in 2000,[43] despite opposition from the Scottish Conservatives and the activity of the public campaign 'Keep the Clause', supported by Cardinal Thomas Winning, businessman Brian Souter, and the editor of the *Daily Record*.[44] In 2001 Blair's Labour Party won a second gen-eral election, with a commitment to repeal Section 28 in its manifesto. With a Labour majority in the Commons, the bill to repeal Section 28 passed easily, and there was no longer significant opposition to it in the Lords. The clause was repealed in England and Wales in 2003.[45] In 2009 Prime Minister David Cameron of the Conservative Party apologized for the legislation. 'We got it wrong,' he said.[46]

Notes

1. Local Government Act 1988, s 28.
2. Richard Gutch and others, *Publish and Still Not Be Damned: A Guide for Voluntary Groups on the Provisions of the 1986 and 1988 Local Government Acts Regarding Political Publicity and the Promotion of Homosexuality* (London: National Council for Voluntary Organisations, 1989), p. 43.
3. Madeleine Colvin, *Section 28: A Practical Guide to the Law and its Implications* (London: National Council for Civil Liberties, 1989), p. 13.
4. HC Deb 15 December 1987, vol 124, col 1006.
5. HC Deb 9 March 1988, vol 129, col 421.
6. HC Deb 8 May 1987, vol 115, col 997.
7. HC Deb 8 May 1987, vol 115, col 997.
8. Geoffrey Robertson, *The Justice Game* (London: Vintage, 1999), pp. 154–56.
9. HL Deb 1 February 1988, vol 492, col 878.
10. Shan Lancaster, 'Vile Book in School', *Sun*, 6 May 1986, pp. 1–2 (ellipsis original).
11. 'Report on Gays [*sic*] Books Criticized', *The Times*, 3 February 1987, p. 7. See also Sebastian Buckle, *The Way Out: A History of Homosexuality in Modern Britain* (London: I. B. Tauris, 2015), pp. 104, 135–36.

12. HC Deb 8 May 1987, vol 115, col 997.

13. 'Sex Clause Wrangle Hits Tories', *The Times*, 16 September 1986, p. 2.

14. Edward Vulliamy, 'Parents Protest over "Gay Lessons"', *Guardian*, 14 October 1986, p. 3.

15. 'Gay Book Is Recalled', *The Times*, 12 August 1987, p. 2.

16. Susanne Bösche, *Jenny Lives with Eric and Martin*, trans. Louis Mackay (London: Gay Men's Press, 1983), pp. 38, 44.

17. James Meek, 'Happy Ever After for "Gay Breakfast" Child', *Guardian*, 29 January 2000, p. 29.

18. HC Deb 8 May 1987, vol 115, col 997; Lancaster, p. 1. See also HL Deb 7 May 1986, vol 474, col 726; HL Deb 1 February 1988, vol 492, col 878.

19. Rachel Tingle, *Gay Lessons: How Public Funds Are Used to Promote Homosexuality among Children and Young People* (London: Pickwick, 1986), p. 22.

20. 'Jenny Lives with Eric and Martin', *In Living Memory*, BBC Radio 4, 5 August 2009, www.bbc.co.uk/archive/gay_rights/12030.shtml, accessed 12 March 2017.

21. Bösche, p. 40.

22. Alan Travis, 'Abseil Demo by Women as Lords Confirm Gay Ban', *Guardian*, 3 February 1988, p. 3.

23. Vicki Carter, 'Abseil Makes the Heart Grow Fonder: Lesbian and Gay Campaigning Tactics and Section 28', in *Modern Homosexualities: Fragments of Lesbian and Gay Experiences*, ed. Ken Plummer (London: Routledge, 2002), pp. 217–26 (p. 221).

24. John Peacock and Graham Barnes, 'Here Is the Six O'Clock News.. BEEB MAN SITS ON LESBIAN.. While Sue Reads On with Woman Chained to her Desk', *Daily Mirror*, 24 May 1988, p. 1.

25. Carter, pp. 220–21.

26. Nicholas de Jongh, 'Thousands Join Protest against Section 28 Curb on Gay Rights', *Guardian*, 2 May 1988, p. 4.

27. Buckle, pp. 111–15, 165–79.

28. 'Gay Groups Claim Court Victory', BBC News, 6 July 2000, http://news.bbc.co.uk/1/hi/scotland/821896.stm, accessed 26 December 2016.

29. Colvin, p. 5.

30. Ian Warwick and others, 'Playing It Safe: Addressing the Emotional and Physical Health of Lesbian and Gay Pupils in the UK', *Journal of Adolescence*, 24.1 (2001), 129–40 (p. 136).

31. Colvin, pp. 5–6.

32. Philip Thomas and Ruth Costigan, *Promoting Homosexuality: Section 28 of the Local Government Act 1988* (Cardiff: Cardiff Law School, 1990), p. 29.

33. Arabella Thorp and Gillian Allen, 'The *Local Government Bill* [HL]:
     The "Section 28" Debate', Bill 87 of 1999–2000, House of Com-
     mons Library Research Paper 00/47, p. 19, http://researchbriefings.
     parliament.uk/ResearchBriefing/Summary/RP00-47, accessed 26
     December 2016.

34. Thomas and Costigan, pp. 28–31.

35. Thomas and Costigan, p. 30.

36. HL Deb 1 February 1988, vol 492, col 891.

37. Adam Lent, 'Chronology', in *Section 28 and the Revival of Gay, Lesbian
     and Queer Politics in Britain*, ed. Virginia Preston (London: Institute of
     Contemporary British History, 2001), pp. 13–16.

38. Valerie Grove, 'If I Had a Homosexual Son, I'd Love Him, but . . .', *The
     Times*, 29 January 2000, p. 21.

39. James Clark, 'Labour May Open School Gates to Gay Propaganda:
     Family Campaigners' Fury over Plans to Repeal Section 28', *Daily Mail*,
     30 May 1998, p. 11.

40. Steve Smith, 'I'll Make Sure Every School in Scotland Has a Copy of
     Jenny Lives with Eric and Martin: Pledge by Gay Activist', *Daily Record*, 25
     January 2000, p. 8.

41. Susanne Bosche [*sic*], 'Jenny, Eric, Martin . . . and Me', *Guardian*, 31
     January 2000, p. B5.

42. HL Deb 7 February 2000, vol 609, col 477.

43. Buckle, p. 180.

44. Arnold Kemp and Alex Bell, 'Gay Battle Splits Scotland', *Observer*, 23
     January 2000, p. 19; Kirsty Scott, 'Edinburgh Rejects Private Section
     28 Poll', *Guardian*, 31 May 2000, p. 6; 'MSPs Abolish Section 28', BBC
     News, 21 June 2000, http://news.bbc.co.uk/1/hi/scotland/800673.stm,
     accessed 12 March 2017.

45. Buckle, pp. 180–83.

46. Brian Wheeler, 'Tory Anger over Homophobia Claim', BBC News,
     3 July 2009, http://news.bbc.co.uk/1/hi/uk_politics/8132582.stm,
     accessed 31 December 2016.

21

The Satanic Verses
Salman Rushdie

Mary Whitehouse's prosecution of Denis Lemon and Gay News
Ltd for blasphemy in 1977 left the law in an untenable state
(see Chapter 19). Offending the religious feelings of Christians, even
unintentionally, was a crime, but it was not a crime to offend anybody
else. Parliament had two clear choices. It could endorse blasphemy
law, and, as Lord Scarman advised in the *Gay News* case, extend its
protection to all religions. Or, as the Law Commission recommended
in 1985, Parliament could prioritize the freedom of speech, and abolish the blasphemy offence altogether. Instead, legislators did nothing.[1] This inaction left the United Kingdom in an awkward position
in 1988 when Salman Rushdie published *The Satanic Verses*, which
became the focus of controversy, first in India and then around the
world. The novel's opponents accused Rushdie of insulting religious
figures and injuring the feelings of believers. In the United Kingdom,
these arguments had been effective against *Gay News*, but the law
that still defended the religious feelings of Christians did not defend
Muslims. While at home the escalating conflict included attacks on
bookshops and violence against Muslims, and abroad the Ayatollah
Khomeini of Iran called for Rushdie's death, British officials continued to hedge their bets, mouthing defences of the freedom of speech

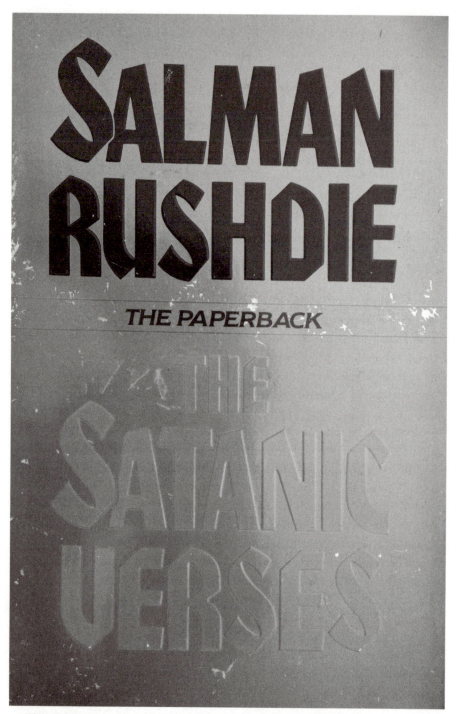

The Consortium edition of *The Satanic Verses*, which Salman Rushdie arranged when Penguin declined to publish a paperback.

while implying that Rushdie should not have written the novel in the first place.

Rushdie, winner of the Booker Prize for *Midnight's Children*, had taken five years to write *The Satanic Verses*, and the novel was eagerly anticipated. It was published in Britain on 26 September 1988 by Viking, an imprint of Penguin, and initially received good reviews praising its style, humour, and depiction of London and Bombay.[2] The novel was due to be released in India shortly after its British publication, but the Indian Ministry of Finance abruptly banned its import on the grounds that it would 'offend the religious sentiments of some sections of the people'. According to the Indian press, the ban was prompted by complaints from 'prominent persons', including three Muslim politicians.[3] In an open letter to the Prime Minister of India, Rajiv Gandhi, Rushdie accused the Indian government of placating people whom he called 'extremists, even fundamentalists'. The politicians had not read the book, he pointed out, and he didn't believe that they cared about his novel one way or another. His book had become 'a political football', and he claimed that it was being used to try to win Muslim votes. He also objected strongly to the accusation that his book attacked Islam. *The Satanic Verses* was a novel, he explained, not a work of history:

> The section of the book in question (and let's remember that the book isn't actually about Islam, but about migration, metamorphosis, divided selves, love, death, London and Bombay) deals with a prophet who is not called Muhammad living in a highly fantasticated city— made of sand, it dissolves when water falls upon it—in which he is surrounded by fictional followers, one of whom happens to bear my own first name. Moreover, this entire sequence happens in a dream, the fictional dream of a fictional character, an Indian movie star, and one who is losing his mind, at that. How much further from history could one get?[4]

The allegations that *The Satanic Verses* is blasphemous focus on one section of the novel, a dream sequence that expresses the religious doubt of a Bollywood star who calls himself 'Gibreel Farishta' and is starting to believe that he really is the Archangel Jibreel or Gabriel, who delivered the text of the Quran to the Prophet Muhammad. As

Farishta descends into psychosis, he experiences increasingly vivid hallucinations, based on the early history of Islam but distorted by his doubt and personality. The prophet he thinks he is talking to is a fallible figure who bears the name 'Mahound', an insulting name for Muhammad used by Christians in the Middle Ages. This imaginary Mahound, who is not Muhammad, is a visionary, but also a politician and a businessman whose visions tend to serve his worldly interests. When it is convenient to do so, he declares that certain verses in his scripture that exalt pagan goddesses are inventions of the devil.[5] Some historians have claimed that such 'Satanic verses' were introduced to and then withdrawn from the fifty-third *sura* (chapter) of the Quran.[6] Farishta also dreams that a scribe (named Salman) mischievously alters the text.[7] To the novel's opponents, Rushdie's depiction of Mahound and his flawed scripture appeared to be a deliberate slur on Muhammad and the Quran.

One of the politicians who had called for the ban, Syed Shahabuddin, responded with his own open letter to Rushdie. He saw the book as an insult to his faith, its founders, and its followers, poorly disguised as a novel. The 'very title' of the novel was 'suggestively derogatory' to those who believe the Quran is the 'Word of God', he said, and he took Mahound to be a depiction of the Prophet as 'an imposter'. And Rushdie 'had the nerve to situate the wives of the Prophet, whom we Muslims regard as the mothers of the community, in a brothel'. Rushdie had not in fact placed the Prophet's wives in a brothel, but only their names. Farishta dreams of an enterprising madam who calls her brothel the *Hijab* and gives the women who work there the names of the Prophet's wives, predicting that the thrill of religious transgression will be good for business. But Shahabuddin had not read the book, nor did he intend to. 'I do not have to wade through a filthy drain to know what filth is,' he wrote. He accused Rushdie of having committed a criminal offence under Article 295A of India's Penal Code, which punishes those who outrage the religious feelings of Indian citizens or insult their religion, and wished that Rushdie were in India 'to face the music'.[8]

News of the Indian controversy reached Faiyazuddin Ahmad, the public relations director of the Islamic Foundation in Leicester. He photocopied passages from the novel and sent them to Muslim

organizations in Britain. In London, the Union of Muslim Organisations were alarmed by the package they received. They called a crisis
meeting and formed the United Kingdom Action Committee on
Islamic Affairs (UKACIA) to co-ordinate a British campaign against
the book.[9] On 28 October 1988, UKACIA wrote to affiliated groups
to alert them to what they called 'the most offensive, filthy and abusive book ever written by any hostile enemy of Islam'. Like Shahabuddin, UKACIA depicted the novel as an insult 'thinly disguised
as a piece of literature'. *The Satanic Verses* distorted Islamic history,
UKACIA wrote, portrayed the Prophet Ibrahim and the Prophet
Muhammad in 'the worst possible colours', disfigured the characters
of the Prophet's companions and wives, and described 'the Islamic
creed and rituals in the most foul language'. UKACIA asked affiliated
organizations to demand that Penguin withdraw, pulp, and undertake not to republish the book, apologize to Muslims for the injury
to their feelings, and pay damages to a British Islamic charity. They
asked Prime Minister Margaret Thatcher to prosecute Rushdie and
Penguin under the Public Order Act 1986 and the Race Relations
Act 1976.[10] Throughout December 1988, UKACIA and their affili-
ates delivered petitions, lobbied politicians, and organized marches
calling for the book to be banned. There was little media interest. Ken
Hargreaves, Conservative MP, expressed regret for the distress caused
by the book in an early-day motion in the House of Commons, but
Margaret Thatcher told UKACIA that there were 'no grounds' for
the government to ban it, and on 23 December the Attorney General
confirmed that no action could be taken against the publisher.[11]

Frustrated by the legal impasse and the national press's lack of interest in UKACIA's campaign, Muslim organizations in Bradford tried a
new tactic. According to the *Observer*, a solicitor suggested that, 'if what
they wanted was publicity, they could always try burning the book in
public'.[12] On 14 January 1989 protesters bearing anti-Rushdie signs
gathered outside police headquarters in the centre of Bradford. As
police watched, a local councillor, Mohammad Ajeeb, commended the
crowd for their peaceful protest and promised to persuade the council
to ban the book in Bradford libraries. Then the protesters burned a
copy of the book.[13]

Now the protesters had the media's attention. The demonstration may have been legal and peaceful, but the provocative act of
book burning met with alarm and anger, and the protesters were
derided as fanatics and fascists. Rushdie condemned what he called
'zealot protests', both for the threat they posed to secular values and
for confirming 'in the Western mind, all the worst stereotypes of the
Muslim world'.[14] Photographs of the protesters burning a book in a
British town square circulated widely, accompanied by critical editorials comparing them to the Nazi sympathizers who held ceremo-
nial book burnings in the Bebelplatz in Berlin in 1933. Deploring
'Bradfordian bibliocide', the poet Tony Harrison reminded the pro-
testers that 'The works of Kafka, Brecht and Mann | were burned
by zealots like yourselves'.[15] In the *Daily Mail*, the author Anthony
Burgess quoted Heinrich Heine, the German author whose words
appear on the Berlin memorial to the Nazi book burnings: 'That was
a prelude only; where they burn books, they will in the end also burn
people.' There is a hidden irony here: in Heine's 1821 play *Alman-
sor*, from which these lines are taken, the burned book is the Quran
and the book burners are the Catholic Inquisition. Glossing over this
context, Burgess made it seem as if Heine had been addressing the
Nazis in 1933, and claimed that such 'barbarous rituals' were foreign
to Western traditions of intellectual freedom.[16] Heine's words were
also deployed by Education Secretary Kenneth Baker, even though
three years earlier he had joined the campaign against *Jenny Lives with
Eric and Martin*, during which the *Guardian* reported that a group
of parents had burned the book (see Chapter 20).[17] Unlike the parents, the Bradford book burners were portrayed as un-British. Islamic
organizations pointed out that their demonstration had been legal
and that they were exercising their right to free speech.[18] Bhikhu
Parekh, deputy chairman of Britain's Commission for Racial Equality,
warned that dismissing the Bradford protesters as 'barbarians, illiter-
ates, enemies of free speech' was socially divisive, creating a 'chasm'
between protesters and their critics.[19] This chasm would grow wider
as British protests became entangled with international events.

When Faiyazuddin Ahmad wrote to British Muslim groups about
The Satanic Verses, he also contacted the Organisation of the Islamic
Conference,[20] which asked member states to ensure that the book was

withdrawn and the book and its author banned from entering Islamic countries.[21] Some member states ignored the conference's call, but many, including Pakistan, banned the book.[22] On 12 February 1989 demonstrators in Islamabad marched to the American Cultural Centre to protest against the publication of the novel in the United States. Some protesters wanted to deliver a petition, others were throwing stones, and some police officers threw stones back at the protesters. When the protesters began to move forward, the police caught themselves in the tear gas they used against protesters, and fired guns into the crowd. More than eighty people were injured, and five died.[23] Benazir Bhutto, whose Pakistan People's Party had recently won a general election, claimed that the protest's organizers were attempting more to 'destabilize the process of democracy' than to suppress the book.[24] The next day, in Srinagar, demonstrators and police clashed again. At least three people died, and sixty were injured. Again, the protest was depicted as an anti-*Satanic Verses* protest, but it was also influenced by regional politics, this time the dispute between India and Pakistan over control of Kashmir.[25] In the early days of the controversy, Rushdie had complained that his novel was being used as a political football. Now it had become a geopolitical football.

On 14 February 1989, the Ayatollah Khomeini, the religious leader of Iran's Islamic Revolution, entered the fray, issuing a *fatwa* calling for Muslims to execute Rushdie and 'those publishers who were aware of' the contents of *The Satanic Verses*.[26] The conventional meaning of '*fatwa*' is a non-binding legal opinion given by a scholar of Islamic law.[27] Khomeini had the authority only to give an opinion, not a command, and those he condemned lived outside the lands where Islamic law applied.[28] But the next day Hassan Sanei of the Fifth of Khordad Foundation, an Iranian charity, offered one million dollars to any non-Iranian who would kill Rushdie. (Iranian assassins were promised a larger reward.)[29] In the coming weeks, groups in Lebanon and Syria would claim that they were ready to kill him.[30]

Rushdie left his home on 14 February to attend the funeral of his close friend and fellow author Bruce Chatwin. He did not return home. He took the name 'Joseph Anton', and went into hiding, making only occasional public appearances. He was given (but often had to fight to retain) police protection by the British government, and

was obliged to move regularly, living in hotels and rented accommo-
dation, which he paid for. The popular misconception that he lived at
taxpayers' expense in lavish safe houses was a myth fostered by hostile
British newspapers. Rushdie lost the right to vote because he could
not reveal his home address.[31] The *fatwa* also affected Penguin. Police
were posted outside Penguin's offices, and its mail was scanned for
explosives. The publisher's chief executive, Peter Mayer, and his family
endured an intimidation campaign.[32] The company committed itself
to support the book nonetheless, Mayer recalled, because it believed
that more was at stake than the fate of one book:

> How we responded to the controversy over *The Satanic Verses* would
> affect the future of free inquiry, without which there would be no
> publishing as we knew it, but also, by extension, no civil society as we
> knew it. We all came to agree that all we could do, as individuals or as a
> company, was to uphold the principles that underlay our profession and
> which, since the invention of movable type, have brought it respect. We
> were publishers. I thought that meant something. We all did.[33]

Everyone at Penguin understood the issues at stake, Mayer added—'not
just the editors or the executives, but the secretaries and the people
moving boxes, too.'[34]

Writing in March 1989, shortly after the *fatwa* was issued, the
critic and intellectual Homi Bhabha warned that 'the tragic events'
surrounding *The Satanic Verses* were polarizing public opinion and
generating 'implacable antagonism' between groups. He deplored
both 'demands for censorship' and 'anti-Muslim statements', criticizing the media's depiction of the controversy as a war between
'Western liberalism' and 'what has been identified as a Muslim fundamentalist position'. 'Neither of these perspectives is adequate,' he
warned.[35] In fact, the 'Western liberal' position was often reluctant
to support Rushdie. British freedom of speech was asserted, but with
the implication that Rushdie had abused it. Roald Dahl wrote that
Rushdie 'knew exactly what he was doing'. A writer 'has an absolute right to say what he likes,' he said, but to protect that right
'we all have a moral obligation to apply a modicum of censorship
to our own work'.[36] The historian Hugh Trevor-Roper agreed that

Rushdie 'knew what he was doing', and, though he defended the author's freedom of expression in theory, 'would not shed a tear if some British Muslims, deploring his manners, should waylay him in a dark street and seek to improve them'.[37] Hidden from the violence that Khomeini was calling for and that Trevor-Roper was fantasizing about, Rushdie was coerced into making an apology. His protection officers told him that unnamed people 'upstairs' (the government or the police) were concerned for British and Irish hostages in Iran and Lebanon.[38] The hostages' imprisonment was unconnected to *The Satanic Verses*, but the *fatwa* was making it more difficult to communicate with Iran.[39] The officers suggested that, if Rushdie published an apology (which those 'upstairs' had already prepared for him), it might help the hostages as well as him. Reluctantly, he issued a statement of regret for the distress felt by sincere followers of Islam. As he expected, the statement helped no one.[40] Khomeini and his supporters had been strengthened by the *fatwa*, and were not about to back down.[41] As Iran began to move towards breaking diplomatic relations with Britain, the British government began to criticize Rushdie.[42] Arguing that 'great religions' could 'withstand these kinds of events', Margaret Thatcher invoked the hurt feelings of Christians: 'We have known in our own religion people doing things which are deeply offensive to some of us, deeply offensive, and we felt it very much. And that is what has happened in Islam.' Foreign Secretary Geoffrey Howe defended the freedom of expression, but added that you didn't have to be Muslim to find the book 'distressing and anger-making'.[43] British people did not like *The Satanic Verses*, he said, because it was 'extremely rude' about Britain and 'compares Britain with Hitler's Germany'.[44] In hiding, unable to respond, Rushdie raged: 'Where? On what page?'[45] He feared that the government's support for him was weakening, and called the leader of the Liberal Democrat party, Paddy Ashdown, who made a public statement of concern that the government was not prepared to stand up for Rushdie.[46] The government's language did not ease international tensions. On 7 March 1989, four days after Thatcher's statement, Iran ended diplomatic relations with Britain. Bilateral relations would not be fully restored until 1998.[47]

The *fatwa* amplified extreme voices, giving them a platform they had not had before. A previously low-profile figure, Kalim Siddiqui, became the media's reliable source of inflammatory statements and startling images for the evening news.[48] He acknowledged British law, stating that 'it is not for Muslims in Britain to execute Rushdie',[49] but he also absurdly claimed that Khomeini had spoken for global Islam: 'Virtually every Muslim man, woman and child agreed Rushdie should die.'[50] On 21 October 1989, at a meeting of 300 Muslim activists at Manchester Town Hall, Siddiqui asked the audience if they thought Rushdie should die. Footage of the majority raising their hands in agreement was broadcast on the BBC national news that evening.[51] Muslim views on the *fatwa* and *The Satanic Verses* were more diverse than this image suggested. Many British Muslims, including those who were calling for Penguin to withdraw the book, deeply disapproved of the *fatwa*, criticized it as contrary to Islamic law, and spoke out against violence.[52] A 'World Writers' Statement', signed by thousands, including Muslim writers, declared the signatories to be 'involved in the publication' of *The Satanic Verses*, 'whether we approve the contents of the book or not'.[53] Essays by Muslim and Arab writers from the Middle East and North Africa, gathered together and translated in 1994 under the title *For Rushdie*, expressed solidarity with the author and other dissenting and progressive writers whose voices had been suppressed.[54] But, as Homi Bhabha had pointed out, Muslim expressions of solidarity with Rushdie received relatively little attention in the press. They were overshadowed by acts of violence carried out by those who heeded Khomeini's command.[55]

Throughout 1989, booksellers and the press were targeted. Two bookshops in Berkeley, California, and three bookshops in London were bombed, as was Riverdale Press in New York, the headquarters of a paper that had printed a condemnation of the *fatwa*. An arsonist attacked a Penguin bookshop in London, there was an explosion at a Penguin bookshop in York, and bombs were defused in Guildford, Peterborough, and Nottingham.[56] In response, some bookshops stopped selling the novel, while others sold it under the counter.[57] Libraries took special precautions. The British Library, the Bodleian Library in Oxford, and the National Library of Scotland permitted visitors to read the novel only under secure conditions. In Bradford libraries, it was taken off the shelves and available only upon request.[58] Bradford, Sheffield, and Halifax libraries placed 'warning' stickers on it, Bradford's sticker stating that the novel was a work of imagination and that, although the library regretted the offence it had caused, the public library had a duty to provide the public with books, subject to the law of the land.[59]

Despite threats and violence, Penguin continued to support *The Satanic Verses*. But the paperback proved contentious. Liaqat Hussain, general secretary of the Bradford Council of Mosques, said a paperback would be 'incitement'. Max Madden, Labour MP, agreed it would be a 'contemptuous provocation'.[60] Alistair Darling, future Labour Chancellor, asked Penguin not to publish it.[61] Michael Meacher, Labour MP, said it would be 'helpful' if Rushdie 'voluntarily' prevented further publication.[62] A survey of booksellers revealed that 40 per cent would not sell the paperback edition, and *Publishers Weekly* advised Penguin to 'consider honour satisfied' and 'resume a normal life: without a paperback'.[63] Penguin wanted to wait for the media frenzy to calm down, but Rushdie thought it would be safer, and more consistent with Penguin's commitment to free inquiry, to publish the paperback and remove the incentive to protest. He fell out with the publisher and formed a consortium to publish an English paperback edition, which eventually appeared in 1992.[64]

The *fatwa* threatened anyone involved in the publication of the book, not just the author or its distributors. The first murders took place just weeks after the *fatwa*. Abdullah Al Ahdal, a Belgian Islamic leader who had resisted calls to ban the book, and his aide, Salem el-Behir, were murdered in March 1989.[65] In the years that followed, those involved with publication of translations were targeted. In 1991 the novel's Italian translator, Ettore Capriolo, was attacked, and the Japanese translator, Hitoshi Igarashi, was murdered. The novel's Norwegian publisher, William Nygaard, was shot and seriously injured in 1993. In July of that year, in Sivas, Turkey, a mob attacked a hotel where a gathering of secularists and Alevis, a minority religious group in Turkey, were celebrating the life of a sixteenth-century Alevi poet.[66] In Turkey, this attack is known as the 'Sivas massacre'. But the world's press, Rushdie wrote, called it a 'Rushdie riot'. Aziz Nesin, the editor of a newspaper that had recently published extracts from *The Satanic*

Verses (without Rushdie's permission) was at the gathering. Nesin may well not have been the mob's target, and he escaped when they set fire to the hotel. Thirty-seven people, two of them members of the mob, died.[67]

British Muslims were also facing intolerance, intimidation, and violence. White racists assaulted Muslims and British Asians and hurled Rushdie's name at them as a term of abuse.[68] There were death threats against Muslims who had opposed the book, the London Central Mosque and Islamic Cultural Centre in Regent's Park was fire-bombed, and the Bradford Council of Mosques office was attacked four times in one year. A painted message read 'Leave Salman Rushdie alone—or else'.[69] John Townend, Conservative MP, said it was time to 'start to fight back' and tell Muslims who 'say they cannot live in a country when Salman Rushdie is free to express his views' to 'go back from whence you came'.[70] Rushdie was disgusted. 'There has been too much name-calling,' he wrote. 'Muslims have been called savages and barbarians and worse.' Rushdie rejected the view that *The Satanic Verses* controversy was 'a struggle between Western freedoms and Eastern unfreedom'. The people of the 'East' were no less passionate about freedom than the people of the 'West', he pointed out, and many in the 'West' were 'excluded from full possession' of Western liberties.[71]

Rushdie's statement acknowledged inequality in Britain. The ongoing inequality in blasphemy law, which protected only Christians, was a case in point. Since the *Gay News* decision, there had been calls to remedy the inequality by abolishing blasphemy law, but *The Satanic Verses* controversy prompted some politicians and religious groups to argue that the law should be expanded. In a letter to the *Independent* signed by representatives of the Christian, Jewish, Muslim, Hindu, Sikh, and Jain faiths, the 'World Conference on Religion and Peace' proposed that 'inequalities' in blasphemy law be addressed so that 'all minority religions will be fully protected'.[72] Jack Straw, future Labour Home Secretary, and Teddy Taylor, Conservative MP, both called for the expansion of blasphemy law.[73] The British Muslim Action Front, a campaigning group convened by Abdal Hussain Choudhury of the East London Mosque, organized a march for blasphemy law reform from Hyde Park to Downing Street on 27 May 1989.[74] Choudhury also attempted to test whether he could persuade a court that English blasphemy law could protect Islam, by prosecuting Rushdie and Penguin for blasphemous and seditious libel. At the magistrate's court, and then at judicial review, his case was rejected,[75] and when he appealed to the European Commission of Human Rights the Commission ruled that freedom of religion did not guarantee the right to bring blasphemy prosecutions, even if members of another religion had that right.[76] The only way that the law could protect Islam was if Parliament voted to expand it, which the government did not intend to do. John Patten, Minister of State at the Home Office, stated the government's position in a strikingly condescending letter to 'influential British Muslims'. After a lecture on the importance of learning English, understanding British rights and responsibilities, and condemning violence (which, he acknowledged, they had done), he told them that the law was 'inappropriate [...] for dealing with matters of faith and individual belief', concluding that Christians did not rely on the law, 'preferring to recognise that the strength of their own belief is the best armour against mockers and blasphemers'.[77] The government was admonishing Muslims as if blasphemy law had not been used to protect Mary Whitehouse's religious feelings in 1977. UKACIA was quick to remind Patten that it was only asking for the same protection afforded to the Church of England.[78] But Thatcher's government opted to leave English blasphemy law unreformed. Seventeen years later, Tony Blair's Labour government attempted to pass religious hatred legislation that would have criminalized 'threatening', 'abusive or insulting' language 'likely' to stir up religious hatred, which could have applied to language that insulted any religion.[79] Rushdie described it as an 'appalling bill', with dangerous implications for books like *The Satanic Verses*, and went to the Home Office to protest.[80] He was relieved when the House of Lords inserted a capacious 'freedom of expression' clause against the government's will. A vote in the House of Commons would have removed the clause, but Blair left early, and the government lost by one vote. The bill passed with the Lords' amendments in place.[81] In its final form the Racial and Religious Hatred Act 2006 does not protect religious beliefs from criticism, insult, or abuse. It protects *people* from threatening words and behaviour intended to stir up hatred against them based on their religious belief or lack of religious belief. But the common law, through the blasphemous libel offence, still protected Christianity, and in 2007 a Christian group attempted to prosecute the BBC for broadcasting *Jerry Springer the Opera*. In 2008, without fanfare, Gordon Brown's Labour government abolished blasphemy law.[82]

The threat to Rushdie began to recede on 24 September 1998, when the Iranian government declared it would neither carry out nor hinder the *fatwa*,[83] but British intelligence services did not feel able to withdraw his protection until 2002.[84] His protection officers threw a party at Scotland Yard and gave Rushdie a souvenir: a bullet fired accidentally in his home by an officer who was cleaning his gun.[85] The ban on importing *The Satanic Verses* into India still stands, and periodically the controversy is revived. In 2012 Rushdie withdrew from the Jaipur Literature Festival when he was warned of a credible threat to his life. He agreed to be interviewed via live-streamed video, but the venue's owner cancelled the event because police told him there would be violence if the interview were broadcast.[86] Four writers at the festival, Ruchir Joshi, Jeet Thayil, Hari Kunzru, and Amitava Kumar, read passages from *The Satanic Verses* in protest.[87] Rushdie thanked them for their solidarity and spoke of his sadness at the infringement of the 'liberty of ordinary Indian citizens to engage in discourse'. Arguing that, in a free society, people had a right to demonstrate, but not to silence those with whom they disagreed, he criticized the police for failing to ensure the safety of those who had come to hear him, and of those who had come to protest against him. 'Both voices can be heard,' he said.[88]

Notes

1. The Law Commission, *Criminal Law: Offences against Religion and Public Worship*, Law. Com. No. 145 (House of Commons, 1985); *Whitehouse v Lemon* [1979] AC 617 (HL) 658, 665. See also Leonard W. Levy, *Blasphemy: Verbal Offense against the Sacred, from Moses to Salman Rushdie* (New York: Knopf, 1993), pp. 551–54, 558.

2. Angela Carter, 'Angels in Dirty Places', *Guardian*, 23 September 1988, in *The Rushdie File*, ed. Lisa Appignanesi and Sara Maitland (London: Fourth Estate, 1989), pp. 10–12; Nisha Puri, 'Magnificent Puzzle', *Indian Post*, 2 October 1988, in *The Rushdie File*, pp. 13–15.

3. 'Rushdie's Book Banned', *Times of India*, 6 October 1988, p. 1.

4. Salman Rushdie, 'An Open Letter to PM', in *The Rushdie File*, pp. 42–45.

5. Salman Rushdie, *The Satanic Verses* (London: Viking, 1988), pp. 91–126, 359–93.

6. Joel Kuortti, '*The Satanic Verses*: "To Be Born Again, First You Have to Die"', in *The Cambridge Companion to Salman Rushdie*, ed. Abdulrazak Gurnah (Cambridge: Cambridge University Press, 2007), pp. 125–38 (p. 134).

7. Rushdie, *The Satanic Verses*, pp. 367–68.

8. Syed Shahabuddin, 'You Did This with Satanic Forethought, Mr Rushdie', *Times of India*, 13 October 1988, in *The Rushdie File*, pp. 45–49. See also Indian Penal Code Act 1860, s 295A.

9. Amit Roy and Deirdre Fernand, 'Satanic Curses', *Sunday Times*, 19 February 1989, pp. A15–A17 (p. A16); Paul Weller, *A Mirror for our Times: 'The Rushdie Affair' and the Future of Multiculturalism* (London: Continuum, 2007), pp. 25, 27.

10. Mughram Al-Ghamdi to 'Brother in Islam' (28 October 1988), in *The Rushdie File*, pp. 58–60.

11. Roy and Fernand, p. A16; Weller, pp. 25–28.

12. Robin Lustig and others, 'War of the Word', *Observer*, 19 February 1989, p. 15.

13. Steven Teale, 'Fury as Book Is Set Ablaze', *Telegraph & Argus* (Bradford), 14 January 1989, in *The Rushdie File*, pp. 66–67; 'What Happened to the Book Burners?', BBC News, 13 February 2009, http://news.bbc.co.uk/1/hi/magazine/7883308.stm, accessed 31 January 2017.

14. Salman Rushdie, 'Choice between Light and Dark', *Observer*, 22 January 1989, in *The Rushdie File*, pp. 74–75 (p. 75).

15. Tony Harrison, 'Satanic Verses', *Observer*, 19 February 1989, p. 45.

16. Anthony Burgess, 'The Burning Truth', *Daily Mail*, 31 January 1989, p. 6.

17. Kenneth Baker, 'Argument before Arson', *The Times*, 30 January 1989, p. 12.

18. Ibrahim B. Hewitt, letter to the editor, *The Times*, 20 January 1989, in *The Rushdie File*, p. 69.

19. Sheila Rule, 'Muslims Find Deep Isolation in British Life', *New York Times*, 8 March 1989, p. A3.

20. Roy and Fernand, p. A16.

21. M. H. Faruqi, 'Publishing Sacrilege Is Not Acceptable', *Impact International*, 28 October–10 November 1988, in *The Rushdie File*, pp. 60–61.

22. Weller, p. 34.

23. Derek Brown, 'Five Shot Dead in Rushdie Protest', *Guardian*, 13 February 1989, p. 1; Barbara Crossette, 'Muslims Storm U.S. Mission in Pakistan', *New York Times*, 13 February 1989, p. A12.

24. Kenan Malik, *From Fatwa to Jihad: The Rushdie Affair and its Legacy* (London: Atlantic, 2009), p. 5.

25. '3 Die and 60 Hurt in Indian Protest', *New York Times*, 14 February 1989, p. A14.

26. Lustig and others, p. 15; Weller, p. 35.

27. John L. Esposito, *The Oxford Dictionary of Islam* (Oxford: Oxford University Press, 2014).

28. Malcolm Yapp, 'The Hubris of the Hidden Imam', *Independent*, 22 February 1989, in *The Rushdie File*, pp. 95–98.

29. Harvey Morris and others, 'Salman Rushdie—The Satanic Verses: Iranian Cleric Puts Price on Rushdie's Head', *Independent*, 16 February 1989, p. 1.

30. Weller, p. 39.

31. Salman Rushdie, *Joseph Anton* (London: Vintage, 2013), pp. 6, 145–46, 163–64.

32. Malik, p. 12.

33. Malik, pp. 13–14.

34. Malik, p. 14.

35. Yasmin Alibhai, 'Beyond Fundamentalism and Liberalism', *New Statesman*, 3 March 1989, pp. 34–35.

36. Roald Dahl, letter to the editor, *The Times*, 28 February 1989, p. 15.

37. Hugh Trevor-Roper, 'Home Thoughts', *Independent Magazine*, 10 June 1989, quoted in Weller, p. 21.

38. Rushdie, *Joseph Anton*, p. 144.

39. Weller, p. 39.

40. Rushdie, *Joseph Anton*, pp. 144–45; Weller, pp. 70–71.

41. Weller, pp. 37–38.

42. Weller, p. 42.

43. Richard Ford, 'Rushdie Fears Backdown by Government', *The Times*, 4 March 1989, p. 1.

44. 'Rude, as in Rudimentary', *Guardian*, 4 March 1989, p. 22; Rushdie, *Joseph Anton*, p. 152.

45. Rushdie, *Joseph Anton*, p. 152.

46. Ford, p. 1. See also Weller, pp. 71–72.

47. 'Timeline: Iran and UK Relations', BBC News, 20 August 2015, http://www.bbc.co.uk/news/uk-15949285, accessed 31 January 2017; Weller, p. 42.

48. Malik, pp. 124–25, 185; Ruvani Ranasinha, 'The *Fatwa* and its Aftermath', in *The Cambridge Companion*, pp. 45–59 (p. 48).

49. Hugo Young, 'Life, Death and Mr Rushdie', *Guardian*, 24 November 1989, p. 23. See also Kalim Siddiqui, 'The Implications of the Rushdie Affair for Muslims in Britain' (London: The Muslim Institute, [1989]), p. 12.

50. Kalim Siddiqui, *Crescent International*, 1–15 March 1989, quoted in Malik, pp. 124–25 (p. 125). See also Siddiqui, 'Implications', p. 6.

51. Tom Sharratt, 'BBC Ordered to Hand Over Rushdie Film', *Guardian*, 18 November 1989, p. 2; Weller, p. 63.

52. Weller, pp. 64–65.

53. 'World Writers' Statement', in *The Rushdie File*, pp. 137–38. See also Weller, p. 20.

54. Anouar Abdallah and others, *For Rushdie: Essays by Arab and Muslim Writers in Defense of Free Speech* (New York: George Braziller, 1994).

55. Ranasinha, p. 48.

56. Weller, pp. 34, 45–47.

57. Sarah Boseley and others, 'Rushdie Sells under Cover', *Guardian*, 16 March 1989, p. 4.

58. Martin Bailey, 'Library Puts Rushdie Book with Porn', *Observer*, 5 March 1989, p. 1.

59. Bailey, p. 1; Weller, pp. 26, 29.

60. Andrew Cuif, 'Muslims Reject Rushdie Plea', *Guardian*, 5 February 1990, p. 1.

61. Weller, p. 77.

62. Anthony Bevins, 'Labour on the Rack over Rushdie', *Independent*, 22 July 1989, p. 19.

63. Weller, p. 77.

64. Malik, p. 14; Rushdie, *Joseph Anton*, pp. 200–5, 327.

65. Weller, p. 45.

66. Malik, pp. 15–16. See also Rushdie, *Joseph Anton*, pp. 296–97, 393–95.

67. Özgün Özçer, 'The Sivas Massacre in Five Questions', *Hürriyet Daily News*, 2 July 2013, http://www.hurriyetdailynews.com/the-sivas-massacre-in-five-questions.aspx?pageID=238&nID=49923&NewsCatID=341, accessed 25 February 2017; Rushdie, *Joseph Anton*, pp. 389–91.

68. Abdul Ali, 'Open Letter to Salman Rushdie', *New Life*, 11 August 1989, p. 1; Amit Roy, 'Rushdie Taunts Widen Racial Gap', *Sunday Times*, 2 July 1989. See also Weller, pp. 30, 68.

69. Julie Flint, 'Tragedy in the Name of Allah', *Observer*, 11 February 1990, p. 53; Weller, p. 46.

70. Patrick Wintour, 'MP in Furore over "Muslims Go Home"', *Guardian*, 29 August 1989, p. 20.

71. Salman Rushdie, 'In Good Faith', in Rushdie, *Imaginary Homelands: Essays and Criticism 1981–91* (London: Granta, 1992), pp. 393–414 (pp. 395–96).

72. Gordon Wilson and others, letter to the editor, *Independent*, 17 March 1989, in *The Rushdie File*, pp. 152–53 (p. 153).

73. Weller, p. 75.

74. British Muslim Action Front, 'Allahu Akbar: Greatest International March to Parliament' (London: British Muslim Action Front, [1989]), in *The Rushdie File*, p. 158; Malik, p. 19; David Rose, 'Rushdie Protest "to Pull 500000"', *Guardian*, 2 May 1989, in *The Rushdie File*, pp. 157–59; Weller, p. 29.

75. *R v Chief Metropolitan Stipendiary Magistrate, ex p Choudhury* [1991] 1 QB 429 (QB).

76. *Choudhury v United Kingdom*, App No 17439/90 (Commission Decision 5 March 1991). See also Peter G. Danchin, 'Islam in the Secular *Nomos* of the European Court of Human Rights', *Michigan Journal of International Law*, 32.4 (2011), 663–747 (pp. 664–65).

77. John Patten to Iqbal Sacranie (4 July 1989), in *Need for Reform: Muslims and the Law in Multi-Faith Britain* (London: UK Action Committee on Islamic Affairs, 1993), pp. 28–30 (p. 30).

78. Iqbal Sacranie to John Patten (19 July 1989), in *Need for Reform*, pp. 31–33.

79. Lucinda Maer, 'The Racial and Religious Hatred Act 2006', House of Commons Library SN/PC/03768, 6 November 2009, p. 7. See also Neil Addison, *Religious Discrimination and Hatred Law* (London: Routledge-Cavendish, 2007), p. 140.

80. Rushdie, *Joseph Anton*, p. 522. See further pp. 521–22.

81. Addison, pp. 140, 144. See also Maer, pp. 6–17; Rushdie, *Joseph Anton*, p. 522.

82. Russell Sandberg and Norman Doe, 'The Strange Death of Blasphemy', *Modern Law Review*, 71.6 (2008), 971–86 (pp. 971, 979–84).

83. Weller, p. 52.

84. Rushdie, *Joseph Anton*, p. 631.

85. Rushdie, *Joseph Anton*, p. 632.

86. William Dalrymple, 'Why Salman Rushdie's Voice Was Silenced in Jaipur', *Guardian*, 26 January 2012, https://www.theguardian.com/books/2012/jan/26/salman-rushdie-jaipur-literary-festival, accessed 31 January 2017.

87. Hari Kunzru, 'Why I Quoted from *The Satanic Verses*', *Guardian*, 22 January 2012, https://www.theguardian.com/commentisfree/2012/jan/22/i-quoted-satanic-verses-suport-rushdie, accessed 31 January 2017.

88. 'Full Transcript: I'm Returning to India, Deal with It—Salman Rushdie to NDTV', NDTV, 25 January 2012, http://www.ndtv.com/india-news/full-transcript-im-returning-to-india-deal-with-it-salman-rushdie-to-ndtv-568445, accessed 31 January 2017.

22

Hit Man

Rex Feral

The First Amendment to the Constitution of the United States prohibits government from 'abridging the freedom of speech, or of the press'.[1] First Amendment advocates acknowledge that speech can do harm, but hold that the free and open exchange of ideas outweighs the harms that can result. There are limits, however, to the First Amendment's protections, and limits to the harm the courts find acceptable. In 1996 the courts were asked to decide whether the Constitution protected even speech that was intended to assist murder. Was the freedom of speech absolute? If a publisher of a technical guide to contract killing knew and intended that it would be used by a hit man to plan and carry out a murder, could that publisher really take refuge in the freedom of speech? If a guide to killing were prohibited, however, would this expose crime fiction writers, producers of films about murder, and journalists who reported on crime to the risk of prosecution and litigation?

On 3 March 1993, a hit man broke into the Maryland home of Mildred (Millie) Horn and murdered three people: Horn, her eight-year-old son Trevor, and Janice Saunders, a nurse who provided medical care for Trevor. Trevor and Millie Horn were the hit man's targets. In the event of their deaths, Trevor's father, Lawrence Horn,

Poster for *Natural Born Killers*, directed by Oliver Stone. Despite fears that the *Hit Man* case would threaten artistic expression, the film's First Amendment protection was upheld in court.

would receive a two million dollar insurance settlement.[2] Investigating Lawrence, the police discovered a connection with James Perry, a conman from Detroit. Phone records showed that Lawrence and Perry had been in regular contact, and on the night of the murder Perry had called Lawrence from a motel near Millie's home. When they searched Perry's apartment, the police found a collection of books and magazines about crime and weapons. The police called the publisher of a catalogue in Perry's possession, Paladin Press, of Boulder, Colorado. Paladin confirmed that in January 1992 Perry had paid for two books with a bad cheque: *Hit Man: A Technical Manual for Independent Contractors* and *How to Make Disposable Silencers*.[3] Perry had taken his modus operandi from *Hit Man*.

Paladin Press asserts its constitutional right to publish books that might be used to carry out illegal or harmful acts. According to its website, the company was founded on the principle that 'the First Amendment guaranteed Americans the right to read about whatever subjects they desired'.[4] Paladin publishes books, videos, and DVDs on weapons, combat, martial arts, survival, identity creation, and espionage.[5] At the time of the murders, it carried an extensive list of instructional manuals on killing techniques and the manufacture and use of explosives, weapons, and poisons. Paladin's president, Peder Lund, called these titles 'burn and blow books'.[6] *Hit Man*, published by Paladin in 1983, was a popular title in this genre. It purports to be an instruction manual authored by a contract killer under the pseudonym 'Rex Feral'. The real author of *Hit Man*, who remains anonymous, was a divorced mother of two who needed money to pay property taxes. She pitched Paladin a fictional memoir of an assassin. She wasn't a hit man, she told Paladin—she didn't even own a gun—but the publisher suggested that she transform the text into an instructional manual.[7] The book provided step-by-step instructions on how to find clients, secure contracts, construct weapons, carry out assassinations, torture victims, and conceal bodies.[8] Paladin's catalogue told readers that they would 'Learn how a pro gets assignments, creates a false identity, makes a disposable silencer, leaves the scene without a trace, watches his mark unobserved and more. Feral reveals how to get in, do the job and get out without getting caught.'[9] Caveats in the catalogue and the book itself warned that

Hit Man was 'for informational purposes only', that manufacture of a silencer without a licence was against the law, and that 'neither the author nor the publisher assumes responsibility for the use or misuse of information contained in this book'.[10] A novice assassin, Perry used the information in the book to plan his first assassination. He followed Rex Feral's directions closely. He used the model of rifle *Hit Man* recommended and made a silencer using its instructions. Two of the murders were carried out according to the book's recommended method. Perry had also followed the book's directions on expenses, disposal of the weapon, and removal of evidence. Altogether, Perry's method matched *Hit Man's* instructions in twenty-two respects.[11] *Hit Man* became the cornerstone of the prosecution's case against Perry, presented in evidence as his 'blueprint for murder'.[12] Perry and Lawrence Horn were both found guilty.[13]

Two families had been devastated. Millie Horn left two children, and Janice Saunders left a husband and young son. Together, the families brought a pioneering civil suit against Paladin for aiding and abetting the murders by publishing *Hit Man* and *Silencers*. The case is known as *Rice* v. *Paladin* because Millie's daughter's guardian, Vivian Rice, was the first-named party in the complaint. *Rice* v. *Paladin* was a tort case, and, if it made it to trial, the jury would be asked to consider Paladin's liability for the deaths. Before it could be referred for trial, however, the case would have to clear the hurdle of the First Amendment. The families' legal representatives, John Marshall, Howard Siegel, and Thomas Heeney, were joined by Rodney Smolla, a First Amendment scholar and lawyer.[14] Smolla was responsible for elucidating First Amendment law and arguing the case for excluding *Hit Man* from First Amendment protection.

Paladin's legal team was led by Thomas Kelley and Lee Levine, media law and First Amendment experts.[15] They asked the District Court for Maryland to grant a summary judgment in their favour, arguing that Paladin could not be held liable because it had a First Amendment right to publish *Hit Man* and *Silencers*. The court's task, Judge Alexander Williams said, was 'both novel and awesome; the Court must balance society's interest in compensating injured parties against the freedom of speech guaranteed by the First Amendment'.[16]

To enable the judge to focus on the First Amendment question, the plaintiffs and defendants presented the court with a 'Joint Statement of Facts', a set of statements that both parties agreed were true, and which each party thought supported their interpretation of First Amendment law. Paladin stated that its marketing strategy was designed to maximize sales, and that it marketed books like *Hit Man* to a wide range of readers who could have legitimate reasons for their interest in a book about contract killers: authors who were writing about crime, law enforcement officers and agencies seeking information about criminal methods, people who enjoyed reading about crime for the purposes of entertainment, people who 'fantasize about committing crimes', criminologists, and others who study criminal methods and psychology. But, in a concession that surprised the families' legal team, and which they thought was fatal to Paladin's claim that it was not liable for damages, the company acknowledged that their books were targeted at 'criminals', and that they knew that their books would be used to help them commit crimes.[17] Paladin stated that they 'engaged in a marketing strategy intended to attract and assist criminals and would-be criminals who desire information and instructions on how to commit crimes', and that 'in publishing, marketing, advertising and distributing *Hit Man* and *Silencers*' they 'intended and had knowledge that their publications would be used, upon receipt, by criminals and would-be criminals to plan and execute the crime of murder for hire, in the manner set forth in the publications'.[18] Paladin's statement demonstrated their belief that the First Amendment protected even speech intended to aid and abet murder. The judge's task was to decide whether they were right.

The First Amendment does not afford absolute protection to all forms of speech, but it sets a high bar for excluding speech from protection. Judge Williams condemned the book in strong terms, finding it 'loathsome', 'enough to engender nausea', 'reprehensible and devoid of any significant redeeming social value', but when he applied the definitive standard of unprotected speech to the case, he found that he had to protect *Hit Man*.[19] In the case of *Brandenburg* v. *Ohio*, the Supreme Court had held that the First Amendment protected even speech that advocated criminal action, unless it was also 'directed to inciting or producing imminent lawless action and is likely to incite or produce such action'.[20] The case concerned a Ku Klux Klan leader who had said, 'We're not a revengent organization, but if our President, our Congress, our Supreme Court, continues to suppress the white, Caucasian race, it's possible that there might have to be some revengeance taken.'[21] This speech, however abhorrent, was lawful: the court had ruled that advocacy and incitement of criminal action were protected. Only advocacy inciting *imminent* criminal action and that was *likely* to achieve its end was unprotected. For Judge Williams, *Hit Man* was like the Klansman's words: reprehensible, but not language that incited imminent lawless action or was likely to achieve that end. Noting that the murders occurred a year after Perry ordered *Hit Man*, Judge Williams held that the test of 'imminence' had not been met. Furthermore, the book did not incite violence, it merely taught readers how to carry out hits. 'Nothing in the book says "go out and commit murder now",' he wrote; rather, 'the book seems to say [...] "if you want to be a hit man this is what you need to do".' While the judge acknowledged that it had been shown that the information in the book could be 'fatal' in 'the wrong hands', First Amendment protection could not be 'eliminated simply because publication of an idea creates a potential hazard'. He granted summary judgment for Paladin.[22]

The plaintiffs appealed. Paladin obtained supporting briefs and statements from groups who had an interest in the result of the case: *amici curiae*, or 'friends of the court'. Media organizations, authors, and civil liberties groups were concerned that the case risked chilling legitimate forms of speech. They argued that *Hit Man* was indistinguishable from works of fiction and entertainment, journalism, and crime non-fiction.[23] Paladin's supporters included the Horror Writers Association, the Freedom to Read Foundation, the American Civil Liberties Union, the National Association of Broadcasters, the Newspaper Association of America, and the Society of Professional Journalists.[24] The Horror Writers believed that a decision against Paladin would permit the 'chilling and silencing of writers and publishers through tort litigation'.[25] The brief submitted on behalf of media and broadcasters warned that there was no meaningful way to distinguish *Hit Man* from works of crime fiction and satire, such as Thomas Harris's *The Silence of the Lambs* and Jonathan Swift's *A Modest Proposal*.[26] Smolla called this the 'Tom Clancy' argument, after the thriller novelist, whose works might lie on the slippery slope the defenders of *Hit Man* feared the case would create.[27] At the Court of Appeal, the text of *Hit Man*, including its mode of address, language, ideas, and overall tendency, were examined closely.

Hit Man's detailed instructions are delivered in a distinctive voice, that of 'Rex Feral'. Like a professional who is mentoring and advising a promising novice, Feral speaks in the second person to the reader, whom he assumes to be a man. He describes the person the reader will become after his first kill:

> The people around you have suddenly become so *aggravatingly ordinary*. You start to view them as an irritating herd of pathetic sheep, doing as they are told, doing what is expected, following someone, anyone, blindly. You can't believe how dumb your friends have become, and your respect diminishes for people you once held in awe. [...] Your experience in facing death head-on has taught you about life. You have the power and ability to stand alone. *You no longer need a reason to kill.*[28]

If *Hit Man* can be read as fiction, as Paladin's supporters argued, then passages like these can be taken as the words of a fictional character, and the reader of the fictional hit man's narrative can be expected to understand that they are not actually the person Feral addresses as 'you'. Other parts of the book use techniques that are also used in fiction, such as dialogue, characterization, and shifts in narrative perspective. Feral illustrates technical instructions with gruesome anecdotes, and the Prologue describes an exemplary assassination in the form of a short narrative. Excerpted, these passages are indistinguishable from fiction. In court, it proved hard to sustain the argument that *Hit Man* was fiction. Read alongside the instructional passages that make up the bulk of the book, Feral's address to the reader looked to the Appeals Court like incitement to violence.

Criminal actions that are carried out using speech are not protected by the First Amendment. The classic example of a criminal speech act was described by Oliver Wendell Holmes: 'the most stringent protection of free speech would not protect a man in falsely shouting fire in a theatre and causing a panic.'[29] Where the Paladin legal team and its supporters had sought to represent *Hit Man* as expressive, imaginative speech, the plaintiffs argued that it should be treated as speech that aided and abetted crime. They had powerful support. The plaintiffs submitted a report by the Department of Justice on the regulation of information about bomb making. The Department of Justice was examining an analogous problem to that contested in *Rice*: could a publisher of a guide to bomb making be found liable if someone used it to make a bomb and commit murder? Timothy McVeigh, who destroyed the Alfred P. Murrah Federal Building in Oklahoma City using a truck bomb, killing 168 people, had owned a Paladin book on the manufacture of improvised explosives.[30] The Department of Justice was emphatic, arguing that criminal speech acts—criminal acts that took the form of speech, such as speech used to arrange a conspiracy—could 'be proscribed without much, if any, concern about the First Amendment'.[31] The Department of Justice's reasoning proved persuasive in court.

The appeal was heard by Judges William W. Wilkins Jr., Karen J. Williams, and J. Michael Luttig. In Smolla's record of the hearing, the gruelling, combative discussion was dominated and driven by Luttig, who had read *Hit Man* so thoroughly that he had committed passages to memory. Luttig referred closely to a dog-eared and annotated copy of the text in his questioning, putting particular pressure on Paladin's interpretation of the book as fantasy.[32] The court's decision, which was written by Luttig, rebuked both Paladin and *amici* for their assessment of the text:

> After carefully and repeatedly reading *Hit Man* in its entirety, we are of the view that the book so overtly promotes murder in concrete, nonabstract terms that we regard as disturbingly disingenuous both Paladin's cavalier suggestion that the book is essentially a comic book whose 'fantastical' promotion of murder no one could take seriously, and amici's reckless characterization of the book as 'almost avuncular'.[33]

Not only did *Hit Man* instruct its reader in killing, the court emphasized, it encouraged him to kill. The court described the text's mode of address as 'like a parent to a child', noting that *Hit Man* 'admonishes',

'reassures', and 'allays' the reader's concerns, systematically addressing and overcoming all obstacles to the commission of murder.[34] The
book combined instruction with exhortation to commit crime, and
that combination, the court reasoned, was not actually protected by
Brandenburg. *Hit Man* crossed *Brandenburg*'s line between permissibly
advocating violence in the abstract, and impermissibly 'preparing a
group for violent action and steeling it to such action'.[35] 'As *Hit Man*
instructs,' the court wrote, 'it also steels its readers to the particular violence it explicates, instilling in them the resolve necessary to carry out
the crimes it details, explains and glorifies.' Specifically, Feral's motiva-
tional addresses to the reader ('This is your job and you are a professional', 'everything you have been taught about life and its value was
a fallacy') exemplified speech that steeled the reader to action.[36] *Hit
Man* was not expressive speech. It was 'speech brigaded with action'.[37]
If the constitution forbade regulation of criminal speech acts, then the
government would be powerless to protect citizens from blackmail,
threats, perjury, conspiracy, harassment, forgery, and other crimes that
are carried out using words. Every court that had examined the protection of 'speech brigaded with action', Luttig wrote, had concluded
that the First Amendment posed no bar to liability for aiding and
abetting crime:

> Paladin's protests notwithstanding, this book constitutes the archetypal
> example of speech which, because it methodically and comprehen-
> sively prepares and steels its audience to specific criminal conduct
> through exhaustively detailed instructions on the planning, commis-
> sion, and concealment of criminal conduct, finds no preserve in the
> First Amendment.[38]

The court took particular issue with the support given to Paladin
by media, civil liberties organizations, and writers, expressing astonishment that they would have allied themselves with a defendant
that had aided and abetted murder, and had openly acknowledged
that was their intent. 'That the national media organizations would
feel obliged to vigorously defend Paladin's assertion of a constitutional right to *intentionally and knowingly* assist murderers' was 'to say
the least, breathtaking'.[39] The court did not believe that Paladin's

supporters needed to fear a plague of litigation. Artistic depictions of crime might glamorize or indirectly promote criminal conduct, but this was not the same as directly and affirmatively promoting such conduct. The court wrote, '[F]or almost any broadcast, book, movie, or song that one can imagine, an inference of unlawful motive from the description or depiction of particular criminal conduct therein would almost never be reasonable.' *Rice* v. *Paladin* was 'unique in the law', distinguished by Paladin's stipulations of intent; the 'extraordinary comprehensiveness, detail, and clarity of *Hit Man*'s instructions'; 'the boldness of its palpable exhortation to murder'; 'the alarming power and effectiveness of its peculiar form of instruction'; the absence of ideas that were entitled to protection; and the book's lack of any purpose beyond the teaching of murder.[40] The district court's summary judgment in Paladin's favour was reversed: *Hit Man* was not protected speech. *Rice* v. *Paladin* was sent back to the district court, to be tried before a jury.

The Supreme Court refused to hear Paladin's appeal against the decision, and *Rice* v. *Paladin* moved towards a trial. Peder Lund was deposed and questioned about Paladin's catalogue—what legitimate purpose was there for books that taught readers how to make bazookas, flamethrowers, explosives, disposable silencers, 'baby bottle bombs', and poisons? He was asked, 'Does it matter to you for what purpose your books are being ordered when you sell them?' His answer was 'no'—he did not care. When asked if he would sell his books on killing to children, he confirmed that he might, possibly, because his books were 'pure information'. If the Libyan dictator Muammar Gaddafi asked for the latest literature on explosives, he would sell it to him.[41] The day before the trial began, Paladin's insurance company insisted on settling with the plaintiffs, against Paladin's wishes.[42] The insurance company made a significant compensation payment to the bereaved families. Paladin agreed to make annual charitable donations to charities chosen by the plaintiffs, and withdrew *Hit Man* from circulation.[43] Although second-hand copies would continue to circulate and the book was not banned, the publisher would no longer market and distribute it.

Paladin's supporters had argued that the principle established in *Rice* would be used to harass producers of artistic works. It was not long before *Rice* was brought into play in a civil suit against the producers of a work of unambiguous artistic expression, the film *Natural Born Killers*. The case was noticed by national media, but did not mark the dawning of a new era of legal suppression of artistic representations of crime. Patsy Ann Byers had been seriously injured by two teenagers, who had gone on a crime spree after watching the film repeatedly. She brought a suit for damages against the director Oliver Stone, Time Warner, Inc., and others (collectively known as 'the Hollywood defendants') for having produced a film that 'they knew, intended, were substantially certain, or should have known' would incite crime sprees.[44] The case was initially dismissed, but an appeals court, following the *Rice* decision, referred it for trial.[45] Superficially, this looked like a serious setback for the freedom of artistic expression and the First Amendment, fulfilling the prophecy of Paladin's supporters. Bumped back down to the lower court, Stone and Warner asked the judge to issue a summary judgment on First Amendment grounds. The court subjected the film to the *Brandenburg* test, and found that, unlike *Hit Man*, *Natural Born Killers* was not speech intended to incite criminal action, and was therefore protected by the First Amendment. An appeals court affirmed this decision, and the nightmare scenario prophesied by Paladin did not materialize.[46]

Paladin Press now operates in a different legal climate. The Department of Justice's interest in *Rice* was an early sign of shifting opinion on instruction manuals. The law now prohibits distributing information pertaining to the manufacture or use of explosives, destructive devices, and weapons of mass destruction, with the intent that the information be used for violent crimes.[47] In response to this law and the outcome of the *Hit Man* case, Paladin has stopped publishing some titles, particularly books on explosives, demolitions, improvised weaponry, and self-defence. A legal statement on the company's website declares that 'Paladin does not intend for any of the information contained in its books or videos to be used for criminal purposes'. Paladin still asserts its founders' belief that Americans have the right to read whatever they want, without government interference, but warns its customers that the law recognizes a significant difference between criminal intent and personal or academic interest in topics covered in the Paladin catalogue. 'To put it bluntly,' the company warns, 'under current U.S. law you still have the right to read about these topics; you do not have the right to use what you've learned to commit a crime.'[48]

Notes

1. U.S. Const. amend. I.
2. Rice v. Paladin Enterprises, 128 F.3d 233, 239 (4th Cir. 1997).
3. Rod Smolla, *Deliberate Intent: A Lawyer Tells the True Story of Murder by the Book* (New York: Crown, 1999), pp. 24–25; David Montgomery, 'If Books Could Kill: This Publisher Offers Lessons in Murder: Now He's a Target Himself', *Washington Post*, 26 July 1998, pp. F1, F5.
4. Paladin Press, 'Paladin Press: A Brief History', https://www.paladin-press.com/company_history, accessed 15 December 2016.
5. Paladin Press, Fall 2016 catalogue (Boulder, CO: Paladin Press, 2016).
6. Smolla, p. 241. See further pp. 240–43.
7. Montgomery, p. F5. See also Smolla, pp. 229–35.
8. *Rice*, 128 F.3d at 256–61.
9. Paladin Press, catalogue, 26.2, p. 41, quoted in *Rice*, 128 F.3d. at 254.
10. Rex Feral, *Hit Man: A Technical Manual for Independent Contractors* (Boulder, CO: Paladin Press, 1983), p. v; *Rice*, 128 F.3d at 254, 263 n. 10.
11. Montgomery, p. F1; Smolla, pp. 26, 65–67.
12. Smolla, p. 65.
13. Montgomery, p. F1; Smolla, p. 72.
14. Smolla, p. 88; Rice v. Paladin Enterprises, 940 F. Supp. 836, 837 (D. Md. 1996).
15. Smolla, pp. 101–2.
16. *Rice*, 940 F. Supp. at 840.
17. Smolla, pp. 121–22.
18. *Rice*, 128 F.3d at 241 n. 2.
19. *Rice*, 940 F. Supp. at 849.
20. Brandenburg v. Ohio, 395 U.S. 444, 447 (1969).
21. *Brandenburg*, 395 U.S. at 446.
22. *Rice*, 940 F. Supp. at 847, 848.
23. Smolla, p. 166.
24. Brian Saccenti, 'Erosion on the Slippery Slope of First Amendment Protection for Books', in 'Recent Decisions The United States Court of Appeals for the Fourth Circuit', *Maryland Law Review*, 58 (1999), 1221–332 (p. 1265 notes 340 and 341).
25. Brief Amicus Curiae of the Horror Writers Association in Support of Affirmance at 9, *Rice*, 128 F.3d (No. 96-2412), quoted in Saccenti, p. 1265 note 341.
26. Brief Amici Curiae of ABC, Inc. et al. in Support of Affirmance at 4–5, 7–8, *Rice*, 128 F.3d (No. 96-2412), quoted in Saccenti, p. 1273 note

395, p. 1275 note 404; Brief Amici Curiae of ABC, Inc. et al. in Support of Affirmance at 2, *Rice*, 128 F.3d (No. 96-2412), quoted in Amy K. Dilworth, 'Murder in the Abstract: The First Amendment and the Misappropriation of *Brandenburg*', *William & Mary Bill of Rights Journal*, 6.2 (1998), 565–92 (p. 573 note 38).

27. Smolla, p. 221.
28. Feral, p. 111.
29. Schenck v. United States, 249 U.S. 47, 52 (1919).
30. Smolla, p. 241.
31. Department of Justice, *Report on the Availability of Bombmaking Information, the Extent to which its Dissemination Is Controlled by Federal Law, and the Extent to which Such Dissemination May Be Subject to Regulation Consistent with the First Amendment of the United States Constitution*, 37 (April 1997), quoted in *Rice*, 128 F.3d at 246 n. 3.
32. Smolla, pp. 186–201.
33. *Rice*, 128 F.3d at 254.
34. *Rice*, 128 F.3d at 261–62.
35. *Brandenburg*, 395 U.S. at 448 (quoting Noto v. United States, 367 U.S. 290, 297–98 (1961)).
36. *Rice*, 128 F.3d at 261.
37. *Rice*, 128 F.3d at 244.
38. *Rice*, 128 F.3d at 256.
39. *Rice*, 128 F.3d at 265.
40. *Rice*, 128 F.3d at 266, 267.
41. Smolla, pp. 240–44.
42. 'Frequently Asked Questions', Paladin Press, https://www.paladin-press.com/faqs, accessed 15 December 2016.
43. Smolla, p. 272.
44. Byers v. Edmondson, 712 So. 2d 681, 685 (La. Ct. App. 1998).
45. *Byers*, 712 So. 2d at 692.
46. Byers v. Edmondson, 826 So. 2d 551, 558 (La. Ct. App. 2002).
47. 18 U.S.C. § 842 (p)(2).
48. 'Legal Statement', Paladin Press, https://www.paladin-press.com/legal_statement, accessed 15 December 2016.

23

Beijing Coma
Ma Jian

When publishers do business across national borders, the demands of trade and the freedom of speech can come into conflict. What concessions, if any, should publishers make in order to access markets in states that regulate speech differently? For publishers in the United Kingdom, the People's Republic of China (PRC) is a particularly important emerging market. According to the UK Publishers Association, in 2014 the United Kingdom was China's single largest source of imported books and China was the United Kingdom's fifteenth largest export market for books. China has also become a more attractive place for foreign publishers to do business since it joined the World Trade Organization in 2001 and began protecting intellectual property more rigorously. China's stance on censorship, however, raises practical and ethical problems for potential business partners. As the association notes, in China, 'there are many political, religious and sexual issues and opinions that are unacceptable in publications'.[1]

The question of how far publishers should accommodate censorship in the interests of trade was thrown into sharp relief at the 2012 London Book Fair, which showcased Chinese publishing. China sent a delegation of officials, over one hundred and eighty publishers, and thirty-one authors. The authors had been selected by the British Council, an organization that promotes cultural exchange and education, in

Ma Jian photographed in 2009 at the Frankfurt Book Fair. He was not one of the invited authors.

consultation with the General Administration of Press and Publication of China (GAPP), which regulates publishing in mainland China and is, in effect, responsible for the censorship of printed literature. The London Book Fair's press release said that the 'selection of writers aims to showcase the very best of Chinese literature today representing the diversity of Chinese writing'.[2] Although the selection was diverse insofar as it included writers from different regions of China who work in various genres, it did not include any dissident or exiled writers, an omission that was criticized by writers' organizations such as Independent Chinese PEN and English PEN.[3] Dissident writers protested at the fair, including Ma Jian, whose books are banned in China and who lives in exile in London. He tried to give the head of GAPP a copy of his latest novel, *Beijing Coma*, which is about the Tiananmen Square massacre of 1989 and violations of human rights in the lead-up to the Beijing Olympics in 2008.

The night of 3 June and morning of 4 June 1989 saw the government deploy the army against a civilian uprising of students and workers, who had been calling for democratic reforms and workers' rights. The government suppressed their movement with lethal force at Tiananmen Square, where pro-democracy encampments had become the symbol of the movement; elsewhere in Beijing; and around the country. The real death toll is unknown.[4] The massacre and the crackdown on dissent that followed drove many into exile in what Shuyu Kong has called 'the biggest intellectual diaspora in modern Chinese history'.[5] Exiled writers are a sensitive subject for GAPP, and it has made its disapproval of their presence at international book fairs clear. In an effort to raise its profile and to encourage bilateral trade, the PRC has sent large delegations to international book fairs in recent years. China has been the guest of honour at the Frankfurt Book Fair in 2009, the London Book Fair in 2012, and BookExpo America in 2015.[6] At Frankfurt, the organizers invited two dissident writers, disinvited them after pressure from China, then reinvited them after criticism from human rights organizations. The delegation of GAPP officials and authors walked out in protest.[7] In contrast, at the London Book Fair in 2012, where no dissident writers had been invited, GAPP was satisfied with the British Council's list. But dissidents and writers' groups were not. Bei Ling, an exiled writer, accused the fair of 'self-censorship to keep Chinese authorities on board'.[8] In an open letter to the council, the Independent Chinese PEN Center and other PEN organizations criticized the council's close collaboration with GAPP, and questioned its concept of 'Chinese literature'. 'Chinese literature must include independent literature, beyond official censorship and banning,' they argued. That included 'heretical literature, underground literature, prison literature and exile literature'.[9] In response to criticism from writers and journalists, the council's director of literature, Susie Nicklin, expressed support for the freedom of expression ('a very important part of British values developed since the Enlightenment'[10]), and assured critics that there had been 'no disagreement' between the council and 'the Chinese government' about who to invite. Noting that the invited writers made regular appearances on 'lists of the best novelists and poets in China', she added: 'These writers live in China and write their books there; others have left China.'[11] The book fair had in fact invited writers who lived outside China but were not dissidents: Guo Xiaolu and Yan Geling.[12] Although Nicklin stated that the council respected both writers in China and writers outside China, and would be organizing events for exiled writers (but outside the fair),[13] journalists and activists found the council's language disturbing, particularly the neutral statement that uninvited writers had simply 'left' China, rather than been forced into exile.[14]

Ma Jian was banned from entering China in 2011,[15] but has lived in exile since 1987, when his books were prohibited in China after he published his collection of stories about Tibet, *Stick Out your Tongue*.[16] As Ma explains in the afterword to this collection, staggered by the poverty he had witnessed in Tibet, he 'wrote without thought of what the repercussions might be'. His stories depict sexual violence, dispossession, and the 'dehumanising' effects of 'extreme hardship'.[17] Shortly after publication, the government announced a campaign against 'bourgeois liberalism', and Ma's stories were the first target.[18] The government denounced *Stick Out your Tongue* as 'a vulgar, obscene book' that defamed Tibetans and failed to depict 'civilised Socialist Tibet'.[19] All copies of the magazine in which the stories had been published were ordered to be seized and destroyed, and the editor of the magazine, Liu Xinwu, was fired. Ma later learned that a blanket ban had been placed on all his publications. The Tiananmen Square massacre, on top of this censorship, drove him into exile.[20] 'One can't write in a totalitarian society unless one writes as a rebel', he says. The only way for writers 'to keep some moral conscience is to flee'.[21]

Ma's rebellious writing challenges the version of history promoted by the Communist Party in China. Not only does his work discuss the atrocities committed during the era of Mao Zedong, some of which can be discussed with caution in China, but it also explores violations of human and civil rights in the post-Mao era, including the persecution of religious minorities, the abuse of women carried out through enforcement of the 'one child policy', and the exploitation of workers in modern factories. The state's stifling of intellectual life, art, and dissent is a thread running through Ma's work, reflecting his personal experience. Writers working in mainland China cannot speak so freely. Those who criticize the Party or call openly for political reform and civil rights have been imprisoned and harassed.[22] Ma explained to British journalists that it was highly unlikely that the writers invited by the British Council would 'express their true feelings or opinions' at the London Book Fair, because writers published in mainland China have been 'forced to enter a silent pact with the regime'.[23] Writers must co-operate with the expurgation and modification of their work if the publisher—who is answerable to GAPP—deems it necessary. If publishers displease GAPP, they may find that their supply of ISBNs dries up, making it impossible to distribute their books to reputable booksellers. Publishers may be blacklisted or closed down altogether.[24] The official regulations governing publishing include a long list of prohibitions against, among other things, damaging the honour of the state, propagating obscenity, and endangering cultural traditions.[25] The prohibitions are broad, and some editors find them difficult to interpret. The writer Murong Xuecun was infuriated by his nervous editor, who struck out 'peasants' (pejorative), 'stealth plane' (too military), and a fart that had 'the flavour of India' (likely to provoke a diplomatic incident). The mangled text approved by his publisher, Murong said, was nonsensical.[26] Foreign works published in translation are subject to the same process, which has surprised some authors. Hillary Clinton demanded her book be withdrawn from sale when she discovered it had been expurgated. Other authors, like Peter Hessler and Ezra Vogel, accepted a degree of expurgation.[27] Ma once co-operated with a Chinese publisher on an edition of his novel *The Noodle Maker* to find out 'what the censors would find objectionable'. Five people examined the book and struck out the same words from a conversation between an artist and his talking dog:[28] '"But when it comes down to it, Chairman Mao was just a human being like any other," the dog said.'[29] As Ma explains, 'Each of the five censors ruled out "the dog said". They did not feel a dog should have the right to pass judgment on Chairman Mao.'[30] Ma won the tussle with his censors over the dog's speech, but two weeks after publication, the authorities discovered Ma was the book's author. *The Noodle Maker* was removed from bookstores and pulped.[31]

Writing in exile, Ma is free to write critically about China without negotiating with its censors. His novel *Beijing Coma*, published in 2008, documents and challenges attempts to erase history, and was awarded the TR Fyvel Book Award by Index on Censorship in 2009.[32] Narrated by Dai Wei, a pro-democracy protester paralysed by a soldier's bullet in the Tiananmen Square massacre, the novel draws a direct line between the horrors of the Cultural Revolution, the suppression of the 1989 protests, and the silencing of critical voices in the following decades. 'In this police state,' Dai thinks, 'I've managed to gain freedom of thought by pretending to be dead. My muteness is a protective cloak.'[33] Because he cannot speak, he poses no threat and, unlike those around him, he is at liberty to remember the violence of the recent past and the present. The novel lingers over the abuse and mutilation of the bodies of dissidents to remind readers that, as Ma puts it, 'In a tyranny, in the end what will be destroyed is your flesh, if you oppose the state.'[34] In its unflinching examination of the darkest moments of China's recent history, *Beijing Coma* insists on remembering that which the state wants its citizens to forget.

Such acts of remembrance were not welcome at the London Book Fair. On 16 April 2012 the Minister of GAPP, Liu Binjie, was due to give a keynote speech at the fair alongside Ed Vaizey, the British Under Secretary of State for Culture, Communications and Creative Industries.[35] But protesters had made it known that they would attend the event, and Liu's speech was read out by another Chinese official. Video of the event shows that an audience member held up signs that said 'Free Speech Is Not a Crime' and 'Stop Literary Persecution'. A security guard tried to force the protester's arm down and ordered him to leave his seat, but, as the protester silently resisted, other audience members raised signs. Their silent protest was allowed to continue for the rest of the talk.[36] One protester held up a picture of Liu Xiaobo,[37] the Nobel peace laureate, who was sentenced to eleven years in prison in 2009 for 'inciting subversion of state power' after he called for constitutional reform and free elections.[38] Ma was in the audience.[39]

After the keynote address, dissident writers gathered at a performance area that was designated for the use of the Romanian delegation, who allowed them to use it for a public reading of their banned works.[40] Ma staged a protest against the silencing of Liu and other writers. 'No Chinese writers enjoy freedom of speech,' he said. Although he was pleased that the British Council was trying to establish a dialogue with China, he wished that the London Book Fair had enabled its visitors to 'get a real understanding of China, not a censored one, and for there to be a genuine dialogue'. The dialogue at the book fair would not be mentioning the Tiananmen Square massacre, Tibetan lamas who had set fire to themselves, or imprisoned writers. The fair would not be exhibiting any book that had not been censored by the authorities. Holding up a copy of Beijing Coma, Ma explained that he had been forcibly prevented from giving it to the head of GAPP. He drew a large red x on the cover to symbolize the banning of his book, not only in China, but also, by implication, at the fair. Then he drew a red x over his face, explaining that he shared his book's fate and was now also banned in China. He described 'books, literature, publishing' as a 'forum' that should be defined by 'integrity and honour', uncontaminated by 'money' and 'corrupt politicians'. 'What happens to a civilization when this forum is itself corrupted?' he asked.[41]

Ma's vision of publishing as a forum protected from economics and politics is not the mission statement of an international trade fair. The London Book Fair had invited China to be its 'Market Focus', and the emphasis of the event was on trade. Yet, even if international trade fairs function as 'shop windows' rather than as festivals of ideas,[42] many of the people who visit them aspire to Ma's vision of the fair as an honourable forum. For the writer Boyd Tonkin, those invited to the London Book Fair deserved a warm welcome, and he thought that the British Council had 'done its diplomatic job as well as it could'. But his job, as a writer, was 'a rather different one'. He pointed out that visitors were under no obligation to be diplomatic and should condemn the persecution of writers and demand the immediate release of imprisoned dissidents. 'At a global literary gathering, this demand cannot be a sideshow. It should take centre-stage,' he declared.[43] Many visitors to the fair made this demand. Visitors took part in silent protests and asked the promoted writers about their experiences of censorship. They attended parallel events featuring uninvited writers and listened to an alternative panel discussion, featuring Ma, hosted off-site by English PEN.[44] Journalists asked GAPP officials pointed questions about absent writers. Jonathan Mirsky, writing for the *New York Review of Books*, pushed one official too far, and his souvenir panda was confiscated.[45]

The British Council could not have hosted China at the London Book Fair without making some concessions to GAPP, but, by adopting GAPP's ground rules, the council did not attempt to balance trade and diplomacy with the freedom of expression. The issues raised by the book fair are only becoming more pressing in light of China's recent actions against booksellers from Hong Kong. Now a semi-autonomous region of the People's Republic of China, Hong Kong was until 1997 a British colony, and it continues to operate under the legal system imposed by Britain and guaranteed by the Sino-British Joint Declaration of 1984, which affords greater protection for the freedom of expression than in mainland China. Until recently, books forbidden on the mainland but legal in Hong Kong were popular with Chinese tourists. But in late 2015 five Hong Kong booksellers disappeared, only to reappear in detention in mainland China in February 2016. They were all associated with companies that sold books about Chinese political scandals. The incident was a problem for Britain for two reasons. The Joint Declaration Britain had co-signed was supposed to guarantee Hong Kong citizens due process and freedom of speech. And one of the booksellers, Lee Bo, holds dual British and Chinese citizenship.[46] Britain has stated that it regards China's treatment of Lee as a serious breach of the Joint Declaration, and has signed a United Nations Human Rights Council statement condemning China's 'extraterritorial actions'.[47] But only Hong Kong can protect its citizens, and it appears that the Hong Kong book trade is not confident that it will. Since the booksellers disappeared, publishers have been less likely to issue books that might be disapproved of on the mainland. Books that support the Communist Party line are being promoted more enthusiastically than critical books, which tourists are less likely to buy. Most Hong Kong bookshops are no longer displaying forbidden books.[48]

Notes

1. Paul Richardson and Chu Xiaoying, *PA Market Report: China* (London: Publishers Association, 2015), pp. ix, 1–4.

2. Midas PR, 'The London Book Fair Announces China Market Focus Programme', http://www.midaspr.co.uk/news-stories/the-london-book-fair-announces-china-market-focus-programme, accessed 6 February 2017. See also Jianhua Yao, *Knowledge Workers in Contemporary China: Reform and Resistance in the Publishing Industry* (Lanham, MD: Lexington Books, 2014), p. 48.

3. Todd Foley, 'The London Book Fair and the Question of Chinese Literature', *Comparative Critical Studies* (2014), 61–75 (pp. 61, 64).

4. Timothy Brook, *Quelling the People: The Military Suppression of the Beijing Democracy Movement* (Stanford: Stanford University Press, 1998), pp. 121–69.

5. Shuyu Kong, 'Ma Jian and Gao Xingjian: Intellectual Nomadism and Exilic Consciousness in Sinophone Literature', *Canadian Review of Comparative Literature*, 41.2 (2014), 126–46 (p. 126).

6. Richardson and Chu, p. 106.

7. Jonathan Fenby, 'Seeking Soft-Power, but Not by the Book', YaleGlobal Online, 26 October 2009, http://yaleglobal.yale.edu/content/seeking-soft-power-not-book, accessed 6 February 2017.

8. Charlotte Williams, 'British Council Responds to Criticism over LBF Line-Up', *Bookseller*, 21 March 2012, http://www.thebookseller.com/news/british-council-responds-criticism-over-lbf-line, accessed 6 February 2017.

9. Independent Chinese PEN Center and others, 'A Letter to the British Council on the London Book Fair', 4 December 2012, Independent Chinese PEN Center, http://www.chinesepen.org/english/a-letter-to-the-british-council-on-the-london-book-fair#more-4263, accessed 27 January 2017.

10. Richard Lea, 'Is the London Book Fair Supporting Chinese Censorship?', *Guardian*, 13 April 2012, https://www.theguardian.com/books/2012/apr/13/london-book-fair-china-censorship, accessed 6 February 2017.

11. Williams.

12. British Council Literature, 'China Market Focus at the London Book Fair 2012', pp. 28, 48, http://www.slideshare.net/bcartsliterature/the-london-book-fair-2012-china-market-focus, accessed 30 January 2017; Foley, pp. 61–64.

13. Lea; Williams.

14. Nick Cohen, 'The British Council Brings More Shame on Us', *Observer*, 15 April 2012, p. 37; Jonathan Mirsky, 'Bringing Censors to the Book Fair', *New York Review of Books*, 18 April 2012, http://www.nybooks.com/daily/2012/04/18/chinese-writers-london-book-fair, accessed 6 February 2017.

15. Tania Branigan, 'Exiled Author Ma Jian Banned from Visiting China', *Guardian*, 29 July 2011, https://www.theguardian.com/world/2011/jul/29/author-ma-jian-banned-from-china, accessed 6 February 2017.

16. Ma Jian, 'Afterword', in Ma, *Stick Out your Tongue*, trans. Flora Drew (London: Vintage, 2014), pp. 82–90.

17. Ma, 'Afterword', pp. 83, 85.

18. Ma, 'Afterword', p. 86.

19. Ma, 'Afterword', p. 85.

20. Ma, 'Afterword', pp. 86–87. See also Bonnie S. McDougall and Kam Louie, *The Literature of China in the Twentieth Century* (London: Hurst, 1997), p. 391.

21. Ma Jian, quoted in Kong, p. 138.

22. Sarah Hoffman and Larry Siems, *The PEN Report: Creativity and Constraint in Today's China* (London: PEN International, 2013), pp. 9–10.

23. Lea.

24. PEN America, *Censorship and Conscience: Foreign Authors and the Challenge of Chinese Censorship* (PEN America, 2015), p. 8, https://www.pen.org/sites/default/files/PEN%20Censorship%20and%20Conscience%202%20June.pdf, accessed 7 February 2017.

25. 'Regulation on the Administration of Publishing', *Congressional–Executive Commission on China*, http://www.cecc.gov/resources/legal-provisions/regulation-on-the-administration-of-publishing-chinese-and-english-text, accessed 6 February 2017.

26. 'Murong Xuecun's Acceptance Speech for the 2010 People's Literature Prize', *New York Times*, 6 November 2011, http://www.nytimes.com/2011/11/06/world/asia/murong-xuecuns-acceptance-speech-for-the-2010-peoples-literature-prize.html, accessed 6 February 2017.

27. PEN America, *Censorship and Conscience*, pp. 11–21. See also Peter Hessler, 'Travels with my Censor', *New Yorker*, 9 March 2015, http://www.newyorker.com/magazine/2015/03/09/travels-with-my-censor#, accessed 6 February 2017.

28. Ma Jian and Flora Drew, 'The Grand Illusion', *Index on Censorship*, 37 (2008), 74–78 (p. 77).

29. Ma Jian, *The Noodle Maker*, trans. Flora Drew (London: Chatto & Windus, 2004), p. 157.

30. Ma and Drew, p. 77.

31. Ma and Drew, p. 78.

32. Index on Censorship, 'Freedom of Expression Awards 2009', https://www.indexoncensorship.org/2009/03/awards-2009, accessed 6 February 2017.

33. Ma Jian, *Beijing Coma*, trans. Flora Drew (London: Chatto & Windus, 2008), p. 514.

34. Boyd Tonkin, 'Ma Jian: Slaughter and Forgetting', *Independent*, 1 May 2008, http://www.independent.co.uk/arts-entertainment/books/features/ma-jian-slaughter-and-forgetting-819385.html, accessed 6 February 2017.

35. Midas PR.

36. hhl13, *Chinese, Uyghurs, Tibetans and Supporters Protest at London Book Fair 2012*, online video recording, YouTube, 17 April 2012, https://www.youtube.com/watch?v=vuWRMoLzYtI&feature=youtu.be, accessed 6 February 2017. See also Amnesty International UK, 'Protests Give Voice to Tibetan, Chinese and Uyghur Writers at the London Book Fair', 18 April 2012, https://www.amnesty.org.uk/blogs/countdown-china/protests-give-voice-tibetan-chinese-and-uyghur-writers-london-book-fair, accessed 6 February 2017.

37. hhl13, *Chinese, Uyghurs, Tibetans and Supporters Protest*.

38. Steven Mufson, 'Chinese Dissident Liu Xiaobo Sentenced to 11 Years on "Subversion" Charges', *Washington Post*, 25 December 2009, http://www.washingtonpost.com/wp-dyn/content/article/2009/12/24/AR2009122401564.html, accessed 6 February 2017.

39. hhl13, *Chinese, Uyghurs, Tibetans and Supporters Protest.*

40. Mirsky.

41. hhl13, *Banned Novelist Ma Jian Speaks at Independent Cultural Event Criticizing London Book Fair,* online video recording, YouTube, 17 April 2012, https://www.youtube.com/watch?v=G9IwEZXau7A, accessed 6 February 2017.

42. Erdener Kaynak and Paul Herbig, *Handbook of Cross-Cultural Marketing* (Hoboken: Taylor & Francis, 2014), p. 131 [e-book].

43. Boyd Tonkin, 'Fill the Book Fair's Empty Chairs', *Independent,* 12 April 2012, http://www.independent.co.uk/arts-entertainment/books/features/boyd-tonkin-fill-the-book-fairs-empty-chairs-7640237.html#, accessed 6 February 2017.

44. A. A., 'A Loud Hush', *Economist,* 23 April 2012, http://www.economist.com/blogs/prospero/2012/04/china-and-london-book-fair-0, accessed 27 February 2017; A. A., 'Playing It by the Book', *Economist,* 13 April 2012, http://www.economist.com/node/21552663, accessed 6 February 2017; English PEN and others, 'China Inside Out', www.freewordonline.com/assets/public/files/PEN_ChinaPROG_Web4.pdf, accessed 6 February 2017.

45. Mirsky.

46. PEN America, *Writing on the Wall: Disappeared Booksellers and Free Expression in Hong Kong* (2016), pp. 4–6, 8–9, 12–19, 25–27, 29–31, https://pen.org/sites/default/files/PEN-America_Writing-on-the-Wall_Hong-Kong-Report.pdf, accessed 7 February 2017. See also C. L. Lim, 'The Sino-British Treaty and the Hong Kong Booksellers Affair', *Law Quarterly Review,* 132 (2016), 552–56.

47. 'Joint Statement—Human Rights Situation in China', quoted in PEN America, *Writing on the Wall,* p. 28. See also PEN America, *Writing on the Wall,* p. 26.

48. Ilaria Maria Sala, 'In Hong Kong's Book Industry, "Everybody Is Scared"', *Guardian,* 28 December 2016, https://www.theguardian.com/books/2016/dec/28/in-hong-kongs-book-industry-everybody-is-scared, accessed 6 February 2017.

24

Persepolis: The Story of a Childhood
Marjane Satrapi

On 15 March 2013, students protested outside Lane Tech, a high
school in Chicago. They held up banners reading 'Honk if you
love free speech', 'Let us read', and 'Free Persepolis'.[1] At Social Justice
High School, students held a 'read-in', gathering together to read a
'banned' book.[2] Chicago students were asserting their right to read
the acclaimed graphic novel *Persepolis: The Story of a Childhood*, the
first volume of Marjane Satrapi's memoir of life in Iran during the
Islamic Revolution and the Iran–Iraq War. *Persepolis* had been held in
many Chicago school libraries and taught in classes from the seventh
grade upwards. Earlier that week, however, managerial staff of Chicago
Public Schools (CPS) had ordered principals to retrieve every copy of
the book from classrooms and school libraries. The order was urgent,
unexpected, and unexplained. As school officials began collecting the
books, students asked why the book was being withdrawn and on
whose authority. Students at Lane Tech checked out copies from the
school library and used social media to publicize the withdrawal.[3] A
student journalist, Matthew Wettig, obtained a written comment from
Satrapi herself: 'SHAME ON THEM!'[4] When international media picked
up on the story, a local reporter dubbed it 'Persepolgate'.[5] On the day
of the students' protest, CPS changed its stance. The book was to be
removed from the seventh grade curriculum but, crucially, not from

The cover of the single-volume *Persepolis* by Marjane Satrapi, containing *The Story of a Childhood* and its sequel, *The Story of a Return*.

school libraries.[6] *Persepolis* had been unbanned. Later that year, the Illinois Library Association awarded Lane Tech students and the school's 451 Degrees Banned Books Club its Intellectual Freedom Award in recognition of their advocacy.[7]

The banning and unbanning of *Persepolis* is a familiar story. Disputes about school curricula and school library materials in the United States make regular appearances in news media. There is less interest in school book challenges in the United Kingdom, but this does not mean that there is less interference with students' reading. For instance, in 2008 the Assessment and Qualifications Alliance (AQA), an exam board, directed schools to stop using the 2005 edition of its *Anthology* of poetry and prose, which was used by students around the country to prepare for the English Literature General Certificate of Secondary Education (GCSE) examination assessed by the AQA. In the 2008 school year, 339,676 students were preparing for that examination, and many would have studied the *Anthology*.[8] The recall was prompted by one exam invigilator, who complained about the poem 'Education for Leisure', a dramatic monologue by Carol Ann Duffy that expresses the psychological state of a disenfranchised school-leaver who kills animals and then takes to the street with a bread knife. Andrew Robathan, the MP who took up the invigilator's complaint, claimed that, though he was 'certainly not in favour of censorship', the poem made carrying a knife 'seem normal and acceptable'.[9] In response, AQA issued a new anthology, removing Duffy's poem and the accompanying image of a knife, and marking the excision with the note 'this page intentionally left blank'.[10] Duffy's public profile in the United Kingdom as a popular and widely taught poet, later to be the British Poet Laureate, ensured that the incident was noticed.[11] Other acts of censorship by exam boards or in UK libraries and schools may well go unrecorded. In contrast, in the United States, every September a coalition of anti-censorship organizations and professional bodies sponsors Banned Books Week, a programme of events that challenges censorship in US libraries. The American Library Association (ALA) announces the top ten 'most frequently banned and challenged books' of the year, based on media reports and records of challenges submitted by librarians to the ALA's Office for Intellectual Freedom.[12] The ALA defines 'challenge' as 'an attempt to remove or restrict materials, based upon the objections of a person or group'. Challenges can be directed at school curriculum as well as library holdings. 'Censorship', for the ALA, is a 'change in the access status of material, based on the content of the work and made by a governing authority or its representatives. Such changes include exclusion, restriction, removal, or age/grade level changes.'[13] According to the Office for Intellectual Freedom, there were 311 challenges to library books in 2014, the year in which *Persepolis* made its first appearance on the frequently challenged list. Between 2000 and 2009, there were 5,099 challenges in total. The ALA estimates that up to 85 per cent of challenges go unrecorded, and therefore warns that its data cannot be treated as comprehensive.[14] Its expanding database of censorship does, however, keep censorship in the public eye. The contrast between the United States, where school censorship is widely reported, and the United Kingdom, where only exceptional cases make the news, is striking.

Each challenge is a record of a local dispute. Like the Chicago *Persepolis* case, US challenges are shaped by the circumstances of particular states, communities, school districts, and schools. Although national advocacy groups may become involved, and are sometimes the initiators of complaints, school censorship disputes are inevitably affected by the concerns of parents, students, librarians, teachers, school boards, and elected officials. Therefore, any single case cannot stand in for all the cases recorded (and not recorded) by the Office for Intellectual Freedom. But the challenges to *Persepolis*, in Chicago and elsewhere, exemplify some larger patterns and trends. According to the ALA, 'authors of color, as well as books with diverse content, are disproportionately challenged and banned'.[15] The ALA's definition of diversity is in flux, but 'diverse content' broadly designates the representation of people of various races, ethnicities, sexualities, genders, abilities, and religions.[16] In September 2014, for example, a parent in Chatham, Illinois, who objected to *Persepolis*'s presence on a reading list, asked why a teacher would assign a book about Muslims on September 11. (His request to remove the book from the curriculum was denied.)[17] Most challenges are initiated by parents, as in the Chatham case, but a significant number are made by library patrons and institutional administrators, as was the case in the recall of *Persepolis* in Chicago. Although there is no single common property linking the books that are the subject of challenges and bans, the most common reasons for objections are, in order of frequency: 'sexually explicit' content, 'offensive language', 'unsuitability for age group', and 'violence'.[18] Book challengers' individual motivations vary, but they often rationalize their attempts to censor books as protective acts—of their children, and of their community's values.[19] When library and information scientist Emily Knox interviewed book challengers, she found that they shared certain beliefs about morality and childhood: morality was under threat, parents were responsible for controlling what their children were exposed to, schools should be places of safety, and innocent children should be protected from adult knowledge.[20] Some of these beliefs can be seen at work in the banning of *Persepolis*. CPS believed they needed to act urgently to protect the children in their care. But their action was seen by librarians, teachers, and the children themselves as a violation of students' rights and the ideal of intellectual freedom.

People who call for restrictions on access to certain books do not necessarily see themselves as censors. Knox has shown that they tend to define censorship narrowly as a total ban on a book. As long as the book continues to be held somewhere, in some library or bookshop, it has not, in their view, been censored.[21] The US courts disagree. They have been asked to consider a number of school book bannings in the context of the First Amendment's protection of the freedom of speech, and their decisions convey a different idea of censorship from that expressed by book challengers.

School book censorship in the United States can involve curricular decisions, where a school board decides to remove a book from its curriculum, and library access changes, where a school removes or restricts access to a book in the library. The final outcome of the *Persepolis* case—dropped from the curriculum, retained in the library—is consistent with the current state of US case law. A line of cases descending from *Board of Education* v. *Pico* (see Chapter 14) and *Hazelwood* v. *Kuhlmeier* has established that the constitutional threshold for excluding and restricting access to books is set far higher in libraries than it is in classrooms.[22] Courts do not generally interfere with pedagogical judgements, though they will examine school boards' motivations to confirm that their judgements *are* pedagogical. In *Pico*, the Supreme Court ruled that there should be a trial to examine a school board's motivations for removing books from a school library. *Pico*'s plurality opinion (the argument made by the only three justices who agreed on the reasoning behind the decision) is not legally binding, but has guided later cases, particularly the argument that it is unconstitutional for a school board to remove books from libraries in a 'narrowly partisan or political manner'. The plurality also argued that the constitution's protection of the freedom of speech necessarily involved the freedom to 'receive ideas', an interpretation of the constitution that the ALA and intellectual freedom organizations have embraced, using it to advocate for the 'freedom to read'.[23] Courts have used the *Pico* plurality's reasoning to establish that school boards cannot remove books from school libraries or restrict students' access to them simply because they dislike or disagree with their contents. Cases have involved the removal of Jim Haskins's *Voodoo and Hoodoo* in response to the objections of Christians,[24] the removal of Nancy Garden's *Annie on my Mind* because of its positive representation of lesbian relationships,[25] and an attempt to restrict students' access to J. K. Rowling's Harry Potter series because the books dealt with 'witchcraft' and 'the occult', and might 'promote disobedience and disrespect for authority' (one school board member predicted 'anarchy' if the Harry Potter books were allowed to circulate freely).[26] In these cases, the courts affirmed the library's special status as a place where students can exercise a considerable degree of autonomy. In contrast, courts are reluctant to interfere with schools' management of curricula, regardless of the courts' view of the merits of the texts in question. Curricular cases often draw on the reasoning of the Supreme Court in *Hazelwood*, where the majority decided that schools could limit students' expression in 'school-sponsored expressive activities' for reasons 'reasonably related to legitimate pedagogical concerns'. For instance, when the school board of Columbia County, Florida, voted to stop using a class textbook because it objected to 'vulgarity and sexual explicitness' in extracts from Chaucer's 'The Miller's Tale' and Aristophanes' *Lysistrata*, the court of appeal quoted generously from the bawdiest parts of the texts and asked whether 'young persons just below the age of majority' could really be harmed by 'these masterpieces of Western literature'. Even so, citing *Hazelwood*, the court accepted that, because the school board's action was 'reasonably related to legitimate pedagogical concerns', its action was constitutional.[27] Chaucer and Aristophanes could be dropped from the curriculum, even if the court thought that this was unwise.

Because Jarrett Dapier, a graduate student, submitted a freedom of information request for materials relating to the meeting in which Chicago Public Schools decided to ban *Persepolis*, we now know what motivated CPS and why they eventually reversed the decision to remove the book from school libraries.[28] The initial complaint was made by an elementary school 'network chief', who emailed CPS early on the morning of 9 March 2013, attaching two pages from *Persepolis* that contained strong language and depicted torture. The first page, she noted, contained 'language such as, *bastards* and *push her against a wall to be fucked*'. The second page showed 'images of a man's penis urinating on another man's back and other torturous images, lashings, ideas'. *Persepolis* had been sent to her schools as a seventh-grade text, she said, but it was 'not suitable at all', and she requested permission to 'pull' the book from her schools.[29] CPS responded quickly. Later that day officials removed the book from the seventh-grade curriculum and recommended reading list across the entire CPS system.[30] The next day, CPS sent a memo to all network chiefs: 'the novel *Persepolis* contains some graphic language and content that is inappropriate for children. [...] It is imperative that we remove the books from the classroom and from the school, to decrease the likelihood of the books getting into the hands of students.'[31] This direction applied to all schools in the district, and was not limited to the seventh-grade curriculum. On 12 March, CPS sent an email to all chiefs directing them to collect *Persepolis* from 'classrooms and libraries'.[32] What had begun as a request to make a curriculum change affecting younger students had escalated into, in effect, a blanket ban on *Persepolis* in classrooms and libraries, affecting all students indiscriminately.

The two pages CPS found inappropriate for children depict a child's first encounters with state violence. The young Satrapi learns about the brutal suppression of political dissent during the Shah's regime, and, after the Shah is overthrown, of religious and political dissent in the new Islamic Republic. The first page shows Satrapi's mother's distress after she is verbally abused in the street. Satrapi does not illustrate the incident itself, but she tells the story in her mother's words. Two 'fundamentalist bastards', her mother says, threatened her with sexual assault because she was not wearing the veil. 'They insulted me,' she tells her husband and daughter: 'They said that women like me should be pushed up against a wall and fucked, and then thrown in the garbage.' A panel on the same page shows a spokesman for the Islamic Republic regime announcing that wearing the veil is now obligatory in order to protect women from rapists. The page makes clear that sexual and political violence are intertwined, connecting a street assault with the misogynistic and paternalist rhetoric of the regime. Similarly, the second page to which CPS objected connects physical violence with assaults on personal freedom. The page depicts a frank conversation about torture between political prisoners who had been incarcerated during the Shah's rule and released after the Islamic Revolution. A large panel depicts the 'worst torture' described by the prisoners, which was inflicted on their friend Ahmadi: he was whipped, urinated on, and burned with an iron. Satrapi listens to the prisoners, unnoticed. She struggles to cope with what she has over-heard, first enacting their stories in violent games, then trying (and failing) to forgive the torturers as she thinks she ought to, only partly consoled by her mother's promise that the torturers will pay.[33] *Persepolis* is a book about a young girl who is forced to confront a violent reality at a young age. The question for educators in CPS was whether the children in their care should learn about this reality, and if so at what age and how. There were genuine curricular and pedagogical issues for CPS management to consider, but its rapid, unilateral action angered students, and raised constitutional questions for librarians.

CPS's order to recall the book came as an unwelcome surprise to students and teachers. *Persepolis* is recommended by the National Council of Teachers of English and was widely used in Chicago public schools.[34] It was on the recommended reading list for seventh-grade students, was used in Advanced Placement French, English Literature, and Comparative Government courses,[35] and had been a foundational text in the Chicago curriculum since 2011. It was used in classes on human rights, equality, and violence against women.[36] Because *Persepolis* is rapidly acquiring the status of a modern classic, having won comic-book prizes and library awards, and having been adapted into an acclaimed animated film, its banning was newsworthy.[37] Some found it ironic that a book that meditates on the effects of censorship in Iran should be censored in the United States.[38] Activists and supporters circulated panels from the book on social media, especially scenes in which the young Satrapi is given books or told that she is old enough to understand difficult ideas.[39]

The book recall was in progress when CPS realized that it should not have ordered principals to remove the book from school libraries. The student protests and international attention may have influenced CPS, but the deciding factor was its own policy on libraries. On 13 March 2013 CPS circulated an urgent update:

> It appears that while we can collect the copies of the book from the classrooms, we *cannot* collect them from the school libraries without going through the process outlined in the policy for 'New Collection Development Policy for School Libraries (604.7)'. [...] High School Chiefs, should you get push back from school librarians, please know that they have the rights outlined in the policy. It is advised that you adhere to the policy.[40]

The collection development policy contained strong protections against the unconstitutional removal of books from school libraries. It set out criteria for the selection, removal, and replacement of materials in school libraries, following principles set out in the ALA's Library Bill of Rights and Illinois School Library Media Association guidelines. When considering individual works, the value of the work as a whole was supposed to be considered and given greater weight than isolated excerpts. The policy also directed librarians to consider factors such as the reputation of the author, appeal to library users, artistic and literary quality, reading level, and educational significance. If a formal challenge were made to a book, a review committee would consider these factors before deciding to remove the book from the library.[41] CPS had not followed this procedure with *Persepolis*, and so, according to its own policy, it had exceeded its authority by trying to remove *Persepolis* from school libraries without consultation.

On 15 March, while students protested outside Lane Tech, CPS CEO Barbara Byrd-Bennett issued a public statement. 'We are not banning this book from our schools,' she told principals. *Persepolis* contained 'graphic language and images that are not appropriate for general use in the seventh grade curriculum', but, referring to the New Collection policy, she told them: 'do not remove this book or any other book from the central school library, unless you have complied with the policy.'[42] CPS did not consider *Persepolis* banned because it was still available in the library for any student who wanted to read it. To teachers, however, the curricular removal still looked like censorship. 'Enough with the Orwellian doublespeak,' said Chicago Teachers Union spokesperson Stephanie Gadlin. She pointed out that the return of *Persepolis* to libraries did not help those students who attended the 160 elementary schools in Chicago that did not have libraries. 'We support our educators who are fighting to ensure their students have access to ideas about democracy, freedom of speech and self-image. Let's not go backward in fear.'[43] The ALA and the Freedom to Read Foundation issued a joint statement: 'The CPS directive to remove this book from the hands of students represents a heavy-handed denial of students' rights to access information, and smacks of censorship. Censorship results in the opposite of true education and learning.'[44]

Chicago Public Schools' curricular decision did not just 'smack of censorship'. It was censorship—but censorship is inevitably part of curriculum management. School boards are expected to make informed judgements about the age appropriateness and educational suitability of reading materials when they compile curricula, which necessarily involves judgements about the potential effects of the material on children. Parties may disagree about those judgements—the ALA may think that *Persepolis* is suitable for twelve-year-olds, and CPS may think it is not. CPS's decision may well be over-cautious or misguided, yet if the responsibility for making judgements about school books were taken away from school boards, the result could be more widespread censorship. In recent years, legislators have developed new strategies that have the potential to undermine schools' control over what students read in classrooms.

In Virginia in 2016, House Bill 516 required teachers to notify parents of any course materials containing 'sexually explicit' content, and to provide children with alternative assignments if the parents objected.[45] The bill became known as the 'Beloved Bill', because those who proposed and supported it cited Toni Morrison's novel

Beloved as the kind of book parents should be able to prevent their children reading in school. One parent had complained to her son's school board when he was required to read *Beloved* for his Advanced Placement English Literature class. When the school did not remove *Beloved* from the reading list, she lobbied the Virginia Board of Education and state legislators to allow parents to opt their children out of sexually explicit assigned reading, in the same way that Virginia parents are allowed to remove their children from sex education classes.[46] *Beloved*, which won the Pulitzer Prize in 1988, is a historical novel set before the abolition of slavery in the United States. It tells the story of Sethe, a formerly enslaved woman who kills her child, Beloved, in order to save her from enslavement. The ghost of Beloved, or a being who pretends to be her, returns to live with Sethe, forcing her community to confront memories of slavery they would rather suppress. *Beloved* imaginatively remembers an African American history that has been denied, forgotten, and written out of the historical record. Its depictions of psychological, sexual, and physical violence recall the brutality of slaveholders and the suffering of enslaved people.[47] But many of those who promoted the Beloved Bill were uninterested in the purpose of sexual violence in a book about slavery, and *Beloved*'s most vocal opponents would not admit any justification for its sexual content. In an email exchange with his constituent Jessica Berg, a teacher who was dismayed that legislators were condemning the book based on passages they had taken out of context, Senator Richard H. Black insisted that 'slavery was a terrible stain on this nation but to teach it does not mean you have to expose children to smut'. He vilified the novel:

> That book is so vile—so profoundly filthy—that when a Senator rose on the Senate Floor and began reading a single passage, several other Senators leapt to their feet to interrupt the reading. Susan Schaar, the Senate Clerk, quickly had embarrassed Senate Officials rush the teenage Senate Pages from the Senate Floor in order to protect them from exposure to this moral sewage.[48]

Speaking in the Senate Public Education Committee, Senator Charles Carrico shared a parable: 'Evil is just—when you plant the seed, it's a kitten. You feed it, it becomes a lion and it eats you.'[49] Other supporters of the Beloved Bill acknowledged the book's literary merit, but saw it as unsuitable for children. Legislators were adamant that the bill was not an attempt to ban books, only to enshrine parental rights in state law.[50] They dismissed the concerns of librarians and teachers, who argued that the bill set teachers an impossible task: to guess what material parents would consider 'sexually explicit'. Opponents of the Beloved Bill were concerned that it would inevitably lead to self-censorship by teachers and the deselection of books on the basis of isolated passages and the objections of individuals.[51] The opponents of the bill failed to move the legislature, but Virginia Governor Terry McAuliffe was more sympathetic. He was critical of the idea that an artistic work could be labelled 'sexually explicit' based on a single scene taken out of context. And school boards in Virginia, he pointed out, already worked with parents to address their concerns.[52] As of 2013, 48 per cent of Virginia schools gave parents advance notice of 'potentially sensitive or controversial material' in classrooms.[53] McAuliffe thought the bill was unnecessary, and used his governor's veto.[54] The Beloved Bill is dead, for now, though its supporters have said that they will reintroduce the bill if the state school board does not adopt it as a state-wide policy.[55] Even if it is not enshrined in state law or education policy, many Virginia schools will continue to offer parents the chance to opt their children out of assigned reading, and some teachers will choose unobjectionable texts in order to avoid disputes.

Legislators in Arizona have developed a law that enables the State Superintendent of Public Instruction to interfere with curriculum design. In 2010 the House of Representatives passed House Bill 2281, prohibiting schools from teaching courses that 'Promote the overthrow of the United States government', 'Promote resentment against a race or class of people', 'Are designed primarily for pupils of a particular ethnic group', or 'Advocate ethnic solidarity instead of the treatment of pupils as individuals'.[56] The law, which we discuss in Chapter 25, targeted the Mexican American Studies Department at Tucson Unified School District. Under the threat of losing funding, the school board withdrew textbooks and shut down the programme.

Such blanket prohibitions, made at the legislative level, have the potential to produce more widespread, indiscriminate, and partisan forms of censorship than the more common practice of school boards making judgements about the educational suitability of particular books. These judgements will always have the potential for controversy, because there will never be consensus about what limitations on children's reading are acceptable. Somebody who believes that the images in *Persepolis* are appropriate for twelve-year-old students will be likely to draw a line at some other image, or some other age. The question is who gets to draw the lines. For now, school boards exercise their discretion, subject to their own policies and the Constitution, overseen by the courts. The ALA and other intellectual freedom organizations will continue to champion students' freedom to read and lobby against censorship decisions that they perceive to threaten that freedom. Their activism keeps censorship in the public eye, encouraging vigilance and awareness of the constitutional implications of book removals. The database of bans and challenges will continue to grow, but not all challenges will become bans, and not all bans will survive popular outcry or judicial review. The constitutional threshold for removing books from libraries remains higher than the threshold for removing books from curricula. *Persepolis*, 'freed', is read in the libraries of Chicago schools and in some classrooms.

Notes

1. Lolly Bowean and Kim Geiger, 'CPS Students Were Driving Force in Protest against Book Ban', *Chicago Tribune*, 15 March 2013, https://web.archive. org/web/20161229122155/http://articles.chicagotribune.com/2013-03-15/news/ct-met-persepolis-book-students-0317-20130317_1_cps-students-executive-officer-barbara-byrd-bennett-graphic-novel, accessed 29 December 2016; National Coalition Against Censorship, 'Chicago Public Schools Demands *Persepolis* Be Removed from Classrooms', Blogging Censorship, https://ncacblog.wordpress.com/2013/03/18/chicago-public-schools-demands-persepolis-be-removed-from-classrooms, accessed 31 December 2016; Patty Wetli, '*Persepolis* Ban Protest Earns Lane Tech Intellectual Freedom Award', DNAInfo, 1 November 2013, https://www.dnainfo.com/chicago/20131101/roscoe-village/persepolis-ban-protest-earns-lane-tech-intellectual-freedom-award, accessed 31 December 2016.
2. Ellyn Fortino, 'Lane Tech Students Hold Morning Sit-In to Protest *Persepolis* Ban', *Progress Illinois*, 18 March 2013, http://progressillinois.com/quick-hits/content/2013/03/18/lane-tech-students-hold-morning-sit-protest-persepolis-book-ban, accessed 31 December 2016.

3. Noreen S. Ahmed-Ullah, 'CPS Order to Pull Graphic Novel Sparks Protests, Outrage', *Chicago Tribune*, 16 March 2013, http://webcache. googleusercontent.com/search?q=cache:i_X50Sy5y1kJ:articles. chicagotribune.com/2013-03-16/news/ct-met-persepolis-book-schools-2-20130316_1_graphic-novel-book-barbara-byrd-bennett+& cd=1&hl=en&ct=clnk&gl=uk, accessed 31 December 2016; Bowean and Geiger.

4. Bowean and Geiger. See also Office for Intellectual Freedom, American Library Association, 'Chicago, Illinois', *Newsletter on Intellectual Freedom*, 62.3 (May 2013), 103–4.

5. Eric Zorn, 'CPS Mishandles *Persepolis* Ban', *Chicago Tribune*, 20 March 2013, http://articles.chicagotribune.com/2013-03-20/news/ct-oped-0320-zorn-20130320_1_persepolis-graphic-novel-school-libraries, accessed 31 December 2016.

6. Barbara Byrd-Bennett, 'Message from CEO regarding *Persepolis*', 15 March 2013, http://cps.edu/News/Announcements/Pages/3_15_2013_PR1. aspx, accessed 31 December 2016.

7. Wetli.

8. Assessment and Qualifications Alliance, 'Exam Results Statistics—June 2009: GCSE Full Course', http://store.aqa.org.uk/over/stat_pdf/AQA-GCSE-FC-STATS-JUNE09.PDF, accessed 31 December 2016.

9. Michael Shaw, 'Board Ditches Knife Poem', *Times Educational Supplement*, 5 September 2008, p. 7.

10. Assessment and Qualifications Alliance, *Anthology: English and English Literature* (Oxford: Oxford University Press, 2002; repr. 2008), p. 37. See also Assessment and Qualifications Alliance, *Anthology: English and English Literature* (Oxford: Oxford University Press, 2002; repr. 2005), p. 37.

11. Esther Addley, 'Poet's Rhyming Riposte Leaves Mrs Schofield "Gob-smacked"', *Guardian*, 6 September 2008, https://www.theguardian. com/education/2008/sep/06/gcses.poetry.carol.ann.duffy, accessed 31 December 2016; Polly Curtis, 'Top Exam Board Asks Schools to Destroy Book Containing Knife Poem', *Guardian*, 4 September 2008, https:// www.theguardian.com/education/2008/sep/04/gcses.english, accessed 31 December 2016; 'GCSE Poem Dropped over Knife Fear', BBC News, 3 September 2008, http://news.bbc.co.uk/1/hi/education/7594566. stm, accessed 31 December 2016.

12. American Library Association, 'Banned Books Week', http://www.ala.org/ bbooks/banned, accessed 27 February 2017; American Library Association, 'Frequently Challenged Books', http://www.ala.org/bbooks/frequent lychallengedbooks, accessed 31 December 2016.

13. American Library Association, 'Challenge Support', http://www.ala.org/tools/challengesupport, accessed 27 February 2017.

14. American Library Association, 'Top Ten Most Frequently Challenged Books Lists', http://www.ala.org/bbooks/frequentlychallengedbooks/top10, accessed 27 February 2017.

15. *The State of America's Libraries: A Report from the American Library Association 2015*, ed. Kathy Rosa, http://www.ala.org/news/sites/ala.org.news/files/content/0415_StateAmLib_0.pdf, accessed 31 December 2016, p. 3.

16. James LaRue, 'Defining Diversity', http://www.ala.org/bbooks/diversity, accessed 31 December 2016.

17. Office for Intellectual Freedom, American Library Association, 'Success Stories', *Newsletter on Intellectual Freedom*, 63.6 (2014), 171–72 (p. 171).

18. American Library Association, 'Infographics', http://www.ala.org/bbooks/frequentlychallengedbooks/statistics, accessed 31 December 2016.

19. Emily Knox, '"The Books Will Still Be in the Library": Narrow Definitions of Censorship in the Discourse of Challengers', *Library Trends*, 62.4 (2014), 740–49 (p. 740).

20. Emily J. M. Knox, *Book-Banning in 21st-Century America* (Lanham, MD: Rowman & Littlefield, 2015), pp. 11–12, 65–91.

21. Knox, '"The Books Will Still Be in the Library"', pp. 743–49.

22. Herbert N. Foerstel, *Banned in the U.S.A.: A Reference Guide to Book Censorship in Schools and Public Libraries* (Westport, CT: Greenwood, 1994), pp. 11–16, 90–100. See also Office for Intellectual Freedom of the American Library Association, *Intellectual Freedom Manual*, 8th edn (Chicago: American Library Association, 2010), pp. 351–56.

23. Bd. of Educ., Island Trees Union Free Sch. Dist. No. 26 v. Pico, 457 U.S. 853, 867, 870 (plurality opinion). See also Office for Intellectual Freedom of the American Library Association, pp. xix, 337, 341, 351, 362.

24. Campbell v. St. Tammany Par. Sch. Bd., 64 F.3d 184 (5th Cir. 1995).

25. Case v. Unified Sch. Dist. No. 233, 908 F. Supp. 864 (D. Kan. 1995).

26. Counts v. Cedarville Sch. Dist., 295 F. Supp. 2d 996, 1002–3 (W.D. Ark. 2003).

27. Hazelwood Sch. Dist. v. Kuhlmeier, 484 U.S. 260, 273 (1988); Virgil v. Sch. Bd., 862 F.2d 1517, 1518, 1525 (11th Cir. 1989).

28. Deborah Caldwell-Stone, 'Newly Revealed Records Detail 2013 Decision to Remove *Persepolis* from CPS Classrooms', Intellectual Freedom Blog: The Office for Intellectual Freedom of the American Library Association, 18 February 2015, http://www.oif.ala.org/oif/?p=5333,

accessed 31 December 2016. See also Ben Joravsky, 'How CPS Officials Decided to Pull *Persepolis* from the Classroom', *Chicago Reader*, 11 February 2015, http://www.chicagoreader.com/chicago/e-mails-show-cps-officials-pull-persepolis-classrooms/Content?oid=16355626, accessed 31 December 2016; Phil Morehart, 'Persepolis Rising: FOIA Request Reveals Depth of Graphic Novel's Banning', *American Libraries Magazine*, 18 February 2015, https://americanlibrariesmagazine.org/blogs/the-scoop/persepolis-rising, accessed 31 December 2016.

29. Chandra James to Annette Gurley, 9 March 2013, http://www.oif.ala.org/oif/wp-content/uploads/2015/02/CPS-FOIA-DocumentsDapierDec2014v2.pdf, accessed 31 December 2016.

30. Cynthia Slater-Green to Annette Gurley, 9 March 2013, http://www.oif.ala.org/oif/wp-content/uploads/2015/02/CPS-FOIA-DocumentsDapierDec2014v2.pdf, accessed 31 December 2016.

31. Annette Gurley to Denise Little, 10 March 2013, http://www.oif.ala.org/oif/wp-content/uploads/2015/02/CPS-FOIA-DocumentsDapierDec2014v2.pdf, accessed 31 December 2016.

32. Natalia Szymczak to Adrian Willis and others, 12 March 2013, http://www.oif.ala.org/oif/wp-content/uploads/2015/02/CPS-FOIA-DocumentsDapierDec2014v2.pdf, accessed 31 December 2016.

33. Marjane Satrapi, *Persepolis: The Story of a Childhood* (London: Cape, 2003), pp. 51–53, 74.

34. National Coalition Against Censorship and Freemuse, 'NCAC and FREEMUSE Universal Periodic Review Joint Submission', p. 4, http://ncac.org/resource/ncac-and-freemuse-form-universal-periodic-review-joint-submission, accessed 31 December 2016.

35. Leslie Boozer to Annette Gurley, 14 March 2013, http://www.oif.ala.org/oif/wp-content/uploads/2015/02/CPS-FOIA-DocumentsDapierDec2014v2.pdf, accessed 31 December 2016.

36. National Coalition Against Censorship and Freemuse, pp. 4–5.

37. Sarah McNicol, 'Freedom to Teach: Implications of the Removal of *Persepolis* from Chicago Schools', *Journal of Graphic Novels and Comics*, 6.1 (2015), 31–41 (p. 35).

38. Bowean and Geiger; National Coalition Against Censorship.

39. Kenzo Shibata (@KenzoShibata), '#FreePersepolis', Twitter, 15 March 2013; Pantheon Books, 'To Enlighten Me They Bought Books', Tumblr, 20 March 2013, http://pantheonbooks.tumblr.com/post/45839199028, accessed 1 January 2017.

40. Annette Gurley to Adrian Willis and others, 13 March 2013, http://www.oif.ala.org/oif/wp-content/uploads/2015/02/CPS-FOIA-DocumentsDapierDec2014v2.pdf, accessed 1 January 2017.

41. Chicago Public Schools, 'New Collection Development Policy for School Libraries', http://policy.cps.edu/download.aspx?ID=93, accessed 1 January 2017.

42. Byrd-Bennett.

43. CTU Communications, 'UPDATED! CTU Statement Regarding the Chicago Public Schools Sudden Ban of the Graphic Novel "Persepolis"', 15 March 2013, http://www.ctunet.com/blog/ctu-statement-regarding-the-chicago-public-schools-sudden-ban-of-the-graphic-novel-persepolis, accessed 1 January 2017.

44. Barbara Jones to Barbara Byrd-Bennett and others (15 March 2013), in Jonathan Kelley, '*Persepolis* Removed from Chicago Public Schools for "Graphic Illustrations and Language": OIF and FTRF Respond', 15 March 2013, Intellectual Freedom Blog, http://www.oif.ala.org/oif/?p=4651, accessed 1 January 2017.

45. H.B. 516, 2016 Gen. Assemb., Reg. Sess. (Va. 2016).

46. Jenna Portnoy, '"Beloved Bill" Goes to McAuliffe's Desk', *Washington Post*, 3 March 2016, https://www.washingtonpost.com/local/virginia-politics/beloved-bill-goes-to-mcauliffes-desk/2016/03/03/fbc11976-e167-11e5-9c36-e1902f6b6571_story.html?utm_term=.fe645339fd77, accessed 27 February 2017; Jenna Portnoy, 'In Virginia Classrooms, Should Parents Block Sexually Explicit Literature for their Kids?', *Washington Post*, 25 February 2016, https://www.washingtonpost.com/local/virginia-politics/in-virginia-classrooms-should-parents-block-sexually-explicit-literature/2016/02/25/fa5aa396-db67-11e5-81ae-7491b9b9e7df_story.html?utm_term=.8f154397db59, accessed 3 March 2017.

47. Toni Morrison, *Beloved* (London: Vintage Classic, 2007).

48. 'Email Exchange over Virginia's "Beloved" Bill', *Washington Post*, 6 April 2016, https://www.washingtonpost.com/news/local/wp/2016/04/06/email-exchange-over-virginias-beloved-bill/?tid=a_inl, accessed 1 January 2017.

49. Portnoy, 'In Virginia Classrooms'.

50. Travis Fain, 'Legislative Notebook: Sexually Explicit Books, Smoking, and Resumes', *Daily Press*, 4 March 2016, http://www.dailypress.com/news/politics/dp-nws-ga-legis-notebook-0304-20160303-story.html, accessed 1 January 2017; Portnoy, '"Beloved Bill" Goes to McAuliffe's Desk'.

51. Virginia Association of Teachers of English, 'Official Position on House Bill 516', http://vate.org/official-position-on-house-bill-516, accessed 1 January 2017; Virginia Library Association, 'VLA Statement on HB 516', http://www.vla.org/index.php?option=com_content&view=article&id=438:vla-statement-on-hb-516&catid=21:latest-news, accessed 1 January 2017.

52. '2016 Session (HB516) Governor's Veto', LIS: Virginia's Legislative Information System, https://lis.virginia.gov/cgi-bin/legp604.exe?161+amd+HB516AG, accessed 1 January 2017.

53. Linda M. Wallinger, 'Report on Options regarding Parental Notification Related to Controversial or Sensitive Materials', 25 July 2013, http://www.doe.virginia.gov/boe/meetings/2013/07_jul/agenda_items/item_g.pdf, accessed 1 January 2017.

54. '2016 Session (HB516) Governor's Veto'.

55. Jenna Portnoy, 'McAuliffe Vetoes Bill Permitting Parents to Block Sexually Explicit Books in Schools', *Washington Post*, 4 April 2016, https://www.washingtonpost.com/local/virginia-politics/mcauliffe-vetoes-bill-that-would-have-allowed-parents-to-block-sexually-explicit-books-in-school/2016/04/04/8b969316-fa75-11e5-886f-a037dba38301_story.html, accessed 1 January 2017.

56. Ariz. Rev. Stat. § 15-112 (2010).

25

Borderlands/La Frontera: The New Mestiza
Gloria Anzaldúa

In 2010 the Arizona state legislature passed House Bill 2281, designed to shut down Mexican American studies in Tucson schools. In January 2012, threatened with a 10 per cent funding penalty under the statute, the Tucson Unified School District (TUSD) eliminated its Mexican American Studies Department (MASD) and removed copies of seven books from classrooms: *Message to Aztlán* by Rodolfo (Corky) Gonzales, *Occupied America: A History of Chicanos* by Rodolfo Acuña, *Pedagogy of the Oppressed* by Paulo Freire, *Critical Race Theory: An Introduction* by Richard Delgado and Jean Stefancic, *Chicano! The History of the Mexican American Civil Rights Movement* by F. Arturo Rosales, *Rethinking Columbus: The Next 500 Years*, edited by Bill Bigelow and Bob Peterson, and *500 Años del Pueblo Chicano/500 Years of Chicano History in Pictures*, edited by Elizabeth Martinez.[1] Many more books that had been on reading lists for the programme, including Matt de la Peña's *Mexican WhiteBoy* and Gloria Anzaldúa's *Borderlands/La Frontera: The New Mestiza*, simply ceased to be part of the curriculum with the dissolution of the courses.[2] Although the school board vehemently denied that any books were 'banned', an act of state censorship had dismantled the framework in which they were being taught, and only those that went through an approval process could be taught in other courses.[3] Journalist Roque Planas reported on 19 April 2012 that the

Student Mayra Feliciano on 26 April 2011, when she and eight other members of UNIDOS took control of a TUSD board meeting. She holds an image of Cesar Chavez, co-founder (with Dolores Huerta) of the United Farm Workers.

approved list contained 'very few works of Latino literature approved for high school classroom use'.[4] In contrast, most of the students were Latino or Latina: in 2011, 60 per cent of TUSD students and 90 per cent of those enrolled in MASD classes belonged to this ethnic group.[5] Mexican American studies courses tackled the effects of social inequality, improving the academic achievement of the students who took them, who were more likely to be English-language learners and to come from families with lower incomes.[6] Republican politicians, however, targeted the department as racist and seditious. Tom Horne, Arizona State Superintendent of Public Instruction, claimed that teachers were promoting 'ethnic chauvinism' and advancing a 'radical separatist agenda'.[7]

The struggle to teach Mexican American studies was, in large part, a struggle to challenge the conventional history of the United States, with its focus on Anglo-European culture and the heroic figures of the founding fathers. A more critical history recognizes the malignancy of European colonization of the Americas, including the deaths of tens of millions of indigenous people and the implementation of slavery, and exposes the opportunity gaps that continue to divide US society. Though it was only one of the books on the MAS reading list, Gloria Anzaldúa's *Borderlands/La Frontera*, originally written in 1987, offers a resistant history of the land that is now called Mexico and the United States, along with personal reflection and poetry. A Chicana who embraced her Mexican heritage and its indigenous elements, Anzaldúa was sceptical of dominant values in both Anglo-American and Mexican cultures. In *Borderlands/La Frontera*, she opposes the subjection of women to men and of some languages to others—Tex-Mex to Mexican Spanish, all kinds of Spanish to English. Describing the economic exploitation of Mexico by US corporations, she characterizes the migration of Mexican people to the north in search of better opportunity as 'the return odyssey to the historical/mythological Aztlán',[8] 'Aztlán' meaning several things, including a mythical place, the homeland of the Aztecs, and the territory that was once part of Mexico before the United States gained about half of it through the annexation of Texas and the Treaty of Guadalupe Hidalgo, which ended the US–Mexican War. For Anzaldúa, the 'borderlands' of Mexico and the

United States are a metaphor for her own mixed identity and for the relations between different groups:

> The struggle is inner: Chicano, *indio*, American Indian, *mojado*, *mexicano*, immigrant Latino, Anglo in power, working class Anglo, Black, Asian—our psyches resemble the bordertowns and are populated by the same people. The struggle has always been inner, and is played out in the outer terrains. Awareness of our situation must come before inner changes, which in turn come before changes in society. Nothing happens in the 'real' world unless it first happens in the images in our heads.[9]

Similarly, Mexican American studies in Tucson encouraged students to understand their situation and to use their knowledge to effect social change. José Gonzalez, one of the teachers in the programme, explains in the documentary *Precious Knowledge* that his course on American government and social justice 'is based on critical thinking. Students are often taught to read the word, and, Paulo Freire said, you have to teach students to read the world. And in order to make change, you have to look at the structure, the institution.'[10]

In their attacks on Mexican American studies, Republican politicians tried to reassert control over the images in students' heads. Arguing in support of HB 2281 in a meeting of the Arizona State Senate Education Accountability and Reform Committee, Senator Sylvia Allen claimed MAS was teaching students to take history 'personally', and then veered into a defence of the founding fathers' use of slave labour. For Senator John Huppenthal, history education involved celebrating 'heroes from different ethnic groups' and promoting 'basic American values of the melting pot'. Senator Linda Lopez, Democrat, pointed out that the ostensible heroes of the past were 'human beings' who had 'failings', and argued that the nation was more like a tapestry than a melting pot. In the committee meeting and elsewhere, Huppenthal attempted to illustrate the unacceptability of the MAS programme with the anecdote of a teacher who described Benjamin Franklin as a racist.[11] (At least a portion of this incident is documented in *Precious Knowledge*. During a classroom visit, Huppenthal objects to the presence of Che Guevara's image and the absence of

Franklin's among the many posters displayed in the room. MAS co-founder Augustine Romero responds by paraphrasing Franklin's own words, in which he suggests 'excluding all Blacks and Tawneys' from the United States rather than 'darken its People'.[12])

The political campaign against Mexican American studies began in 2006. At the Tucson High Magnet School, Dolores Huerta, labour activist and co-founder of the United Farm Workers, gave a talk during which she said that 'Republicans hate Latinos'. This sound bite made the news, and there were reports that a Republican student, who had taken offence, was prevented from leaving the assembly.[13] In response, the Superintendent of Public Instruction, Tom Horne, sent his associate superintendent Margaret Garcia Dugan to speak at the school. She would not be taking questions. At the assembly, a group of students stood in silent protest. Some raised their fists. Some wore tape over their mouths. Some wore shirts with slogans such as 'You can silence my voice but never my spirit' and 'Prop 203 is anti-Latino'.[14] Proposition 203, passed in 2000, prohibited bilingual education in schools. Horne had leveraged popular support for this policy in his election campaign, and appointed Dugan to oversee enforcement of the law. She was a chairperson of English for the Children, the organization that led the push for anti-bilingual legislation in California and Arizona,[15] and she defended her stance on the issue during her address to the students.[16] Though Dugan spoke as a Republican and a Latina, the protesters understood what Huerta meant: 'Republicans hate Latinos' was a condemnation of Republican policy, including the English-only policy that Dugan was responsible for upholding. The student organization Movimiento Estudiantil Chicanx de Aztlán (MEChA) told the press, 'We believe that the Republican agenda is ANTI-LATINO!' One of the student protesters, a member of MEChA, said, 'I believe that we did get our message through, that these bills are focused on us.'[17]

The Tucson incident was not isolated: in 2006 mass protests were held nationwide against Republican-sponsored immigration legislation, especially federal HB 4437, the Border Protection, Anti-terrorism, and Illegal Immigration Control Act of 2005, which failed in the Senate. In Arizona, ballot measures made English the state's official language and cut off financial assistance to undocumented immigrants for adult education, higher education, and childcare.[18]

Horne had a 'long history of opposing ethnic studies and gender studies', and claimed to have blocked a women's studies programme at a high school in Paradise Valley, where he had served on a school board.[19] He would later refer to his efforts to shut down the MASD as a 'crusade'.[20] In response to the Tucson High protest, he published 'An Open Letter to the Citizens of Tucson', in which he called for the termination of the TUSD's ethnic studies programmes,[21] which also included Native American studies, African American studies, and Pan Asian studies.[22] He described the Tucson High assembly as an 'unhappy case' that demonstrated the students' 'defiance of authority' and 'rudeness', which he was sure they had not learned 'at home, but from their Raza teachers'. (The MAS programme was also known as *Raza* studies, the term '*La Raza*' designating Mexican Americans.) Horne cited former and current TUSD teachers who claimed to have been intimidated or accused of racism by school administrators and ethnic studies staff.[23]

Horne objected in particular to the texts *Pedagogy of the Oppressed*, *Occupied America*, and *The Mexican American Heritage*, which he thought misrepresented history and were, in effect, anti-American. He wrote, 'Those students should be taught that this *is* the land of opportunity, and that if they work hard they can achieve their goals. They should not be taught that they are oppressed.'[24] (In media appearances, he and other politicians tapped into anti-communist sentiment by emphasizing the Marxist perspective of Brazilian educator Paulo Freire, author of *Pedagogy of the Oppressed*.[25]) Under the heading 'Teaching the Wrong Things About Literature', Horne quoted from a letter that an ethnic studies student had written to him, which said, 'All that the English classes teach is mainly about some dead white people.' Horne wrote, 'I believe schools should teach the students to judge literature by its content and not by the race or gender of the author.'[26]

The touchstone for his philosophy, the superintendent explained, was Martin Luther King Jr.'s famous statement, 'I have a dream my four little children will one day live in a nation where they will not be judged by the color of their skin but by the content of their character.'[27] Horne had participated in the March on Washington in 1963, and he turned King's speech into a slogan in the campaign against MAS.[28] Yet a student who complains that there is too much content about 'dead white people' in an English literature class is not 'judging' those books or the people who wrote them. Rather, the student is questioning the process of selection that led to such a homogeneous list of books. (For examples of how gender and race have influenced what books get written, remembered, celebrated, and taught, see Chapters 3 and 5.) King did not pretend to be unable to see race, and he did not believe that Black people could obtain civil rights simply by being polite, respecting authority, or naïvely trusting the American Dream. His 'Letter from Birmingham City Jail', in which he defends civil disobedience and direct action, provides a more complex view of his position:

> I have almost reached the regrettable conclusion that the Negro's great stumbling block in the stride toward freedom is not the White Citizen's Counciler or the Ku Klux Klanner, but the white moderate who is more devoted to 'order' than to justice; who prefers a negative peace which is the absence of tension to a positive peace which is the presence of justice; who constantly says, 'I agree with you in the goal you seek, but I can't agree with your methods of direct action'; who paternalistically feels that he can set the timetable for another man's freedom; who lives by the myth of time and who constantly advised the Negro to wait until a 'more convenient season'.[29]

Quoting King's dream of an equitable world while trying to stamp out a programme that inspires students to engage in political protest is, at the very least, incoherent.

When the electorate did not bring about the change Horne desired, he and other politicians attempted to legislate it. In 2008 Senator Russell K. Pearce, Republican, introduced an amendment to a homeland security bill that would have prohibited schools from challenging 'the values of American democracy and western civilization, including democracy, capitalism, pluralism and religious toleration'.[30] The amendment would also have applied to public universities. This bill did not pass, and a second attempt in 2009 did not make it to a vote. In 2010 Representative Steve Montenegro, Republican, introduced HB 2281. This version was more carefully targeted than the 2008 measure, and it succeeded.[31]

HB 2281 asserted 'that public school pupils should be taught to treat and value each other as individuals and not be taught to resent or hate other races or classes of people'.[32] It prohibited courses or classes that:

1. Promote the overthrow of the United States government.
2. Promote resentment toward a race or class of people.
3. Are designed primarily for pupils of a particular ethnic group.
4. Advocate ethnic solidarity instead of the treatment of pupils as individuals.[33]

The bill applied to public school districts and charter schools. The State Superintendent of Public Instruction (still Tom Horne) would have the authority to determine if a school board was in violation and to apply a penalty of 10 per cent of the district's funding. Some explicit qualifications limited the bill's scope. The bill would not prohibit 'Courses or classes that include the history of any ethnic group and that are open to all students' as long as they complied with the four provisions. It would not restrict federally mandated courses for Native American students, '[c]ourses or classes that include the discussion of controversial aspects of history', or 'the instruction of the holocaust [sic], any other instance of genocide, or the historical oppression of a particular group of people based on ethnicity, race, or class'.[34] It was clear in legislative debates that the bill was designed specifically to deal with the MASD. It passed in the House and the Senate, with votes dividing almost entirely along party lines. Weeks after signing Arizona's controversial immigration enforcement bill, SB 1070, Governor Jan Brewer signed HB 2281 into law.[35] Its key components became sections 15-111 and 15-112 of the Arizona Revised Statutes. The next day, at least one hundred and fifty people protested at the state building, where Horne was holding a press conference. Fifteen of the protesters, including MAS students and teachers, held a sit-in, and were arrested for trespassing.[36]

There had been an election campaign underway during the HB 2281 debates, and Horne was elected state Attorney General. On his campaign website he posted a video in which he talked about fighting to 'put a stop to' *Raza* studies, and promised, 'as the attorney general, I will give the legal aid to the Department of Education to be sure that we do put a stop to it'.[37] On 30 December, Horne's last day as superintendent, which was the day before HB 2281 came into effect, he issued a finding that the TUSD was in violation of the statute.[38] This finding was largely symbolic, because it would be up to the new Superintendent of Public Instruction to make his own.

Horne's successor as superintendent was John Huppenthal, formerly Senator, who had run a campaign ad on the radio claiming that he would 'Stop *La Raza*', a slogan that was perhaps intended to apply specifically to *Raza* studies but that effectively means 'Stop the Mexican American people'.[39] Huppenthal's practice of posting inflammatory comments on blogs under pseudonyms would be exposed, to his chagrin, in 2014.[40] For instance, in December 2010, shortly before taking office as superintendent, Huppenthal posted as 'Falcon9', 'We all need to stomp out balkanization. No spanish radio stations, no spanish billboards, no spanish tv stations, no spanish newspapers. This is America, speak English.'[41] (Anzaldúa: 'So, if you want to really hurt me, talk badly about my language. Ethnic identity is twin skin to linguistic identity—I am my language.'[42]) In May 2011, reflecting on the effects of the Arizona Employer Sanctions Law, which permitted employers to be penalized for hiring undocumented workers, he wrote, 'We have a whole lot fewer caucasians working now that the hispanics have left. But, crime is much lower. No money and no one is stealing it.'[43]

Huppenthal supported Horne's finding, but attempted to substantiate it further by commissioning a curriculum audit of the MASD from a private firm, Cambium Learning. Cambium's assessment of the programme turned out to be different from his. Despite doubts about the educational suitability of some of the textbooks, the term *Raza* studies, and 'tones of personal activism and bias' in curriculum documents—including criticism of SB 1070 and HB 2281—the auditors concluded that there was no evidence that TUSD was in violation of the law. They observed the teaching of an inclusive ethics that revolved around the Mayan concept *In Lak'ech* as expressed in a poem by Luis Valdez: 'You are my other me. If I do harm to you, I do harm to me. If I love and respect you, I love and respect myself.' Moreover, the auditors found that the programme was closing the 'achievement gap' between students of different races, ethnicities, and socioeconomic classes.[44]

While Huppenthal's finding was pending, TUSD board president Mark Stegeman pre-emptively moved to downgrade MAS courses into electives, which would have meant that students could no longer take them as alternatives to non-MAS courses in the same subjects. On 26 April 2011, when the board was scheduled to vote on Stegeman's resolution, nine members of United Non-Discriminatory Individuals Demanding Our Studies (UNIDOS), a student activist group formed in response to the anti-ethnic studies bill, chained themselves to the board members' chairs, and shouted, 'Our education is under attack! What do we do? Fight back!' Other community protesters entered the room, and the meeting did not take place.[45] At the next meeting, on 3 May, most of the hundreds of attendees were forced to stand outside the building, where the proceedings were broadcast by loudspeaker.[46] Local pastors made a statement to the press and held a vigil nearby in support of MAS.[47] The TUSD's School Safety Department had requested that the Tucson Police Department provide security, and police presence was heavy: approximately one hundred and fifty to two hundred officers were deployed, some in riot gear, with helicopter support.[48] Inside the meeting room, thirty minutes were allotted for community members to speak, at three minutes per person.[49] Seven women continued to defend MAS and to indict the board after the end of the designated time, and, apparently at the direction of TUSD superintendent John Pedicone, police arrested them.[50] One of these women was sixty-nine-year-old Chicana activist and professor Lupe Castillo, who attempted to read out Martin Luther King Jr.'s 'Letter from Birmingham Jail', saying, 'This is what you need to hear!' Students in shirts that read 'You can silence my voice but never my spirit', some with tape over their mouths, reprised the 2006 Tucson High Magnet School protest.[51] Outside, police had erected barriers to keep the crowd away from the doors to the building. Video footage records officers using force against protesters, and injuries were reported.[52] Stegeman's proposal was deferred.[53]

On 15 June 2011, rejecting the conclusions of the Cambium audit, Huppenthal issued a finding that the MASD had violated subsections 2, 3, and 4 of 15-112(a), based on evidence discussed in the audit and on further materials gathered by the Department of Education. (He did not find that any courses were advocating the overthrow of the US government.) Huppenthal gave the TUSD board sixty days' notice that he would be withholding 10 per cent of the district's funding if they did not comply with the statute.[54] Two groups challenged this decision in two different ways. The TUSD board appealed Huppenthal's finding to an administrative law judge, and a group of MAS teachers complained to the courts, which would examine whether section 15-112 and its use against the MASD were constitutional. In December the administrative law judge supported Huppenthal's finding in a non-binding decision that cited a variety of decontextualized passages from MAS materials, including a student essay that was critical of SB 1070 and the Treaty of Guadalupe Hidalgo.[55] On 10 January 2012 the TUSD board terminated the programme. The seven books listed above were removed from classrooms, and teachers were no longer permitted to teach the curriculum.[56]

For two weeks, hundreds of students walked out of classes in protest. UNIDOS organized an event called the School of Ethnic Studies, which included music, poetry readings, and lectures by University of Arizona professors on the proscribed material. In one breakout session at the School of Ethnic Studies, participants wrote their own poems after reading and discussing Anzaldúa's 'To live in the Borderlands means you', which ends:

> To survive the Borderlands
>   you must live *sin fronteras*
>   be a crossroads.[57]

In Texas, author Tony Diaz and others formed a group called the *Librotraficantes* (book smugglers), who drove a bus containing books from the MAS reading lists from San Antonio to Tucson, donating copies along the way.[58] MAS teacher Curtis Acosta carried on his work outside the classroom through a programme that he offered at a youth centre on Sundays.[59] He resigned from the TUSD after attempting to teach under the new restrictions. He said, 'They took away everything; we were banned from our own curriculum, our intellect, our own selves. It was dehumanizing.'[60]

The teachers' legal complaint, which proceeded under the name of Maya Arce, daughter of MAS co-founder Sean Arce, still offered hope. MAS had been found to be in violation of section 15-112—but what if that statute, or the use of it against MAS, were unconstitutional? Judge A. Wallace Tashima struck down only subsection 3 of the statute, the prohibition on courses designed primarily for a particular ethnic group, which he found overbroad, and the Court of Appeals for the Ninth Circuit affirmed this ruling. With respect to the application of the statute, however, the appeals court noted that 'the legislative history of § 15-112 and the sequence of events (including the administrative history) leading to its enactment reasonably suggest an intent to discriminate'. The court mentioned several red flags, including Horne's use of the original 2006 Tucson High protest in arguments for HB 2281, Huppenthal's 'Stop *La Raza*' radio ad, and his rejection of the Cambium report. Judge Tashima had made an error that meant the plaintiffs did not have a full opportunity to present their evidence that those responsible for the statute were motivated by 'discriminatory intent' or 'racial animus'. Therefore, the court ruled, there would have to be a trial to determine whether section 15-112 had been applied in a discriminatory way.[61] This trial is due to occur in 2017 on 26-30 June and 17-21 July.[62]

The *Atlantic* reported in 2015 that the elimination of MAS in Arizona inspired teacher Jose Lara and *Librotraficante* Tony Diaz to introduce ethnic studies in California and Texas.[63] Several of the MAS teachers, Curtis Acosta, Norma Gonzalez, José Gonzalez, and Sean Arce, are now associated with the Xicanx Institute for Teaching and Organizing, which offers consulting on topics that include ethnic studies implementation.[64] As of the time of our writing, the Mexican American Studies Department is gone, but the TUSD board has been forced to design a replacement as a consequence of a lawsuit that goes back to 1974. The original settlement with the plaintiffs required that the TUSD correct the effects of the school segregation to which both Black and Mexican American students had been subjected. In 2011 a judge found that the district had not made a good faith effort to comply with its federal desegregation order, noting that it was receiving millions of dollars in tax money for the purpose of desegregation.[65] The courts appointed an expert to oversee a new plan for the TUSD to eliminate residual segregation, which included 'culturally relevant courses of instruction designed to reflect the history, experiences, and culture of African American and Mexican American communities'.[66] In 2013 the TUSD board officially approved the seven books they had removed from classrooms for use as supplementary materials in all classes, including culturally relevant ones.[67] Having lost a Republican primary election in 2014,[68] on his last day as superintendent, 2 January 2015, Huppenthal wielded section 15-112 one more time, singling out culturally relevant courses for promoting racial resentment and the overthrow of the government and advocating ethnic solidarity instead of treating students as individuals. His evidence included an essay prompt about the effects of European colonization on indigenous peoples, the continued use of *In Lak'ech*, the song 'Take the Power Back' by Rage Against the Machine, and 'An Introduction to Hip Hop Presented by Master Teacher, KRS-One'.[69]

Notes

1. 'Reports of TUSD Book Ban Completely False and Misleading', Tucson Unified School District, 17 January 2012, http://www.tusd.k12.az.us/contents/news/press1112/01-17-12.html, accessed 31 January 2017.
2. Teri Casteel and others, *Curriculum Audit of the Mexican American Studies Department, Tucson Unified School District*, Cambium Learning Inc. in Collaboration with National Academic Educational Partnership, 2 May 2011, pp. 116–20.
3. 'Reports of TUSD Book Ban Completely False and Misleading'.
4. Roque Planas, 'Neither Banned nor Allowed: Mexican American Studies in Limbo in Arizona', Fox News, 19 April 2012, http://www.foxnews.com/world/2012/04/19/neither-banned-nor-allowed-mexican-american-studies-in-limbo-in-arizona.html, accessed 5 March 2017.
5. Casteel and others, pp. 5, 6.
6. Nolan L. Cabrera and others, 'Missing the (Student Achievement) Forest for All the (Political) Trees: Empiricism and the Mexican American Studies Controversy in Tucson', *American Education Research Journal*, 51.6 (2014), 1084–118 (pp. 1101, 1107).

7. Tom Horne, 'An Open Letter to the Citizens of Tucson', State of Arizona Department of Education, 11 June 2007, p. 2, http://web. archive.org/web/20101122020444/http://electtomhorne.com/ open_letter_01.pdf, accessed 31 January 2017, also repr. in Valerie Strauss, 'Why Arizona Targeted Ethnic Studies', *Washington Post*, 25 May 2010, http://voices.washingtonpost.com/answer-sheet/ civics-education/why-arizona-targeted-ethnic-st.html, accessed 31 January 2017; 'Latest Plan to Plug Gulf Oil Leak? Arizona Culture Clash', CNN, 12 May 2010 (transcript), http://transcripts.cnn.com/ TRANSCRIPTS/1005/12/acd.01.html, accessed 31 January 2017. See also Ray Stern, 'Tom Horne Struggles in CNN Debate on Latino Studies with Georgetown Prof Michael Dyson', *Phoenix New Times*, 13 May 2010, http://www.phoenixnewtimes.com/news/tom-horne-struggles-in-cnn-debate-on-latino-studies-with-georgetown-prof-michael-dyson-6628701, accessed 31 January 2017.

8. Gloria Anzaldúa, *Borderlands/La Frontera: The New Mestiza*, 2nd edn (San Francisco: Aunt Lute Books, 1999), p. 33.

9. Anzaldúa, p. 109.

10. *Precious Knowledge*, dir. Ari Luis Palos (Dos Vatos, 2011).

11. *Hearing on HB 2281 Before S. Ed. Accountability and Reform Comm.*, 49th Leg., 2d Reg. Sess. (Ariz. 2010), http://azleg.granicus.com/Media-Player.php?view_id=13&clip_id=7405, accessed 16 January 2017.

12. Benjamin Franklin, 'Observations concerning the Increase of Mankind', in *Autobiography and Other Writings*, ed. Ormond Seavey (Oxford: Oxford University Press, 1993), pp. 251–60 (p. 260).

13. Eric Sagara, '"Hate-Speak" at School Draws Scrutiny', *Tucson Citizen*, 13 April 2006, http://tucsoncitizen.com/morgue/2006/04/13/9256-hate-speak-at-school-draws-scrutiny, accessed 31 January 2017.

14. Jeff Commings, 'Silent Protest by Students Greets State Official's Speech', *Arizona Daily Star*, 13 May 2006, http://tucson.com/news/ local/education/precollegiate/silent-protest-by-students-greets-state-official-s-speech/article_0132cca7-c8a3-53f6-b001-883fa0ca86a0. html, accessed 31 January 2017; Eric Sagara, '"Equal-Time" Talk Fuels Protest', *Tucson Citizen*, 13 May 2006, http://tucsoncitizen.com/ morgue/2006/05/13/12461-cqual-time-talk-fuels-protest, accessed 31 January 2017.

15. Wayne E. Wright, 'Proposition 203 (Arizona)', in *Encyclopedia of Bilingual Education*, ed. Josué M. González, 2 vols (Los Angeles: SAGE, 2008), II, 684–88 (pp. 686–87).

16. Margaret Garcia Dugan, 'Full Text of Dugan's Speech', http://tucson. com/news/full-text-of-dugan-s-speech/article_e7b06f08-d7eb-593a-9aea-c2d69ba6f757.html, accessed 31 January 2017.

17. Commings; Sagara, '"Equal-Time" Talk Fuels Protest'.

18. Anna Ochoa O'Leary and others, 'Assault on Ethnic Studies', in *Arizona Firestorm: Global Immigration Realities, National Media, and Provincial Politics*, ed. Otto Santa Ana and Celeste González de Bustamante (Lanham, MD: Rowman & Littlefield, 2012), pp. 97–120 (pp. 97–98, 101–3).

19. George B. Sánchez, 'Horne Seeks Info on Ethnic Studies Programs in TUSD', *Arizona Daily Star*, 15 November 2007, http://tucson. com/news/local/education/precollegiate/horne-seeks-info-on-ethnic-studies-programs-in-tusd/article_8307409c-9594-5e9c-8290-04ea41fcc575.html, accessed 31 January 2017. See also Doug Carroll, 'School Uniforms', *Arizona Republic*, 2 May 2006, http://archive. azcentral.com/families/education/articles/0502eduniforms0502. html, accessed 10 March 2017.

20. Paul Ingram, 'Horne Vows to Continue "Crusade" vs. Ethnic Studies', *Tucson Sentinel*, 22 August 2014, http://www.tucsonsentinel.com/ local/report/082114_arpaio_horne/horne-vows-continue-crusade-vs-ethnic-studies, accessed 31 January 2017.

21. Horne, 'Open Letter', p. 1.

22. Augustine F. Romero, 'At War with the State in Order to Save the Lives of our Children: The Battle to Save Ethnic Studies in Arizona', *Black Scholar*, 40.4 (2010), 7–15 (p. 7).

23. Horne, 'Open Letter', p. 2. See further pp. 3–4.

24. Horne, 'Open Letter', p. 2 (emphasis original).

25. 'Latest Plan to Plug Gulf Oil Leak? Arizona Culture Clash'. See also Anita Fernández and Zoe Hammer, 'Red Scare in the Red State: The Attack on Mexican-American Studies in Arizona and Opportunities for Building National Solidarity', *Association of Mexican American Educators Journal*, 6.1 (2012), 65–70 (pp. 67–68).

26. Horne, 'Open Letter', p. 3.

27. Martin Luther King Jr., 'I Have a Dream', in *A Testament of Hope: The Essential Writings of Martin Luther King, Jr.*, ed. James Melvin Washington (San Francisco: Harper & Row, 1986), pp. 217–20 (p. 219).

28. Horne, 'Open Letter', p. 1.

29. Martin Luther King Jr., 'Letter from Birmingham City Jail', in *A Testament of Hope*, pp. 289–302 (p. 295).

30. S.B. 1108, 48th Leg., 2d Reg. Sess. (as reported by Ariz. H. Comm. on Appropriations 16 April 2008), http://www.azleg.gov/legtext/48leg/2r/adopted/h.1108-se-approp.pdf, accessed 31 January 2017.

31. O'Leary and others, pp. 98–99.

32. Ariz. Rev. Stat. § 15-111 (2010).

33. Ariz. Rev. Stat. § 15-112(a) (2010).

34. Ariz. Rev. Stat. § 15-112(b) (2010).

35. 'HB 2281—Ethnic Studies Ban—Key Vote', https://votesmart.org/bill/11398/30470/ethnic-studies-ban#30470, accessed 31 January 2017.

36. Nolan L. Cabrera and others, 'The Fight for Mexican American Studies in Tucson', *NACLA Report on the Americas*, November–December 2011, p. 22. See also *Precious Knowledge*; Dylan Smith, '15 Arrested after Horne Press Conference on Ethnic Studies Ban', *Tucson Sentinel*, 12 May 2010, http://www.tucsonsentinel.com/local/report/051210_horne_sitin/15-arrested-after-horne-press-conference-ethnic-studies-ban, accessed 31 January 2017.

37. Tom Horne, quoted in Arce v. Douglas, 793 F.3d 968, 980 (9th Cir. 2015).

38. *Arce*, 793 F.3d at 980.

39. *Arce*, 793 F.3d at 979.

40. Cathryn Creno, 'School Superintendent Huppenthal Acknowledges Anonymous Blog Posts', *Arizona Republic*, 19 June 2014, http://www.azcentral.com/story/news/arizona/politics/2014/06/18/huppenthal-acknowledges-anonymous-blog-posts/10749057, accessed 31 January 2017; Mary Beth Faller and Cathryn Creno, 'Huppenthal Breaks Down in Tears over Blog Posts', *Arizona Republic*, 26 June 2014, http://www.azcentral.com/story/news/arizona/politics/2014/06/25/arizona-huppenthal-blog-posts-tears-press/11373231, accessed 31 January 2017.

41. 'Falcon9' [John Huppenthal], comment on Greg Patterson, 'Mission Accomplished', 10 December 2010 (14 December 2010), http://www.espressopundit.com/2010/12/mission-accomplished.html, accessed 31 January 2017. See also Laurie Roberts, 'John Huppenthal Is Sorry, but for What Really, I Wonder?', *Arizona Republic*, 25 June 2014, http://www.azcentral.com/story/laurieroberts/2014/06/25/huppenthal-apologizes-blog-comments/11378667, accessed 20 March 2017.

42. Anzaldúa, p. 81.

43. 'Falcon9' [John Huppenthal], comment on Greg Patterson, 'An Epic Victory', 26 May 2011 (27 May 2011), http://www.espressopundit.

com/2011/05/an-epic-victory.html, accessed 31 January 2017. See also Roberts.

44. Casteel and others, pp. 34, 43, 78. See further pp. 34–37, 39–41, 66, 85, 89.

45. Cabrera and others, 'The Fight for Mexican American Studies in Tucson', pp. 20, 23. See also Three Sonorans News, *UNIDOS Takes Over TUSD School Board*, online video recording, YouTube, 27 April 2011, https://www.youtube.com/watch?v=tPZxCDMbZec&feature=youtu. be, accessed 31 January 2017; UNIDOS Tucson, 'Who We Are', https:// unidostucson.wordpress.com/who-we-are, accessed 31 January 2017.

46. Cabrera and others, 'The Fight for Mexican American Studies in Tucson', p. 20.

47. Three Sonorans, *The TUSD Tragedy—Save Ethnic Studies*, online video recording, Vimeo, 9 May 2011, https://vimeo.com/23516724, accessed 31 January 2017.

48. Cabrera and others, 'The Fight for Mexican American Studies in Tucson', p. 20; Julie C. Tolleson to Governing Board, TUSD, Re: 'Investigative Findings—Case No. 08-12-1080 (Access to Board Meetings) United States Department of Education, Office of Civil Rights', [February 2014], pp. 4–5, 12–13.

49. Cabrera and others, 'The Fight for Mexican American Studies in Tucson', p. 20.

50. Mari Herreras, 'Calling for More', *Tucson Weekly*, 26 September 2013, http:// www.tucsonweekly.com/tucson/calling-for-more/Content?oid=3880864, accessed 1 February 2017; Three Sonorans, *The TUSD Tragedy—Save Ethnic Studies*. See also Cabrera and others, 'The Fight for Mexican American Studies in Tucson', pp. 20–21.

51. Three Sonorans, *The TUSD Tragedy—Save Ethnic Studies*. See also Cabrera and others, 'The Fight for Mexican American Studies in Tucson', pp. 20–21.

52. Tolleson to Governing Board, p. 5; Three Sonorans, *The TUSD Tragedy— Save Ethnic Studies*.

53. Cabrera and others, 'The Fight for Mexican American Studies in Tucson', p. 21.

54. Arizona Department of Education, Office of Superintendent of Public Instruction John Huppenthal, 'Superintendent of Public Instruction John Huppenthal Rules Tucson Unified School District Out of Compliance with A.R.S. § 15-112', 15 June 2011, https://www.azed.gov/public-relations/files/2011/08/pr06-15-11.pdf, accessed 1 February 2017.

55. Tucson Unified School Dist. No. 1, No. 11F-002-ADE ¶ 147 (Off. of Admin. Hearings, Ariz. December 27, 2011).

56. Planas, 'Neither Banned nor Allowed'.

57. Anzaldúa, p. 217. See also Nolan L. Cabrera and others, '"If There Is No Struggle, There Is No Progress": Transformative Youth Activism and the School of Ethnic Studies', *Urban Review*, 45 (2013), 7–22 (pp. 8, 13, 18), accessed 1 February 2017.

58. J. Weston Phippen, 'How One Law Banning Ethnic Studies Led to its Rise', *Atlantic*, 19 July 2015, http://www.theatlantic.com/education/archive/2015/07/how-one-law-banning-ethnic-studies-led-to-rise/398885, accessed 1 February 2017.

59. Curtis Acosta, 'Dangerous Minds in Tucson: The Banning of Mexican American Studies and Critical Thinking in Arizona', *Journal of Educational Controversy*, 8.1 (2004), art. 9 (p. 1).

60. Jing Fong, 'When This Teacher's Ethnic Studies Classes Were Banned, his Students Took the District to Court—and Won', *Yes! Magazine*, 25 April 2014, http://www.yesmagazine.org/issues/education-uprising/interview-with-curtis-acosta, accessed 1 February 2017.

61. *Arce*, 793 F.3d at 970, 976, 979. See further pp. 978–81, 985, 990.

62. Lorraine Kasprisin, 'Trial Date Set: Latest Action on the Banning of Mexican American studies in Tucson, Arizona', Journal of Educational Controversy Blog, 13 April 2017, http://www.journalofeducationalcontroversy.blogspot.co.uk/2017/04/trial-date-set-latest-action-on-banning.html

63. Phippen.

64. Phippen; XITO: Xicanx Institute for Teaching and Organizing, 'Who is XITO?', http://www.xicanoinstitute.org/about, accessed 1 February 2017.

65. Fisher v. Tucson Unified Sch. Dist., 652 F.3d 1131, 1134, 1137 n. 11 (9th Cir. 2011).

66. *Tucson Unified School District Unitary Status Plan (USP)*, 6 November 2014, p. 37, http://tusd1.org/contents/distinfo/deseg/Documents/USP.pdf, accessed 1 February 2017.

67. Alexis Huicochea, 'TUSD's Revised Book Policy Draws State Concern', *Arizona Daily Star*, 24 October 2013, http://tucson.com/news/local/education/tusd-s-revised-book-policy-draws-state-concern/article_1c78100b-5bac-5ece-aaf8-6ca93a2a2d0c.html, accessed 1 February 2017.

68. Roque Planas, 'Man Behind Mexican–American Studies Ban Won't Head Arizona Schools Anymore', *Huffington Post*, 27 August 2014, http://www.huffingtonpost.com/2014/08/27/john-huppenthal-loses_n_5721762.html, accessed 12 March 2017.

69. John Huppenthal to H. T. Sanchez, 'Notice of Noncompliance', 2 January 2015, pp. 3–5, http://archive.azcentral.com/persistent/icimages/news/TUSD%20Notice%20of%20Noncompliance%201-2-2015.pdf, accessed 1 February 2017. See also Roque Planas, 'Teaching Hip Hop Illegally Promotes Ethnic Solidarity, Arizona Official Says', *Huffington Post*, 5 January 2015, http://www.huffingtonpost.com/2015/01/05/arizona-hip-hop-illegal_n_6419558.html, accessed 1 February 2017.

Afterword

Oppressors don't just want to do their deed, they want to take a bow: they want their victims to sing their praises. This doesn't change, and it seems there are no new thoughts, no new struggles with censorship and self-censorship, only the old struggles repeating: half-animated corpses of forbidden childhood thoughts crawling out of the psychic trenches we have dug for them, and recurring denials by the great of the truths written on the bodies of the small.

Hilary Mantel[1]

It would be a mistake to assume that the censorship of literature in the United Kingdom and the United States progresses steadily towards greater freedom. The days of theatrical jury trials over the obscenity of a novel like *Lady Chatterley's Lover* appear to be behind us—and we don't burn heretics anymore. Yet, because many factors influence censorship practices, including politics, the law, special interest groups, public opinion, and new technologies, these practices can develop in surprising ways. UK blasphemy law is now buried, but it was obsolete for much of the twentieth century until Mary Whitehouse breathed life into it in the *Gay News* case. As the novelist Hilary Mantel suggests, the conflict between subversion and control is an old one, and it plays out in large patterns that we hope this book has made recognizable. The details of that struggle, however, are perpetually shifting. Here are some frontiers of censorship that literature faces in our time.

Fear of terrorist attacks committed by extremist Islamist groups has now become a significant force in politics, resulting in broad restrictions on intellectual freedom in the United Kingdom. The Terrorism Act 2006 prohibits the direct or indirect encouragement of terrorism, including through dissemination of 'terrorist publications'. In 2008 criminology scholar Rizwaan Sabir was arrested while researching terrorism as a master's student at Nottingham University. He and a university administrator were detained for six days without charges for downloading 'a document referred to as the "al-Qaida training manual"', which Sabir describes as a 'bog-standard source' that is 'widely available' on reputable websites and through Amazon.[2] An inquiry found that police officers had fabricated statements from Sabir.[3] In 2015, citing legal advice and the Terrorism Act, the British Library turned down a digital collection of documents related to the Taliban, including magazines and poetry, even though 'the archive was recognised as being of research value'.[4] Where reading and research are threatened, so is imaginative literature. In July 2016, using powers granted by Schedule 7 of the Terrorism Act 2000, police detained and questioned a British Muslim woman on her return to Doncaster airport because she had been reading *Syria Speaks: Art and Culture from the Frontline*, edited by Malu Halasa and others, on her outbound flight.[5]

In the United States, the First Amendment continues to present a higher bar for direct restrictions on speech. Robust government surveillance, however, can extend to what people read. Section 215 of the Patriot Act, passed in 2001 after the 11 September attacks, allows law enforcement to obtain records from any entity for national security purposes.[6] (This was the section that, as the whistleblower Edward Snowden revealed, permitted the National Security Agency to collect bulk metadata about telephone calls in the United States.) Unlike an ordinary subpoena, a section 215 order does not require a reasonable suspicion that the subject of the search has committed a crime.[7] Section 215 became known as the 'library provision', and librarians, who feared that the state would monitor patrons' reading behaviour, vocally opposed it.[8] Requests under section 215 automatically impose a gag order: anyone required to yield up records is prohibited from saying that they have done so.[9] With the renewal in modified form of Patriot Act surveillance powers in 2015, the potential for abuse remains.[10] In the United Kingdom, in addition to bulk data collection, the Investigatory Powers Act 2016 allows records of what websites a user visits to be preserved for up to a year and to be provided to government agencies and law enforcement. The mere existence of these powers is likely to create a chilling effect on reading. Though chilling effect remains difficult to measure, researchers have recently begun to develop methods to do so. A 2016 study found a statistically significant drop in web traffic to Wikipedia pages on topics related to terrorism after the Snowden revelations in June 2013, suggesting that internet users' reading practices changed when they were aware that their activity might be monitored.[11]

Speech continues to be restricted by obscenity law, though standards of obscenity in the United Kingdom and the United States have largely shifted away from written literature to focus on pornographic images and videos. According to the Miller test of obscenity, now current in the United States, only 'serious' social value can save a work, not any social value at all.[12] Aside from the older obscenity statutes, laws now criminalize child pornography and forms of 'extreme' pornography. US and UK child pornography laws apply not only to photographs but also to cartoons and other drawings, and there have been convictions in both countries for obtaining or possessing Japanese manga or manga-style drawings.[13] Obscenity laws also encompass publications on the internet. In 2009 a man was unsuccessfully prosecuted under the UK Obscene Publications Act 1959 for posting a fictional story online that depicted the murder of the members of pop group Girls Aloud.[14]

A medium of communication in itself as well as a marketplace for books, the internet has vastly amplified speech while also creating a labyrinthine tangle of restrictions, many dealing with copyright and privacy. As legal scholars Anupam Chander and Uyên P. Lê write, 'Cyberlaw is today's speech law.'[15] US public libraries and schools cannot receive federal funding for internet access unless they use content filters, and many states have their own filtering requirements for libraries and schools. These filters, designed to block 'materials harmful for minors',[16] can prevent students from accessing social media and LGBT resources.[17] Filtering is also routinely implemented in public libraries in the United Kingdom, and can block children's access to categories of content such as 'gay or lesbian or bisexual interest'.[18] Filtering in the United Kingdom is not limited to libraries. In addition to blocking the Internet Watch Foundation's blacklist of sites with illegal content, such as child pornography, major internet service providers (ISPs) now implement filters that block a variety of legal content. These 'family-friendly' filters are the result of pressure from Prime Minister David Cameron, and users who do not wish to use them need to opt out.[19] These filters can mistakenly block sexual education websites.[20]

The internet also makes especially clear the role that large technology corporations now play in channelling speech. Google and Facebook's algorithms, in addition to censoring content, select what users see in web searches or on their Facebook feeds.[21] While bookshops have always been able to exercise or defy censorship, online retailers can do so on a vast scale. Electronic books, or e-books, are especially vulnerable to censorship. In 2009 Amazon deleted George Orwell's *1984* and *Animal Farm* from users' e-book readers without warning. Though the reason for this intervention had to do with a copyright error, it was an apt illustration of how, in a totalitarian state like the ones Orwell describes, governments or corporations can deprive the public of access to digital information.[22]

And students? Some would have it that a generation of censorious young people is threatening intellectual freedom on university campuses. Should instructors notify students in advance about material that might trigger past traumas? Is it okay to reject potential guest speakers whose speech has crossed from opinion into hate? Much has been said on either side of these questions, but the danger posed by students has been overblown. To focus on students as a censorship threat is to lose sight of power, which increasingly rests neither with them nor with their instructors. For example, in the United Kingdom the widely criticized 'Prevent' counter-terrorism strategy requires institutions of higher education, among other public authorities, to 'have due regard to the need to prevent people from being drawn into terrorism'. In practice, despite a section in the statute protecting academic freedom and the freedom of expression at universities, the Prevent strategy results in thought policing, and can extend to monitoring staff and student activity on institutional computer systems.[23] In 2015 an official at Staffordshire University questioned a postgraduate student about his views and reported him to security because he was reading a book called *Terrorism Studies* in the library, an incident that deeply distressed the student and caused him to abandon his course of study.[24] In Wisconsin, Republican politicians, threatening funding cuts, have repeatedly attacked academic content at the University of Wisconsin–Madison, including a course on race called 'The Problem of Whiteness'.[25] In Arizona, in January 2017, Republican Bob Thorpe proposed a bill to expand the anti-ethnic studies statute used against Mexican American studies in Tucson schools, and to apply it to universities (see Chapter 25). The measure failed—for now.[26] If universities become instruments of party politics or business, academic freedom will truly be lost, along with the literary culture that it fosters.

When they were first written, many of the books that we have discussed challenged orthodoxies and were unwelcome to those in power. Authoritarian politics, disregard for human rights, and political systems in which money translates into influence mean that, however free speech might be in theory, only the speech of the powerful is assured. To see the future of censorship, look up.

Notes

1. Hilary Mantel, 'Blot, Erase, Delete', *Index on Censorship*, 45.3 (2016), 64–68 (p. 68).
2. Rizwaan Sabir, 'This Is No Way to Fight Terror', *Guardian*, 16 September 2008, https://www.theguardian.com/commentisfree/2008/sep/16/uksecurity.terrorism, accessed 1 February 2017.
3. Mark Townsend, 'Police "Made Up" Evidence against Muslim Student', *Guardian*, 14 July 2012, https://www.theguardian.com/uk/2012/jul/14/police-evidence-muslim-student-rizwaan-sabir, accessed 1 February 2017.
4. Emma Graham-Harrison and Kevin Rawlinson, 'Terror Law Prompts British Library to Reject Unique Taliban Archive', *Guardian*, 28 August 2015, https://www.theguardian.com/world/2015/aug/28/terror-law-prompts-british-library-to-reject-unique-taliban-archive, accessed 1 February 2017.

5. Liam O'Hare and Ted Jeory, 'British Muslim Woman Detained under Terror Laws after Cabin Crew Report Her Reading Syrian Art Book on Plane', *Independent*, 3 August 2016, http://www.independent.co.uk/news/uk/home-news/british-muslim-woman-detained-terror-laws-syrian-art-book-plane-cabin-crew-faizah-shaheen-a7168751.html, accessed 1 February 2017.

6. Susan Nevelow Mart, 'Protecting the Lady from Toledo: Post-USA PATRIOT Act Electronic Surveillance at the Library', *Law Library Journal*, 96 (2004), 449–73 (p. 461).

7. Christopher Cooke, 'Securing Liberty: A Response to Debates on Section 215 of the Patriot Act', *Georgetown Journal of Law & Public Policy*, 12 (2014), 889–96 (pp. 889–91).

8. Anne Klinefelter, 'The Role of Librarians in Challenges to the USA PATRIOT Act', *North Carolina Journal of Law & Technology*, 5.2 (2004), 219–26 (pp. 219, 222–23).

9. Mart, p. 461.

10. Dustin Volz and others, 'Senate Passes Major NSA Reform Bill', *Atlantic*, 2 June 2015, https://www.theatlantic.com/politics/archive/2015/06/senate-passes-major-nsa-reform-bill/445959, accessed 1 February 2017.

11. Jonathon W. Penney, 'Chilling Effects: Online Surveillance and Wikipedia Use', *Berkeley Technology Law Journal*, 31 (2016), 117–82 (pp. 157, 159, 161).

12. Miller v. California, 413 U.S. 15, 24 (1973).

13. Marc H. Greenberg, 'Comics, Courts & Controversy: A Case Study of the Comic Book Legal Defense Fund', *Loyola of Los Angeles Entertainment Law Review*, 32 (2012), 121–87 (pp. 166–74); Gareth Lightfoot, 'Fan of Japanese Anime Makes British Legal History after Conviction for Having Pictures of Cartoon Children', *Mirror*, 20 October 2014, http://www.mirror.co.uk/news/uk-news/fan-japanese-anime-makes-british-4470102, accessed 2 February 2017.

14. 'Man Cleared over Girls Aloud Blog', BBC News, 29 June 2009, http://news.bbc.co.uk/1/hi/england/tyne/8124059.stm, accessed 2 February 2017.

15. Anupam Chander and Uyên P. Lê, '*Free* Speech', *Iowa Law Review*, 100 (2014–15), 501–49 (p. 505).

16. 'Children and the Internet: Laws Relating to Filtering, Blocking and Usage Policies in Schools and Libraries', National Conference of State Legislatures, 16 November 2016, http://www.ncsl.org/research/

telecommunications-and-information-technology/state-internet-filtering-laws.aspx, accessed 2 February 2017.

17. Melinda D. Anderson, 'How Internet Filtering Hurts Kids', *Atlantic*, 26 April 2016, https://www.theatlantic.com/education/archive/2016/04/internet-filtering-hurts-kids/479907, accessed 2 February 2017.

18. Daniel Payne and others, 'Content Filtering in UK Public Libraries', 17 February 2016, https://figshare.com/articles/Content_filtering_in_UK_public_libraries/2059998, accessed 2 February 2017.

19. Philip Chwee, 'Bringing In a New Scale: Proposing a Global Metric of Internet Censorship', *Fordham International Law Journal*, 38 (2015), 825–88 (pp. 849–53). See also David Cameron, 'The Internet and Pornography: Prime Minister Calls for Action', 24 July 2013, https://www.gov.uk/government/speeches/the-internet-and-pornography-prime-minister-calls-for-action, accessed 2 February 2017.

20. Mike Deri Smith, 'Porn Filters Block Sex Education Websites', BBC News, 18 December 2013, http://www.bbc.co.uk/news/uk-25430582, accessed 2 February 2017.

21. Will Oremus, 'Who Controls your Facebook Feed', *Slate*, 3 January 2016, http://www.slate.com/articles/technology/cover_story/2016/01/how_facebook_s_news_feed_algorithm_works.html, accessed 2 February 2017; Olivia Solon and Sam Levin, 'How Google's Search Algorithm Spreads False Information with a Rightwing Bias', *Guardian*, 16 December 2016, https://www.theguardian.com/technology/2016/dec/16/google-autocomplete-rightwing-bias-algorithm-political-propaganda, accessed 2 February 2017.

22. Brad Stone, 'Amazon Erases Orwell Books from Kindle', *New York Times*, 17 July 2009, http://www.nytimes.com/2009/07/18/technology/companies/18amazon.html?_r=0, accessed 2 February 2017.

23. Counter-Terrorism and Security Act 2015, ss 26(1), 31; Sally Weale, 'London University Tells Students their Emails May Be Monitored', *Guardian*, 20 January 2017, https://www.theguardian.com/uk-news/2017/jan/20/university-warns-students-emails-may-be-monitored-kings-college-london-prevent, accessed 2 February 2017.

24. Randeep Ramesh and Josh Halliday, 'Student Accused of Being a Terrorist for Reading Book on Terrorism', *Guardian*, 24 September 2015, https://www.theguardian.com/education/2015/sep/24/

student-accused-being-terrorist-reading-book-terrorism, accessed 2 February 2017.

25. Edward Helmore, 'Republicans Condemn University's Masculinity Program as a "War on Men"', *Guardian*, 9 January 2017, https://www.theguardian.com/us-news/2017/jan/09/university-of-wisconsin-masculinity-program-republicans, accessed 2 February 2017.

26. Hank Stephenson, 'Arizona Bill to Ban School "Social Justice" Courses Dies Quickly', *Arizona Capitol Times*, 17 January 2017, http://azcapitoltimes.com/news/2017/01/17/thorpe-social-justice-course-ban, accessed 2 February 2017.

Index